Symmetry/Asymmetry in Computer-Aided Industrial Design

Symmetry/Asymmetry in Computer-Aided Industrial Design

Guest Editors

Yanpu Yang

Dengkai Chen

MDPI

Basel • Beijing • Wuhan • Barcelona • Belgrade • Novi Sad • Cluj • Manchester

Guest Editors

Yanpu Yang
School of Construction Machinery
Chang'an University
Xi'an
China

Dengkai Chen
Department of Industrial Design
Northwestern Polytechnical University
Xi'an
China

Editorial Office
MDPI AG
Grosspeteranlage 5
4052 Basel, Switzerland

This is a reprint of the Special Issue, published open access by the journal *Symmetry* (ISSN 2073-8994), freely accessible at: https://www.mdpi.com/journal/symmetry/special_issues/OUH7J0N3RO.

For citation purposes, cite each article independently as indicated on the article page online and as indicated below:

Lastname, A.A.; Lastname, B.B. Article Title. *Journal Name* **Year**, *Volume Number*, Page Range.

ISBN 978-3-7258-7250-3 (Hbk)
ISBN 978-3-7258-7251-0 (PDF)
https://doi.org/10.3390/books978-3-7258-7251-0

Contents

About the Editors vii

Yanpu Yang and Dengkai Chen
Symmetry/Asymmetry in Computer-Aided Industrial Design
Reprinted from: *Symmetry* **2026**, *18*, 346, https://doi.org/10.3390/sym18020346 1

Xiu Miao, Wenjun Hou and Zhichun Li
Fine-Grained Implicit Intention Pattern Recognition for Key Interactive Tasks in Industrial Human–Machine Collaboration
Reprinted from: *Symmetry* **2026**, *18*, 317, https://doi.org/10.3390/sym18020317 3

Yihang Fang and Yundong Qu
Symmetric Alignment Between Affective Semantics and Biomimetic Forms: Sustainable Packaging Design and Decision Support
Reprinted from: *Symmetry* **2026**, *18*, 19, https://doi.org/10.3390/sym18010019 42

Yanpu Yang, Yueming Zhuo, Jialing Liu, Wenhao Meng and Zhihong Wu
A Hybrid Quantitative Method for Evaluating HMI Layout Design in Service Robots
Reprinted from: *Symmetry* **2025**, *17*, 2102, https://doi.org/10.3390/sym17122102 65

Bo Li, Zhen Hu, Yuhang Liu and Zewei Wang
Integrating Kansei Engineering and AI-Generated Image for Commercial Vehicle Body Morphology Design
Reprinted from: *Symmetry* **2025**, *17*, 1971, https://doi.org/10.3390/sym17111971 97

Lei Fu, Xinyan Yang, Ling Zhu and Jiufang Lv
An Intelligent Optimization Design Method for Furniture Form Considering Multi-Dimensional User Affective Requirements
Reprinted from: *Symmetry* **2025**, *17*, 1406, https://doi.org/10.3390/sym17091406 120

Mengqi Qin, Jianfang Wang, Xueying Ding and Haihong Zhang
Symmetrical Traditional Patterns and User Perception: A Study on Innovation in Home Textile Design
Reprinted from: *Symmetry* **2025**, *17*, 960, https://doi.org/10.3390/sym17060960 146

Lei Wang, Jingluan Wang, Dengkai Chen and Jie Song
A Cognitive Load Assessment Method for Airtight Cabin Operators Based on a One-Dimensional Convolutional Neural Network
Reprinted from: *Symmetry* **2025**, *17*, 915, https://doi.org/10.3390/sym17060915 168

Yu Chen, Haotian Liu, Jianwei Zhang and Jiang Wu
A Data-Driven Methodology for Industrial Design Optimization and Consumer Preference Modeling: An Application of Computer-Aided Design in Sustainable Refrigerator Design Research
Reprinted from: *Symmetry* **2025**, *17*, 621, https://doi.org/10.3390/sym17040621 194

Zheng Wen, Jianming Yang, Bowen Sun and Yuanwei Liu
Research on Symmetry Optimization of Designer Requirements and Prototyping Platform Functionality in the Context of Agile Development
Reprinted from: *Symmetry* **2025**, *17*, 502, https://doi.org/10.3390/sym17040502 233

Zhuo Liu, Suihuai Yu, Wenjun Du and Fangmin Cheng
A Failure Touchpoint Identification and Reconfiguration Approach for Enhancing Product–Service Symmetry
Reprinted from: *Symmetry* **2025**, *17*, 485, https://doi.org/10.3390/sym17040485 . . . . **259**

About the Editors

Yanpu Yang

Yanpu Yang is a professor and doctoral supervisor at the School of Construction Machinery, Chang'an University, holding a Ph.D. in Engineering with postdoctoral experience. A senior member of the Chinese Mechanical Engineering Society and committee member of its Ergonomics Special Committee, he specializes in ergonomics and innovative design, particularly optimizing human-machine systems for heavy construction machinery. Professor Yang has hosted three national-level projects, including grants from the National Natural Science Foundation of China, and five provincial initiatives like the Shaanxi Innovation Capability Support Program, while participating in key national R&D plans. His scholarly impact includes over 70 papers in SCI/SSCI/EI-indexed journals and more than 10 authorized patents. He currently serves on the early-career editorial boards of *Advanced Design Research*, the *Journal of Mechanical Design*, and *Packaging Engineering*, acts as a guest editor for *Symmetry*, and reviews for top-tier journals such as *Advanced Engineering Informatics* and *Expert Systems With Applications*. Through these multifaceted roles, he continues to advance the fields of industrial design and ergonomics while mentoring the next generation of researchers.

Dengkai Chen

Dengkai Chen is a professor and doctoral supervisor at the School of Mechanical Engineering, Northwestern Polytechnical University, where he serves as the head of the Design discipline and the Department of Industrial Design. Recognized as a leading talent in Shaanxi Province, he directs the Key Laboratory of Industrial Design and Ergonomics under the Ministry of Industry and Information Technology and the Shaanxi Provincial Engineering Laboratory for Industrial Design. His research focuses on industrial design and ergonomics within manned closed spaces, addressing critical challenges in extreme environments such as weightlessness, high pressure, and long-duration missions for national projects in aerospace, aviation, deep-sea exploration, and naval engineering. Professor Chen has successfully led or participated in over 30 major national initiatives, including projects for the National Key R&D Program, manned spaceflight, and deep-sea submersibles. His distinguished career includes four provincial-level scientific and technological awards, the publication of over 100 academic papers, 7 books, 11 registered product designs, 6 software copyrights, and more than 130 patents. Through his work, he has established significant expertise in system integration and human–machine performance enhancement for extreme environment applications.

symmetry

MDPI

Editorial

Symmetry/Asymmetry in Computer-Aided Industrial Design

Yanpu Yang [1,*] and Dengkai Chen [2]

[1] School of Construction Machinery, Chang'an University, Xi'an 710064, China
[2] School of Mechanical Engineering, Northwestern Polytechnical University, Xi'an 710072, China; chendengkai@nwpu.edu.cn
* Correspondence: yangyanpu@chd.edu.cn

In the ever-evolving landscape of industrial design, the interplay between symmetry and asymmetry serves as both a philosophical cornerstone and a practical compass. This Special Issue of *Symmetry*, titled "Symmetry/Asymmetry in Computer-Aided Industrial Design," brings together cutting-edge research that interrogates these dual forces—not merely as visual attributes but as systemic principles shaping user experience, design cognition, decision-making, and technological integration.

Symmetry, long celebrated for its harmony, balance, and intuitive appeal, continues to underpin successful design across products, interfaces, and services [1–3]. However, in an age defined by personalization, complexity, and dynamic user contexts, rigid symmetry can sometimes obscure nuance or stifle innovation. Conversely, asymmetry—often perceived as disruptive or chaotic—emerges here not as a flaw but as a fertile ground for addressing real-world mismatches, particularly those between designer intent and user need, between system output and human perception, and between functional requirements and emotional resonance.

The contributions featured in this Special Issue exemplify this duality with remarkable depth and diversity. From failure touchpoint reconfiguration aimed at enhancing product–service symmetry [4] to data-driven methodologies aligning sustainable refrigerator design with consumer preferences [5], each paper navigates the tension between order and variation. Several works tackle information asymmetries directly: one investigates the alignment gap between agile prototyping platforms and designer requirements [6], while another proposes fine-grained recognition of implicit user intentions in human–machine collaboration [7]. Complementing these, studies on the hybrid evaluation of HMI layout design in service robots [8] and cognitive load assessments in airtight cabins via a one-dimensional convolutional neural network [9] demonstrate how computational methods can reconcile aesthetic symmetry with functional and perceptual demands. Notably, multiple papers explore affective dimensions: furniture forms shaped by multi-dimensional emotional responses [10], biomimetic packaging aligned with affective semantics [11], AI-augmented Kansei engineering for vehicle morphology [12], and the reinterpretation of symmetrical traditional patterns in home textiles through user perception [13]. Together, they reveal a field increasingly attuned to human nature within human-centred designs.

This Special Issue also reaffirms that symmetry and asymmetry are not binary opposites but complementary strategies. Strategic asymmetry can drive innovation where symmetry risks homogeneity; conversely, intentional symmetry can restore clarity in complex systems. The challenge—and opportunity—for designers and researchers lies in discerning when to embrace each, guided by empirical data, user empathy, and computational insight.

We extend our sincere gratitude to all authors, reviewers, and editorial staff whose rigour and vision made this collection possible. We hope these works inspire further interdisciplinary dialogue at the intersection of design theory, artificial intelligence, ergonomics, and human factors—ultimately advancing a more responsive, equitable, and meaningful design practice for the future.

Author Contributions: Y.Y.: conceptualization, investigation, and writing—original draft. Y.Y. and D.C.: discussion and writing—review and editing. All authors have read and agreed to the published version of the manuscript.

Funding: This research received no external funding.

Data Availability Statement: No new data were created.

Conflicts of Interest: The authors declare no conflicts of interest.

References

1. Ngo, D.C.L.; Teo, L.S.; Byrne, J.G. Modelling interface aesthetics. *Inf. Sci.* **2003**, *152*, 25–46. [CrossRef]
2. Hu, H.; Liu, Y.; Lu, W.F.; Guo, X. A quantitative aesthetic measurement method for product appearance design. *Adv. Eng. Inf.* **2022**, *53*, 101644. [CrossRef]
3. Yang, C.; Yuan, B.; Wu, K.; Ye, J. Aesthetic evaluation method for interactive interface layouts on the basis of visual cognitive multi-attribute fusion decision making. *Int. J. Ind. Ergon.* **2025**, *105*, 103673. [CrossRef]
4. Liu, Z.; Yu, S.; Du, W.; Cheng, F. A Failure Touchpoint Identification and Reconfiguration Approach for Enhancing Product–Service Symmetry. *Symmetry* **2025**, *17*, 485. [CrossRef]
5. Chen, Y.; Liu, H.; Zhang, J.; Wu, J. A Data-Driven Methodology for Industrial Design Optimization and Consumer Preference Modeling: An Application of Computer-Aided Design in Sustainable Refrigerator Design Research. *Symmetry* **2025**, *17*, 621. [CrossRef]
6. Wen, Z.; Yang, J.; Sun, B.; Liu, Y. Research on Symmetry Optimization of Designer Requirements and Prototyping Platform Functionality in the Context of Agile Development. *Symmetry* **2025**, *17*, 502. [CrossRef]
7. Miao, X.; Hou, W.; Li, Z. Fine-Grained Implicit Intention Pattern Recognition for Key Interactive Tasks in Industrial Human–Machine Collaboration. *Symmetry* **2026**, *18*, 317. [CrossRef]
8. Yang, Y.; Zhuo, Y.; Liu, J.; Meng, W.; Wu, Z. A Hybrid Quantitative Method for Evaluating HMI Layout Design in Service Robots. *Symmetry* **2025**, *17*, 2102. [CrossRef]
9. Wang, L.; Wang, J.; Chen, D.; Song, J. A Cognitive Load Assessment Method for Airtight Cabin Operators Based on a One-Dimensional Convolutional Neural Network. *Symmetry* **2025**, *17*, 915. [CrossRef]
10. Fu, L.; Yang, X.; Zhu, L.; Lv, J. An Intelligent Optimization Design Method for Furniture Form Considering Multi-Dimensional User Affective Requirements. *Symmetry* **2025**, *17*, 1406. [CrossRef]
11. Fang, Y.; Qu, Y. Symmetric Alignment Between Affective Semantics and Biomimetic Forms: Sustainable Packaging Design and Decision Support. *Symmetry* **2026**, *18*, 19. [CrossRef]
12. Li, B.; Hu, Z.; Liu, Y.; Wang, Z. Integrating Kansei Engineering and AI-Generated Image for Commercial Vehicle Body Morphology Design. *Symmetry* **2025**, *17*, 1971. [CrossRef]
13. Qin, M.; Wang, J.; Ding, X.; Zhang, H. Symmetrical Traditional Patterns and User Perception: A Study on Innovation in Home Textile Design. *Symmetry* **2025**, *17*, 960. [CrossRef]

https://doi.org/10.3390/sym18020346

symmetry

MDPI

Article

Fine-Grained Implicit Intention Pattern Recognition for Key Interactive Tasks in Industrial Human–Machine Collaboration

Xiu Miao [1], Wenjun Hou [2,*] and Zhichun Li [1]

[1] School of Architecture and Art Design, Inner Mongolia University of Science and Technology, Baotou 014020, China; 18547290825@163.com (X.M.)
[2] School of Intelligent Engineering and Automation, Beijing University of Posts and Telecommunications, Beijing 100876, China
* Correspondence: hwj1505@bupt.edu.cn; Tel.: +86-18547290825

Abstract

The information symmetry between humans and machines can enhance mutual perception and understanding, leading to more robust cooperation. Intention recognition is a key technology in natural human–machine collaboration (HMC). However, as the complexity of the system increases, the amount of information and the types of tasks become numerous, which leads to continuous dynamic changes in interaction intentions. New sensing technologies such as electroencephalogram (EEG) have provided a continuous and unobtrusive monitoring approach to accurately and effectively identify intentions. But the complexity of physiological responses and the uncertain nature of intention make cross-subject recognition difficult, resulting in poor generalization performance and coarse-grained recognition patterns. To address these limitations, we proposed a framework for modeling tasks in complex systems and applied it to model tasks in an industrial system. Then, we use operators' EEG data to effectively recognize the fine-grained intention patterns within different typical task scenarios, such as monitoring production and communication tasks. By inputting the improved multi-channel phase synchronization features into a machine learning classifier, cross-subject accuracy rates of 99.42% and 99.91% were achieved. This work furnishes systematic, field-tested cases for task modeling in the industrial field, demonstrates high-performance implicit intention recognition with a single EEG modality, and refines the granularity of implicit intention recognition. It provides theoretical underpinnings and technical support for both human–machine information symmetry and the advancement of HMC hybrid intelligence.

Keywords: industrial human–machine collaboration; electroencephalogram; intention recognition; phase synchronization

1. Introduction

As a key milestone of the "China Manufacturing 2025" strategy, the past year has seen a series of policies introduced around its core objectives to promote the digital transformation, intelligent upgrading, and high-quality development of manufacturing. For example, the "Steel Industry Steady Growth Work Plan (2025–2026)", the "14th Five-Year Plan for Intelligent Manufacturing Development", the "Guiding Opinions on Accelerating the Transformation and Upgrading of Traditional Manufacturing", and the "Industrial Internet Innovation and Development Action Plan" have elevated artificial intelligence technology from an auxiliary tool to a core engine of new productive forces. The intelligent upgrading of industry and manufacturing is a crucial measure to enhance national core competitiveness, playing a vital role in promoting the development of related industries and economic prosperity, advancing technological progress, and improving people's living standards [1].

The ultimate goal of industrial intelligence is to achieve full-process automation and even "unmanned" production. However, multiple pieces of evidence—including system complexity, domain-specific differences, dynamic environments, situational diversity, and social-ethical and legal constraints—indicate that fully autonomous intelligent systems remain an unattainable ideal in the foreseeable future [2,3]. In current major scenarios, critical tasks and processes require human intervention to ensure complete and correct behavior under all circumstances, and dynamic human–machine collaboration to maximize system safety and efficiency [4,5]. How to integrate human intelligence into intelligent systems has become a core challenge for next-generation industrial systems, urgently requiring breakthroughs to support real-time human–machine–environment mapping, adaptive interaction, and efficient collaboration.

Intention recognition technology is the key technology of HMC, which can help enhance mutual perception, understanding, and adaptation between the two intelligent entities, and improve the level of information symmetry of the system [6]. Information symmetry refers to the degree of equality in information acquisition, understanding, and feedback abilities. It serves as an indicator of whether both parties maintain complete transparency and information symmetry, thereby achieving "symmetrical communication" at the information level to minimize misunderstandings and enhance collaborative efficiency.

In human–computer interaction (HCI), intention refers to the goals and expectations users wish to achieve when interacting with computer systems [7]. Based on whether intentions are explicitly stated, they can be further categorized into explicit and implicit intentions. Explicit intentions refer to those clearly expressed by users through text or actions, which are determined by integrating textual input, voice commands, machine actuator behaviors, and environmental signals during interactions. Implicit intentions, however, are not explicitly stated by users, making them more elusive and harder to recognize [8]. They exhibit non-obvious characteristics, lack clear triggers, and rely on situational and physiological signals, resulting in high ambiguity that makes direct identification challenging. Consequently, the recognition process involves significant ambiguity and technical difficulties. Unlike explicit intentions that require behavioral cues and thus exhibit certain delays, implicit intentions recognition holds great significance for predicting user behavior, enabling natural HCI, and facilitating efficient collaboration. As system intelligence continues to advance, most human–computer communication relies on interfaces. This interface-based display and interaction format inherently manifests HCI through implicit intentions. Given their concealed nature, difficulty in detection, and ambiguous uncertainty, recognizing implicit intentions presents immense challenges.

Physiological sensing technology provides innovative perspectives and practical solutions for embedding implicit intentions. The dynamic physiological changes during interactions enable the integration of intentions into environmental and system models. Among various physiological measurement techniques, electroencephalography (EEG) serves as a crucial neurophysiological signal reflecting brain cognitive processes. Due to its direct correlation with central nervous system activity and cognitive functions, EEG demonstrates superior sensitivity and accuracy in capturing cognitive states compared to other physiological signals, providing vital human factors for HMC [9]. With advantages including non-invasiveness, portability, simplicity, cost-effectiveness, and high temporal resolution, EEG has become the preferred technology for modeling intentions, paving the way for engineering applications.

https://doi.org/10.3390/sym18020317

Research on EEG-based implicit intention recognition traces back to the five-category cognitive task paradigm proposed by Keirn and Aunion [10]. Scholars have successfully decoded five cognitive task intentions using single-modal EEG through this framework. Building on this research, HCI scholars have extended the experimental paradigm to both human–computer interaction and brain-controlled computer domains. In the study of decoding implicit intentions from physiological signals, motor cognitive intention has received the most attention and the highest decoding effect. For example, Zheng et al. enhanced the classification performance of motor imagery (MI) intention EEG signals through improved feature extraction algorithms [11]. Wang et al. expanded the MI research boundary by combining the experimental paradigm with the task characteristics of human–machine systems, and the multi-category recognition of three kinds of intentions, such as imaging left turn, right turn and shooting, was realized by the aircraft operator via eye movement and EEG signal fusion [7].

Current research on implicit intentions predominantly focuses on cognitive task intentions, MI, target preferences, and behavioral decision-making. Intentions that can be well-recognized are mostly those with significant physiological response differences across different tasks, for example, users imagine left and right, perform various cognitive tasks [12,13]. However, within a specific task, there are also different intention patterns. The cognitive components involved in these subdivided intention patterns are similar to the induced physiological signals, so it is more difficult to identify. Most studies employ multi-modal physiological signal fusion modeling, with single-modal recognition yielding limited results, which restricts the implementation of intention experiments and the application of recognition technologies.

In the field of fine-grained intention pattern recognition, Park et al. developed an intention recognition system based on eye movement and EEG, addressing two types of implicit intentions during user browsing: purposeful visual search and aimless general browsing [14]. However, single-modal EEG yielded limited results. Slanzi et al. investigated click decision-making intention patterns when users browse websites naturally based on eye movement and EEG [12]. They found that eye movement features demonstrated good discriminative power, though the final recognition accuracy remained low. Kang et al. employed a phase-synchronous multi-channel EEG signal processing method to extract intention features, achieving 63.6% accuracy in cross-subject model recognition by collecting EEG signals induced during visual browsing under various target scenarios [15]. Current research on fine-grained intentions demonstrates limited diversity in pattern types, with most studies focusing on synchronizing multi-channel and multi-domain EEG features. While individualized modeling approaches can achieve high recognition accuracy, their generalization performance across subjects remains suboptimal.

Furthermore, intention recognition is domain-specific and task-oriented. Current research predominantly focuses on simple systems or everyday applications, with limited attention paid to security-centric complex systems in industrial and applied fields. This gap results in existing quantitative computational dimensions of operators' physiological, psychological, behavioral, and intent characteristics being unsuitable for modeling complex systems. There remains insufficient analysis of domain-specific brainwave patterns for intent detection and inadequate exploration of intent modeling techniques. To bridge this gap, it is essential to integrate task-specific features, expand current research paradigms, and deepen the scope and breadth of HCI studies.

Against this backdrop, this study addresses the requirements of human-centered Industry 5.0 and safety-focused industrial intelligent systems. By leveraging single-modal EEG signals, it aims to achieve fine-grained recognition of implicit intention patterns in critical tasks within industrial HMC systems. The research explores natural human integra-

https://doi.org/10.3390/sym18020317

tion into intelligent systems, enhances human–machine hybrid intelligence, and promotes quantified human computation and bidirectional robust human–machine understanding. This work furnishes systematic, field-tested cases for task modeling in the industrial field, demonstrates high-performance implicit intention recognition with a single EEG modality, and refines the granularity of implicit intention recognition. It provides theoretical underpinnings and technical support for both human–machine information symmetry and the advancement of HMC hybrid intelligence.

2. Related Research

2.1. EEG Induction and Acquisition

The evolution of intention-based experimental paradigms is intrinsically linked to the iterative upgrading of systems. As complexity increases, these experiments have progressed from static material demonstrations and imagination exercises to prototype systems with interactive support. The experimental environments—featuring materials, task designs, and interaction mechanisms—now increasingly mirror real-world system applications. Figure 1 illustrates the developmental trajectory of intention-based experiment paradigms.

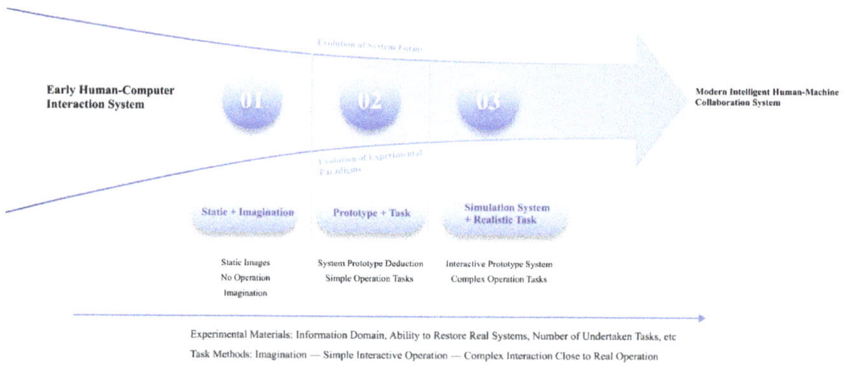

Figure 1. Evolution of the intention experiment paradigms.

In early experiments, given the simplicity of the system's characteristics, intention-evoked EEG stimuli were created through basic interaction scenarios. Participants primarily relied on cognitive imagination or performed simple tasks to complete the experiments.

Researchers like [15,16] focused on user intentions in visual browsing scenarios. They used common real-life scene images as stimulus materials, sequentially presenting five scene images per intention category. Participants completed two types of EEG signal collection—target search and random browsing—following experimental instructions, with the entire process requiring no physical operation. The intention-evoked materials and experimental procedures are illustrated in Figure 2a. The mental tasks intention experiment paradigm designs corresponding intention-inducing materials based on the characteristics of each mental task [17]. Figure 2b shows the intention-inducing materials for the geometric body spatial rotation. Participants sit in front of the display, visually process static materials, and mentally perform the cognitive task as required by the experimental task. The motor cognitive intention paradigm primarily employs motor imagery experiments, where participants visualize specific body movements to activate corresponding brain regions. The standard procedure involves establishing a baseline in a relaxed state, triggering motor imagery through auditory cues, and then performing the imagery task.

https://doi.org/10.3390/sym18020317

(a) (b)

Figure 2. Early stage intention triggering way: (**a**) informational intention and navigational intention; (**b**) geometric control rotation intention triggering materials for Keirn's mental task classification experiment.

As HCI systems handle increasingly complex information and tasks, display methods and interaction modes have become more sophisticated. EEG experiments are now being conducted in real-world scenarios. By simulating system interfaces and interaction methods, experimental stimuli and tasks are presented through prototype interfaces, interactive prototype systems, or even real-world systems, while providing interaction support (such as mouse movement, clicks, and joystick tracking) to capture participants' task EEG signals. Prototype systems maintain close resemblance to real HCI environments while avoiding excessive system details that could compromise the transferability and generalizability of recognition models.

Wang et al. utilized driving simulation software to capture drivers' braking intentions in real-world scenarios [18]. See Figure 3a. By implementing varied external conditions (including different road conditions and speed levels), they induced three types of driving intentions: normal driving, adaptive braking, and emergency braking. The experiment captured EEG activity patterns under these conditions and classified braking intentions using EEG signals. Wang et al. developed an experimental stimulus interface prototype based on typical pilot-aircraft interaction scenarios. The prototype incorporated two types of intentions—motor imagery and shooting intent—along with three intention patterns: imagining a left turn, imagining a right turn, and shooting intent [7]. The experimental scenario is illustrated in Figure 3b.

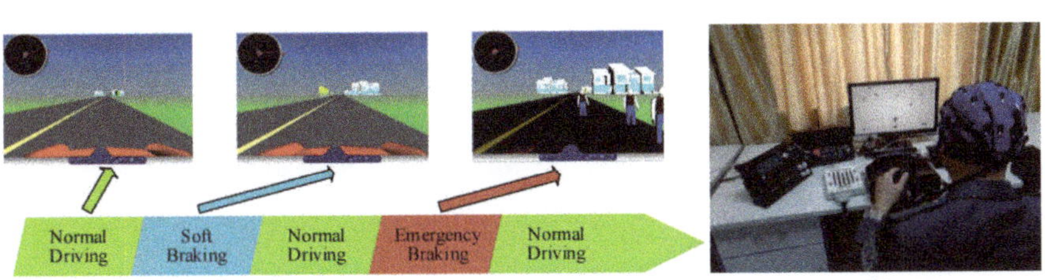

(a) (b)

Figure 3. Induce user's task-related EEG signals through carrying out interactive tasks: (**a**) Braking intention during driving; (**b**) simulated military aircraft intent scenario.

Complex systems often carry out multiple tasks simultaneously. The multi-tasking paradigm such as the Multi-attribute Task Battery (MATB) [19] enables precise control over module difficulty levels with multiple attributes, which has been widely adopted and evolved into various variants due to its controllable nature. See Figure 4a. For instance, in a NASA project, Liao designed four concurrent tasks: tracking, selection reaction, arithmetic calculation, and simulated radar observation [20]. The experimental program interface featured two tiled displays: the right screen presented compensation tracking and selection reaction tasks, while the left screen displayed simulated radar imagery and arithmetic operations, allowing all four tasks to be executed simultaneously. Liang et al. developed

https://doi.org/10.3390/sym18020317

a prototype system for military aircraft based on typical operational task patterns and interface design principles [21]. The prototype features four functional zones: radar, table, icon, and control areas, along with five operational scenarios covering rest, visual search, table lookup, communication, and control. This system successfully identified pilot intentions, as demonstrated in Figure 4b.

(a) (b)

Figure 4. EEG induced forms in the multi-task environment of complex systems: (**a**) MATBII; (**b**) pilot intention experiment simulating military aircraft environment.

Some intention experiments are conducted in real human–machine system environments, identifying intentions by collecting task-state physiological signals from subjects during natural human–machine interactions. These experiments focus on natural human-system interactions but face challenges such as data annotation difficulties and poor signal-to-noise ratios in physiological signals induced by real-world environments. Typically, physiological intention signals are supplemented with other physiological, behavioral, or subjective records to label intention types. However, due to implementation difficulties, low data quality, and processing challenges, such experiments are rarely applied.

Slanzi et al. documented EEG and eye movement signals from users browsing five real-world websites in natural browsing scenarios [22]. They innovatively labeled intent data using eye-tracking technology to capture physiological signals of gaze behavior. Whether a mouse click occurred after a gaze event was used as an intent classification label, thereby modeling click intent. This combination of eye-tracking and mouse click behavior served as the annotation method for intent types.

2.2. Data Analysis and Modeling

In EEG recording, multiple electrodes are distributed in different locations of the scalp, and the EEG signals recorded by each electrode contain information about neural activity in different regions of the brain. The generation of intention leads to specific changes in the EEG signals of different regions of the brain.

Traditional EEG analysis methods focus on detecting differences in brain regions and channels, identifying distinct features through comparative analysis. For instance, Slanzi et al. used pupil diameter data in eye movement analysis as features and extracted 789 EEG feature values across time-domain, frequency-domain, and complexity metrics from 5 frequency bands and 14 channels [22]. Using a logistic regression model, they achieved 71.09% accuracy in intent recognition. Wang et al. integrated time-domain EEG features with frequency-domain power spectral density (PSD) characteristics to classify three driving intentions: emergency braking, soft braking, and normal driving [18]. The study revealed that braking intentions significantly enhance PSD in the 40–60 Hz range, with emergency braking showing more pronounced PSD increases and shorter durations. By screening EEG features with significant differences and applying a Support Vector Machine (SVM) classifier, the researchers achieved over 74% accuracy in identifying braking intentions.

https://doi.org/10.3390/sym18020317

However, intention involves complex information processing and multiple cognitive stages, with information exchange occurring between different brain regions and channels. Traditional EEG feature extraction methods use significantly different brain regions or channels as modeling inputs, neglecting the underlying mechanisms of intent generation, which results in low recognition accuracy. EEG spatial domain features focus on synchronicity between brain regions and multi-channel interactions [23]. Phase information in EEG is highly effective for pattern recognition [24]. Phase locking values (PLVs) reflect the degree of phase synchronization between channels, which has been proven to better represent implicit intentions and is widely applied in motor intention and attention intention recognition. For instance, Park et al. compared the magnitude and variation in PLV values under two visual browsing intentions, finding that the accuracy of classification improved by approximately 5% when integrating EEG and eye movement signals compared to single EEG signal modeling [14]. Kang et al. employed a multi-channel EEG phase synchronization method to extract intention features [15]. The experiment collected EEG signals induced by subjects during two scenarios: target-driven visual search and target-free visual browsing. They extracted PLV values across four frequency bands (theta, alpha, beta-1, and beta-2), identified electrode pairs with maximum phase locking values, and constructed intention features using these PLV values. The features were input into three classifiers: SVM, GMM, and NB. The study revealed that SVM achieved the highest classification accuracy with an average rate of 63.6%, demonstrating that brainwave phase synchronization was more pronounced during target-driven visual search than during target-free visual browsing.

This method makes full use of the synchronization of multi-channel signals and has been proven to be effective in the recognition of implicit intention, especially in the conversion of different types of implicit intention. However, current research shows that the accuracy of such algorithms remains relatively low. While individualized models achieve good recognition rates, cross-subject intent recognition rates only reach around 60%. Therefore, how to leverage the advantages of spatial domain features in individual modeling to improve cross-subject algorithms and achieve higher recognition accuracy remains a key challenge in implicit intent research that requires urgent breakthroughs.

2.3. Task Modeling Method

Traditional task modeling relies on subjective requirements and functional descriptions, neglecting quantitative task calculations and human physiological responses. This overdependence on researchers' prior knowledge results in poor reproducibility and reliability in the extraction process. Consequently, the constructed task models exhibit coarse granularity, only providing a macroscopic view of the overall framework. Such limitations significantly restrict their value in HCI research.

Task analysis based on conceptual models helps clarify system task structures, hierarchical relationships, dynamic execution processes, and predict task outcomes. Current approaches for structurally describing task hierarchies primarily include hierarchical task analysis (HTA), task knowledge structure models (TKS), and predictive error-avoidance models like the GOMS model [25] and HAMSTERS methodology. While these methods define complete task structures and hierarchies, their static nature overlooks external changes and dynamic human–machine–environment interactions. Methods focusing on task execution dynamics better capture human-system interactions. For instance, the CTT model integrates model-based user interface design with formal HCI methods, providing symbols to express subtask execution sequences, transient relationships, and interdependencies [26]. The Rule-Enhanced Task Model extends CTT by embedding business logic through rule-based languages, offering more precise task execution descriptions [27]. The DynaMo-AID model incorporates dynamic device awareness into task analysis frameworks [28]. The

Executable Task Model proposed by Klug and Kangasharju [29] adds input/output ports to each task. Although the above model can describe the dynamic interaction process between human and machine, it lacks consideration of the changes in the external environment and the research on the relationship between human and machine.

The PCTBTA (Perceptual Control Theory-based Task Analysis) model, grounded in perceptual control theory, synthesizes the strengths of both aforementioned models by unifying task hierarchy and task execution frameworks while emphasizing dynamic processes. This methodology incorporates all external factors influencing user goal achievement—including environmental, technological, or social relationships—into its analytical model, enabling comprehensive descriptions of user tasks in dynamic environments. By prioritizing perceptual dynamics and integrating external information into task analysis, the model expands its descriptive scope beyond static system-user interactions to encompass dynamic task execution processes. However, the model's design lacks foundational support in the task objective formulation stage, as both environmental and task specifications rely on subjective expert knowledge and require manual proposal. This top-down approach neglects core elements of HCI systems, particularly the critical focus on operators' behavioral and physiological data.

In view of the problems in the above task modeling, the complex system needs to combine multiple dimensions, such as the system hierarchy and structure, task execution process and operator physiology.

3. Task Analysis and Modeling

3.1. Method

3.1.1. Dimension, Structure and Elements

Building upon the PCTBTA modeling process, this section outlines a three-tiered framework comprising task extraction, task analysis, and task modeling. It specifies the hierarchical structure, implementation procedures, dynamic response analysis, and multi-source heterogeneous data sources with corresponding analytical methods for each phase, as illustrated in Figure 5.

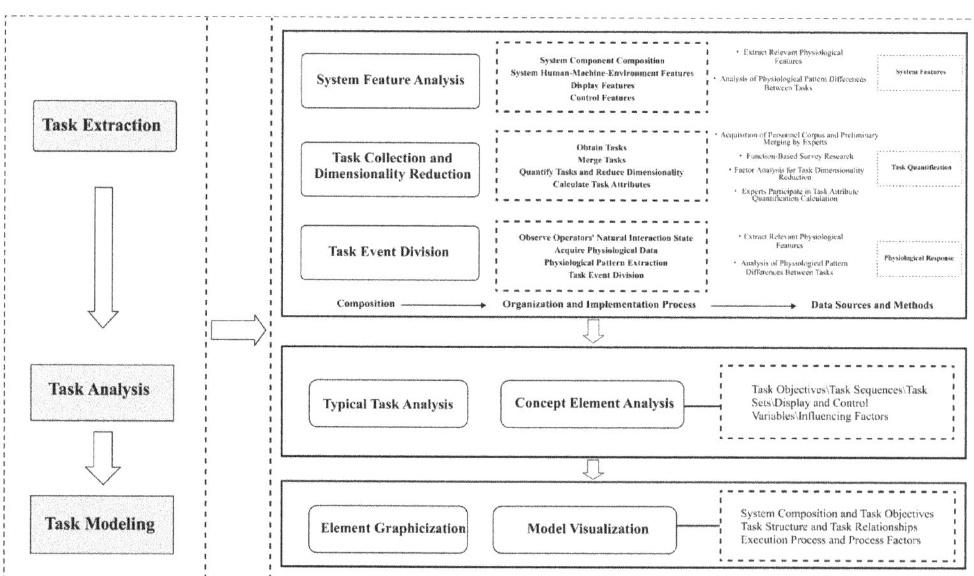

Figure 5. Task modeling method.

https://doi.org/10.3390/sym18020317

Task extraction is based on the analysis of system features. It conducts a three-level coupling analysis at the system, task, and personnel levels. Through subjective analysis, quantitative calculation, and physiological response analysis, it accomplishes steps such as system feature analysis, task collection and dimension reduction, and task event extraction to achieve task convergence.

After completing the extraction of primary tasks through the aforementioned steps, it needs to conduct a comprehensive analysis by integrating conceptual tuple frameworks. This methodology defines five key components: task objectives, task sets, task sequences, display and control variables, and influencing factors. The analysis systematically examines five dimensions: task decomposition and composition, temporal execution flow, conditional constraints based on dependent variables, and external influencing factors. By identifying critical implementation checkpoints, this approach establishes a robust foundation for task modeling and process optimization.

The task modeling layer visually presents the five conceptual elements through a graphical representation. It establishes standardized graphical modeling methods to visually demonstrate the system's task architecture, workflow processes, and interaction relationships. Creating a unified graphic symbol library, it establishes connections between different types of conceptual elements and graphical components. Through visual modeling, complex task logic is transformed into clear graphical expressions, enabling stakeholders to quickly grasp the system's overall architecture. This approach also provides intuitive task model references for subsequent HCI interface design.

3.1.2. Technology Implementation Path

The task modeling process follows the linear execution flow illustrated in Figure 6. After four rounds of subjective and objective dimension reduction calculations, the task achieves convergence, and the key tasks of the complex system are extracted. This process involves the knowledge of researchers and experts, algorithmic computation, and analysis of physiological patterns. Through the integration of qualitative and quantitative analyses, it collectively derives key mission scenarios for complex systems using the concept of the tuple analysis method to analyze the main task scenarios and the subtask patterns of each task. After standardizing the visual elements of the model, the main tasks are modeled and presented.

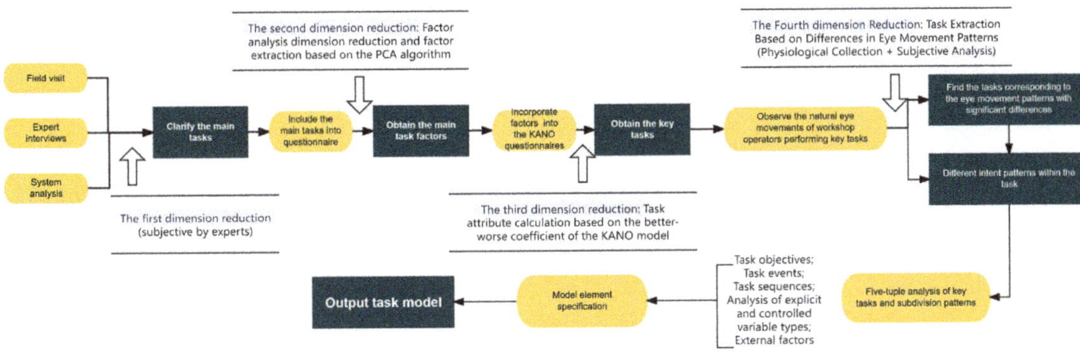

Figure 6. The linear execution flow.

3.2. *Task Extraction*

3.2.1. System Composition Analysis

Industrial HMC systems are multidimensional complex systems integrating human resources, computing, networks, and physical environments [30]. The entire manufactur-

https://doi.org/10.3390/sym18020317

ing lifecycle involves factors characterized by complexity and diversity. Key technologies encompass manufacturing engineering, machine intelligence, and human–machine collaboration. Core components include personnel, production equipment, sensors, industrial software, materials, semi-finished products, and finished products. These elements interact and support one another to accomplish manufacturing tasks for products of various specifications. The constituent elements belong to personnel systems, physical systems, and information systems. Through the organic integration and in-depth collaboration of communication technologies, computer technologies, and control technologies, industrial systems achieve real-time perception, dynamic control, and information services [31].

The human dimension describes the personnel involved in the manufacturing process, including production management personnel, technical R & D personnel, equipment maintenance personnel, production operation personnel, quality inspection personnel, procurement and sales personnel, etc. It involves the knowledge, experience, technology, behavior, and physiological data attributes of these personnel.

The physical dimension describes the flow and transformation of raw materials, sensors, actuators, semi-finished products, and finished products throughout the manufacturing process. Raw materials refer to the initial materials involved in production. Sensors and actuators vary depending on the product type and manufacturing process. For example, in metal rolling, key actuators include rolling mills, welding machines, uncoiler machines, tension rollers, and baling machines, while sensors consist of position detectors and weld seam inspection devices. Semi-finished and finished products refer to items that have been processed on the production line after initial manufacturing and final processing.

The information dimension encompasses both measurable static data generated by personnel, equipment, and environmental factors during production processes and dynamic information that evolves with manufacturing execution. This process involves data perception, acquisition, storage, and computation, and data visualization is achieved through industrial software interfaces. Key components include programmable logic controllers (PLCs), production monitoring and data acquisition systems, management systems, and human–machine interfaces. Personnel utilize the data provided by the software to perform critical operations such as real-time monitoring, control, troubleshooting, and emergency response.

Information systems serve as vital bridges connecting human systems with physical infrastructure, embodying the essence of digitalization, informatization, and intelligent development. They act as essential digital tools supporting smart manufacturing operations. The software components within these systems provide user interfaces that integrate production data visualization and physical system control channels. As the most user-engaged elements, they form the core components and primary interfaces of industrial human–machine interaction systems, as illustrated in Figure 7.

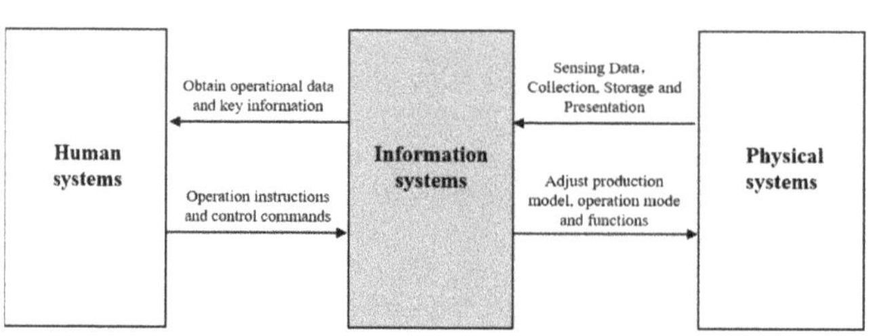

Figure 7. Core interaction patterns of industrial HMC systems.

In information systems, the component that has the closest contact with users is industrial software. Operators use dedicated peripherals such as keyboards, mice, and joysticks to convert their commands into machine control signals, enabling the physical system to respond. Software interfaces typically include system menus, status bars, visual production line modules, control zones, and data display areas. These interfaces present real-time, dynamic, and complex information with diverse operational modes. See Figure 8.

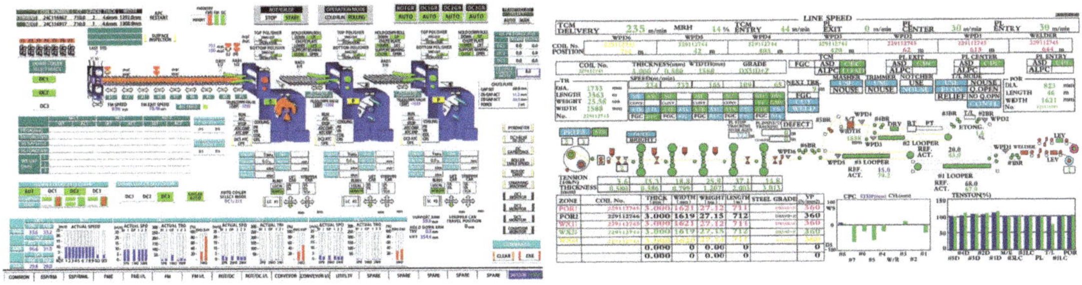

Figure 8. Industrial software interface.

3.2.2. Task Collection and Dimension Reduction

(1) Data acquisition

Task objectives encompass all responsibilities assumed by personnel involved in production activities and human–machine interaction processes. Through literature review and field investigations, we collaborated with operators and automation experts to understand the system's operational status, evaluate the current state of industrial intelligence, and identify specific tasks carried out using industrial software.

Finally, we identified 47 tasks from interview transcripts, including:

- Monitoring real-time production status via industrial software;
- Tracking operational data from systems, equipment, and sensors;
- Reviewing parameter configurations;
- Adjusting operational modes;
- Modifying production models;
- Reviewing warning messages and troubleshooting recommendations;
- Identifying abnormal targets;
- Resolving anomalies;
- Accessing historical production records;
- Inspecting finished and semi-finished product information;
- Comparing preset equipment parameters with actual performance;
- Performing maintenance operations.

Experts were invited to preliminarily merge the tasks according to the correlation and obtain 17 main tasks, as shown in Table 1.

(2) Dimension reduction

To further refine the computational process, the aforementioned tasks were incorporated into a survey questionnaire distributed nationwide to industrial manufacturing personnel. The responses were organized using a 7-point Likert scale format.

In this experimental round, 135 questionnaires were distributed, and 126 valid responses were collected. Feedback from participants demonstrated that the questionnaire questions were well-designed and comprehensively covered the relevant tasks.

The survey participants represented diverse demographics in terms of gender, age, and job roles. The sample had a balanced gender representation, with 50.79% male and 49.21% female. Regarding age distribution, 58.73% of respondents were aged 31–40, followed by 24.6% in the 26–30 age bracket. Job classification showed that managers were

https://doi.org/10.3390/sym18020317

the predominant group (57.94%), followed by software monitoring operators (16.67%), workshop production staff (13.49%), and automation developers (16.67%). In terms of tenure, 50% had 6–10 years of experience, and 26.19% had 11–15 years of experience.

Table 1. Main tasks from expert consolidation.

Task Number	Main Tasks
T1	View production status through the graphical production line
T2	View real-time system and subsystem data
T3	View important device status
T4	View real-time sensor data
T5	View system and subsystem parameter settings
T6	View device parameter settings
T7	Control device functions
T8	Adjust production model
T9	Control production line mode
T10	Abnormal production information alert
T11	Handle, recommend, and take emergency actions for abnormal alerts
T12	View data in a table
T13	View production information through the symbol
T14	View production status with symbols, text, numbers, and other formats
T15	View information about the product being produced
T16	Historical production information storage and query
T17	Compare device preset parameters with actual data

To simplify the task structure, factor analysis was employed to reduce the dimension of questionnaire data. In this section, SPSS19.0 (IBM's statistical software) was used to perform principal component analysis (PCA) on the dataset, extracting common factors for human–machine interaction tasks in industrial systems. Considering the independence between task factors, PCA combined with variance-maximizing rotation (Varimax, Baotou Iron and Steel Company, Baotou, China) was applied for factor extraction. Convergence was achieved after 18 iterations [32].

The Kaiser-Meyer-Olkin (KMO) test yielded a value of 0.807, indicating strong correlations among variables ($p < 0.000$). This confirms the suitability of the collected questionnaire data for factor analysis. Through iterative factor extraction experiments, combined with the scree plot and cumulative variance contribution analysis, the optimal solution was identified at six common factors, achieving 65.380% cumulative variance contribution. The rotated pattern matrix is presented in Table 2.

Table 2. Pattern Matrix.

Task Number	Factor 1	Factor 2	Factor 3	Factor 4	Factor 5	Factor 6
T9	0.794					
T8	0.698					
T7	0.637					
T1		0.810				
T4		0.779				
T12		0.683				
T2		0.561				
T3		0.494				
T15			0.832			
T6			0.633			
T5			0.539			
T11				0.720		
T10				0.653		
T17					0.760	
T16					0.739	
T14						0.828
T13						0.557

Note: Extraction method: Principal Component Analysis (PCA); Rotation method: Orthogonal Rotation with Kaiser normalization; The rotation converges after 18 iterations.

Factor 1 consists of three operational tasks: "controlling the actual operation of production lines via interface controls and buttons", "selecting production models and adjusting production modes for the entire production line using interface controls and buttons", and "modifying equipment functions and operational modes through interface controls and buttons". These tasks indicate that operators adjust production models, system/subsystem configurations, and equipment/subequipment operation modes via industrial software interfaces. Since all three tasks are related to control execution tasks, this factor is named "Control execution task".

Factor 2 comprises five operational tasks: "monitoring production status through graphical production lines", "accessing real-time sensor data", "viewing live operational metrics of production lines", "analyzing real-time system/subsystem performance", and "tracking critical equipment status". These tasks are all closely integrated with operators' real-time monitoring of production lines, systems, subsystems, equipment, and sensors via industrial software, collectively referred to as the "Production monitoring task".

Factor 3 comprises three tasks: "reading product-related data from the table", "viewing preset parameter values of important equipment", and "inquiring and communicating about production conditions". These tasks involve communicating with operators after querying information via the industrial software interface, so they are named "Communication task".

Factor 4 consists of two components: "Abnormal Alert Handling Suggestions" and "Abnormal Information Warnings", both of which pertain to production anomalies. Therefore, it is called the "Abnormal Issue Handling Task". This factor refers to the industrial software's alert notifications and handling recommendations for abnormal situations.

Factor 5 consists of two components: "Display and Comparison of Equipment Preset Parameters with Actual Operational Data" and "Historical Production Information Storage and Query". These tasks employ bar charts, line charts, and other visual formats to help operators make informed decisions via comparative analysis and trend assessment. Therefore, they are labeled as "Comparison and Review Task".

Factor 6 consists of two components: "Integrating visual symbols, text, and numerical data to present production line information" and "Displaying such information through universally understandable graphic symbols". These elements relate to graphical and symbolic production line presentation methods and data retrieval processes. Thus, they are designated as "Symbol Reading Task".

(3) Task attribute quantification

The Kano model was employed to quantitatively analyze the functional attributes of the six task factors. Through the Kano model questionnaire, we examined users' attitudes toward industrial software in both positive and negative dimensions when the software provides or fails to provide specific task functionalities. This survey consisted of 4 basic information questions and 12 task-related questions (6 positive and 6 negative dimensions). Targeting industry professionals via an online survey platform, 84 questionnaires were distributed nationwide to individuals working in industrial manufacturing monitoring and complex operation software roles, and 81 valid responses were collected. Task attributes were quantified using the Better-worse algorithm to identify task positioning within attribute quadrants. The calculation formula is as follows:

$$Better = \frac{A+O}{A+O+M+I} \tag{1}$$

$$Worse = \left(\frac{M+O}{A+O+M+I}\right) \times (-1) \tag{2}$$

In the formula, M means required attributes, O means expected attributes, A means charismatic attributes, and I means unimportant attributes. Through the analysis and calculation of the task attributes, the six task attributes are shown in Table 3.

https://doi.org/10.3390/sym18020317

Table 3. Task Factor Classification Using the KANO Model.

Task Factors	Attributes	*Better*	*Worse*
Production monitoring task	Essential	50%	−58.87%
Communication task	Essential	51.2%	−63.2%
Control execution task	Expect	50%	−53.23%
Abnormal issue handling task	Attractiveness	50%	−50%
Comparison and reviewtask	Indifferent	52.85%	−49.59%
Symbol Reading Task	Indifferent	50.4%	−45.6%

Figure 9 illustrates the distribution of six task factors across the Better-worse coefficient quadrant. Monitoring production and information queries are key tasks in human-industrial software interactions, having the greatest impact on operators. They are followed by control execution and anomaly resolution tasks. The comparison view and multi-display mode are considered attribute tasks with no significant differences.

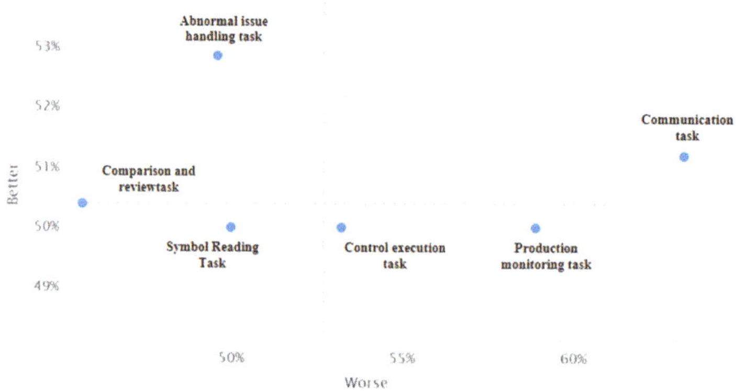

Figure 9. Better-worse Distribution.

The experimental results revealed no significant differences in task attributes between the comparison review task and the graphic symbol reading task, indicating that both tasks were evaluated as having relatively low importance. This narrowed the scope of the six task factor categories to four primary types. Among these, monitoring, communication, and control tasks were prioritized over anomaly issue-resolution tasks.

(4) Task event division based on natural eye movement behavior

A task event refers to a collection of task sequences that achieve specific objectives within a given context. These events can serve as independent descriptive primitives to establish connections with other tasks. Due to their autonomy, task execution naturally triggers unique physiological signal patterns.

This study utilizes eye-tracking technology to observe industrial software operators in real workshop monitoring environments, tracking their natural eye movements while performing four core tasks: monitoring, control execution, communication, and anomaly resolution. By collecting eye movement data during software operation, the research identifies that tasks sharing similar behavioral patterns belong to the same event category, while distinct events exhibit differentiated eye movement metrics. Through eye-tracking visualization, the study analyzes variations in eye movement patterns.

The desktop eye tracker was positioned centrally below the monitor. The Tobii Nano Pro desktop eye tracker (60 Hz sampling rate) was used, with the scene software shown in Figure 8. Eye-tracking materials for the four task categories were sourced from industrial

https://doi.org/10.3390/sym18020317

production monitoring software developed by Hitachi, which was implemented in a certain Iron and Steel Company's intelligent steel rolling production line in China.

To ensure adequate physiological signal induction for observers under natural production conditions and achieve sufficient task type coverage, while facilitating task-related eye movement data labeling during processing, this experimental design collects task-related eye movement data by having staff members watch typical task operation interface videos. The videos are captured from the production interface screen recordings. After expert verification, the video content corresponds to the task type.

The experiment participants were workshop production monitoring personnel, and there were two participants. Both had extensive experience in production monitoring and using experimental software.

The study examines the horizontal (x) and vertical (y) positions of fixation points and instantaneous gaze points, analyzes eye movement speed metrics to identify differences in eye movement patterns across tasks, and identifies typical eye movement pattern characteristics. Time-scale segments (horizontal axis) and absolute vertical axis segments of pattern features are extracted, with the visualization of these metrics shown in Figure 10.

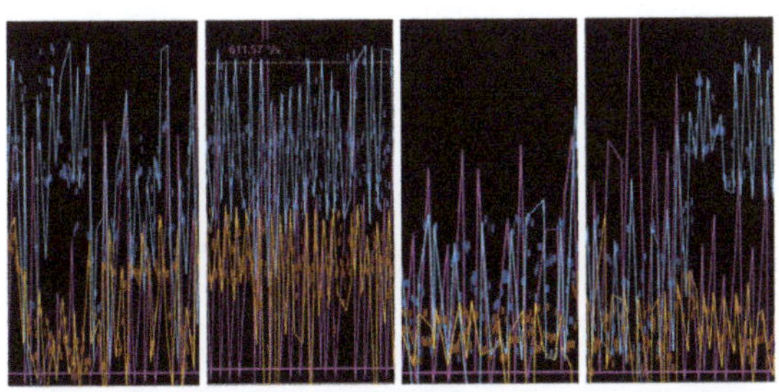

(a)

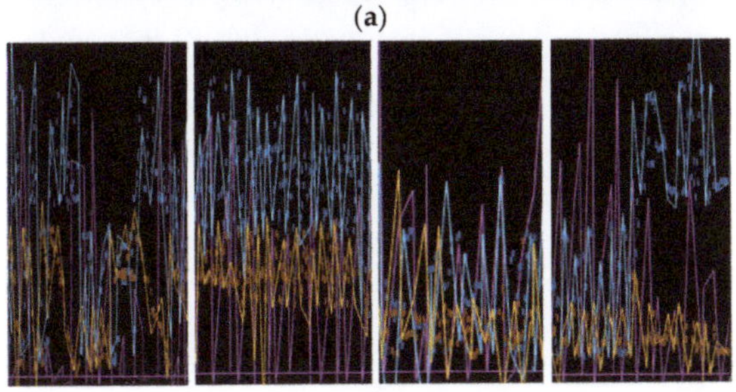

(b)

Figure 10. Visualized eye movement patterns across four tasks: (**a**) Subject 1; (**b**) Subject 2. Note: In the figure, the blue line represents the horizontal position of the instantaneous gaze, and the yellow line represents the vertical position of the instantaneous gaze. The wider blue line indicates the horizontal position of the gaze behavior, while the wider yellow line indicates the vertical position of the gaze behavior. The purple line represents the eye movement speed.

The dynamic eye movements of two participants reveal that the instantaneous fixation positions during monitoring tasks exhibited significant horizontal and vertical variations. This indicates that the visual focus of the task covers the entire monitoring interface.

In contrast, control execution tasks, communication tasks, and complex problem-solving tasks displayed localized fixation patterns. This suggests that these tasks rely on stable interface functional modules. Post-interview analysis confirmed that control execution tasks predominantly utilize centralized button operations in the control module area, while communication tasks primarily depend on the text and numerical information displayed in the table section of the interface.

https://doi.org/10.3390/sym18020317

In terms of fixation points, Task 1 has a scattered fixation area, while Tasks 2 and 3 have a more concentrated fixation area. This clarifies the main functional modules corresponding to the tasks and provides a basis for the design of task-based evocative materials.

In terms of eye movement speed, production monitoring and communication tasks exhibit significantly lower eye movement rates, while control execution and anomaly handling demonstrate higher rates. This indicates that these task behaviors require rapid eye movements to locate targets and perform operations, suggesting higher task demands for the latter two categories. Research shows that eye movement speed correlates positively with cognitive load, indicating that these tasks involve more scenarios requiring cognitive load management and fine-grained intention pattern analysis.

The instantaneous gaze positions and fixation points in complex problem-solving tasks involve multiple regions with significantly different spatial distributions, which allows for more detailed task event categorization. Post-event interviews with monitoring personnel validated the experimental findings: complex problem-solving tasks are highly correlated with the monitors' knowledge, experience, and skills, involving intricate cognitive processing and multiple cognitive stages.

Conventional execution paths engage multiple functional areas, covering task units beyond the aforementioned three categories, thus constituting composite task types. Due to the lack of distinct separable patterns from other tasks, they are not considered typical candidates for further interactive task modeling.

At this point, the industrial HMC tasks related to fine-grained intention are further narrowed down to task 1: monitoring production task and task 2: communication task.

3.3. Different Pattern Analysis Within Tasks

In the context of digital, information-based, and intelligent manufacturing, monitoring automated production lines serves as a critical basis for assessing production status and making scientific decisions. It is a prerequisite for safe and efficient production and the foundation for preventing major accidents. By inspecting, surveilling, and controlling the monitored objects, this monitoring task effectively enhances production efficiency and product quality, representing a primary human–machine interaction scenario in industrial systems.

According to different production scenarios, there are two types of task units for production task monitoring, corresponding to refined task modes. They are the visual browsing mode of the monitor in normal production scenarios and the target search mode of the monitor in abnormal production scenarios, as shown in Figure 11.

In normal production scenarios, monitors carry out routine monitoring tasks by extracting target elements such as the entire system, subsystems, equipment, and sensors to analyze production conditions. During abnormal production situations, monitors conduct browsing and troubleshooting through real-time data analysis and comparison of production data with preset parameters to identify anomalies. Subsequently, human intervention is employed for resolution.

Communication tasks occur between personnel at the control and execution layers. While execution layer personnel have real-time yet transient access to production site conditions through immediate signals, control layer personnel can retrieve sensor data via industrial software interfaces. This includes system and equipment parameters, real-time operational data, and product data—information that is delayed but long-term. The information held by these two groups exhibits differences in granularity, credibility, transparency, and asymmetry, as illustrated in Figure 12.

https://doi.org/10.3390/sym18020317

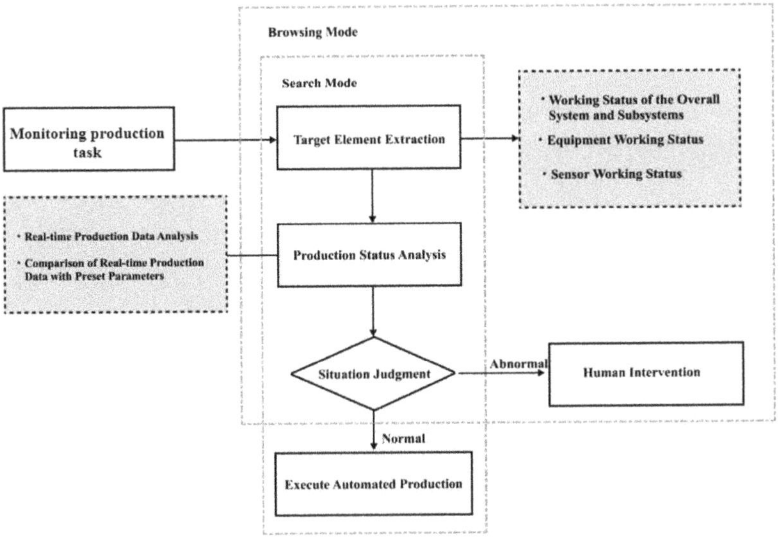

Figure 11. Monitoring production task and fine task pattern.

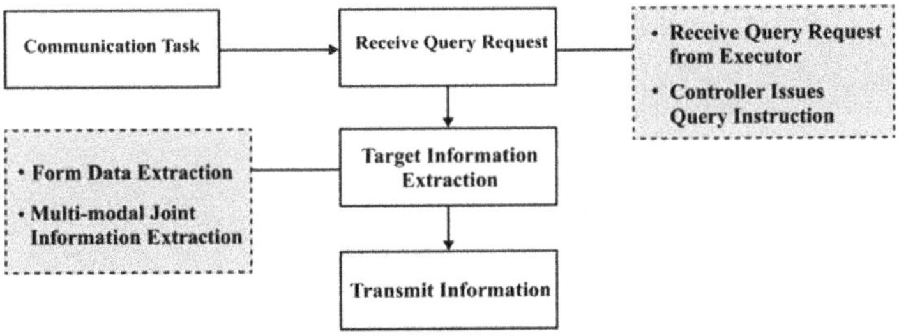

Figure 12. Communication task and fine task mode analysis.

Information retrieval and interaction between control-layer personnel and executive-layer personnel primarily rely on data sources provided by industrial software. The information to be verified typically includes preset process parameters and real-time operational data. This information is generally presented through graphical symbols, textual symbols, numerical symbols, or combinations of these formats.

For complex human–machine interfaces, tabular data serves as the most common information organization format. Another approach combines tabular data with visual graphics and other modalities, such as displaying near production line systems, equipment, or sensors to facilitate real-time interpretation of production status.

Based on differences in operator interpretation behaviors caused by presentation formats, communication tasks are further categorized into tabular communication and multimodal information communication.

3.4. Interaction Model Construction

Analyze the detailed patterns of the above two tasks using the task concept meta-analysis method. After comprehensively analyzing the task objectives, sets, sequences, display control variable properties and influencing factors, model the task visually. The graphic elements in the model are standardized as shown in Table 4:

https://doi.org/10.3390/sym18020317

Table 4. Model Diagram Meaning.

Item	Symbol	Meaning	Detailed Explanation
Task objectives		Typical major tasks	The main tasks produced during the task extraction stage
Task sets		Task units	The detailed task patterns contained within each main task
Task sequences		Task process	The sequence in which users complete the tasks
Influencing Factors		Internal/external conditions	The conditions that affect task completion
Display Control Variable Properties		Controller tasks	The tasks completed by users have controllable attributes
		System tasks	The tasks completed by the system internally have only output variables

The standardized graphics are combined with the task concept meta to visualize the task model. The system interaction task model is built around the two main types of HMC tasks in the industrial system, as shown in Figure 13.

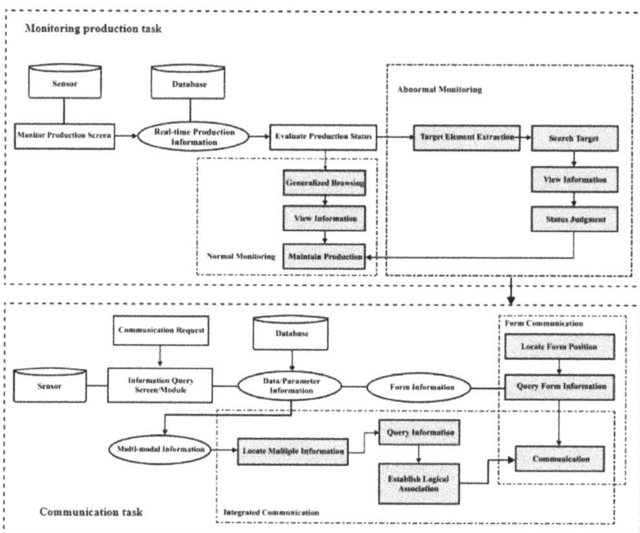

Figure 13. Industrial HMC Interaction Model.

4. Materials and Methods

4.1. Experimental Procedure

Based on the two types of task intentions with fine-grained intention patterns proposed, an EEG experiment was designed. The materials used in the intention-evoking experiment were all taken from the interface of the automatic production line's supporting industrial software of the factory (Baotou Iron and Steel Company, Baotou, China). To avoid redundant stimulation, the interface was processed as a prototype interface.

The task model reveals that Task 1 exhibits two distinct fine-grained intention patterns: visual browsing under normal conditions and target search under abnormal conditions. Visual browsing refers to the aimless, generalized scanning by monitors. In the experimental design, participants must maintain continuous monitoring throughout the task period for a specified duration. To ensure that participants generate task-related EEG signals, they are

https://doi.org/10.3390/sym18020317

required to diligently complete two tasks after the monitoring ends, which evaluates the task execution quality.

For the purposeful target search intention experiment, participants must sustain focused target search during task execution. Drawing from Liang et al.'s complex multi-tasking system paradigm [21] featuring target search subtasks, the experimental procedure is structured as follows: First, participants receive target requests, visually search for corresponding targets, verify if the number of identified targets matches the given quantity, and provide key feedback. The experimental flow is illustrated in Figure 14.

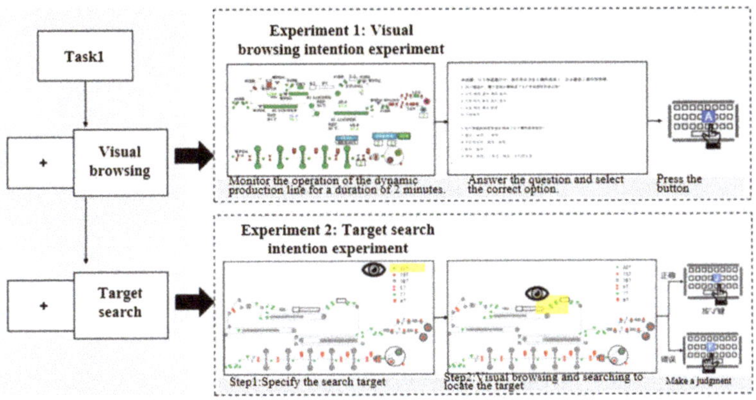

Figure 14. EEG experimental protocols for task 1.

The communication task patterns emerge from interaction scenarios and presentation modalities. They include tasks such as reading table information and providing responses, as well as processing multimodal data (combining tables, production lines, symbols, and text) to formulate answers.

Participants receive communication requests, clarify their objectives, locate target objects within the data presented in tables, and ultimately provide responses. The experiment requires setting up a sufficient number of verifiable table objects and preparing communication questions to keep participants continuously engaged in the communication request-response cycle.

The multimodal communication experiment involves participants receiving requests and responding via a multimodal interface that integrates tables and visual production lines, combining information from both modalities. When encountering abnormal data, participants visually locate the corresponding equipment positions on the dynamic production line. The experimental procedure is illustrated in Figure 15.

The detailed intention experiment was programmed using Tobii Pro Lab software (Version 1.241.54219, x64). The procedure commenced with the experimenter explaining the process, after which participants logged into the computer and completed a pre-experiment. Once confirmed as ready, participants initiated the experiment by pressing the space bar.

The procedure starts with the recording of resting-state EEG signals. Participants then undertake two sub-experiments under the monitoring production task, followed by two sub-experiments under the communication task. Before each experimental task, the instructions for the current task are displayed. Participants can initiate the task by pressing the spacebar once they are prepared.

The EEG annotation system is pre-configured in the software, which automatically marks physiological signals at both the beginning and end of each task. After finishing a task, users can take a rest and resume the experiment by pressing the space bar when they are ready. The system records resting-state EEG data and captures two distinct EEG patterns for fine-grained intention classification during the execution of two types of tasks.

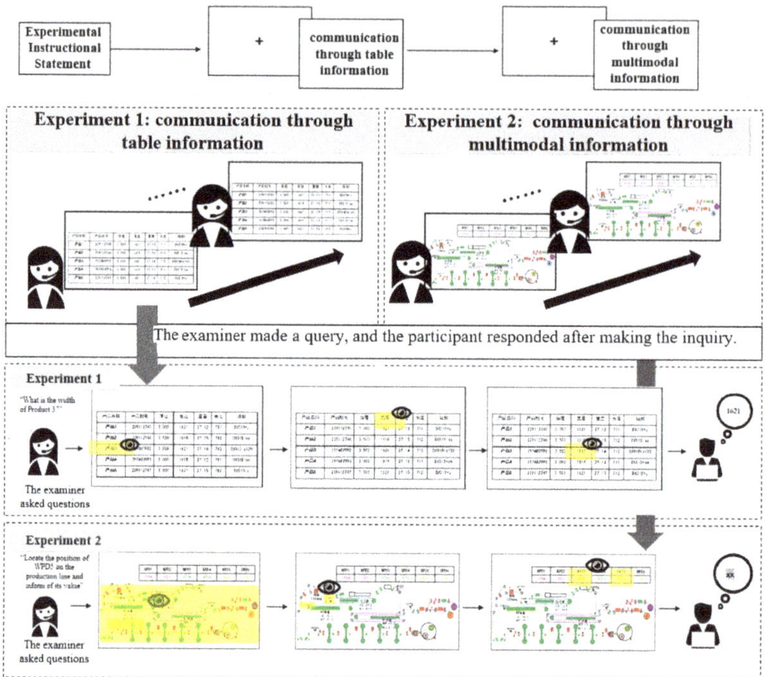

Figure 15. EEG experimental protocols for two types of fine-grained intentions in communication tasks.

4.2. Experimental Environment

This experiment utilized Brain Products' EEG amplifiers and a 64-electrode cap to collect the participants' brainwave data. The data was sampled across cortical channels using the international 10–20 lead system, with the TP9 and TP10 electrodes serving as reference points. All impedance measurements remained below 5 kΩ, and the sampling rate was set at 1000 Hz.

A Tobii Pro Nano eye tracker was employed to verify the induction of fine intention patterns. Two Lenovo desktop computers were used: one for data acquisition and recording, and the other for running experimental programs.

The participants completed tasks using a mouse and keyboard while seated approximately 60 cm from the screen. Twenty participants took part in the experiment, and all equipment specifications and setup details are shown in Figure 16.

(a) (b) (c)

Figure 16. Experimental scenario: (**a**) Experimental data acquisition channel points; (**b**) experimental scenario and BP EEG Signal Collector; (**c**) eye tracker.

https://doi.org/10.3390/sym18020317

4.3. Validity Verification of EEG Data Set

It is challenging to verify whether participants accurately provided EEG data that reflects their intention patterns during experiments. To address this issue, the experimental design integrated post-task performance evaluation with eye movement data collection, ensuring that the EEG data used in subsequent analyses was strongly correlated with task performance.

4.3.1. Performance

In terms of task performance, most of the 20 participants successfully comprehended the requirements and completed the tasks assiduously. Notably, 18 participants attained 100% accuracy in answering questions during the visual scanning task. Participants 4 and 6 each made one error, leading to a 50% accuracy rate. Through post-experiment follow-up interviews and retrospective analysis of video recordings, researchers confirmed that both participants understood the experimental requirements and attentively monitored the task throughout. Subsequent inquiries disclosed that their errors originated from misunderstandings of the test questions and insufficient review of answer options. Therefore, neither participant was excluded from the study.

4.3.2. Eye Movement Behavior Analysis

Eye-tracking technology was employed to analyze the participants' eye movement patterns during task execution, including fixation duration, saccade speed, and gaze trajectories. This enabled the evaluation of whether the participants' intention states aligned with the experimental requirements and whether EEG patterns could be utilized for subsequent fine intention modeling.

Through visual analysis of the eye movement data, we examined fine intention execution from three perspectives: (1) cumulative fixation duration heat maps, (2) saccade path analysis, and (3) gaze trajectory monitoring. The findings revealed the following insights.

For Task 1, a visual mode comparison between Figures 17 and 18 reveals that visual browsing tasks exhibit an extensive distribution of fixation points, predominantly concentrated on graphic symbols along the production line. The scanning paths show random full-screen scanning trajectories.

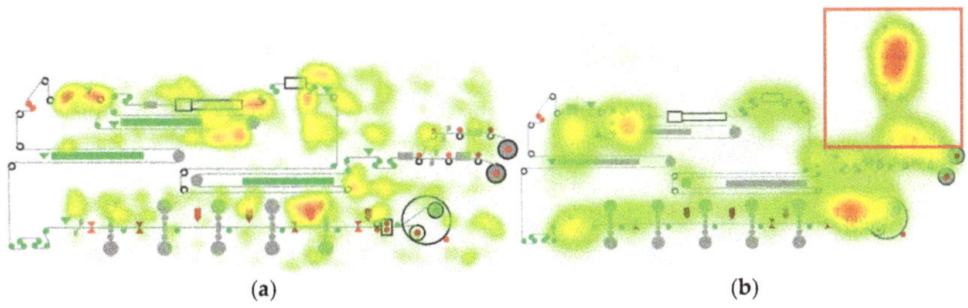

Figure 17. Cumulative heat map: (**a**) Visual browsing pattern; (**b**) visual search pattern.

In contrast, visual search tasks demonstrate concentrated fixation points in two primary areas: the search target region in the upper right corner and graphic elements across the production line. Although search tasks involve fewer fixation points than browsing tasks, the majority of these points occupy larger areas, indicating longer fixation durations. The scanning paths in search tasks frequently cross multiple regions and extend further, yet they maintain clear patterns.

This confirms that participants maintain a certain level of goal orientation during the browsing process.

https://doi.org/10.3390/sym18020317

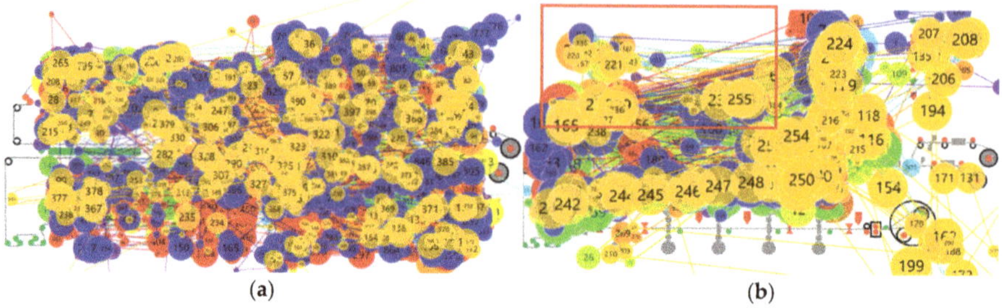

Figure 18. Cumulative scanning path map: (**a**) Visual browsing pattern; (**b**) visual search pattern.

For Task 2, as shown in Figures 19 and 20, during the cumulative task duration, the table-based tasks demonstrated a more concentrated gaze distribution pattern. Specifically, attention was focused on the headers of both rows and columns, as well as the locations of numerical values in the experimental tasks. The scanning paths were widely spread, with trajectories mainly ending at the headers of the table rows.

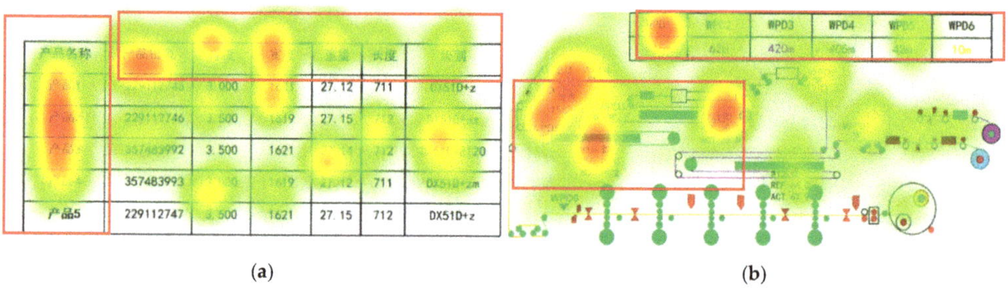

Figure 19. Cumulative thermal map: (**a**) Table communication pattern; (**b**) multimodal information communication pattern.

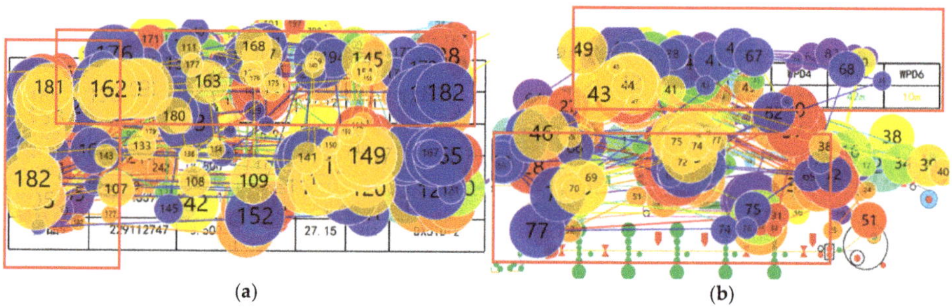

Figure 20. Cumulative scanning path diagram: (**a**) Table communication pattern; (**b**) multimodal information communication pattern.

The fixation point distribution in multimodal communication tasks exhibits concentrated patterns, mainly focusing on two areas: the visual production line and the table. Regarding cumulative scanning paths, both task types display scanning trajectory patterns consistent with the experimental requirements. For example, in the table communication task, the connections of fixation points predominantly cluster between the header and data sections of the scanning trajectory. In contrast, the multimodal information communication task shows fixation point connections that bridge the visual production line and the table display modes, indicating eye movements between these two visual domains.

The results showed that the fixation position, fixation trajectory, fixation time, and scanning path of the 20 subjects in this round of experiment were highly consistent with the experimental task setting, indicating that the subjects performed the task well. The collected EEG signals were correlated with fine intention and could reflect the EEG feedback under fine intention.

4.4. Data Description and Preprocessing

The raw EEG data was preprocessed using the EEGLAB toolbox in Matlab R2013b. The workflow consisted of electrode localization, exclusion of active electrodes, band-pass filtering (0.5–45 Hz), data slicing, artifact removal, and re-referencing using the TP9 and TP10 electrodes, which left 61 remaining channels. ICA algorithms were utilized to eliminate artifacts like blinking, ECG, and eye movement, and outliers were removed at $\pm 100\ \mu V$. A subject-wise approach was adopted to construct multi-subject training sets and leave-one-subject test sets.

4.5. Improved Algorithm

Phase Locking Value (PLV) quantifies the phase consistency between two signals over time, with values ranging from 0 to 1 [33]. MSPs-PLV is an enhanced method for multi-channel electrode phase synchronization. The preprocessing EEG signals undergo Hilbert transform to extract phase values, which are then used to calculate phase synchronization between electrode pairs across multiple channels. The most synchronized electrode pairs are selected, and their PLV values form a feature space. Machine learning classifiers are then applied to categorize implicit intentions. The workflow is illustrated in Figure 21.

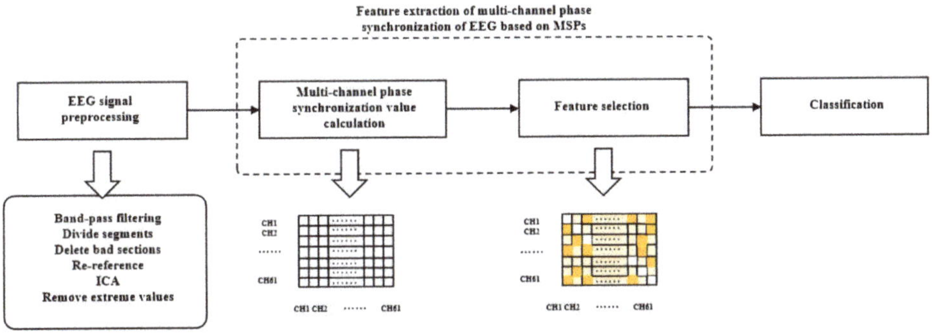

Figure 21. Schematic illustration of MSPs-PLV feature extraction. Note: The yellow-marked channels represent the selected synchronous channel pairs. The darker the color, the stronger the synchronization, and the PLV value approaches 1.

The specific steps of this method are as follows:

4.5.1. Calculate the Phase-Locking Value (PLV) Between Channels

The PLV quantifies the synchronization of two signals' phases, reflecting phase consistency across channels and brain regions. In this study, we analyzed the phase synchronization patterns of EEG signals across channels to identify distinct intentional EEG synchronization modes.

The calculation process is as follows:

For an EEG signal sequence in a specific $x(t)$, use the Hilbert transform to find the imaginary part of the corresponding complex signal $\hat{x}(t)$. The original signal after inversion can be expressed as:

$$\widetilde{x}(t) = x(t) + i\hat{x}(t) = a(t)e^{i\Phi_x(t)} \quad (3)$$

Use the arctan function to calculate the instantaneous phase $\phi_x(t)$ and Amplitude $a(t)$, obtain the phase difference between the two signals by combining the instantaneous phase and amplitude of the complex signal.

$$\phi_{xy}(t) = \phi_x(t) - \phi_y(t) \tag{4}$$

Compute the unit-modulus signal on the complex plane $X(t) = e^{i\phi_{xy}(t)}$ and then calculate the mathematical expectation of the temporal values. The calculation formula is as follows:

$$\text{PLV} = \left\| \frac{1}{\text{T}} \int_0^{\text{T}} X(\tau) d\tau \right\| \tag{5}$$

The PLV value ranges from 0 to 1. A value closer to 1 indicates better phase synchronization between the two signals, while a value closer to 0 indicates worse synchronization.

4.5.2. Select Most Significant Pairs (MSPs) with the Maximum Difference

To classify intents, we calculate the difference PLV between channel pairs of two intent categories and select MSPs with the largest differences as dimensions for intent feature construction. Fifteen pairs of MSPs are extracted from each frequency band, as shown in Figure 22.

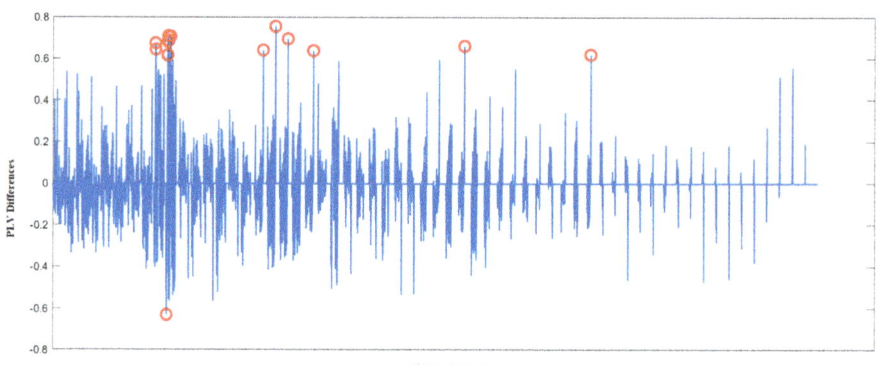

Figure 22. The electrode pair with the greatest PLV difference identified through two fine intention searches in Trial 14's monitoring production task is shown as an example.

Assume two fine-grained intention patterns and N-channel EEG signals. Each pair of PLV channels can be represented by a matrix:

$\text{PLV}_{ij}^{(1)}$ indicates the PLV value between channel i and channel j under intention 1. $\text{PLV}_{ij}^{(2)}$ indicates the PLV value between channel i and channel j under intention 2. $\Delta\text{PLV}_{ij}(i,j)$ means a difference in PLV values for the channel pair (i,j) under the two types of intentions. PLV represents the PLV value between channel i and channel j under intention 1. N is the total number of channels.

For each channel (i,j) pair, calculate the PLV difference between the two types of intent:

$$\Delta\text{PLV}_{ij} = \left| \text{PLV}_{ij}^{(1)} - \text{PLV}_{ij}^{(2)} \right| \tag{6}$$

Identify the MSPs with the largest PLV difference among all possible channel pairs. Specifically, the task is to determine:

$$(i^*, j^*) = \text{argmax}(\Delta\text{PLV}_{ij}) \tag{7}$$

https://doi.org/10.3390/sym18020317

The (i^*, j^*) dimension will be constructed as an intention feature. The final intention phase difference can be expressed as:

$$\mathrm{PLV_{diff}} = \Delta \mathrm{PLV}_{i^* j^*} \tag{8}$$

4.5.3. Reconstructing Intention Features Using MSPs

To expand the model training dataset, we partitioned the intent task state samples into time windows with 1-s interval PLVs and no repetition. For each intent category, we extracted 15 pairs of MSP channels with the maximum difference and calculated the corresponding MSPs for each intent category.

The calculation formula is as follows:

Let $\mathrm{MSPs}_{i,j}(i \neq j, i, j \in \{1,2\})$ represent the channels between the i-th intention and the j-th intention. For the i-th intention, we need to aggregate its MSPs channel pairs with those of other intentions. Let MSPs_i denote the complete set of MSPs channel pairs for the i-th intention, which can be expressed as:

$$\mathrm{MSPs}_i = \bigcup_{j \neq i} \mathrm{MSPs}_{i,j} \tag{9}$$

where $\cup$ represents the union of sets.

Next, the PLV is extracted from the intention feature set. Let $\mathrm{PLV}_{i,k}$ represent the phase locking value feature of the i-th channel pair for the j-th intention. For the i-th intention, extract the phase-locking value characteristics of all channel pairs in MSPs_i. Let PLV_i represent the complete feature vector of the i-th intention, which can be expressed as:

$$\mathrm{PLV}_i = [\mathrm{PLV}_{i,1}, \mathrm{PLV}_{i,2}, \ldots, \mathrm{PLV}_{i,15}] \tag{10}$$

Among them, 1 to 15 represent 15 pairs of channels for the first intention.

The schematic diagram of feature construction is shown in Figure 23:

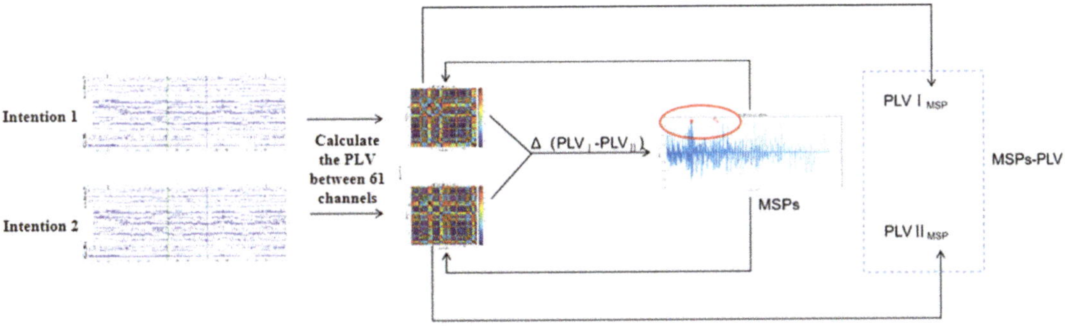

Figure 23. Schematic diagram of feature construction.

4.6. Model Data Construction

To prevent data leakage, the subject-wise approach was employed to construct training and test sets. Parameter optimization was performed using 5-fold cross-validation and grid search to determine the optimal c and g values for the RBF-SVM model. Given SVM's high requirement for sample balance, this study employs the SMOTE technique to equalize sample quantities across different class labels. The final training and test set sizes for each inter-subject modeling experiment are presented in Table 5.

https://doi.org/10.3390/sym18020317

Table 5. Sample capacity of train and test sets.

Subject ID	Task 1		Task 2	
	Test Sets	Train Sets	Test Sets	Train Sets
Subject 1	225	6776	167	4960
Subject 2	66	6956	94	5069
Subject 3	104	6917	116	5034
Subject 4	68	6960	84	5094
Subject 5	108	6911	149	4993
Subject 6	100	6924	166	4966
Subject 7	446	6387	314	4751
Subject 8	215	6715	153	4985
Subject 9	326	6573	215	4898
Subject 10	230	6743	87	5079
Subject 11	162	6841	137	5013
Subject 12	379	6424	189	4942
Subject 13	266	6667	213	4895
Subject 14	327	6585	233	4876
Subject 15	319	6510	207	4909
Subject 16	274	6617	190	4932
Subject 17	301	6623	279	4812
Subject 18	349	6556	216	4898
Subject 19	353	6541	210	4818
Subject 20	355	6514	228	4870

5. Results and Discussion

5.1. Algorithm Performance

This study included 20 participants to evaluate the recognition performance of two fine-grained intention patterns: visual browsing/target search and table communication/multi-modal information communication, as shown in Table 6.

Table 6. The performance of the method.

Subject ID	Task 1				Task 2			
	Train Acc%	Test Acc%	*c*	*g*	Train Acc%	Test Acc%	*c*	*g*
Subject 1	99.62	99.56	0.06	2.00	100.00	100.00	0.03	0.50
Subject 2	100.00	100.00	0.06	0.25	100.00	100.00	0.06	1.00
Subject 3	100.00	100.00	0.06	0.50	100.00	100.00	0.03	1.00
Subject 4	100.00	100.00	0.13	0.25	100.00	100.00	0.03	0.50
Subject 5	98.44	98.15	0.06	0.50	98.58	97.99	0.03	2.00
Subject 6	99.13	99.00	0.25	1.00	100.00	100.00	0.03	0.06
Subject 7	95.09	93.95	8.00	0.25	100.00	100.00	0.03	1.00
Subject 8	100.00	100.00	0.03	0.25	100.00	100.00	0.03	2.00
Subject 9	100.00	100.00	0.03	0.06	100.00	100.00	0.03	0.06
Subject 10	100.00	100.00	0.03	0.25	100.00	100.00	0.03	0.50
Subject 11	100.00	100.00	0.03	0.50	100.00	100.00	0.03	0.25
Subject 12	99.84	99.74	0.03	2.00	100.00	100.00	0.03	0.06
Subject 13	100.00	100.00	0.03	2.00	100.00	100.00	0.03	0.13
Subject 14	98.78	98.02	0.5	4.00	100.00	100.00	0.03	0.06
Subject 15	100.00	100.00	0.03	0.06	99.66	99.52	0.03	1.00
Subject 16	100.00	100.00	0.03	0.13	100.00	100.00	0.03	0.06
Subject 17	100.00	100.00	0.03	0.06	100.00	100.00	0.03	1.00
Subject 18	100.00	100.00	0.03	0.06	100.00	100.00	0.03	0.06
Subject 19	100.00	100.00	0.03	1.00	100.00	100.00	0.03	0.06
Subject 20	100.00	100.00	0.03	0.13	100.00	100.00	0.03	0.03
Mean	99.54	99.42	0.48	0.76	99.91	99.88	0.03	0.57
Std	1.14	1.42	1.77	1.01	0.32	0.46	0.01	0.63

The two types of fine-grained intent recognition models achieved an average accuracy rate exceeding 96% across both training and test sets. In the monitoring production

https://doi.org/10.3390/sym18020317

task, the training and test accuracies for the two fine-grained intents were 99.54 ± 1.14% and 99.42 ± 1.42%, respectively. For the communication task, the accuracies reached 99.91 ± 0.32% and 99.88 ± 0.46%. The method proposed in this research demonstrates exceptional accuracy in fine-grained intent pattern recognition, with its small standard deviation further validating its generalization performance. A small standard deviation indicates that the MSPs-PLV feature's inherent cross-subject stability is naturally or through preprocessing normalized to a common scale and individuals exhibit high consistency in their optimal decision boundary.

The table presents the optimal coefficients c and g of the Gaussian kernel function RBF-SVM determined through grid search after training. In the production monitoring task for fine intention pattern recognition, the average coefficients are c = 0.48 and g = 0.76, while in the communication task, the average coefficients are c = 0.03 and g = 0.57. The consistency of parameters c and g proves that there are no fundamental differences in the feature space regarding which RBF kernel width and regularization parameter to use in which interval. Their separability and margin are highly similar. This demonstrates well-controlled experimental conditions, providing a basis for cross-species recognition. Using these parameters to train a leave-one-subject-out (LOSO) general SVM can prevent performance collapse caused by hyperparameter drift.

5.2. Baseline Method Comparison

The baseline comparison method is the traditional PLV method, while integrating it with the aforementioned RBF-SVM. The performance of each method in the frequency domain was observed. The three baseline methods for comparison are:

(1) The traditional PLV method;

(2) The traditional PLV in the frequency domain (FDPLV);

(3) MSPs-PLV in frequency domain (FDMSPs-PLV);

Comparison results are shown in Figure 24.

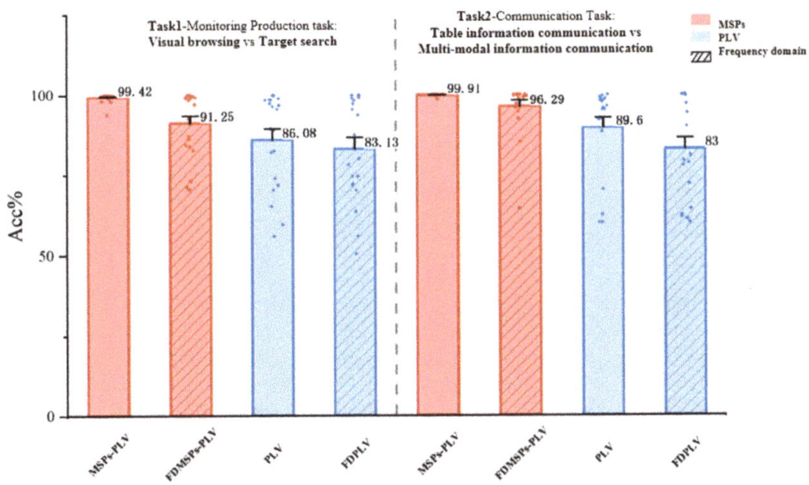

Figure 24. Comparison of results with the baseline methods.

The experimental results show that the feature information enriched by frequency segmentation cannot improve the recognition accuracy, and the whole frequency band of PLV features has better discrimination ability for implicit intention.

The MSP method, which identifies electrode pairs with maximum PLV differences for constructing fine-grained intention features, outperforms traditional PLV algorithms.

https://doi.org/10.3390/sym18020317

While frequency-domain PLV under the same feature screening method does not provide richer feature information, it still demonstrates higher recognition accuracy and smaller standard deviation compared to the two conventional time-domain PLV methods.

Figure 24 comprehensively demonstrates the high performance and stability of the MSPs-based approach in fine-grained intention pattern recognition across two task categories.

5.2.1. Comparative Analysis of Methods for Task 1

The recognition model developed using time-domain PLV based on MSPs achieved 99.42% accuracy, outperforming frequency-domain PLV's 91.25% by 8.17 percentage points. In contrast, the traditional time-domain PLV algorithm (before optimization) recorded 86.08% accuracy, surpassing frequency-domain PLV's 83.13% by 2.95 percentage points. See Table 7.

Table 7. Method comparison for Task 1.

	MSPs-PLV		**PLV**	
	MSPs-PLV	**FDMSPs-PLV**	**PLV**	**FDPLV**
Acc%	99.42 ± 1.42	91.25 ± 10.43	86.08 ± 14.74	83.13 ± 15.96
F1	1.00 ± 0.01	0.92 ± 0.10	0.90 ± 0.09	0.88 ± 0.11

The experimental results demonstrate that the fine intention pattern features of electrode pairs selected by the MSPs method significantly outperform those of traditional multi-electrode pair PLV algorithms.

Figure 25a compares the accuracy of four recognition models across 20 experimental groups. The MSP-based feature space construction method for synchronous electrode pairs demonstrates significantly better performance than the traditional PLV method in both recognition accuracy and stability.

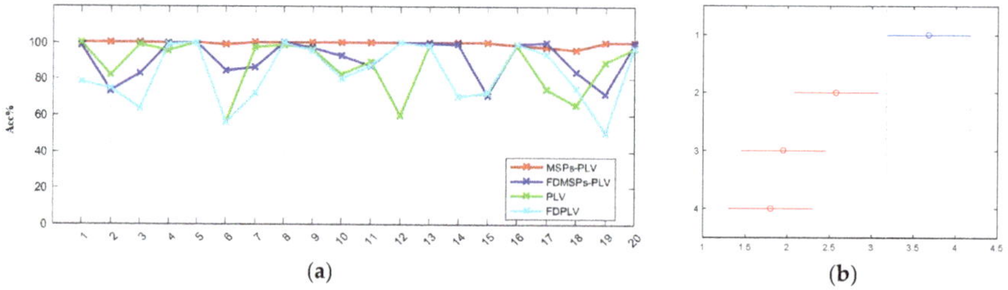

Figure 25. Subject-wise test Acc and Difference test: (**a**) Subject-wise modeling results for 20 groups; (**b**) Friedman's test result. The blue line represents the method of this paper. Note: The vertical axis indicates: 1 for the proposed method MSPs-PLV, 2 for FDMSPs-PLV, 3 for PLV, and 4 for FDPLV.

We conducted a Friedman's nonparametric test on the identification accuracy rates of 20 experimental groups across four methods to determine if statistically significant differences existed. The p-value of 2.75×10^{-6} (significantly lower than 0.001) led to the rejection of the null hypothesis that all methods had identical accuracy rates, indicating substantial differences in identification performance.

The post hoc test using pairwise comparisons revealed that, as shown in the Friedman test plot, the proposed algorithm did not overlap with the other three algorithms, while the latter exhibited mutual overlaps. This demonstrates the superiority of our method over the three alternatives. There were no significant differences in recognition performance among the three alternatives, as illustrated in Figure 25b.

https://doi.org/10.3390/sym18020317

5.2.2. Comparative Analysis of Methods for Task 2

In the task of fine-grained intent recognition from multimodal information communication in tables, our method achieves the highest F1 recognition accuracy (99.88 ± 0.46%) and value compared with the other three methods. See Table 8.

Table 8. Method comparison for Task 2.

	MSPs-PLV		**PLV**	
	MSPs-PLV	**FDMSPs-PLV**	**PLV**	**FDPLV**
Acc%	99.88 ± 0.46	86.08 ± 14.74	89.60 ± 13.92	83.00 ± 15.38
F1	1.00 ± 0.00	0.97 ± 0.06	0.87 ± 0.17	0.88 ± 0.11

The frequency-domain phase synchronization features failed to provide sufficient discriminative characteristics for this classification task. Both frequency-domain PLV methods performed worse than time-domain approaches. The recognition accuracy of these two PLV methods in the frequency domain was only 86.08% and 83.00%, respectively, significantly lower than that of the time-domain MSPs-PLV algorithm (99.88%) and the PLV algorithm (89.60%).

As shown in Figure 26a, the comparison of the test accuracy rates of the four methods in the identification model of 20 groups of experiments shows that the method based on MSPs screening synchronous electrode pairs to constitute the feature space is significantly better than the other three methods in terms of identification accuracy and stability.

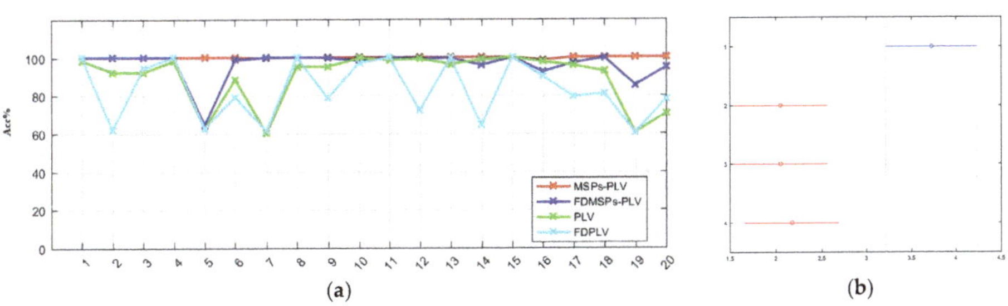

Figure 26. Subject-wise test Acc and Difference test: (**a**) Subject-wise modeling results for 20 groups; (**b**) Friedman's test result. The blue line represents the method of this paper. Note: The vertical axis indicates: 1 for the proposed method MSPs-PLV, 2 for FDMSPs-PLV, 3 for PLV, and 4 for FDPLV.

The Friedman's non-parametric test was employed to determine whether there were statistically significant differences in the accuracy of the four methods for fine intention pattern recognition. The test yielded a p-value of 1.36×10^{-5}, which is below the 0.001 threshold. This result rejects the null hypothesis that all four methods have identical recognition accuracy, thereby indicating significant differences in performance.

We conducted pairwise comparisons among the four methods. The post hoc test results, as shown in Figure 26b (Friedman's test plot), revealed no overlapping regions between our method and the other three approaches, indicating that our method significantly outperforms them in recognition performance. The overlapping regions among the other three methods suggest that there are no significant differences in their recognition performance.

https://doi.org/10.3390/sym18020317

5.3. Discussion

5.3.1. MSPs-PLV Characteristics Identified by Visualization

Twenty participants were assigned 15 pairs of MSP channels each to a 61 × 61 EEG coordinate system. The study examined the similarities and differences between major intention categories and fine intention patterns within tasks. The comparison results are shown in Figure 27.

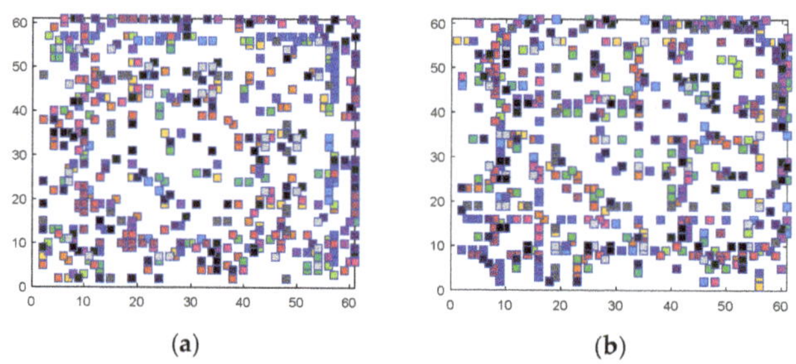

Figure 27. Most significant feature channel of 20 subjects: (**a**) Task 1; (**b**) Task 2. Note: To distinguish them, the MSP channels of 20 subjects are labeled with different colors.

The channel pairs of 20 screened subjects were displayed in different colors, revealing that MSPs screening exhibited individual specificity: each subject's 15 pairs of MSPs differed. During training, the personalized PLV values of each subject's MSPs channel pairs were used to form intention features.

By comparing the MSPs diagrams of production monitoring and communication tasks, we observe that the MSPs of the same subjects vary across different tasks. The distribution of MSPs exhibits significant differences between these two task categories. This indicates that feature selection based on MSPs in fine intention modeling should be determined by the broad category of interaction tasks. Different task types lead to distinct pairs of phase-synchronized channels even among the same subjects. In practical applications, fine intention recognition should be built on the foundation of broad task category intention recognition, using a two-tier cascade model approach for identification.

5.3.2. Functional Connectivity Analysis

The FieldTrip [34] toolkit was employed for brain power source localization. For volume conductor modeling, the standard BEM head volume conductor model provided by FieldTrip was utilized. Source space definition and lead field matrix calculation were subsequently performed, where potential neural activity sources in the brain were modeled as equivalent current dipoles. The theoretical potential distribution generated by each equivalent current dipole at all EEG electrode positions constituted the numerical solution of the EEG forward problem. Based on the obtained lead field matrix, the linearly constrained minimum variance (LCMV) beamformer algorithm was applied for source activity estimation [35]. According to the AAL atlas [36], the time series of source current density from the estimated 1149 dipoles were assigned to their corresponding 76 brain regions. The singular value decomposition method was then employed to extract the most representative source activity time series for each brain region.

The brain regions with phase synchronization are observed by tracing the intention patterns in two key task scenarios, and the functional channels that constitute the real-time flow or integration of information are observed.

The paired T-test [37] was employed to identify statistically significant functional connectivity subnetworks, detect phase synchronization differences across broad frequency bands, and trace brain origins of significantly different frequency bands. The thresholds

https://doi.org/10.3390/sym18020317

used were Edge $p < 0.005$ and Component $p < 0.05$, with 10,000 permutation trials. The specific procedures were as follows:

- First, conduct paired T-tests on each edge in the functional connectivity network, identifying edges with Edge $p < 0.005$ as candidate differential edges.
- Based on the principle of connectivity, the candidate difference edges are divided into different network components (subnetworks).
- Calculate the size of each network component, that is, the number of connected edges contained in each subnetwork.
- To determine the significance of network components, we conducted 10,000 permutation tests to construct the empirical null distribution of maximum component sizes under random grouping. If a component size exceeds the 95th percentile of the maximum observed sizes from these tests (i.e., Component $p < 0.05$), the component is considered statistically significant between the two groups.

(1) Target searching pattern (Pattern 1) vs. Visual browsing pattern (Pattern 2)

Statistical analysis revealed statistically significant differences between the two patterns in the connection strength of PLV pathways, as illustrated in Figure 28; the related data is listed in Table 9.

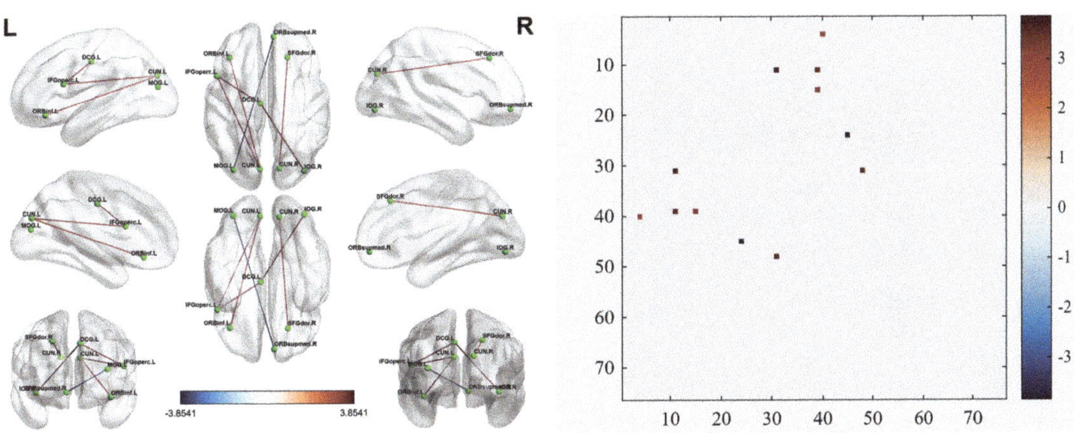

(**a**) (**b**)

Figure 28. Connected edge diagram with significant differences for Task 1's two patterns (t-value): (**a**) significant edge connection; (**b**) link strength. The name of brain regions is derived from the AAL atlas.

Table 9. The brain region with the strongest phase synchronization between intention patterns for Task 1.

Node1	Node2	t-Value	*p*-Value
SFGdor.R	CUN.R	3.177397857	0.00495905
IFGoperc.L	DCG.L	3.755840969	0.001338031
IFGoperc.L	CUN.L	3.543256793	0.002171253
ORBinf.L	CUN.L	3.25131374	0.004201297
ORBsupmed.R	MOG.L	−3.854118414	0.001069169
DCG.L	IOG.R	3.560457875	0.002088015

The red edge connection involved the primary node locations, such as the Superior Frontal Gyrus, Cuneus, Inferior Frontal Gyrus, Middle Cingulate Gyrus, etc. These brain regions are involved in working memory, attention regulation, higher cognitive control,

https://doi.org/10.3390/sym18020317

visual attention, and visual information integration. The synchronous enhancement in these brain regions indicates a wide range of functional coordination and information exchange. Pattern 1 induced broader synchronization because it has more red connecting edges. It suggests that pattern 1 demands higher cognitive resource with enhanced phase locking and involvement of attention, memory, and cognitive control.

The blue connecting edges indicate brain regions where pattern 2 surpasses pattern 1. The brain region distribution in Figure 28 suggests that pattern 2 relies more heavily on the selective allocation of visual attention and the priority processing of visual information. The two brain regions with significant connectivity (ORBsupmed.R-MOG.L) are involved in value assessment and higher visual processing, visual-spatial integration, and visual-cognitive information integration, respectively. This transhemispheric and trans-network-phase synchronization is a crucial neural mechanism for visual-cognitive integration. It shows that the monitoring task calls for visual browsing and cognitive integration. These results suggest distinct task-related information routing strategies and may reflect a central–peripheral attentional reallocation mechanism.

The group average of functional connectivity strength of 20 subjects is shown in Figure 29. The results show that the functional connectivity of the brain regions in pattern 1 is stronger than that in pattern 2, with more significant task states and stronger phase synchronization between brain regions.

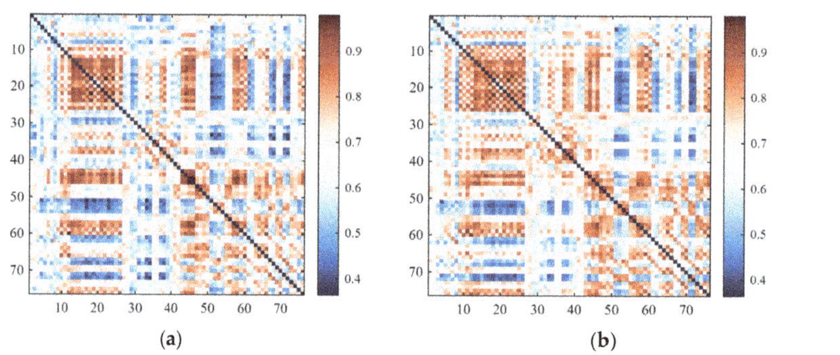

Figure 29. Group average connection diagram for Task 1: (**a**) pattern 1; (**b**) pattern 2.

(2) Multi-modal information communication pattern (pattern 1) vs. Table information communication pattern (pattern 2)

The most synchronized brain region nodes under the two patterns are shown in Table 10. As shown in Figure 30, the two intention patterns of Task 2 were traced to functional connections involving the central prefrontal cortex, superior parietal cortex, superior frontal cortex, inferior frontal cortex, angular gyrus, insula, central posterior cortex, anterior cingulate cortex, and middle cingulate cortex, forming a complex frontal–parietal–lobal system network.

Table 10. The brain region with the strongest phase synchronization between intention patterns for Task 2.

Node1	Node2	T-Value	p-Value
PreCG.R	SMG.L	3.23126137	0.00439488
SFGdor.R	IFGoperc.R	3.261405149	0.004107056
SFGdor.R	ANG.R	3.316502729	0.003627893
INS.L	PoCG.R	3.332614894	0.003498442
ACG.L	DCG.R	−4.475790585	0.000259035

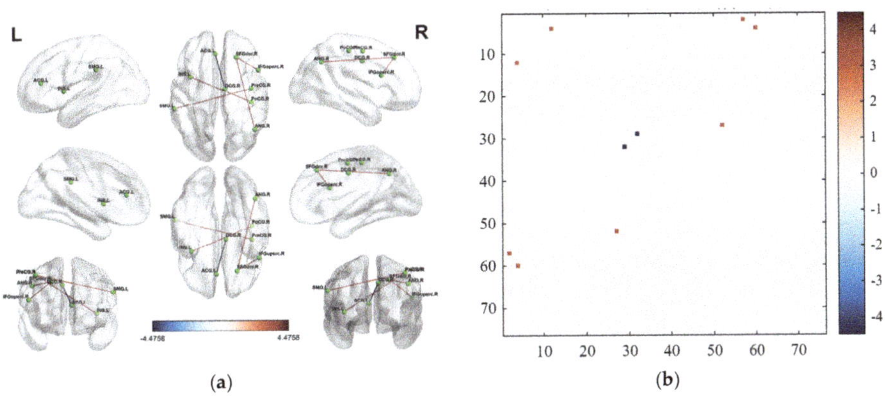

Figure 30. Connected edge diagram with significant differences for Task 2's two patterns (t-value): (a) significant edge connection; (b) link strength. The name of brain regions is derived from the AAL atlas.

The phase synchronization of the aforementioned brain regions suggests that communication tasks involve cognitive processes such as working memory maintenance and response inhibition, task switching and attentional balance, proprioceptive processing, as well as error monitoring and adaptive control. This indicates that in this communication task scenario, the operator requires efficient cross-network information integration, flexible task switching capabilities, and robust cognitive control reserves. The synchronization pattern reflects the high cognitive load of the operator in task 2.

More red edges indicate that pattern 1 has more extensive functional connections and information exchange than pattern 2. Through analysis of brain networks and functions, it demonstrates the integration of three major networks: the Executive Control Network (ECN), the Sensory-Motor Network (SMN), and the Salience Network (SN). Details include cognitive control–language execution–semantic integration; executive planning–sensory integration; conflict monitoring–cognitive control.

Pattern 2 shows a significant phase synchronization between two brain regions (ACG.L-DCG.R), which is a hemispheric coordination of the cingulate cortex. These two brain regions are associated with error monitoring and adaptive control, and their functional connectivity represents the integration of conflict detection and cognitive control.

The average group connectivity between patterns showed a large difference from task 1, as shown in Figure 31. But the difference in the average group connectivity within tasks was very weak, reflecting the similar physiological response of fine intention patterns and the difficulty of fuzzy classification.

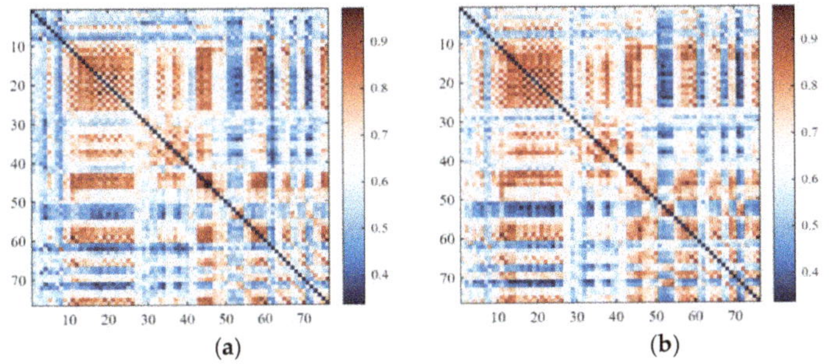

Figure 31. Group average connection diagram for Task 2: (a) pattern 1; (b) pattern 2.

https://doi.org/10.3390/sym18020317

5.3.3. Significance Analysis of Frequency Band Function Connection

NBS correction revealed a significant difference in only the gamma (30–45 Hz) frequency band connectivity between multi-modal communication and table communication, with the difference component being positive (indicating stronger connectivity under multimodal communication compared to tabular communication), at $p = 0.043$.

High-frequency functional connectivity indicates that multi-modal information communication demonstrates significantly stronger information integration compared to other tasks. It suggests that this task involves a high level of operator consciousness, potentially generating substantial cognitive workload. The edge connection of gamma-band communication tasks with significant differences is shown in Figure 32. This visualization displays the T-value distribution of statistically significant edges, where edge colors indicate T-value magnitudes. T-values > 0 indicate stronger multi-modal communication than tabular communication.

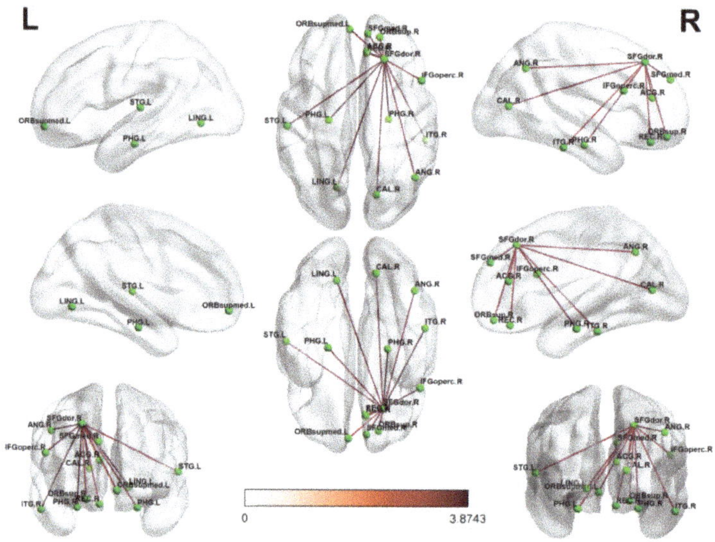

Figure 32. Connected edge diagram with significant differences.

Further analysis revealed that most internal connections within this component were associated with SFGdor.R (Frontal Supramarginal Region, right dorsolateral prefrontal gyrus), indicating SFGdor.R as a key brain region for communication tasks. This region is typically considered part of the dorsolateral prefrontal cortex (DLPFC), which is involved in working memory, cognitive control, executive functions, attention regulation, decision-making, and understanding others' intentions.

5.3.4. Cross-Domain Generalization Performance

The public intention EEG datasets are mostly coarse categories with significant physiological response differences, such as motor imagery intention datasets and cognitive task datasets [10]. This study conducted experiments based on the visual browsing intent experimental paradigm by Kang, Park et al., constructing a visual browsing intent dataset. Following the photo scenes from the original experiment, we carefully generated five similar scene photos using AIGC, designed the experimental procedure according to the paradigm, and collected EEG data. The experimental flow is shown in Figure 33.

https://doi.org/10.3390/sym18020317

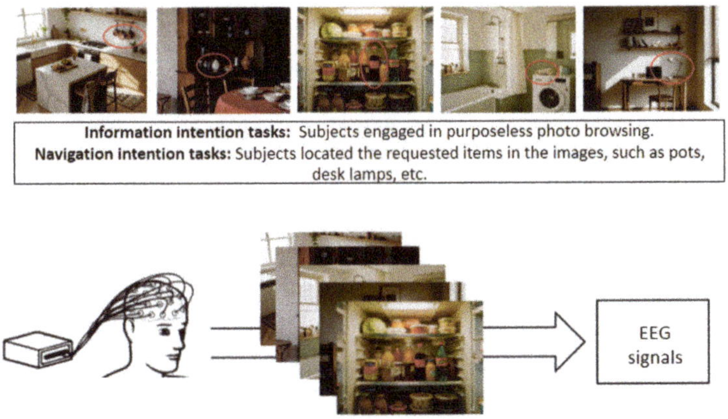

Figure 33. Baseline data set.

A total of five participants were enrolled in the study, and each completed two experimental sessions. Each session consisted of 10 trials (five trials for each of the two fine intention patterns). In the visual search task, the text was presented in ascending order to avoid the repetition of target items, thus eliminating the influence of prior experience on physiological signal induction. The 64-channel EEG data were collected using the Brain Product system at a 1000 Hz sampling rate. When applying the proposed method to this dataset, the experimental results are presented in Table 11.

Table 11. Cross-scene generalization performance of the proposed method.

	Subject 1	Subject 2	Subject 3	Subject 4	Subject 5
test Acc	94.12%	72.22%	88.24%	94.44%	76.47%
F1	0.92	0.62	0.92	0.96	0.78
mean Acc			85.09 ± 10.23%		
mean F1			0.84 ± 0.14%		

The proposed method achieves an accuracy rate of 85.09 ± 10.23% on the EEG dataset from this experiment, surpassing the 83.9 ± 0.07% result obtained by Park et al. in their single-modal EEG classification study.

Although the method's accuracy (90.9 ± 0.07%) is lower than Park et al.'s implicit intention recognition approach that combines EEG phase synchronization and eye-movement multimodal features, it still shows 1.19 percentage points higher performance than their single-modal EEG modeling. This confirms the effectiveness of our method in fine-grained intention pattern recognition.

6. Conclusions

6.1. Main Work

This paper proposes a task modeling method for complex HMC, which includes task extraction, task analysis, and task visualization modeling. It integrates operators' natural eye movement behaviors and multi-source heterogeneous data into the modeling process, making the model construction a repeatable process. The approach standardizes reliable input and execution methods while providing scientific foundations for optimizing HMC designs in complex industrial scenarios. In typical industrial HMC scenarios, we applied this method for task modeling.

https://doi.org/10.3390/sym18020317

This research also proposes a fine-grained implicit intention recognition method, which addresses the multi-channel functional connectivity characteristics of intentional EEG. Experimental results demonstrate that the MSPs-based PLV method outperforms both time-domain and frequency-domain PLV approaches in recognition accuracy. When applied to two typical industrial system-specific intention classification, the method achieves 99.42% and 99.88% accuracy rates, respectively.

By integrating functional connectivity sub-networks and brain source localization techniques with visualizations, this study employs multiple methodologies, including MSPs localization, PLV temporal dynamics, group-averaged PLV analysis, and functional connectivity tracing. The research precisely identifies task-specific frequency bands and key brain regions, while revealing functional connectivity differences and source activity variations between tasks and across patterns within tasks. Through visual analysis and differential verification, the study confirms the inherent ambiguity in fine-grained intention patterns and further validates the effectiveness of the proposed methodology.

6.2. Innovation

By taking human intention as our lens, we explore ways to weave human intelligence into HMC, fostering bidirectional perception and understanding that heighten information symmetry between the two agents and, ultimately, enhance overall performance.

The system-task-physiological multi-dimensional task-modeling framework overcomes existing limitations by incorporating physiological feedback and system-wide interaction characteristics. It effectively integrates multi-level information that combines subjective cognition, objective data, and physiological responses. The model achieves a leap from subjective requirements and functional descriptions to computable and verifiable task specifications, establishing a paradigm for extracting, analyzing, and modeling tasks in complex systems. This advancement drives the hierarchical convergence of industrial system interactions, enables concept-based tuple-driven task refinement, and provides reliable inputs for intention recognition.

This research refines the granularity of intention recognition technology, enabling more nuanced and precise interpretation of human intentions. The MSPs-PLV method addresses the limitations of existing methods by establishing a framework that identifies electrode pairs with maximum phase synchronization differences, enabling high-precision recognition of nuanced intention patterns. Furthermore, it reveals the neural mechanisms underlying these patterns through functional connectivity analysis, source localization, and identification of key brain regions and frequency bands.

6.3. Future Study

This research focuses on the transformation and upgrading of human-centered industrial systems in Industry 5.0, conducting experimental and exploratory studies on the theories and methods of integrating humans into intelligent systems. From the perspective of operators' physiological signals, this paper presents a method for identifying refined implicit intentions. With the continuous development of technology, this research will play an increasingly important role in promoting the wide application of artificial intelligence technology.

Due to the limitations of research level, time, and laboratory conditions, this research still has certain limitations that need to be further explored and improved. The following aspects can be explored in future research work:

(1) The requirements for human physiological and cognitive state recognition in industrial human–machine collaborative scenarios are becoming increasingly stringent. The research mainly focuses on the recognition of operators' implicit intentions. Further studies

https://doi.org/10.3390/sym18020317

can be conducted on operator attention modeling, emotion computing, fatigue recognition, etc., and the methods proposed in this paper can be applied to other complex system fields for verification to improve the systematicness and reliability of the research structure.

(2) The sample size is limited, and most of the subjects are college students and young engineers, with a narrow distribution of age, educational background, and operational experience, and the generalization performance of the model still needs to be improved. All experiments (especially EEG experiments) were conducted in a controlled laboratory environment, lacking the noise, vibration, temperature and humidity changes, and multi-task parallelism of real workshops, which has not fully verified the robustness and reliability of the cognitive model in actual industrial scenarios. In future research, we will expand the physiological database by incorporating operators' physiological data from various industrial scenarios, and further investigate the feasibility of combining the feature map proposed in this paper with deep learning models.

(3) Due to the interface conditions of the laboratory physiological sensing equipment, this study only achieves offline intent recognition, without achieving real-time online cognitive state assessment, failing to fully reflect the challenges of non-stationary noise, network latency, and sudden changes in task load in real industrial sites. The online effectiveness, timeliness, and long-term stability of the model have not been empirically verified. In addition, the hybrid intelligent system may introduce the risk of instability in the perception-decision-feedback loop, which needs to be evaluated and suppressed in future work.

In the future, the methods proposed in this paper will be further verified and optimized in diverse complex HMC systems, and problems will be identified in practical applications to continuously improve the theory. At the same time, the experimental paradigms for estimating human cognitive states in complex systems will be further optimized, the scale of the data set will be expanded, and the transformation of theoretical models to engineering-level applications will be promoted.

Author Contributions: Conceptualization, X.M. and W.H.; methodology, X.M.; software, X.M.; validation, X.M.; formal analysis, X.M.; investigation, X.M. and Z.L.; resources, X.M. and Z.L.; data curation, X.M.; writing—original draft preparation, X.M.; writing—review and editing, X.M., W.H. and Z.L.; visualization, X.M.; supervision, X.M., W.H. and Z.L.; project administration, X.M. and Z.L.; funding acquisition, X.M. and Z.L. All authors have read and agreed to the published version of the manuscript.

Funding: This research was funded by Metallurgical Engineering First-Class Discipline Scientific Research Special Project of the Department of Education of Inner Mongolia Autonomous Region China, grant number YLXKZX-NKD-024.

Institutional Review Board Statement: The study was conducted in accordance with the Declaration of Helsinki, and the protocol was approved by the Ethics Committee of Inner Mongolia University of Science ((2023) No.10) on 1 March 2023.

Informed Consent Statement: Informed consent for participation was obtained from all subjects involved in the study.

Data Availability Statement: The data used in this research can be downloaded from the following link, accessed on 1 February 2026: https://pan.baidu.com/s/1x_uPtkVBp0d_rRQuVFzY_w?pwd=0000.

Conflicts of Interest: The authors declare no conflicts of interest. The funders had no role in the design of the study; in the collection, analyses, or interpretation of data; in the writing of the manuscript; or in the decision to publish the results.

https://doi.org/10.3390/sym18020317

References

1. Xu, X.; Lu, Y.; Vogel-Heuser, B.; Wang, L. Industry 4.0 and Industry 5.0—Inception, conception and perception. *J. Manuf. Syst.* **2021**, *61*, 530–535. [CrossRef]
2. Moore, A.; O'Reilly, T.; Nielsen, P.D.; Fall, K. Four Thought Leaders on Where the Industry Is Headed. *IEEE Softw.* **2016**, *33*, 36–39. [CrossRef]
3. World Economic Forum. *Digital Transformation of Industries*; World Economic Forum: Cologny/Geneva, Switzerland, 2016.
4. Miller, D.; Sun, A.; Johns, M.; Ive, H.; Sirkin, D.; Aich, S.; Ju, W. Distraction Becomes Engagement in Automated Driving. *Proc. Hum. Factors Ergon. Soc. Annu. Meet.* **2015**, *59*, 1676–1680. [CrossRef]
5. Bousdekis, A.; Apostolou, D.; Mentzas, G. A human cyber physical system framework for operator 4.0–artificial intelligence symbiosis. *Manuf. Lett.* **2020**, *25*, 10–15. [CrossRef]
6. Liu, Z.; Lou, S.; Yixiong, F.; Song, X.; Tan, J. A closed-loop human-computer interactive design method based on sequential human intention prediction and knowledge recommendation. *J. Eng. Des.* **2024**, *35*, 1–24. [CrossRef]
7. Wang, W.; Zhao, M.; Gao, H.; Zhu, S.; Qu, J. Human-computer interaction:Intention recognition based on EEG and eye tracking. *Acta Aeronaut. Astronaut. Sin.* **2021**, *42*, 292–302.
8. Ma, L.S.; Lv, J.; Pan, W.J.; Shan, J.J.; Ping, Z.Q. Research on Implicit Intention Recognition and Classification Based on Eye Movement Pattern. *J. Graph.* **2017**, *38*, 332–340.
9. Kitamura, Y.; Yamaguchi, Y.; Imamizu, H.; Kishino, F.; Kawato, M. Things Happening in the Brain While Humans Learn to Use New Tools. In *Proceedings of the SIGCHI Conference on Human Factors in Computing Systems, Fort Lauderdale, FL, USA, 5–10 April 2003*; Association for Computing Machinery: New York, NY, USA, 2003; pp. 417–424.
10. Keirn, Z.A.; Aunon, J.I. A new mode of communication between man and his surroundings. *IEEE Trans. Biomed. Eng.* **1990**, *37*, 1209–1214. [CrossRef]
11. Zheng, C.-J.; Xiao, G.-B.; Luo, T.-J. Improved deep neural network with overlapped time slice for pattern recognition of motor imagery EEG. *Comput. Syst. Appl.* **2022**, *31*, 52–64.
12. Miao, X.; Hou, W. Human–Computer Interaction Multi-Task Modeling Based on Implicit Intent EEG Decoding. *Appl. Sci.* **2024**, *14*, 368. [CrossRef]
13. Qu, J.; Guo, H.; Wang, W.; Dang, S. Prediction of Human-Computer Interaction Intention Based on Eye Movement and Electroencephalograph Characteristics. *Front. Psychol.* **2022**, *13*, 816127. [CrossRef]
14. Park, U.; Mallipeddi, R.; Lee, M. Human Implicit Intent Discrimination Using EEG and Eye Movement. In *Proceedings of the 21st International Conference on Neural Information Processing (ICONIP), Kuching, Malaysia, 3–6 November 2014*; Springer International Publishing: Cham, Switzerland, 2014; pp. 11–18.
15. Kang, J.S.; Park, U.; Gonuguntla, V.; Veluvolu, K.C.; Lee, M. Human implicit intent recognition based on the phase synchrony of EEG signals. *Pattern Recognit. Lett.* **2015**, *66*, 144–152. [CrossRef]
16. Park, H.; Lee, A.; Lee, M.; Chang, M.S.; Kwak, H.W. Using eye movement data to infer human behavioral intentions. *Comput. Hum. Behav.* **2016**, *63*, 796–804. [CrossRef]
17. Palaniappan, R. Brain Computer Interface Design Using Band Powers Extracted During Mental Tasks. In Proceedings of the 2nd International IEEE EMBS Conference on Neural Engineering, Pittsburgh, PA, USA, 16–19 March 2005.
18. Wang, H.K.; Bi, L.Z.; Fei, W.J.; Wang, L. An EEG-Based Multi-Classification Method of Braking Intentions for Driver-Vehicle Interaction. In Proceedings of the 2019 IEEE International Conference on Real-Time Computing and Robotics (RCAR), Irkutsk, Russia, 4–9 August 2019; pp. 438–441.
19. Nasa.Gov. MATB-II. Available online: https://matb.larc.nasa.gov/ (accessed on 1 February 2026).
20. Liao, J.Q. Prediction and analysis methods of mental load. *Ind. Eng. J.* **1998**, *1*, 38–42.
21. Liang, Y.Q.; Wang, W.; Qu, J.; Yang, J.; Liu, X.W. Human-Computer Interaction Behavior and Intention Prediction Model Based on Eye Movement Characteristics. *Acta Electron. Sin.* **2018**, *46*, 2993–3001.
22. Slanzi, G.; Balazs, J.A.; Velasquez, J.D. Combining eye tracking, pupil dilation and EEG analysis for predicting web users click intention. *Inf. Fusion* **2017**, *35*, 51–57. [CrossRef]
23. Wang, Y.; Gao, S.; Gao, X. Common Spatial Pattern Method for Channel Selelction in Motor Imagery Based Brain-computer Interface. In Proceedings of the 2005 IEEE Engineering in Medicine and Biology 27th Annual Conference, Shanghai, China, 1–4 September 2005.
24. Chakraborty, B.; Ghosh, L.; Konar, A. Designing Phase-Sensitive Common Spatial Pattern Filter to Improve Brain-Computer Interfacing. *IEEE Trans. Biomed. Eng.* **2020**, *67*, 2064–2072. [CrossRef]
25. Card, S.K. *The Psychology of Human-Computer Interaction*; CRC Press: Boca Raton, FL, USA, 1983.
26. Taylor, M.M. Editorial: Perceptual Control Theory and its application. *Int. J. Hum. Comput. Stud.* **1999**, *50*, 433–444. [CrossRef]
27. Gaulke, W.; Ziegler, J. Rule-enhanced task models for increased expressiveness and compactness. In *Proceedings of the 8th ACM SIGCHI Symposium on Engineering Interactive Computing Systems, Brussels, Belgium, 21–24 June 2016*; Association for Computing Machinery: New York, NY, USA, 2016; pp. 4–15.

https://doi.org/10.3390/sym18020317

28. Clerckx, T.; Luyten, K.; Coninx, K. DynaMo-AID: A Design Process and a Runtime Architecture for Dynamic Model-Based User Interface Development. In *Proceedings of the IFIP International Conference on Engineering for Human-Computer Interaction, Hamburg, Germany, 11–13 July 2004*; Springer: Berlin/Heidelberg, Germany, 2004; pp. 77–95.
29. Klug, T.; Kangasharju, J. Executable task models. In *Proceedings of the 4th International Workshop on Task Models and Diagrams, Gdansk, Poland, 26–27 September 2005*; Association for Computing Machinery: New York, NY, USA, 2005; pp. 119–122.
30. He, G.; Dang, Y.; Zhou, L.; Dai, Y.; Que, Y.; Ji, X. Architecture model proposal of innovative intelligent manufacturing in the chemical industry based on multi-scale integration and key technologies. *Comput. Chem. Eng.* **2020**, *141*, 106967. [CrossRef]
31. Hu, B.; Zhong, R.; Feng, Y.; Yang, C.; Wang, T. Digital shop floor manufacturing capability modeling and adaptive scheduling in human-cyber-physical interconnected environment. *J. Mech. Eng.* **2025**, *61*, 23–39.
32. Jolliffe, I.; Cadima, J. Principal component analysis: A review and recent developments. *Philos. Trans. R. Soc. A Math. Phys. Eng. Sci.* **2016**, *374*, 20150202. [CrossRef]
33. Lachaux, J.P.; Rodriguez, E.; Martinerie, J.; Varela, F.J. Measuring phase synchrony in brain signals. *Hum. Brain Mapp.* **1999**, *8*, 194–208. [CrossRef]
34. Oostenveld, R.; Fries, P.; Maris, E.; Schoffelen, J.-M. FieldTrip: Open source software for advanced analysis of MEG, EEG, and invasive electrophysiological data. *Comput. Intell. Neurosci.* **2011**, *2011*, 156869. [CrossRef]
35. Van Veen, B.; Van Drongelen, W.; Yuchtman, M.; Suzuki, A. Localization of brain electrical activity via linearly constrained minimum variance spatial filtering. *IEEE Trans. Biomed. Eng.* **1997**, *44*, 867–880. [CrossRef] [PubMed]
36. Tzoutio-Mazoyera, N.; Landeau, B.; Papathanassiou, D.; Crivello, F.; Etard, O.; Delcroix, N.; Tzourio-Mazoyer, B.; Joliot, M. Automated anatomical labeling of activations in SPM using a macroscopic anatomical parcellation of the MNI MRI single-subject brain. *NeuroImage* **2002**, *15*, 273–289. [CrossRef] [PubMed]
37. Zalesky, A.; Fornito, A.; Bullmore, E.T. Network-based statistic: Identifying differences in brain networks. *NeuroImage* **2010**, *53*, 1197–1207. [CrossRef] [PubMed]

https://doi.org/10.3390/sym18020317

symmetry

MDPI

Article

Symmetric Alignment Between Affective Semantics and Biomimetic Forms: Sustainable Packaging Design and Decision Support

Yihang Fang [1] and Yundong Qu [1,2,*]

1 Changxin International College of Art, Yunnan University, Kunming 650091, China; 32024236021@stu.ynu.edu.cn
2 School of Architecture and Art, Central South University, Changsha 410083, China
* Correspondence: quyundong@csu.edu.cn

Abstract

The symmetrical relationship between affective semantics and form bionics creates new possibilities for tea packaging. This study proposes a biologically inspired workflow for tea packaging design, effectively integrating natural forms, affective semantics, and sustainability assessment. First, ten natural forms suitable for bionic design were collected. The Affinity Diagram (AD) method was adopted based on evaluations from 20 consumers and tea merchants, yielding nine effective semantic and sustainability evaluation systems. Then, 10 domain experts scored the affective semantics, and the indicator weights were determined via the Precedence Chart (PC) method. The Quality Function Deployment (QFD) method was used to construct a relationship matrix between natural forms and affective semantics, identifying prioritized natural forms. Three biomimetic tea packaging designs were developed based on the three selected priority forms. Subsequently, the Criteria Importance Through Intercriteria Correlation (CRITIC) method calculated the objective weights of sustainability indicators. These weights were combined with Grey Relational Analysis (GRA) for comprehensive ranking to determine the optimal packaging scheme. The results show that stylish design (P1) has the highest weight among affective semantics, while low resource consumption (Q1) ranks first in sustainability evaluation indicators. Bamboo joint packaging was selected as the optimal design solution in the comprehensive ranking. This design process provides a methodological framework for tea packaging design, integrates biological bionics with affective semantics, and demonstrates potential for cross-category applications.

Keywords: packaging design; biomimetic design; sustainability; affective semantics; multi-criteria evaluation

1. Introduction

The symmetry between packaging forms and users' affective semantics is a key channel for designers to receive positive and negative market feedback. Biomimetic forms can better reflect the uniqueness and differentiation of packaging forms. Integrating users' affective semantics with bionic elements narrows the gap between designers' intentions and users' perceptions [1]. ZhaoXian Ren and his team [2] proposed an emotion-driven product form design methodology by combining user emotions with neural networks and applying it to air purifiers. Jixiao Chang and his team [3] converted user affective semantics into design criteria through the Fuzzy KANO model and integrated regional cultural symbols into public seating design. Xuerui Li [4] and others developed a new design pathway for electric garden tools by capturing workers' affective needs and leveraging AI-generated images for inspiration. Natural forms themselves carry emotional associations familiar to users; through the mapping of "natural forms to affective semantics," abstract affective semantics can be transformed into tangible packaging forms. This enables consumers to intuitively perceive designers' intentions and addresses the disconnect in emotional connection. With the growing prominence of green and sustainable principles, more designers are reconsidering the ecological impacts of modern human activities and design practices, proposing and applying sustainable design theories. Meanwhile, the international community emphasizes that green design should adhere to the "3R1D" principle: Reduce, Reuse, Recycle, and Degrade [5]. Numerous green and sustainable packaging solutions have been developed and applied in commercial products. For example, Coca-Cola uses lightweight PET bottles to reduce packaging material consumption and processing energy consumption; KFC's biodegradable straws ensure no environmental burden after disposal; and zero-carbon packaging minimizes material usage while prioritizing the recyclability of materials (Figure 1). Sining Huan [6] and others designed a fruit preservation packaging material using beeswax, leveraging its natural environmental friendliness and strong hydrophobicity. Andreja Pogacar and Diana Gregor Svetec [7] combined green sustainability principles with digital interaction methods to optimize a sustainable gift packaging model, reducing material use and printing while enhancing consumer-packaging interaction without environmental harm. However, most design solutions overly focus on material environmental friendliness and space utilization while neglecting the impact of form on user experience, resulting in packaging that lacks visual appeal; such designs are mostly concentrated in commercial product packaging and fail to cover the high-frequency demand scenario of daily agricultural and sideline products, leaving a long-standing gap in their green and sustainable design. Furthermore, they do not integrate consumers' affective semantics into packaging design, creating a disconnect between designers' intentions and users' perceptions that hinders emotional resonance, and no corresponding relationship between form and affective semantics has been established, making it difficult to convey sustainable values through morphological design. Overall, existing packaging designs tend to be rigid and lack user engagement, with attention primarily focused on commercial applications rather than extending to daily agricultural and sideline product packaging, which also lacks green and sustainable design concepts.

Figure 1. Sustainable Commercial Products.

To address the deficiencies of existing packaging research in form and user affective semantics, this study aims to: (i) systematically collect natural forms suitable for biomimetic packaging design, integrate affective semantics and sustainability evaluation indicators for packaging, and establish a "natural form-affective semantics" mapping matrix; (ii) conduct conceptual practice based on this mapping to develop three biomimetic-form tea packaging conceptual designs; (iii) construct a sustainable multi-criteria evaluation framework to

https://doi.org/10.3390/sym18010019

determine indicator weights and conduct comprehensive evaluations of design schemes, identify the optimal solution, and refine design strategies.

The research process consists of three phases: natural form collection and screening, affective semantics prioritization and sustainability indicator system construction, and concept generation and comprehensive evaluation. First, ten candidate natural forms were collected from plants, animals, and other natural prototypes. The Affinity Diagram method (AD) is used to screen and obtain the initial nine affective semantic terms and nine sustainability evaluation indicators based on user evaluations. Ten domain experts rated the importance of the affective semantics to determine their priority ranking using the Precedence Chart (PC) method, and a "natural form-affective semantics" matrix was constructed. Based on this, three optimal natural forms were selected for conceptual design, leading to three biomimetic tea packaging schemes. Combined with sustainability indicators, objective weighting and comprehensive evaluation were conducted via the Criteria Importance Through Intercriteria Correlation (CRITIC) method and Grey Relational Analysis (GRA) method. Finally, thirty target consumers (18–60 years old, regular tea buyers) were invited to assess the acceptance of the three design schemes.

The remainder of this paper is structured as follows: Section 2 reviews relevant literature on biomimetic design and packaging sustainability, summarizing theoretical and practical advancements in the synergy between packaging form and environmental performance; Section 3 details the research methodology and implementation process; Section 4 presents the results of natural form screening, conceptual design generation, and comprehensive evaluation of the tea packaging prototypes; Section 5 discusses user acceptance results of the optimal scheme, design trade-offs, and strategy optimization; Section 6 presents conclusions and highlights research contributions.

2. Research Background

2.1. Application of User Affective Semantics

User affective semantics are a core and indispensable factor in the design field, reflecting the "user-centered" design philosophy. Affective semantics are typically implicit in users' subjective evaluations and emotional feedback regarding product functions, appearance, and usage details. By systematically collecting and analyzing such feedback, users' psychological demands can be transformed into explicit, objective references for design practice, guiding designers in precise product optimization and iteration. Liem's team [8] conducted qualitative and quantitative research focusing on milk packaging to explore the impact of visual cues on consumers' perception of sustainability. They found that packaging with a cardboard brown color and rough texture is more likely to be judged as sustainable by consumers. Doi Toshihisa and Nagata Aoi [9] used the Evaluation Grid Method to analyze the sequence of product use and predict expected user experiences, optimizing packaging designs for candies and sunscreen. Mengqi Qin [10] and others collected affective vocabulary and integrated traditional patterns to optimize furniture and textile product designs, providing practical guidance for the modernization and innovative transformation of Home Textile Design (HTD) cultural elements. Lei Fu [11] and others enhanced the versatility of user research and the balance of design decisions, applying the approach to furniture design to address the common cognitive asymmetry between designers and users.

From the aforementioned literature, it can be concluded that the impact of users' affective semantics on packaging form design is not an abstract correlation but is realized through direct "demand-form attribute" correspondence. In the field of packaging design, affective semantics directly define the core form attributes of packaging through the chain of "user feedback-demand extraction-form transformation", enabling packaging to evolve

https://doi.org/10.3390/sym18010019

from a mere "container carrier" into a visual expression of users' emotions. However, most existing practices merely integrate products with affective semantics to enhance market acceptance and user satisfaction; while improvements and designs have been made to the visual presentation of packaging forms, an overabundance of similar designs has led to monotony.

This study will establish the core mechanism of affective semantics supporting packaging development, construct a symmetrical relationship between "affective semantics and formal attributes", and transform abstract emotions into quantifiable and operable design indicators. Each lexical term is further decomposed into corresponding dimensions of packaging formal attributes. Design elements of the scheme, such as packaging form, texture, structure, and color, are prioritized according to the weights of affective semantics, providing a clear decision-making basis for packaging development.

2.2. Biomimetic Design Applications

Biomimetic Design, as an emerging interdisciplinary research field, is defined as "an interdisciplinary practice that consciously imitates biological models to address technological and ecological challenges." It emphasizes studying the systematic characteristics of natural organisms, integrating design thinking to transform them into sustainable technical solutions. By exploring the functional and ecological advantages of organisms and leveraging human innovative cognition to convert them into design schemes, it ultimately achieves technological resilience and sustainability [12]. Dhatt Puneet [13] and others drew inspiration from plant leaf structures, simulating the "cellulose skeleton + outer protective layer" synergistic structure using the support of cell walls and hydrophobic cuticles to develop a Layered, Ecological, Advanced, and Multi-Functional Film, which effectively extends food shelf life, reduces packaging costs, and replaces traditional disposable plastic packaging. Chao Liu [14] and others designed flapping-wing micro robots (FWMRs) by mimicking the flapping motion, wing structural parameters, and unsteady aerodynamics of flying insects, enhancing their flexibility and maneuverability. Dongbao Sui [15] and others studied the anatomical characteristics of elephant trunks and designed a continuum manipulator consisting of internally pneumatically driven bellows and externally tendon-driven spiral springs, mimicking the trunk's conical profile to improve variable stiffness and ductility. Zhihong Wang [16] and others designed a biomimetic annular groove sealing structure inspired by the multi-level groove structure and adaptive sealing mechanism of octopus suckers, effectively enhancing adsorption capacity and load-bearing performance.

Currently, most researchers focus on analyzing biological functional attributes and ecological characteristics for product function improvement, leading to widespread application in functional design. However, these studies are limited to enhancing product functionality, neglecting material sustainability and visual design. The natural imagery embodied by biological forms can directly arouse users' emotional resonance, forging a relational chain of "-affective semantics-biomimetic form-user perception" that enables the design to convey warmth and experiential value. In this context, designers should prioritize sustainable materials and biomimetic design based on biological morphological characteristics to improve packaging's visual presentation. This study focuses on tea packaging. We screen biological forms highly aligned with the core emotions of tea consumption and integrate green sustainable materials to construct a new pathway for biomimetic tea packaging characterized by "emotion conveyance through form and environmental friendliness through materials." This approach not only addresses the insufficiency of existing biomimetic designs in emotional communication but also meets users' multiple demands for packaging-encompassing visual appeal, emotional resonance, and sustainability.

https://doi.org/10.3390/sym18010019

2.3. Sustainable Design Applications

In contemporary packaging design, designers are increasingly emphasizing and applying sustainable principles. Amid severe global resource depletion and environmental degradation, numerous packaging designs have adopted material substitution and structural innovation to address environmental challenges. The maturity of "sustainable design" also encourages industries to expand their scope of achievements, including services, product-service systems, and social innovation [17]. Quoc Tai Nguyen, Phuc Nhan Nghiem, and Duong Ngoc Hong [18] influenced consumers' purchasing intentions through eco-labels and promoted environmentally friendly production processes to demonstrate commitment to sustainability. Traditional packaging, a major environmental pollutant and the first point of consumer contact during transportation, must balance product protection, aesthetic needs, and environmental impact. Team of Kossalbayev [19] focused on developing biodegradable packaging from agricultural waste to reduce pollution and carbon emissions associated with traditional plastic packaging. To enhance key properties of such packaging—including tensile strength and thermal stability—to meet transportation requirements, they incorporated nanocellulose additives or adopted composite processes such as extrusion molding. The team of Gholizadeh Sara [20] developed a green packaging preservation technology for fresh beef using zein and inulin electrospun nanofibers incorporated with copper oxide nanoparticles and fennel essential oil. Gungoren Alper [21] and others enhanced the antibacterial and antioxidant properties of chitosan films with borage extract (Borago officinalis extract) for fresh rainbow trout fillet packaging. Qureshi Waseem Akhtar [22] and others coated paper substrates with cellulose nanofibers to fill surface pores and form a barrier film, replacing traditional paper packaging films.

Collectively, these studies indicate that integrating green design into packaging can alleviate environmental pollution and resource waste caused by traditional packaging, a trend that is also reflected in commercial products. However, an overemphasis on green sustainability has led designers to overlook the visual symbolic significance of packaging, equating the green concept with a homogeneous expression of "decorless design, monotonous natural colors, and simplified printing". This not only triggers a trade-off conflict between sustainability and usability—where minimalist designs impair the information transmission function of some packaging, making it difficult for consumers to quickly identify product information—but also results in a loss of distinctive visual recognition and artistic appeal, failing to incorporate consumers' core demands of "natural affinity", "exquisite texture" and "emotional resonance". Without a profound emotional connection between packaging and users, even eco-friendly packaging struggles to stimulate sustained purchase intention and usage loyalty, ultimately limiting the market penetration of green packaging.

Therefore, designers should abandon the inherent misconception that "environmental protection and user experience are opposing forces". While adhering to the concept of green sustainable development, the focus should shift toward the synergistic optimization of "sustainability-usability-consumer appeal". It is essential to thoroughly explore the visual value and structural advantages of natural forms, integrate the core semantics of user emotions, and enhance product appeal through the fusion of visual forms and emotional expression, while ensuring the environmental friendliness of packaging. This approach not only resolves the two key trade-off conflicts but also enriches the design dimensions of green packaging, providing an innovative framework for similar packaging designs that integrates ecological, practical, and emotional values.

https://doi.org/10.3390/sym18010019

2.4. Multi-Criteria Evaluation Methods

Multi-criteria evaluation methods are widely used in packaging design as essential tools for complex decision-making. These methods offer a systematic and structured evaluation framework through multi-dimensional indicators, converting fragmented traditional indicators into comprehensive, objective, and holistic evaluations [10]. Huafeng Quan, Yiting Li, and Qin Li [23] used natural language processing and latent Dirichlet allocation models to analyze users' sensory evaluations of Guizhou red sour soup packaging. They established relationships between sensory vocabulary sets and design elements through Kansei Engineering, evaluated suitable packaging schemes using standard deviation, and completed pattern design using semiotic methods. Harahap [19] and others applied QFD to establish relationships between customer needs and engineering indicators. They then employed the Theory of Inventive Problem Solving (TRIZ) to identify solutions. Engineering indicators from QFD were converted into 39 TRIZ parameter improvement types, leading to green color matching packaging design solutions through TRIZ contradiction matrices. Dollaya Buakum [24] and others combined subjective and objective methods (AHP and QFD) to gather sensory needs and technical plans from diverse customer groups, constructing an evaluation system for temperature-controlled medical packaging design. Byanca Porto de Lima [25] and others addressed uncertainty and expert opinion divergence in decision-making using AHP, QFD, and Preference Ranking Organization Method for Enrichment Evaluations, applying these methods to packaging design selection for automotive companies. Min Qu [26] and others enhanced user satisfaction and product competitiveness by integrating user feedback into air purifier innovation via the FKANO-Decision-Making Trial and Evaluation Laboratory (DEMATEL)-ViseKriterijumska Optimizacija I Kompromisno Resenje (VIKOR) multi-criteria model.

Current multi-criteria evaluation methods in packaging design primarily focus on capturing consumers' sensory vocabulary, constructing matrices, and applying them to design. These methods significantly improve design accuracy and enhance user favorability and attractiveness. However, many existing designs rely excessively on experts' subjective judgments, which compromises data objectivity, and the complex decision-making processes limit the ability to provide actionable insights for other packaging applications.

To overcome these limitations, this study uses the AD method and the CRITIC method to reduce over-reliance on experts' subjective judgments and enhance data objectivity. QFD, PC method, and GRA are integrated to streamline the entire decision-making process. Through these quantitative methods, sensory user needs are translated into biomimetic tea packaging schemes that meet both user demands and sustainable design principles.

3. Methods

3.1. Proposed Framework

This study takes consumers' affective needs as the carrier, synergizes biomimetic design with sustainable concepts as the design entry point, achieves visual symmetry between user affective semantics and packaging form design, and designs a sustainable tea packaging scheme and evaluation system integrating user affective needs and form bionics. The overall research process mainly includes four phases: extraction of biomimetic elements and affective vocabulary, acquisition of three ideal biomimetic forms, biomimetic tea packaging design, and determining the optimal option (Figure 2).

https://doi.org/10.3390/sym18010019

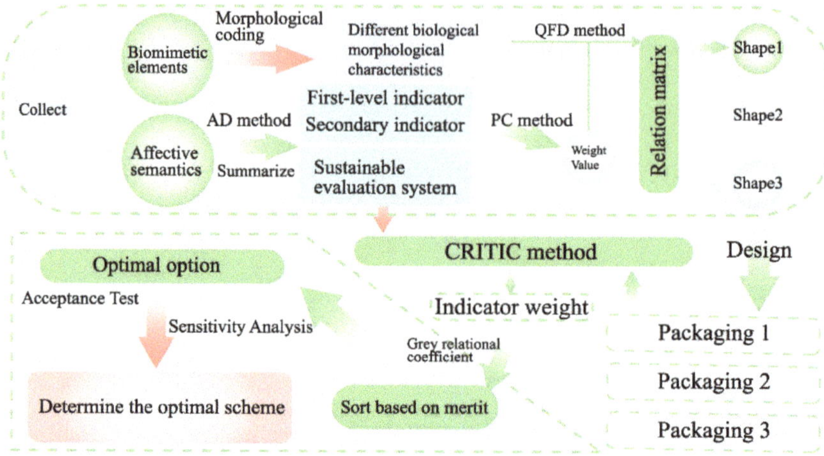

Figure 2. Research Framework Diagram.

(1) Typical ecological characteristics, morphological features, and sustainable values of 10 distinct biological species were analyzed through data collection and observation, from which applicable biomimetic elements were extracted. These 10 elements cover both plants and animals and encompass diverse morphological characteristics, ensuring the "natural form-affective semantics" matrix can capture rich correlation relationships and avoid biased selection of similar forms. Subsequently, affective semantics for packaging design and a sustainability evaluation index system were summarized using the Affinity Diagram method.

(2) The weights of sensory vocabulary were calculated via the PC method. QFD was applied to construct a correlation matrix between biomimetic forms and sensory vocabulary, and 3 ideal biomimetic forms were selected based on ranking.

(3) Three functional and emotional tea packaging schemes were developed corresponding to the 3 selected biomimetic elements.

(4) The CRITIC method was used to calculate the weights of sustainability evaluation indicators. GRA was applied to determine the correlation degree between each scheme and the ideal optimal solution based on these weights, identifying the optimal biomimetic tea packaging design. Finally, through user acceptance testing to assess the market acceptance of the packaging and sensitivity analysis, it was confirmed that the optimal packaging scheme derived from GRA remains the best biomimetic tea packaging option under different weight settings

3.2. *Affinity Diagram (AD) Method*

The AD method is a qualitative analysis method proposed by Professor Jiro Kawakita to summarize the overall meaning of multiple issues, and it enables the systematic integration of diverse pieces of information to uncover underlying patterns and core meanings within complex issues [27]. From a user-centric perspective, it consolidates existing product functional needs and generates new ones, making it highly suitable for capturing user evaluations of biomimetic tea packaging. The basic process of the AD method includes: selecting interviewees, collecting opinions, and summarizing a hierarchical table of user needs (Figure 3).

https://doi.org/10.3390/sym18010019

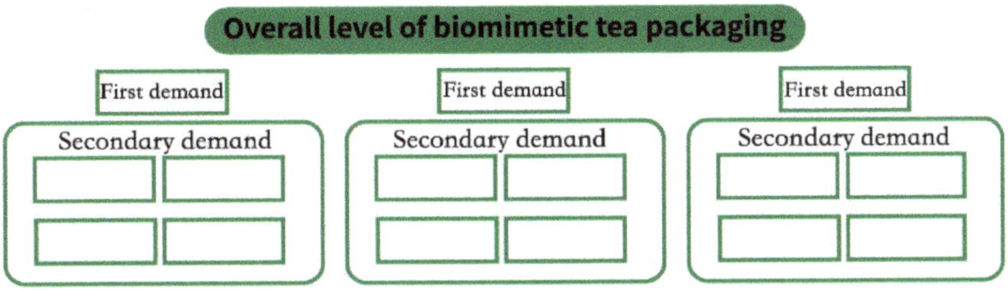

Figure 3. Affinity Diagram Induction.

(1) To ensure perspective diversity and data representativeness, respondents should include tea packaging design professionals, frequent tea consumers, and tea distributors, with a balanced proportion of users from different backgrounds, laying a reliable sample foundation for subsequent analysis.

(2) Systematically gather affective semantics descriptions and keywords regarding the functionality, emotion, and design of 9 biomimetic tea packaging schemes through open-ended questionnaires, in-depth interviews, or focus groups. To enhance data credibility, this study will adopt triangulation and observation notes to ensure the comprehensiveness and consistency of the collected opinions.

(3) At least two researchers will independently decompose, merge, and cluster demand descriptions, eliminate duplicate information, and form a preliminary demand hierarchy, followed by discussions on discrepancies until consensus is reached. After the initial system is established, participant validation will be conducted. Some users will be invited to provide feedback and revisions on the summarized results, ensuring the final demand evaluation system truly and reliably reflects user intentions.

3.3. Precedence Chart (PC) Method

The PC method is a subjective weighting method for multi-objective decision-making that involves pairwise comparisons of all schemes to determine their priority ranking. It handles both quantitative and qualitative issues [28]. The method consists of four steps:

(1) Determine evaluation factors and calculate the average score for each factor: List all influencing factors or alternative schemes, and compute the average of the scores assigned by the experts (X_{ki}: where represents the score given by the k-th expert to the i-th evaluation factor). The average score synthesizes the opinions of all experts to form a more representative and objective group consensus value, providing benchmark data for subsequent pairwise comparisons. The formula for calculating the average score ($\overline{X_i}$) is:

$$\overline{X_i} = \frac{1}{n} \sum_{k=1}^{n} X_{ki} \tag{1}$$

(2) Experts (including three environmental research scholars, three packaging design professors, and four corporate packaging specialists) systematically compared the relative importance of factors in pairs via an online questionnaire. To ensure consistency in experts' understanding of evaluation factors and judgment criteria, an online orientation meeting will be conducted prior to the comparison, providing clear terminological definitions, comparison rules, and scoring standards for each factor. A chessboard format was adopted, containing a total of N blank cells (Table 1). Rows represent comparison objects, and columns represent compared objects. Assign values for pairwise comparisons: 1 for the "better" factor, 0 for the "worse" factor, and 0.5 for equally important factors. Items in the first column represent the comparison subjects, while those in the first row represent the compared objects. For each pairwise comparison, scores were assigned as follows: 1 for the

https://doi.org/10.3390/sym18010019

relatively "superior" factor, 0 for the relatively "inferior" one, and 0.5 when the two factors are equally important.

Table 1. Indicator comparison matrix.

	X1	X2	X3	X4	...	Xn	TTL	Weight
X1								
X2								
X3								
X4								
...								
Xn								

(3) Sum the assigned values horizontally to obtain the final score for each indicator. Rank indicators by score to determine their relative importance. A_i represents the assigned value when the i-th affective vocabulary is compared pairwise with the j-th affective vocabulary, and A_{ij} denotes the total score of the i-th affective vocabulary. The weight (M_i) formulas are:

$$A_i = \sum_{i=1}^{n} A_{ij}(i = 1, 2, \cdots, n) \tag{2}$$

$$M_i = \frac{A_i}{\sum_{i=1}^{n} A_i} \tag{3}$$

(4) The score of the $\boldsymbol{m}$-th design scheme under the dimension of the $\boldsymbol{i}$-th affective vocabulary ($\boldsymbol{D_{mi}}$). Calculate the final subjective weight ($\boldsymbol{H_m}$):

$$\boldsymbol{H_m = \sum_{i=1}^{n} M_i \times D_{mi}} \tag{4}$$

3.4. Quality Function Deployment (QFD)

QFD is a multi-layered deductive method that converts user needs into design requirements, aiming to provide high-quality product services and maximize consumer satisfaction [29]. By mapping designers' needs to functional specifications, it derives optimization strategies for biomimetic tea packaging design [30]. The core of QFD is the House of Quality (HOQ), a matrix framework that intuitively transforms needs during product design. Its structure includes: Left Wall (user needs), Ceiling (design requirements), Roof (correlation between requirements), House (correlation between customer needs and design requirements), Floor (importance of quality characteristics), and Right Wall (product design expectations and evaluations) (Figure 4).

Based on packaging sensory vocabulary and biomimetic design elements obtained via the AD method, QFD was used to convert user needs into achievable design indicators and establish an HOQ matrix. The specific steps are as follows:

(1) Import user needs into the Left Wall of the HOQ.

(2) Quantify the correlation between user needs and biomimetic elements to form the House of the HOQ.

(3) Use "+" and "−" in the Roof to indicate the correlation between product requirements.

(4) $\boldsymbol{W_i}$ represents the weight of the $\boldsymbol{i}$-th user demand, and $\boldsymbol{P_{ij}}$ denotes the correlation degree between the $\boldsymbol{i}$-th user demand and the $\boldsymbol{j}$-th design feature. Calculate the absolute

https://doi.org/10.3390/sym18010019

weight (W_j) and relative weight (W_k) of packaging performance indicators to form the Floor of the HOQ. The formulas are:

$$W_j = \sum_{i=1}^{q} W_i P_{ij} \tag{5}$$

$$W_k = \frac{W_j}{\sum_{i=1}^{q} W_j} \tag{6}$$

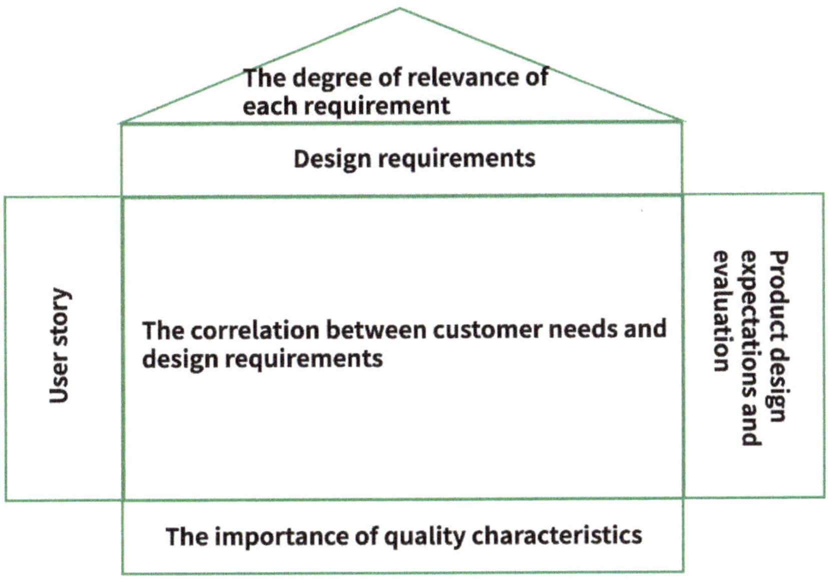

Figure 4. House of Quality Structure.

3.5. Criteria Importance Through Intercriteria Correlation (CRITIC)

The CRITIC method is an objective weighting method based on contrast intensity and conflict indicators. It determines importance based on the objective attributes of data rather than numerical values, effectively complementing the subjective weighting of the PC method [31]. The method involves five steps:

(1) Standardize user evaluation data to eliminate dimensional effects. Common standardization formulas are:

Positive indicator formula:

$$x'_{ij} = \frac{x_{ij} - \min(x_j)}{\max(x_j) - \min(x_j)} \tag{7}$$

Negative indicator formula:

$$x'_{ij} = \frac{\max(x_j) - x_{ij}}{\max(x_j) - \min(x_j)} \tag{8}$$

where x_{ij} is the value in the original decision matrix, x'_{ij} is the standardized value, $\max(x_j)$ and $\min(x_j)$ are the maximum and minimum values of the j-th indicator, respectively.

https://doi.org/10.3390/sym18010019

(2) Standard deviation reflects the degree of dispersion of each indicator; a larger standard deviation indicates stronger discriminative power. The formula for calculating the standard deviation (σ_j) is:

$$\sigma_j = \sqrt{\frac{1}{m}\sum_{i=1}^{n}(x'_{ij} - \sqrt{x'_j})^2} \tag{9}$$

where x'_j is the mean of the j-th indicator, and m is the sample size.

(3) Calculate the correlation coefficient (r_{jk}) between each indicator. The formula is:

$$r_{jk} = \frac{\sum_{i=1}^{m}\left(x'_{ij} - \overline{x'_j}\right)\left(x'_{ik} - \overline{x'_k}\right)}{\sqrt{\sum_{i=1}^{m}\left(x'_{ij} - \overline{x'_j}\right)^2 \sum_{i=1}^{m}\left(x'_{ik} - \overline{x'_k}\right)^2}} \tag{10}$$

(4) Calculate the information amount (C_j). The formula is:

$$C_j = \sigma_j \times \sqrt{\sum_{k=1}^{n}\left(1 - r_{jk}\right)} \tag{11}$$

(5) Calculate the objective weight (w_j). The formula is:

$$w_j = \frac{C_j}{\sum_{j=1}^{n} C_j} \tag{12}$$

3.6. Grey Relational Analysis (GRA)

GRA determines the correlation between data based on the geometric similarity of reference and comparison sequence curves. Higher similarity indicates a stronger correlation [32]. The method includes three steps:

(1) Standardization processing formula (x'_i):

$$x'_i = \frac{x_i - \min(x)}{\max(x) - \min(x)} \tag{13}$$

where x_i is the original data, $\max(x)$ and $\min(x)$ represent the maximum and minimum values, respectively.

(2) Calculate the grey relational matrix formula ($\xi_i(k)$):

$$\xi_i(k) = \frac{\underset{i}{min}\,\underset{k}{min}\,|x_0(k) - x_i(k)| + \rho\,\underset{i}{max}\,\underset{k}{max}\,|x_0(k) - x_i(k)|}{|x_0(k) - x_i(k)| + \rho\,\underset{i}{max}\,\underset{k}{max}\,|x_0(k) - x_i(k)|} \tag{14}$$

where $x_0(k)$ is the reference sequence, $x_i(k)$ is other comparison sequences, ρ is the distinguishing coefficient (set to 0.5), and $|x_0(k) - x_i(k)|$ is the absolute difference.

(3) Calculate the grey relational degree (γ_i):

$$\gamma_i = \frac{1}{m}\sum^{m}\xi_i(k) \tag{15}$$

4. Case Study

4.1. Construction of a Biomimetic Element Library

Ten biological species with bionic potential were collected from nature, and their morphological characteristics were analyzed and summarized. In this study, we first observed the morphological features of these 10 different organisms, then manually drew

https://doi.org/10.3390/sym18010019

their forms based on these features. Among them, special focus was placed on depicting the unique hexagonal structure of honeycombs; for sponges, we referred to their porous morphological features; for pod, we adopted their symmetrical multi-seed form; for gourd, we used the figure-eight shape; for bamboo joints, we extracted their segmented and square characteristics; for mushrooms, penguins, owls, tea seedlings and bergamot, we depicted their external morphological appearances. The forms drawn above constitute the bionic element library presented in the table below (Table 2).

Table 2. Biomimetic Design Element Library.

No.	Name	Morphological Characteristics	Image	Element Extraction
K1	Honeycomb	Hexagonal shape	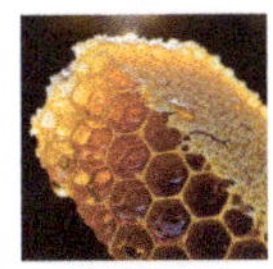	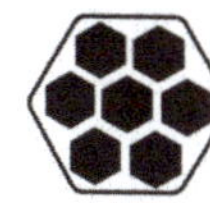
K2	Sponge	Irregular, porous		
K3	Pod	Symmetrical, multi-seeded		
K4	Gourd	"8"-shaped		
K5	Bamboo Joint	Cylindrical tube shape, bamboo joint partitions		
K6	Mushroom	Umbrella-shaped, cylindrical stem		
K7	Penguin	Wide at the bottom, narrow at the top, high stability		
K8	Owl	Round face, large eyes		

https://doi.org/10.3390/sym18010019

Table 2. *Cont.*

No.	Name	Morphological Characteristics	Image	Element Extraction
K9	Tea Seedling	Bamboo shoot-like shape		
K10	Bergamot	Irregular, lobed aggregation		

4.2. Acquisition of Affective Semantics and Sustainability Evaluation System

Accurately and effectively obtaining consumer demand information is the premise for forming biomimetic packaging design. Guided by consumers' affective semantics and applied in the form of biomimetic design, the synergistic alignment between packaging form and affective semantics is realized. Using the AD method, 15 tea packaging consumers and 5 tea merchants were interviewed online and offline to collect affective semantics and sustainability evaluation indicators. After deduplication and ambiguity elimination, 29 valid sensory vocabulary terms were obtained, and 9 core affective semantics terms for biomimetic tea packaging were summarized: Stylish Design (P1), Fine Pattern (P2), Reasonable Color Scheme (P3), Advanced Material (P4), Auspicious Meaning (P5), Comfortable and Convenient (P6), Creative Structural Form (P7), Reliable and Durable (P8), and Novel Functionality (P9). These terms cover the core demand scenarios for tea packaging, from visual appeal and usage experience to cultural identity and functional innovation (Figure 5).

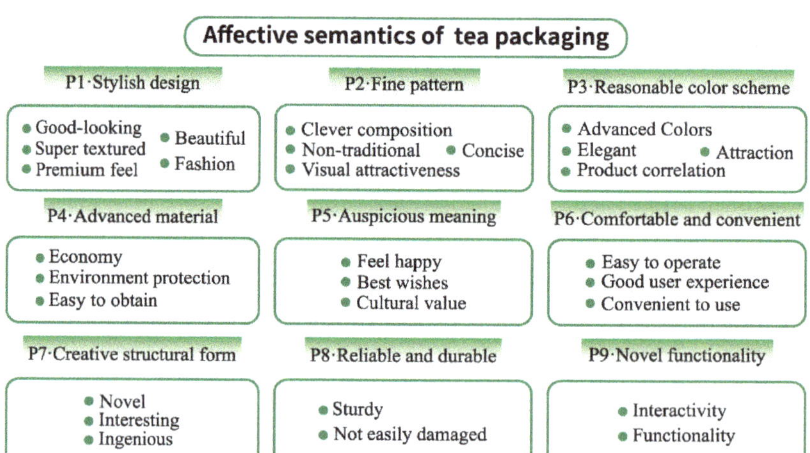

Figure 5. Affective Semantics for Biomimetic Tea Packaging.

Simultaneously, 24 sustainability evaluation indicators were collected from interviews, and 9 core sustainability evaluation indicators for biomimetic tea packaging were generated: Low Resource Consumption (Q1), Environmentally Friendly (Q2), Product Safety (Q3), Material Reduction (Q4), Degradability (Q5), Recyclability (Q6), Reproducibility

https://doi.org/10.3390/sym18010019

(Q7), Simplified Structure (Q8), and Biomimetic Morphology Affinity (Q9). They are consistent with the mainstream evaluation framework for green packaging design, with no redundancy among indicators, and can effectively reflect the core dimensions of packaging sustainability (Figure 6).

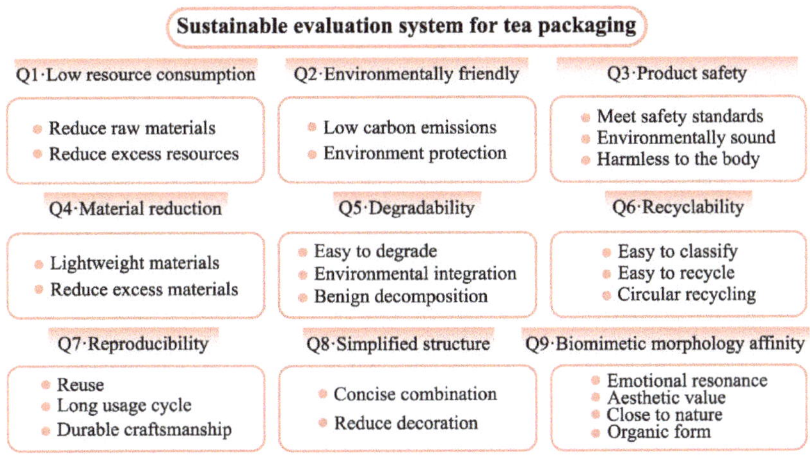

Figure 6. Sustainability Evaluation System for Biomimetic Tea Packaging.

4.3. Sensory Weight Calculation and Biomimetic Element Screening

In total, 10 experts rated the nine core sensory indicators on a 1–10 scale following the PC method. The average score for each indicator was calculated using Formula (1) (Table 3). Pairwise comparisons were conducted based on these averages, and TTL (total score) and weights for each indicator were computed using Formulas (2)–(4) (Table 4).

Table 3. Average scores of primary indicators.

Evaluation Dimension	P1	P2	P3	P4	P5	P6	P7	P8	P9
Average Value	7.2	6.1	6.9	5.8	6.2	5.9	6.3	6.4	6.8

Table 4. Weights of primary indicators.

	P1	P2	P3	P4	P5	P6	P7	P8	P9	TTL	Weight
P1	0.5	1	1	1	1	1	1	1	1	8.5	0.250
P2	0	0.5	0	1	0	1	0	0	0	2.5	0.073
P3	0	1	0.5	1	1	1	1	1	1	7.5	0.220
P4	0	0	0	0.5	0	0	0	0	0	0.5	0.014
P5	0	1	0	1	0.5	1	0	0	0	3.5	0.102
P6	0	0	0	1	0	0.5	0	0	0	1.5	0.044
P7	0	1	0	1	1	1	0.5	0	0	4.5	0.132
P8	0	1	0	1	1	1	1	0.5	0	5.5	0.161
P9	0	1	0	1	1	1	1	1	0.5	6.5	0.191

The biomimetic element library, affective semantics, and need weights were imported into the corresponding positions of the HOQ. The correlation intensity between affective

https://doi.org/10.3390/sym18010019

semantics and biomimetic elements was evaluated, and the correlation intensity was quantified using the scoring system in Table 5. The absolute and relative weights of biomimetic packaging indicators were calculated using Formulas (5) and (6). Three optimal biomimetic elements for packaging design were identified by analyzing the Floor of the HOQ (Figure 7).

Table 5. Correlation scoring between user needs and design indicators.

Correlation Strength	Strong Correlation	Medium Correlation	Weak Correlation	No Correlation
Symbol and Score	● 5	◎ 3	△ 1	0

	User demand weight	K1	K2	K3	K4	K5	K6	K7	K8	K9	K10
P1	0.250	●	△		◎	◎	△				△
P2	0.073				◎			△	●		
P3	0.220	△		●	△	△					●
P4	0.014	◎	△			◎				△	
P5	0.102				●	●				●	△
P6	0.044	△	●	△						◎	
P7	0.132	◎				◎	△	●			
P8	0.161						●				
P9	0.191				△	△			△		
Importance	Absolute weight(X100)	195.2	48.4	114.4	189	210.9	118.7	73.3	55.6	65.6	145.2
	Relative Weight	0.160	0.039	0.094	0.155	0.173	0.097	0.060	0.045	0.053	0.119

Figure 7. Relationship between Biomimetic Elements and User Demand Indicator Weights.

The weight ranking via QFD was K5 > K1 > K4 > K10 > K6 > K3 > K7 > K9 > K8 > K2. The top three design elements were K1 (honeycomb), K4 (gourd), and K5 (bamboo joint).

4.4. Tea Packaging Design

Based on the three biomimetic elements derived from the QFD method as the morphological semantic basis of this biomimetic tea packaging, combined with the user affective semantics dimensions and sustainability evaluation system compiled via the AD method, the structural symmetry between biomimetic forms and user affective experience was achieved through the mapping relationship between form bionics and user affective semantics. Finally, the following three schemes were obtained (Figure 8).

Option A Option B Option C

Figure 8. Biomimetic Tea Packaging Schemes.

https://doi.org/10.3390/sym18010019

(1) Option A: Honeycomb-inspired design-adopting the hexagonal structure of honeycombs as the biomimetic design prototype. The overall packaging uses a hexagonal box shape, with hexagonal texture details on the surface and rounded corners at the edge transitions. This design not only effectively cushions collisions during transportation and enhances structural durability but also conveys the emotional connotations of "stability", "orderliness", and "natural rhythm"-thereby achieving symmetrical resonance with users' affective semantics for "a sense of security" and "a sense of harmony". Tea images are decorated on the top and front of the box, further strengthening the natural context and product recognizability. In terms of material selection, this scheme uses linen paper as the primary packaging material. Composed primarily of flax fibers, this material possesses physical properties including wear resistance, high-temperature resistance, and anti-static performance. Meanwhile, its raw material is easy to cultivate, with a short growth cycle, controllable cost, and complete biodegradability, making it recognized as a sustainable alternative to traditional wood pulp paper [33]. The natural texture and simple visual style of linen paper also elicit a natural affinity at the sensory level, resonating with users' deep-seated affective pursuit of "returning to simplicity" and "eco-friendliness". In this way, a bidirectional symmetric alignment is established between material semantics and users' affective cognition.

(2) Option B: Bamboo joint-inspired design, taking the segmented structure of bamboo joints as the core biomimetic design element. Each independent bamboo joint unit stores a different type of tea bag, achieving functional partitioning and endowing the packaging with modular usability. Freehand bamboo leaf patterns embellish the packaging surface, enhancing the natural artistic conception and overall visual rhythm, which aligns with users' affective semantics for "poetic living" and "natural experience". Bamboo is used as the exclusive material for this packaging scheme. As a typical sustainable material, it not only possesses resource characteristics such as rapid growth, early maturity, and sustained usability after a single planting but also delivers ecological advantages of carbon reduction and sequestration, helping enterprises reduce environmental costs across the entire product lifecycle [34]. Its intrinsic high toughness and structural rigidity can effectively withstand extrusion and impacts during logistics and transportation, ensuring the integrity of tea leaves. Beyond functionality, this design embodies auspicious implications of "steady progress" and "perseverance" through the bamboo joint form and modular functions. Furthermore, it fosters users' value recognition of "sustainable living" and "natural authenticity" through material perception and usage experience, establishing a cohesive link between biomimetic aesthetics, ecological responsibility, and emotional resonance.

(3) Option C: Gourd-inspired design, taking the gourd form as the biomimetic design prototype. A two-piece packaging structure is designed: the upper part acts as a lid, and the lower part serves as a tea storage compartment. The gourd form itself embodies profound affective semantics and auspicious implications. Via morphological translation, this design integrates the auspicious connotations of the gourd into the packaging semantics, thereby achieving emotional symmetry with users' affective semantics for "blessings" and "cultural belonging". In terms of material selection, this scheme adopts bagasse paper as the primary substrate, replacing traditional wood pulp paper. Derived from the recycling of sugarcane fiber by-products, this material features complete biodegradability, along with properties including water resistance, oil resistance, low carbon emissions, and high food safety [35].

4.5. Calculation of Sustainability Indicator Weights

Ten experts (specializing in environmental research, packaging research, and corporate packaging design) scored the 9 sustainability indicators. The data were standardized using Formula (7), and the final weights of sustainability indicators were calculated sequen-

https://doi.org/10.3390/sym18010019

tially using Formulas (9)–(12) to support the selection of the optimal packaging scheme (Tables 6 and 7).

Table 6. Expert Scoring Matrix.

	Q1	Q2	Q3	Q4	Q5	Q6	Q7	Q8	Q9
Expert 1	6	7	4	4	6	6	4	4	2
Expert 2	7	6	5	3	5	5	4	3	2
Expert 3	5	6	6	4	6	5	5	6	3
Expert 4	6	7	5	6	5	7	3	3	3
Expert 5	5	5	7	4	6	6	5	4	5
Expert 6	6	6	6	4	7	5	5	3	4
Expert 7	5	6	5	5	6	5	5	5	3
Expert 8	7	6	5	4	5	4	3	3	4
Expert 9	5	5	7	5	6	7	4	3	3
Expert 10	6	6	4	3	6	5	4	5	4

Table 7. Weights of Sustainability Indicators.

Evaluation Dimension	Indicator Variability	Indicator Conflict	Information Amount	Weight
Q1	0.394	10.810	4.264	0.164
Q2	0.333	9.384	3.128	0.120
Q3	0.358	7.752	2.778	0.107
Q4	0.306	8.058	2.468	0.095
Q5	0.316	7.293	2.306	0.088
Q6	0.324	8.041	2.605	0.100
Q7	0.394	7.577	2.988	0.115
Q8	0.344	8.306	2.859	0.110
Q9	0.316	8.006	2.532	0.097

4.6. Identification of the Optimal Packaging Scheme

A team of experts scored the three biomimetic tea packaging schemes across the 9 evaluation dimensions (1–10 points: 1 = very poor, 10 = very good). Combining the sustainability indicator weights (from CRITIC) with GRA, the correlation degree between each scheme and sustainability indicators was calculated using Formulas (13)–(15), and schemes were ranked based on correlation degrees (Tables 8 and 9).

Table 8. Correlation Coefficients.

Evaluation Dimension	Option A	Option B	Option C
Q1	0.39	1.00	0.45
Q2	0.65	1.00	0.48
Q3	1.00	0.67	0.44
Q4	0.33	0.45	1.00
Q5	0.45	1.00	0.54
Q6	1.00	0.78	0.59
Q7	0.75	0.50	1.00
Q8	0.84	1.00	0.53
Q9	0.55	1.00	0.82

Table 9. Correlation Degree Results.

Evaluation Item	Correlation Degree	Ranking
Option A	0.66	2
Option B	0.82	1
Option C	0.65	3

The GRA results show Option B (0.82) > Option A (0.66) > Option C (0.65), indicating Option B is the optimal biomimetic packaging design.

5. Discussion

5.1. Acceptance Test

To verify the acceptance of the optimal biomimetic packaging scheme among consumers, six evaluation dimensions were established (purchase likehood, perceived aesthetics, environmental satisfaction, likehood of recommending, performance satisfaction, and satisfaction with ease), and an online survey was conducted to invite 30 target consumers to rate the packaging on a 1–5 scale; the demographic distribution of the 30 respondents is as follows: 15 males (50%) and 15 females (50%) in terms of gender, 10 young adults (33.3%), 12 middle-aged adults (40%), 8 middle-aged and elderly adults (26.7%) by age group, and 4 with high school education or below (13.3%), 20 with bachelor's degrees (66.7%), and 6 with master's degrees or above (20%) regarding educational background (Table 10). This balanced configuration of demographic characteristics aims to cover the differentiated perceptions of sustainability and aesthetics among consumers across genders, age groups, and educational backgrounds, ensuring that the evaluation results reflect the attitudes of diverse sub-groups and enhancing the representativeness of the data and the reliability of the conclusions (Figure 9).

Table 10. Process Consumer Structure.

	Item	Frequency	Percentage
Gender	males	15	50%
	females	15	50%
Age	young adults	10	33.3%
	middle-aged adults	12	40%
	middle-aged and elderly adults	8	26.7%
Educational Background	high school education or below	4	13.3%
	bachelor's degrees	20	66.7%
	master's degrees or above	6	20%

Descriptive statistical analysis shows that most consumers approve of this design scheme and are willing to recommend it. As this design focuses primarily on packaging form, its bamboo joint-inspired biomimetic structure adopts a flip-top design, which tends to cause poor sealing performance. Thus, the environmental attribute received the highest score, while performance satisfaction was slightly lower than that of other dimensions.

https://doi.org/10.3390/sym18010019

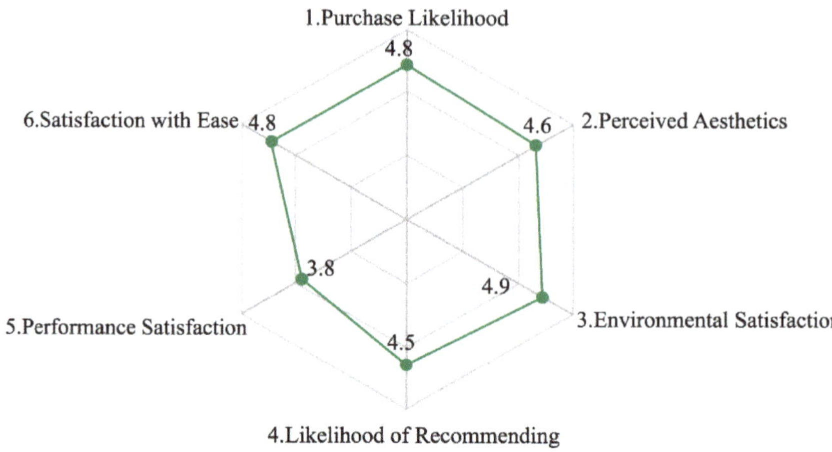

Figure 9. User acceptance test results.

In future market applications, the packaging will retain core morphological features such as the bamboo joint design while integrating modern manufacturing processes. To enhance sealing and moisture resistance, food-grade silicone gaskets will be adopted, along with a recyclable material combination and easy-to-separate structure. This design ensures functional reliability while enabling efficient recycling and controlling material complexity at the source. Visual cues will be added to the packaging surface to clearly guide consumers to separate components after use, as well as to store and dispose of the packaging correctly, thereby indirectly improving product usability, convenience, and user satisfaction. Finally, a new product life cycle assessment method will be continuously integrated into each design iteration, with a focus on evaluating the recycling compatibility of multi-material structures. This will ensure that the packaging is environmentally friendly, can be efficiently processed in existing recycling systems, and maintains a competitive edge in terms of sustainability performance.

5.2. Sensitivity Analysis

To assess the sensitivity of sustainability indicators in the multi-criteria decision-making process and their influence on the final selection decision, a series of sensitivity analysis experiments was designed and implemented. Indicator weights were systematically adjusted to examine their influence on decision outcomes, helping identify the robust optimal biomimetic tea packaging scheme under weight uncertainty.

A total of 14 sensitivity experiments were performed. In the first five experiments, all indicators were assigned the same weight: 1, 3, 5, 7, and 9, respectively. By constructing weight distribution scenarios ranging from uniform to gradient-based, this study covered multiple benchmark scenarios—from equal weights (simulating the absence of prior preferences) to gradually increasing overall weight levels—thereby observing the response trend of decision results to the absolute weight levels. Subsequent experiments (Experiments 6 to 14) involved setting the weight of one indicator to the maximum value of 9 while gradually adjusting the weights of other indicators to the minimum value of 1, aiming to reflect the potential impact of subtle changes in each indicator (Table 11).

Table 11. Sensitivity Analysis Process.

No.	Weight Setting	Packaging Solution			Ranking
		A	B	C	
Expt.1	$w_{Q1\text{–}9} = 1$	0.69	0.83	0.68	B > A > C
Expt.2	$w_{Q1\text{–}9} = 3$	0.69	0.83	0.68	B > A > C
Expt.3	$w_{Q1\text{–}9} = 5$	0.69	0.83	0.68	B > A > C
Expt.4	$w_{Q1\text{–}9} = 7$	0.69	0.83	0.68	B > A > C
Expt.5	$w_{Q1\text{–}9} = 9$	0.69	0.83	0.68	B > A > C
Expt.6	$w_{Q1} = 1, w_{Q2\text{–}9} = 9$	0.73	0.83	0.72	B > A > C
Expt.7	$w_{Q2} = 1, w_{Q1,Q3\text{–}9} = 9$	0.72	0.83	0.72	B > A = C
Expt.8	$w_{Q3} = 1, w_{Q1\text{–}2,Q4\text{–}9} = 9$	0.69	0.86	0.73	B > C > A
Expt.9	$w_{Q4} = 1, w_{Q1\text{–}3,Q5\text{–}9} = 9$	0.67	0.84	0.60	B > A > C
Expt.10	$w_{Q5} = 1, w_{Q1\text{–}4,Q6\text{–}9} = 9$	0.74	0.83	0.72	B > A > C
Expt.11	$w_{Q6} = 1, w_{Q1\text{–}5,Q7\text{–}9} = 9$	0.69	0.85	0.72	B > C > A
Expt.12	$w_{Q7} = 1, w_{Q1\text{–}6,Q8\text{–}9} = 9$	0.71	0.87	0.68	B > A > C
Expt.13	$w_{Q8} = 1, w_{Q1\text{–}7,Q9} = 9$	0.70	0.83	0.72	B > C > A
Expt.14	$w_{Q9} = 1, w_{Q1\text{–}8} = 9$	0.73	0.83	0.70	B > A > C

The above sensitivity experiments not only reveal which indicator weight changes significantly alter the decision ranking but also evaluate the stability of the decision scheme under different weight assumptions. In practical applications, this helps decision-makers identify indicators for which weight determination requires greater caution and supports judgments on resource allocation and design optimization directions.

Based on the results of the 14 experiments, Packaging option B consistently achieved the highest grey relational degree under different weight configurations, confirming that option B is the robust optimal choice across diverse weight scenarios (Figure 10).

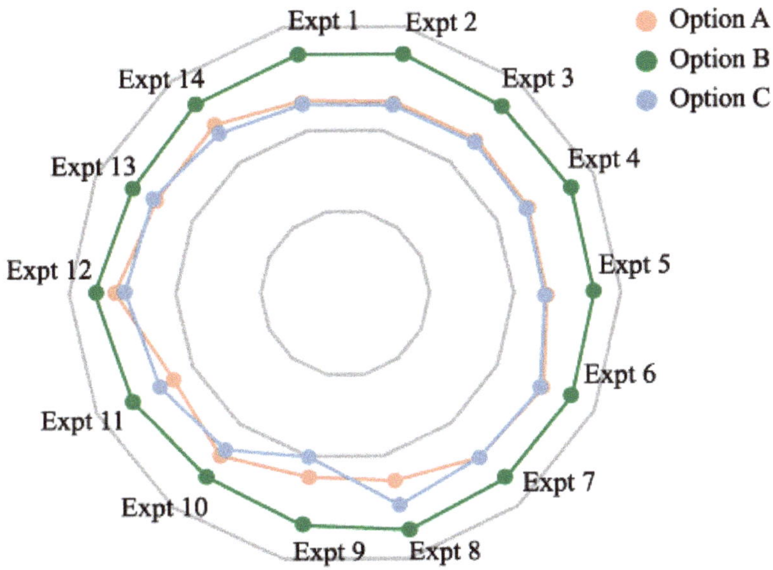

Figure 10. Sensitivity Analysis Results.

https://doi.org/10.3390/sym18010019

6. Conclusions

Based on the results of multi-criteria decision analysis, a tea packaging scheme integrating affective semantics, biomimetic elements, and sustainable materials was developed. Calculation results show that stylish design (P1) has the highest weight in affective semantics, and low resource consumption (Q1) ranks first in sustainability evaluation indicators. For affective semantics, consumers tend to pay more attention to visual presentation when purchasing products, so packaging design should be consistent with the product itself and consumer preferences. In terms of sustainability indicators, consumers attach greater importance to low material consumption, so designers should prioritize low material consumption when selecting packaging materials. Bamboo joints were selected as the biomimetic form; this not only achieves the visual translation of the form, but also matches the form with affective semantics, thereby strengthening the emotional connection between the product and consumers. This study screened the ideal biomimetic form based on users' preferences for affective semantics, avoiding the asymmetry between the two types of semantics. This symmetry emphasizes the integration of "affective semantics and morphological characteristics" to ensure the consistency between design intentions and users' emotions. Sustainable materials were adopted for material selection, in line with the concept of environmental protection. This study provides a morphological carrier for affective semantics, offers design insights for biomimicry, and further broadens the design directions for sustainable design. It breaks the traditional one-way interpretation framework of "symbolic meaning", takes "symmetry" as the core evaluation criterion for the semantic transmission effect, and provides new insights for accurately conveying affective semantics through forms. Finally, the feasibility of the scheme was verified via user acceptance testing and sensitivity statistical analysis. By integrating users' affective semantics, biomimetic design, and sustainable materials, the study promotes the upgrading of agricultural and sideline product packaging and provides a clear approach for similar packaging designs on how to accurately transform affective semantics into form design, rather than a vague "integration of affective semantics". This integration of affective semantics serves as a key supplement to existing research on the "emotion-form" relationship in the design field.

This study only selected 10 biomimetic elements without covering a broader range of biological categories, which affects the diversity and comparative depth of morphological bionics. Meanwhile, as the research focused on integrating users' affective semantics with biomimetic design, it lacked sufficient design research on packaging structure and functional attributes. Finally, only 30 consumers were invited to evaluate the optimal scheme for verifying user acceptance. The small sample size results in insufficient detection sensitivity for key variables such as "the correlation intensity between users' affective semantics and biomimetic forms" and "preference differences for packaging among different groups." It is difficult to exclude the interference of random errors on the results, which may reduce the significance level of relevant statistical tests and prevent accurate verification of the core hypothesis of "symmetrical alignment between morphological semantics and emotional needs." Consequently, the research conclusions are difficult to generalize to broader market scenarios and cannot fully reflect the real needs and acceptance attitudes of different subgroups towards the packaging, requiring further expansion in statistical representativeness and generalizability.

In subsequent design research, biological categories such as marine organisms, microorganisms, and desert plants will be incorporated to expand the biomimetic element library, enhancing the diversity of morphological semantics and scenario adaptability. Additionally, the mapping mechanism of biomimetic forms in terms of packaging functionality and structure will be explored in depth to achieve multi-dimensional symmetry of "form-emotion-function." Meanwhile, larger-scale user experience tests will be conducted, and

https://doi.org/10.3390/sym18010019

attempts will be made to introduce biomimetic packaging into actual market environments. Through continuous tracking of sales data and consumer feedback, a more ecologically valid decision-making basis will be provided for design optimization.

Author Contributions: Writing—original draft, Y.F.; Writing—review and editing, Y.Q. All authors have read and agreed to the published version of the manuscript.

Funding: This research received no external funding.

Data Availability Statement: Data is contained within the article.

Conflicts of Interest: The authors declare no conflicts of interest.

Abbreviations

The following abbreviations are used in this manuscript:

AD	Affinity Diagram
PC	Precedence Chart
QFD	Quality Function Deployment
CRITIC	Criteria Importance Through Intercriteria Correlation
GRA	Grey Relational Analysis
HTD	Home Textile Design
FWMRs	flapping-wing micro robots
TRIZ	Theory of Inventive Problem Solving
DEMATEL	Decision-Making Trial and Evaluation Laboratory
VIKOR	ViseKriterijumska Optimizacija I Kompromisno Resenje
HOQ	House of Quality

References

1. Wang, L.; Gong, Y.; Niu, S.; Ren, Z.-X. Cultural Symbols Migration and User Perception: Innovation in Chinese-Style Furniture Design. *BioResources* **2025**, *20*, 3476–3496. [CrossRef]
2. Ren, Z.; Chen, D.; Gong, Y.; Niu, S.; An, W.; Liu, Z.; Wei, S. Exploring the complex mapping between user perception and product form: A case study of air purifiers. *J. Eng. Des.* **2023**, 1–26. [CrossRef]
3. Chang, J.; Han, H.; Yuan, K. How Can Regional Cultural Symbols be Integrated into Public Seating Design? An Innovative Exploration Using Marbled Porcelain Patterns as an Example. *BioResources* **2025**, *20*, 8420–8438. [CrossRef]
4. Li, X.; Lin, J.; Li, Q.; Cao, W. Research on assist design strategy of electric garden tools driven by data and intelligence. *Adv. Des. Res.* **2024**, *2*, 55–62. [CrossRef]
5. Huang, J. Sustainable Development of Green Paper Packaging. *Environ. Pollut.* **2017**, *6*, 1. [CrossRef]
6. Huang, S.; Lv, J.; Liu, X.; Yuan, H.; Wang, Y.; Huan, S.; Shen, J.; Wang, C. Sustainable and green design of beeswax-based pickering emulsion coating for food packaging. *J. Clean. Prod.* **2025**, *495*, 145096. [CrossRef]
7. Pogacar, A.; Gregor-Svetec, D. Eco-Friendly Design for Sustainable Gift Packaging. *Appl. Sci.* **2025**, *15*, 2973. [CrossRef]
8. Liem, D.G.; In't Groen, A.; Van Kleef, E. Dutch consumers' perception of sustainable packaging for milk products, a qualitative and quantitative study. *Food Qual. Prefer.* **2022**, *102*, 104658. [CrossRef]
9. Doi, T.; Nagata, A. An Analysis Method of Anticipated UX Evoked by Packaging Design Using the Evaluation Grid Method: A Case of the Analysis of Packages of Boxed Flour Confections and Sunscreen. *Appl. Sci.* **2025**, *15*, 1339. [CrossRef]
10. Qin, M.; Wang, J.; Ding, X.; Zhang, H. Symmetrical Traditional Patterns and User Perception: A Study on Innova-tion in Home Textile Design. *Symmetry* **2025**, *17*, 960. [CrossRef]
11. Fu, L.; Yang, X.; Zhu, L.; Lv, J. An Intelligent Optimization Design Method for Furniture Form Considering Mul-ti-Dimensional User Affective Requirements. *Symmetry* **2025**, *17*, 1406. [CrossRef]
12. Gerola, A.; Robaey, Z.; Blok, V. What does it mean to mimic nature? A typology for biomimetic design. *Philos. Technol.* **2023**, *36*, 65. [CrossRef]
13. Puneet, D.; Acadia, H.; Cheng, H.; Huynh, V.; Dai, S.Y.; Yuan, J.S. Biomimetic layered; ecological; advanced, multi-functional film for sus-tainable packaging. *Nat. Commun.* **2025**, *16*, 6649.
14. Liu, C.; Shen, T.; Shen, H.; Lu, B.; Sun, L.; Chen, G.; Chi, W. Mimicking Nature's Insects: A Review of Bio-inspired Flapping-Wing Micro Ro-bots (FWMRs). *J. Bionics Eng.* **2025**, *22*, 458–479. [CrossRef]

https://doi.org/10.3390/sym18010019

15. Sui, D.; Zhao, S.; Wang, T.; Liu, Y.; Zhu, Y.; Zhao, J. Design of a Bio-inspired Extensible Continuum Manipulator with Variable Stiffness. *J. Bionics Eng.* **2025**, *22*, 181–194. [CrossRef]
16. Wang, Z.; Zhang, X.; Mu, Z.; Guan, X.; Liu, J.; Pan, Z.; Wang, J.; Ye, X.; Qi, Z.; Dong, J.; et al. Design and Performance Verification of Bionic Octopus Sucker Sealing Structure for Solenoid Valves. *Biomimetics* **2025**, *10*, 425. [CrossRef]
17. Scherer, K.; Santos, A.D.; Lilley, D. Design for sustainable behaviour: Guidelines for cooking appliances. *Adv. Des. Res.* **2023**, *1*, 94–108. [CrossRef]
18. Quoc, T.N.; Phuc, N.N.; Duong, N.H. Examining green packaging, branding, and eco-labeling strate-gies: The case of young consumers'perceptions and responses in F&B industry. *Clean. Responsible Consum.* **2025**, *16*, 100258.
19. Kossalbayev, B.D.; Belkozhayev, A.M.; Abaildayev, A.; Kadirshe, D.K.; Tastambek, K.T.; Kurmanbek, A.; Toleutay, G. Biodegradable packaging from agricultural wastes: A comprehensive review of processing techniques, material properties, and future prospects. *Polymers* **2025**, *17*, 2224. [CrossRef]
20. Gholizadeh, S.; Ehsani, A.; Amjadi, S.; Ahangari, H.; Panahiazar, V. Green packaging system based on hybrid zein/inulin nanofibers activated with copper oxide nanoparticles and Foeniculum vulgare essential oil for preservation of fresh beef. *Appl. Food Res.* **2025**, *5*, 100724. [CrossRef]
21. Gungoren, A.; Akkemik, Y.; Tufekci, E.F.; Zengin, G.; Emre, G.; Gungoren, G.; Celik Altunoglu, Y.; Baloğlu, M.C. Applying Chitosan-Based Films Enriched with Borago officinalis Extract for Active and Green Packaging of Fresh Rainbow Trout Fillets. *Foods* **2025**, *14*, 639. [CrossRef]
22. Qureshi, W.A.; Radjarejesri, S.; Shanmugam, K.; Elavarasan, P.; Gowrishankar, M.; Gebeyehu, K.B. Central composite design of spraying process to laminate the paper substrates with cellulose nanofibers (CNF) as green packaging wrap. *J. Nanomater.* **2022**, *2022*, 9481983. [CrossRef]
23. Quan, H.; Li, Y.; Li, Q. Satisfying Consumer Preferences: The Packaging Design of Guizhou Red Sour Soup. *Foods* **2024**, *13*, 3806. [CrossRef]
24. Buakum, D.; Daesa, C.; Sinthavalai, R.; Noppasri, K. Designing temperature-controlled medicine bag using an in-tegrated AHP-QFD methodology. *Int. J. Interact. Des. Manuf.* **2024**, *18*, 659–670. [CrossRef]
25. de Lima, B.P.; da Silva, A.F.; Marins, F.A.S. New hybrid AHP-QFD-PROMETHEE decision-making support method in the hesitant fuzzy environment: An application in packaging design selection. *J. Intell. Fuzzy Syst.* **2022**, *42*, 2881–2897.
26. Qu, M.; Ren, Z.-X.; Wu, C.; Li, X. Integrating user feedback into air purifier innovation: The FKA-NO-DEMATEL-VIKOR decision framework. *Eng. Manag. J.* **2025**, 1–18. [CrossRef]
27. Hou, D.; Zhang, B.; Chen, J.; Shi, P. Improved GNN based on Graph-Transformer: A new framework for rolling mill bearing fault diagnosis. *Trans. Inst. Meas. Control* **2024**, *46*, 2804–2815. [CrossRef]
28. Malela-Majika, J.-C.; Chakraborti, S.; Graham, M.A. Distribution-free precedence control charts with improved runs-rules. *Appl. Sto-Chastic Models Bus. Ind.* **2016**, *32*, 423–439. [CrossRef]
29. Singh, A.; Kumar, S. Picture fuzzy set and quality function deploymentapproach based novel framework for multi-criteria group decision makingmethod. *Eng. Appl. Artif. Intell.* **2022**, *104*, 104395. [CrossRef]
30. Wen, Z.; Yang, J.; Sun, B.; Liu, Y. Research on Symmetry Optimization of Designer Requirements and Prototyp-ing Platform Functionality in the Context of Agile Development. *Symmetry* **2025**, *17*, 502. [CrossRef]
31. Wang, T.; Zhang, Q.; Chong, H.; Wang, X. Integrated supplier selection framework in a resilient construction supply chain: An approach via analytic hierarchy process (AHP) and grey relational analysis (GRA). *Sustainability* **2017**, *9*, 289. [CrossRef]
32. Xiong, F.; Zou, X.; Zhang, Z.; Shi, X. A systematic approach for multiobjective lightweight and stiffness optimization of a car body. *Struct. Multidiscip. Optim.* **2020**, *62*, 3229–3248. [CrossRef]
33. More, A.P. Flax fiber–based polymer composites: A review. *Adv. Compos. Hybrid Mater.* **2022**, *5*, 1–20. [CrossRef]
34. Xu, D.; He, S.; Leng, W.; Chen, Y.; Wu, Z. Replacing plastic with bamboo: A review of the properties and green applications of bamboo-fiber-reinforced polymer composites. *Polymers* **2023**, *15*, 4276. [CrossRef]
35. Zhu, Y.; Li, L.; Hou, Y.; Xu, C.; Hu, G.; Man, Y.; Vladimirovich, V.S.; Li, J.; Xiong, Q. Investigation into the characteristics of bagasse processed with 3C-DES and the pro-duction of chemimechanical pulp for pulp molded. *J. Clean. Prod.* **2024**, *447*, 141652. [CrossRef]

https://doi.org/10.3390/sym18010019

symmetry

MDPI

Article

A Hybrid Quantitative Method for Evaluating HMI Layout Design in Service Robots

Yanpu Yang *, Yueming Zhuo, Jialing Liu, Wenhao Meng and Zhihong Wu

The Key Laboratory of Road Construction Technology and Equipment, Ministry of Education, Chang'an University, Xi'an 710064, China; 2023225145@chd.edu.cn (Y.Z.); 2023225004@chd.edu.cn (J.L.); 2023225139@chd.edu.cn (W.M.); 2023225141@chd.edu.cn (Z.W.)

* Correspondence: yangyanpu@chd.edu.cn

Abstract: Evaluating the human–machine interface (HMI) of service robots remains challenging due to the complex integration of perceptual aesthetics and functional rationality. To address this, we propose a hybrid multidimensional HMI evaluation method that quantifies three key dimensions—layout aesthetics, color aesthetics, and functional layout rationality—by integrating visual cognition theory and axiomatic design (AD). The framework operationalizes five layout principles (balance, proportion, unity, regularity, density) and a four-component color model (color difference, distribution, harmony, and personality), complemented by a biologically grounded metric—visual perceptual intensity (VPI)—derived from cone cell response theory. Subjective weights from expert judgments (via analytic hierarchy process, AHP) and objective weights from the entropy weighting method (EWM) are fused within an AD-based information axiom framework to enable balanced, data-driven assessment. Applied to five candidate HMIs for a medical service robot ($N = 15$ participants), the method identified the design scheme x_3 as optimal when the balancing coefficient $\alpha \geq 0.5$ (reflecting greater emphasis on subjective judgment), whereas design scheme x_2 was preferred when $\alpha < 0.5$ (prioritizing objective data). Given the modest sample size, correlation analysis revealed moderate-to-large—though not reaching conventional significance—between evaluation indicator scores and eye-tracking behavior: unity correlated with total fixation duration ($Pearson\_r = 0.682$), and color harmony with first fixation duration ($Pearson\_r = 0.788$), suggesting alignment between design attributes and visual attention patterns. These preliminary findings suggest that key design attributes may influence visual attention patterns, supporting the framework's potential to link aesthetic and visual choices to measurable perceptual outcomes.

Keywords: human–machine interface (HMI); service robots; HMI evaluation; visual aesthetics; visual perceptual intensity; axiomatic design

1. Introduction

The global robotics market is experiencing robust expansion, with service robots projected to play an increasingly prominent role across diverse industries. These advancements are driving innovation, reshaping consumer interactions, and generating substantial economic value [1,2]. Service robots are formally defined as "system-based autonomous and adaptable interfaces that interact, communicate, and deliver services to an organization's customers" [3]. Engineered for socially compliant human–robot interaction, they employ human-recognizable communication modalities to convey intent and collaborate with users in achieving goals or addressing challenges. These technologies are now integral to economic and social progress, with transformative applications spanning healthcare [4], education [5], domestic assistance [6], logistics [7], and commerce [8].

Human–Computer Interaction (HCI) technologies serve as critical mediators in service robots, enabling bidirectional communication between humans and robotic systems [9]. Among various HCI components, human–machine interfaces (HMIs) enable users to control robotic platforms and access information through multimodal channels. The HMI is a technology that facilitates interaction between users and devices, encompassing both hardware components—such as displays, touchscreens, keyboards, and indicator lights—and supporting software systems. Its primary objective is to simplify user operations, enhance task efficiency, and improve operational accuracy. Through graphical interfaces, intuitive controls, and real-time feedback, HMI enables users to readily comprehend device status and issue appropriate commands [10]. These channels include hardware elements such as display screens, touchscreens, keyboards, and indicator lights, as well as associated software [11]. At the same time, HMIs allow robots to process user inputs and deliver contextually appropriate feedback. Current HCI implementations encompass both well-established modalities—such as haptic, visual, and auditory interfaces—as well as emerging approaches like neuro-adaptive systems and brain–computer interfaces [12]. Nevertheless, despite significant technological advancements, traditional HMI designs remain widely used in public service robotics. Importantly, the aesthetic quality, functional coherence, and usability of these interfaces have a direct and measurable impact on the overall user experience in human–robot interactions.

Effective HMI layout design extends beyond superficial visual appeal to prioritize alignment with users' cognitive processes. Through systematic integration of perceptual design principles with iterative usability testing [13], developers can create interfaces that optimize both functional performance and affective engagement. Strategically optimized layouts simultaneously address ergonomic requirements and aesthetic preferences while maintaining task-oriented focus. Such designs demonstrably reduce cognitive load [14] and accelerate information processing [15], thereby enhancing overall interaction efficiency [16]. By minimizing visual clutter and cognitive dissonance, these interfaces enable users to dedicate greater attentional resources to primary tasks rather than interface navigation. However, while understanding and accommodating users' cognitive characteristics—such as attention distribution, memory capacity, and decision-making patterns—is undeniably essential, it should not overshadow the importance of holistic design considerations. A well-rounded HMI layout must also integrate aesthetic coherence, functional clarity, and comprehensive spatial organization. These elements collectively contribute to a unified user experience by ensuring that information is not only cognitively accessible but also visually harmonious and intuitively structured. Neglecting the balance between cognitive responsiveness and overall design quality may lead to interfaces that, while theoretically efficient, fail to engage users effectively or support intuitive interaction in real-world contexts.

Current HMI design methods often overlook two critical dimensions: (1) the integration of visual cognitive patterns with aesthetic considerations, and (2) the systematic alignment between functional hierarchy and the distribution of visual salience. These omissions highlight the limitations of purely algorithmic or heuristic approaches to interface rationalization [17], which frequently fail to account for human perceptual and cognitive behaviors in real-world service robot interaction scenarios. To bridge these gaps, this paper proposes a hybrid quantitative evaluation framework that systematically quantifies the relationship between key HMI layout design features and users' visual cognitive characteristics in service robots. By integrating aesthetic assessment and visual cognitive considerations, the framework enables data-driven evaluation of HMI layout design. This approach advances the field beyond subjective or isolated evaluations, supporting more rational, user-centered HMI development in robotic systems.

The primary contributions of this paper are as follows:

(1) Quantification of aesthetic and cognitive dimensions through computational modeling: This study operationalizes two critical yet often under-quantified aspects of HMI design—layout aesthetics and color aesthetics—into rigorously defined, computationally tractable metrics. Layout aesthetics are quantified using a visual harmony model encompassing five key design principles, while color aesthetics are evaluated via a four-component color assessment model. Furthermore, we introduce a visual perceptual intensity (VPI) model that accounts for the decline in visual sensitivity from fovea to periphery, enabling spatially weighted assessment of functional layout salience in service robot HMIs.

(2) A perceptually grounded evaluation framework for service robot HMIs: This paper proposes a novel hybrid evaluation framework that systematically integrates visual cognitive mechanisms with layout and color-related aesthetic principles in the context of service robot HMIs. By incorporating VPI—based on retinal cone cell distribution—the framework captures bottom-up visual salience driven by human sensory processing. This perceptual model is unified with top-down aesthetic evaluation metrics, including layout and color aesthetics, enabling a comprehensive assessment that bridges sensory response and cognitive appreciation.

(3) A hybrid subjective–objective weighting method within an axiomatic decision structure: To ensure balanced and robust criterion prioritization, we develop a hybrid weighting approach that combines Analytic Hierarchy Process (AHP) for capturing expert-driven subjective preferences and Entropy Weighting Method (EWM) for reflecting objective data variation. The hybrid quantitative method is specifically applied to the evaluation of HMI design quality. This integrated AHP-EWM approach is embedded within an Axiomatic Design (AD) framework, enabling coherent multi-criteria decision-making (MCDM) that satisfies independence axioms while accounting for inter-criterion correlations. The resulting structure enhances both the rationality and reliability of service robot HMI evaluation under complex design constraints.

The proposed methodological framework is illustrated in Figure 1.

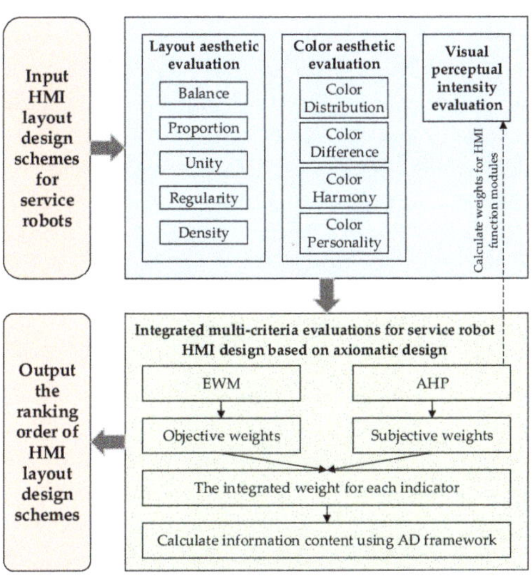

Figure 1. The proposed methodological framework.

2. Literature Review

As the primary medium of interaction between humans and machines, HMIs are typically designed based on principles of functionality and usability. The core objective of an effective HMI is to facilitate user operations and enhance the way functional systems deliver convenience and support to users [11]. However, achieving this objective requires more than just intuitive design or advanced technology—it necessitates systematic evaluation of HMI performance from both a technical and human-centered perspective.

Generally, the evaluation of HMI design encompasses three key dimensions: user cognition, aesthetic measurement, and comprehensive performance assessment. User cognitive evaluation focuses on how effectively the interface supports users' understanding, decision-making, and task execution by aligning with their mental models and information-processing capabilities. The layout of an interactive interface is deliberately designed to engage users' spatial reasoning abilities. As a result, individual cognitive characteristics influence visual attention patterns and the interpretation of interface elements, thereby significantly affecting cognitive processing efficiency [18]. Given that user perceptions are often subconscious or difficult to articulate, designers must employ structured methodologies to uncover and assess latent user requirements [19]. For instance, Chikhaoui and Pigot [20] applied cognitive modeling techniques—including ACT-R, GOMS, and Fitts' Law—to evaluate smart home interfaces, with a primary focus on task execution time. Diego-Mas et al. [21] collected eye-tracking and mouse-tracking data during interface use to determine the optimal arrangement of interface elements, subsequently employing a slicing-trees-based genetic algorithm to generate optimized layouts. Wang et al. [22] assessed the quality of visual encoding in a mixed reality interface designed for human–machine collaborative assembly in complex environments, revealing the relationship between the implementation of visual cues and the cognitive balance of the interface.

Beyond studies centered on cognitive aspects of HMI design, recent research has increasingly emphasized the importance of users' emotional responses and aesthetic impressions elicited by the visual layout of interactive interfaces [23]. Aesthetic measurement quantifies the visual appeal and emotional impact of an interface, both of which play crucial roles in shaping first impressions and sustaining long-term user engagement. Visual aesthetics, as an important branch of design research, holds significant value in the fields of interface design, industrial design, and human–machine interaction. A well-executed visual aesthetic not only enhances user experience but also improves information transmission efficiency and operational comprehensibility. Maria [24] et al. explored how and when visual aesthetic features, such as symmetry and complexity, influence approach-avoidance motivational behavior, examining the relationship between these aesthetic features and user preferences. Chen [25] et al. investigated the impact of shape, contrast, and visual forces on the visual weight of interface elements, finding that polygons and rounded rectangles had no significant effect on visual weight. These related visual aesthetics studies provide a foundation for the quantitative evaluation of layout aesthetics and color aesthetics in service robot HMI. Several relatively subjective perceptual factors—such as interface visual complexity [26], attractiveness [27], and usefulness [28]—have been investigated. Additionally, Ngo et al. [29] proposed a set of quantitative formulas for 13 layout elements to objectively characterize interface design features. Building on this quantitative approach, Ha [30] introduced a balancing principle for HMI design evaluation and optimization. Based on this principle, two metrics—Design Importance Ratio (DIR) and Balancing Index (BI)—were developed and applied in the HMI design of nuclear power plants. Reinecke et al. [31] further advanced the field by developing computational models to assess the colorfulness and visual complexity of website screenshots, with visual complexity calculations linked to webpage structural properties. In their models, symmetry, balance, and equilibrium were computed based on mathematical definitions. Wan et al. [32] proposed a novel Webpage Layout Aesthetic Evaluation (WLAE) model, based on an improved AdaBoost algorithm, capable of automatically predicting the aesthetic quality of webpage layouts. Bauerly and Liu [33] presented computational modeling and two corresponding experimental studies examining the effects of symmetry, balance, and the number of construction elements on aesthetic judgments of interfaces.

When both cognitive aspects and aesthetic qualities of a HMI are considered simultaneously, selecting an optimized design that effectively meets users' cognitive and aesthetic needs becomes a complex task. Comprehensive evaluation integrates both qualitative and quantitative metrics to assess overall usability, functionality, and user satisfaction, ensuring that the HMI not only performs efficiently but also delivers a positive and intuitive interaction experience. Therefore, a comprehensive evaluation method is required to integrate multiple design metrics into a unified assessment framework. In this context, two key challenges emerge: determining the relative weights of HMI design indicators and aggregating the performance scores across these indicators to evaluate overall interface quality. Several studies have explored MCDM approaches to address these challenges. For instance, Liu et al. [34] integrated the Spherical Fuzzy Analytic Hierarchy Process (SF-AHP) with the Spherical Fuzzy AD (SF-AD) method to select a suitable HMI alternative while accounting for uncertainties arising from experts' hesitation. Yang et al. [35] applied the entropy weight method to assess key interaction performance factors relevant to in-vehicle thermal environment evaluation. Pei et al. [36] proposed a framework for evaluating cognitive load in fighter cockpit interfaces using an MCDM approach, in which the SWARA (Step-wise Weight Assessment Ratio Analysis) and MEREC (Method based on the Removal Effects of Criteria) methods were employed to determine subjective and objective indicator weights, respectively. Zhang et al. [37] developed a comprehensive evaluation method for head-up display (HUD) interface layouts by combining the Bayesian Best-Worst Method (BWM) with Gray-TOPSIS (Technique for Order Preference by Similarity to an Ideal Solution). In their approach, Bayesian BWM was used to calculate indicator weights, followed by Gray-TOPSIS to evaluate and rank candidate layout designs. Li [38] proposed a Bayesian classification based method for evaluating the quality of intelligent product interaction interfaces. Introducing an adaptive Gaussian filter, adjusting the color of the intelligent product interaction interface through logarithmic operators, and formalizing the description of the intelligent product interaction interface. This method has high recognition accuracy and fast evaluation time.

Despite significant advancements in HMI design evaluation, a critical gap remains in the development of integrated, quantifiable, and user-centered methods specifically tailored to the HMI layout design in service robots. While prior research has explored cognitive ergonomics, aesthetic principles, and MCDM techniques in isolation, few studies have systematically synthesized these dimensions into a unified evaluation framework within the context of human–robot interaction. Moreover, many existing HMI layout evaluation methods rely on subjective assessments or conventional MCDM models that fail to adequately capture the complexity of visual perception—particularly the interplay between functional efficiency and visual harmony. To address these challenges, this study proposes a hybrid HMI quantitative evaluation method for service robot HMI layouts. The approach integrates layout and color aesthetic measurement, VPI modelling, a structured evaluation framework based on AD, and a hybrid AHP-EWM to determine both qualitative and quantitative criterion weights, balancing expert judgment with data-driven objectivity. The proposed method is empirically validated through eye-tracking experiments, ensuring alignment with actual human visual behavior. This holistic framework not only enhances layout rationality but also supports the design of HMIs that foster user trust, engagement, and long-term satisfaction in service robot interactions.

3. Methods

3.1. Aesthetic Measurement

Aesthetics plays a pivotal role in shaping user experience and interaction quality in HMI design. Fundamental design elements—such as line, shape, and color [39]—serve as the building blocks of visual expression, directly influencing users' perceptual responses, emotional engagement, and overall satisfaction. In service robot HMIs, where first impressions and intuitive interaction are critical, these elements not only enhance visual appeal but also support cognitive processing and functional clarity, effectively bridging the gap between aesthetic attractiveness and usability. Research has consistently demonstrated that visually pleasing interfaces are often perceived as more usable, even when their functional performance remains unchanged—a phenomenon known as the aesthetic-usability effect [40]. In the context of interactive systems such as service robots, aesthetic design significantly contributes to building user trust, satisfaction, and long-term engagement. Building on foundational work, Miniukovich and Angeli [41] proposed eight computational metrics for graphical user interface aesthetic evaluation: visual clutter, color range, number of dominant colors, figure-ground contrast, contour congestion, symmetry, grid quality, and white space. Similarly, Liu et al. [42] identified eight key visual features—graphics-to-text ratio, color difference, color distribution, color harmony, theme style, white space ratio, frame style, and total number of colors—to analyze both visual structure and emotional response in HCI interfaces. An HMI contains a wide variety of these basic design elements, each with distinct colors, shapes, sizes, and lines, which together shape user perception and overall satisfaction with the HMI design. However, we treat layout and color as complementary yet analytically separable dimensions based on their distinct perceptual and functional roles:

(1) Layout aesthetics refers to the spatial organization of interface elements—captured through attributes such as shape, size, position, balance, proportion, unity, regularity, and density. These properties primarily govern structural coherence, compositional stability, and navigational efficiency, and are evaluated independently of chromatic content (e.g., using grayscale or positional analysis).

(2) Color aesthetics, by contrast, focuses on the chromatic qualities of the interface—including color contrast, distribution, harmony, and personality—which convey emotional tone, semantic meaning, and visual salience. This dimension is grounded in color psychology and human spectral sensitivity, and is assessed through metrics such as color difference, color distribution, color harmony, and color personality.

This two-dimensional decomposition does not deny the holistic nature of visual perception; rather, it enables systematic quantification of otherwise entangled aesthetic factors. By decoupling spatial structure from chromatic expression, our method supports targeted design optimization—e.g., improving layout balance without altering color semantics, or tuning color harmony while preserving spatial logic.

Synthesizing these studies, we classify HMI aesthetic evaluation into two primary dimensions: layout aesthetics and color aesthetics. Layout aesthetics encompass structural and spatial properties such as visual balance, proportion, unity, regularity, and density—principles rooted in Gestalt psychology and visual design theory. These attributes not only evoke positive emotional responses but also reduce cognitive load by improving visual scanning efficiency and facilitating rapid information retrieval [43,44], thereby supporting both aesthetic appeal and functional usability in HMI interactions. Color aesthetics, in contrast, focuses on the expressive and psychological dimensions of color, including color difference, color distribution, and color harmony. It also incorporates color personality attributes to construct an evaluative paradigm for assessing the personality impressions elicited by polychromatic HMI appearances in service robots. This dimension aligns with social response theory, where users are more conscious of agents with anthropomorphic visual cues [45]. This two-dimensional classification provides a structured, measurable foundation for integrating aesthetic considerations into the rational design of service robot HMIs.

3.1.1. Layout Aesthetic Evaluation

Building upon the foundational layout characteristics outlined by Ngo et al. [44] and the aesthetic guidelines for display design proposed by Tullis [46], this study identifies balance, proportion, unity, regularity, and density as core aesthetic dimensions for quantitative evaluation. Informed by insights from user interviews, designer focus areas, and the mapping between interface layout and cognitive response, these metrics collectively contribute to the overall visual harmony, usability, and user experience.

(1) Balance

Balance refers to the distribution of visual or optical weight within a design composition, contributing to a sense of stability and aesthetic harmony [47–49]. Rooted in fundamental principles of visual perception and Gestalt psychology, balance reflects the human cognitive tendency to seek equilibrium in structured arrangements. A balanced composition is perceived as evenly distributed across spatial axes—horizontally (left vs. right) and/or vertically (top vs. bottom) —even if the distribution is not perfectly symmetrical. The perception of optical weight is influenced by multiple design attributes, including size, shape, and position. For instance, larger elements tend to carry greater visual weight than smaller ones. In the context of service robot HMI design, achieving visual balance ensures that no single region dominates the interface disproportionately. This prevents user attention from being unintentionally drawn to non-critical areas, thereby enhancing both aesthetic appeal and cognitive ease.

Balance is quantified by computing the difference in visual weight between interface components located on opposite sides of the horizontal and vertical axes of the HMI layout. Typically, HMIs are framed in a rectangular shape, with the centroid of the rectangle serving as the central reference point. Horizontal (left vs. right) and vertical (top vs. bottom) axes are established, dividing the interface space into four regions: top-left, top-right, bottom-left, and bottom-right. The centroid of each functional module is then calculated, and based on its position, the functional module is assigned to one of these four regions—top or bottom, left or right. This allows for the computation of the overall balance of the HMI. Formally, balance can be defined as follows:

$$\begin{cases} BM = 1 - \frac{|BM_{\mathrm{v}}|+|BM_{\mathrm{h}}|}{2} \\ BM_{\mathrm{v}} = \frac{w_{\mathrm{L}}-w_{\mathrm{R}}}{\max(|w_{\mathrm{L}}|,|w_{\mathrm{R}}|)} \\ BM_{\mathrm{h}} = \frac{w_{\mathrm{T}}-w_{\mathrm{B}}}{\max(|w_{\mathrm{T}}|,|w_{\mathrm{B}}|)} \\ w_j = \sum\limits_{i=1}^{n_j} a_{ij}d_{ij}, j \in \{\mathrm{L},\mathrm{R},\mathrm{T},\mathrm{B}\} \end{cases} \quad (1)$$

where BM denotes the overall balance of the HMI layout, while BM_{v} and BM_{h} represent the vertical and horizontal balance components, respectively; L, R, T, and B denote the left, right, top, and bottom regions of the layout, respectively; a_{ij} represents the area of object i on side j; d_{ij} denotes the distance between the centerline of object i and the corresponding frame boundary; and n_j is the total number of objects on side j.

(2) Proportion

Across diverse historical periods and cultural contexts, certain geometric proportional systems have been consistently associated with aesthetic value and visual harmony. Although perceptions of beauty are influenced by cultural and contextual factors, specific mathematical ratios have demonstrated enduring cross-cultural appeal, suggesting a degree of university in human aesthetic preference. Marcus [50] identifies several such ratios widely regarded as visually harmonious, including (1:1), (1:1.414), (1:1.618), (1:1.732), and (1:2). In the context of HMI layout design, applying these proportionally balanced forms to key interface components—such as windows, data regions, and text blocks—can enhance visual coherence, structural clarity, and aesthetic fluency. Thus, proportion serves not only as a formal design principle but also as a cognitive scaffold, reducing visual complexity and guiding attention through spatial hierarchy.

Proportion is defined as the quantitative relationship between the dimensional attributes of HMI layout design elements and a set of reference geometric forms associated with visually harmonious ratios. This relationship can be mathematically formulated as follows:

$$\begin{cases} PM = \frac{|PM_o|+|PM_l|}{2} \\ PM_o = \frac{1}{n_t}\sum_{i=1}^{n_t}\left(1 - 2\min\left(\left|p_j - p_i\right|\right)\right) \\ PM_l = 1 - 2\min\left(\left|p_j - p_l\right|\right) \end{cases} \tag{2}$$

where PM denotes the overall proportion of the HMI layout; PM_o represents the deviation between the proportions of individual interface objects and the nearest established proportional shape, while PM_l indicates the deviation between the overall layout proportion and its closest proportional shape. p_j is the referenced proportion of shape j with $p_j \in$ {(1:1), (1:1.414), (1:1.618), (1:1.732), (1:2)}. For object i, $p_i = \min\{h_i/b_i, b_i/h_i\}$, where b_i and h_i denote the width and height of the object, respectively. Similarly, $p_l = \min\{h_l/b_l, b_l/h_l\}$, with b_l and h_l representing the width and height of the entire layout.

(3) Unity

Unity reflects the degree to which visual components are perceived as a cohesive and harmonious whole, rather than isolated or disjointed elements. Rooted in Gestalt psychology—particularly the principles of proximity, similarity, and continuity—unity emerges when design elements are visually integrated through consistent sizing and spatial organization. A high degree of unity reduces cognitive load by enabling users to intuitively group related components and perceive structural hierarchy without explicit labeling. In HMI layout design, unity is enhanced through consistent sizing of elements and minimizing the spacing between related components relative to the margins. Formally, unity can be defined as:

$$\begin{cases} UM = \frac{|UM_f|+|UM_s|}{2} \\ UM_f = 1 - (n-1)/n_t \\ UM_s = 1 - \left(a_l - \sum_{i=1}^{n} a_i\right) / \left(a_f - \sum_{i=1}^{n} a_i\right) \end{cases} \tag{3}$$

where UM denotes the overall unity of the HMI layout; UM_f reflects the degree of size consistency among interface objects, and UM_s represents the spatial relationship between the margin area of the screen and the space between individual components. a_i, a_l, and a_f refer to the areas of object i, the layout, and the frame, respectively; n is the number of distinct sizes used, and n_t is the total number of objects within the frame.

(4) Regularity

Regularity pertains to the uniformity and predictability of alignment structures within an HMI layout. It reflects the extent to which interface components adhere to a consistent spatial grid system, minimizing arbitrary positioning and promoting visual order. High regularity is achieved through standardized horizontal and vertical alignment lines, uniform spacing, and modular positioning—principles that support rapid visual parsing and reduce cognitive load. In HMI design, regularity emerges when elements align along shared baselines, margins, and column/row guides. A layout with high regularity uses fewer alignment references, meaning that most components share common edges or centers, resulting in a structured and predictable composition. Formally, regularity can be defined as:

$$\begin{cases} RM = \frac{|RM_a| + |RM_s|}{2} \\ RM_a = \begin{cases} 1 & \text{, if } n_t = 1 \\ 1 - (n_v + n_h)/2n_t, & \text{otherwise} \end{cases} \\ RM_s = \begin{cases} 1 & \text{, if } n_t = 1 \\ 1 - (n_s - 1)/2(n_t - 1), & \text{otherwise} \end{cases} \end{cases} \quad (4)$$

where RM denotes the overall regularity of the HMI layout; RM_a reflects the degree to which alignment points are minimized, and RM_s indicates the consistency in spacing between these alignment points. n_v and n_h represent the number of vertical and horizontal alignment references, respectively; n_s is the number of distinct distances between column and row starting points; and n_t is the total number of interface objects within the frame.

(5) Density

Density refers to the degree of spatial compactness within an HMI layout, quantified as the ratio of content area to total available screen space. It plays a pivotal role in shaping visual comfort: excessive density induces visual clutter and cognitive overload, whereas insufficient density leads to fragmented layouts and inefficient use of screen real estate. Empirical studies in HCI and visual perception consistently suggest that a content-to-total-area ratio of approximately 50%—commonly termed optimal visual density—is perceived as most balanced and aesthetically pleasing [51]. This threshold strikes an effective compromise between information richness and perceptual clarity, enabling adequate content display without overwhelming the user's sensory and cognitive systems. The principle is particularly well-established in design disciplines such as graphic design, web design, and advertising, where moderate visual density enhances readability, guides attention, and improves overall user experience. It aligns closely with foundational concepts like visual rhythm and breathing room, which advocate for intentional negative space to support both efficient information processing and perceptual relaxation.

Formally, density DM is defined as:

$$DM = 1 - 2\left|0.5 - \frac{1}{a_f}\sum_{i=1}^{n_t} a_i\right| \quad (5)$$

where a_i denotes the area of object i, a_f represents the total area of the screen frame, and n_t is the total number of objects within the HMI layout.

3.1.2. Color Aesthetic Measurement

Color exerts a profound influence on human cognition and emotion, serving as a powerful non-verbal communication channel within HMIs. It conveys functional meaning, guides attention, shapes brand perception, and evokes emotional responses through its symbolic, cultural, and physiological associations [52]. From a perceptual standpoint, color can be systematically described using three fundamental attributes derived from the Munsell color system and aligned with human visual processing: hue, value, and chroma [53]. These attributes form a perceptually uniform three-dimensional space, enabling objective analysis of color schemes in digital interfaces. The overall visual impression of an HMI's color scheme emerges from the interplay of these dimensions across the layout. To systematically evaluate the aesthetic and functional impact of color, this study adopts a four-component analytical framework [54,55]: color difference, color distribution, color harmony, and color personalities.

(1) Color difference

Color difference is determined by decomposing color into three perceptual dimensions—hue, chroma, and value—and evaluating the differences with each dimension. Based on Munsell color theory [56], a hue difference of up to 144° on the hue circle represents the upper threshold for achieving strong visual distinction, beyond which perceptual benefits plateau. Li and Xue [54] found that chroma differences exceeding 50 (on a 0–100 scale) result in stable color discriminability, with minimal interference, provided hue and value remain constant. For value difference, this study adopts a threshold of 4.5 (on a 0–10 scale) [42], grounded in psychophysical evidence for effective visual discrimination and cognitive processing. Building on these dimension-specific thresholds, the overall color difference between two colors is calculated as follows:

$$\begin{cases} D_{\text{difference}} = (D_{\text{hue}} + D_{\text{chroma}} + D_{\text{value}})/3 \\ D_{\text{hue}} = \gamma_k / 144^\circ \\ D_{\text{chroma}} = \frac{1}{50}\left(\frac{C_x}{\max C_x} - \frac{C_y}{\max C_y}\right) \times 100 \\ D_{\text{value}} = 10 \times (V_x - V_y)/45 \end{cases} \tag{6}$$

where D_{hue}, D_{chroma}, and D_{value} denote the differences in hue, chroma, and value between colors x and y, respectively; γ_k represents the angular separation between the two colors on the hue circle (in degrees); C_x and C_y are the chroma values of colors x and y; and V_x and V_y are their corresponding value measures. The terms $\max C_x$ and $\max C_y$ represent the maximum chroma achievable for each color within the applicable color system.

(2) Color distribution

To compute color distribution, the HMI of a service robot is divided into four quadrants—Q1(X1Y1), Q2(X2Y1), Q3(X2Y2), and Q4(X1Y2)—using the horizontal (X) and vertical (Y) axes intersecting at the screen's center. The spatial distribution of colors across these quadrants is then quantified using image entropy theory [57], as described below:

$$\begin{cases} D_{\text{distribution}} = \frac{1}{n}\sum\limits_{i=1}^{n} E_i \\ E_i = -\frac{1}{\ln 4}\sum\limits_{j=1}^{4} F_{ij} \ln F_{ij} \\ F_{ij} = A_{ij} / \sum\limits_{j=1}^{4} A_{ij} \end{cases} \tag{7}$$

where E_i denotes the entropy associated with the i-th color, and A_{ij} represents the area in the j-th quadrant of the HMI occupied by regions dominated by the i-th color.

(3) Color harmony

To quantitatively assess the aesthetic quality of color combinations, this study employs the color harmony model developed by Moon and Spencer [58], which extends Birkhoff's foundational theory of aesthetic measurement [59]. The model is formulated as follows:

$$\begin{cases} M = O/C \\ C = C_{\text{m}} + C_{\text{h}} + C_{\text{v}} + C_{\text{c}} \\ O = \begin{cases} \sum O_{\text{g}} & \text{, for achromatic colors} \\ \sum O_{\text{h}} + \sum O_{\text{v}} + \sum O_{\text{c}} & \text{, for chromatic colors} \end{cases} \end{cases} \tag{8}$$

where C_{m} denotes the total number of colors in the HMI design scheme; C_{h}, C_{v}, and C_{c} represent the counts of color pairs differing in hue, value, and chroma, respectively; O_{g} is the order term for schemes composed exclusively of achromatic colors; and O_{h}, O_{v}, and

O_c are the order terms derived from hue, value, and chroma differences, respectively, in chromatic color schemes. These order values are determined by the interval relationships among the corresponding color attributes, as defined in prior studies [60–62].

(4) Color personality

Color serves as a powerful medium for conveying psychological meaning through color-personality association [63], a phenomenon that has elevated the intentional design of personality traits to a critical imperative in HMI development. Building on the methodological framework of Wu et al. [55], we employ multi-colored personality indices (MCPIs) as an evaluative paradigm to quantify personality impressions elicited by polychromatic HMI designs. The MCPI model operationalizes perceived personality along five bipolar dimensions: wide interests (NE_1)–narrow interests (PE_1), organized (NE_2)–disorganized (PE_2), extraverted (NE_3)–introverted (PE_3), agreeable (NE_4)–disagreeable (PE_4), and moody (NE_5)–unemotional (PE_5). This model integrates two primary data streams through computational synthesis: (1) RGB histogram analysis of the HMI's chromatic distribution; (2) pre-established color personality indices (CPIs) for individual monochromatic components. The mathematical formalization of this integrative process is as follows:

$$S_p = \begin{cases} MCPI_p & ,\text{if } p \in \{NE_1, NE_2, \cdots, NE_5\} \\ 1 - MCPI_p & ,\text{if } p \in \{PE_1, PE_2, \cdots, PE_5\} \end{cases} \tag{9}$$

where S_p denotes the score for personality impression p, and $MCPI_p$ is the MCPI for trait p, computed according to Equation (10) [64]:

$$MCPI_p = \frac{\sum_{i=1}^{512} \sigma_i \times CPI_i - MIN\_CPI_p}{MAX\_CPI_p - MIN\_CPI_p} \tag{10}$$

where σ_i denotes the ratio of the number of pixels in the i-th bin to the total number of pixels in the service robot's HMI layout, CPI_i is computed using the color attributes—CIE Lightness (L^*), Chroma (C^*), and Hue (h)—evaluated at the midpoint of the i-th bin and the single-color CPI model specified in Table 1; and MAX_CPI_p and MIN_CPI_p denote the maximum and minimum CPI values, respectively, across the 512 color bins for personality trait p, with $p \in \{NE_1, NE_2, \ldots, NE_5, PE_1, PE_2, \ldots, PE_5\}$.

Table 1. The CPI model predicting personality impressions of single colors [55].

Hues	CPI Models
Red ($h > 315°, h \leq 45°$)	$CPI_{NE_1\_PE_1\_R} = -3.7229 + 0.0464L^* + 0.0561C^*$
	$CPI_{NE_2\_PE_2\_R} = 1.5575 - 0.0243L^* - 0.0185C^*$
	$CPI_{NE_3\_PE_3\_R} = -3.4140 + 0.0420L^* + 0.0552C^*$
	$CPI_{NE_4\_PE_4\_R} = -1.3626 + 0.0272L^*$
	$CPI_{NE_5\_PE_5\_R} = -2.0015 + 0.0214L^* + 0.0420C^*$
Yellow ($45° < h \leq 135°$)	$CPI_{NE_1\_PE_1\_Y} = -3.1289 + 0.0496L^* + 0.0316C^* - 0.0092h$
	$CPI_{NE_2\_PE_2\_Y} = 0.8409 - 0.0185L^* - 0.0101C^* + 0.0036h$
	$CPI_{NE_3\_PE_3\_Y} = -2.9373 + 0.0464L^* + 0.0362C^* - 0.0100h$
	$CPI_{NE_4\_PE_4\_Y} = -1.0144 + 0.0203L^* - 0.0061C^*$
	$CPI_{NE_5\_PE_5\_Y} = -1.5858 + 0.0228L^* + 0.0270C^* - 0.0056h$
Green ($135° < h \leq 225°$)	$CPI_{NE_1\_PE_1\_G} = -3.6473 + 0.0439L^* + 0.0441C^*$
	$CPI_{NE_2\_PE_2\_G} = 1.4449 - 0.0189L^* - 0.0088C^*$
	$CPI_{NE_3\_PE_3\_G} = -3.2257 + 0.0371L^* + 0.0466C^*$
	$CPI_{NE_4\_PE_4\_G} = -1.5705 + 0.0224L^* + 0.0167C^*$
	$CPI_{NE_5\_PE_5\_G} = -1.7020 + 0.0185L^* + 0.0142C^*$
Blue ($225° < h \leq 315°$)	$CPI_{NE_1\_PE_1\_B} = -3.4639 + 0.0414L^* + 0.0397C^*$
	$CPI_{NE_2\_PE_2\_B} = 1.7541 - 0.0247L^* - 0.0107C^*$
	$CPI_{NE_3\_PE_3\_B} = -2.0517 + 0.0374L^* + 0.0419C^* - 0.0045h$
	$CPI_{NE_4\_PE_4\_B} = -1.7247 + 0.0236L^* + 0.0129C^*$
	$CPI_{NE_5\_PE_5\_B} = -1.8432 + 0.0195L^* + 0.0246C^*$

3.2. Visual Perceptual Intensity Evaluation

Cone cells on the retina are non-uniformly distributed, with higher density in the central fovea and decreasing density toward the periphery [65]. According to cone perception theory, visual perceptual intensity (VPI) follows this distribution pattern, diminishing gradually from the center to the periphery [66]. When an observer directly views an interface, the angle θ between the line of sight to a given point and the central visual axis—combined with the viewing distance l—can be used to define regions of varying perceptual intensity. By integrating VPI, HMI evaluation can prioritize design elements in the central visual field, where human color and detail perception are strongest, thereby enhancing usability and responsiveness in service robot interfaces.

As illustrated in Figure 2, due to the circular symmetry of cone cell distribution, the visual perceptual field can be modeled as concentric zones of decreasing sensitivity. The radius r of a perceptual zone corresponding to a specific angular eccentricity θ is calculated using the following formula:

$$r = l \tan\theta \tag{11}$$

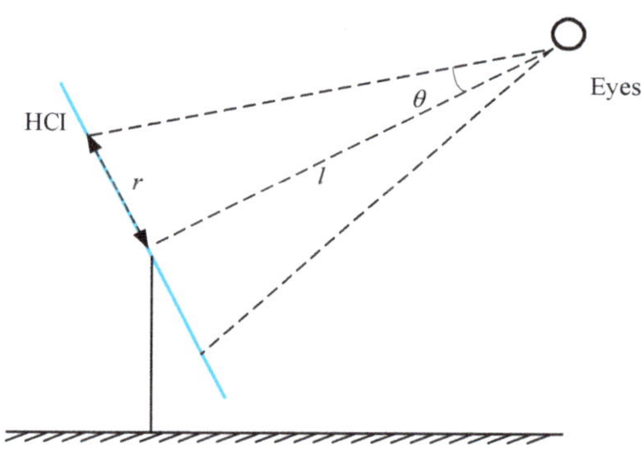

Figure 2. The visual perceptual field.

Based on visual cognition theory and the perceptual intensity zoning criteria of human retinal photoreceptors, the visual field can be divided into five levels when the angular eccentricity from the central gaze axis ranges between 12° and 13° [66], with perceptual intensity increasing toward the foveal center. Four concentric circles are centered on the fovea, defining four annular regions within the 13° gaze limit. The boundary angles—1°, 5°, 9°, and 13°—form an arithmetic sequence. The central 1° region corresponds to the area of highest cone cell density on the HMI and is classified as Level 1; subsequent concentric zones are assigned to Levels 2–5 accordingly. Using Equation (11), radial boundaries can be calculated for eccentricities of 1°, 5°, 9°, and 13°. For HMIs with different aspect ratios, the number of perceptual regions can be adjusted using the proposed method, with angular boundaries extended geometrically (e.g., 17°, 21°) to accommodate additional zones. When more than seven regions are required, adjustment of the viewing distance l should be considered to maintain perceptual resolution and spatial feasibility.

Let H and W denote the lengths of the short and long sides, respectively, of the HMI framework. The radii of the visual perceptual levels are denoted as r_1, r_2, r_3, r_4. The rectangular HMI is partitioned into perceptual levels using a minimum unit—a square of side length a—determined by visual intensity theory and user visual habits. The area of this unit satisfies $a^2 = \pi r_1^2$. Consequently, the visual field is discretized into a grid of these smallest square units, each of side length a, as illustrated in Figure 3. Since the boundaries of the perceptual field may not align perfectly with the edges of the square units, partially overlapping units along the boundary are included in the perceptual field.

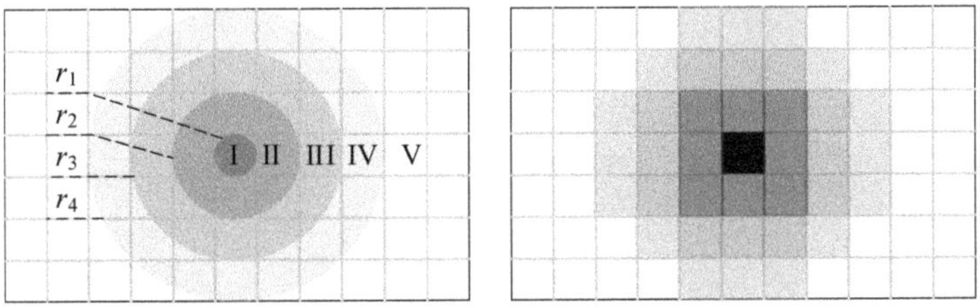

Figure 3. HMI visual perception area classification levels: I, II, III, IV, V.

To comprehensively evaluate the rationality of the HMI layout, we integrate the importance of each function module in the service robot interface with the VPI index. Due to the limitations of human working memory and perceptual capacity, it is essential to minimize the interference of low-priority information in HMI design, thereby reducing the external cognitive load on users. Typically, the function modules in an HMI are arranged according to their importance, with more critical modules placed in the optimal visual regions. The importance weights of the function modules are determined using the AHP method [67], which provides a structured approach for capturing expert judgments on relative significance. A detailed exposition of the AHP procedure is omitted here, as the focus of this study lies in the integration and application of these weights within the visual attention assessment framework.

Let u_τ^z denote the number of discrete units occupied by function module z (where $1 \le z \le Z$) in the τ-th visual perceptual region (where $1 \le \tau \le T$) of a service robot HMI layout. Let q_τ represent the VPI weight associated with τ-th region, with values assigned according to perceptual hierarchy:

$$q_\tau = \begin{cases} 5, \text{perceptual level I} \\ 4, \text{perceptual level II} \\ 3, \text{perceptual level III} \\ 2, \text{perceptual level IV} \\ 1, \text{perceptual level V} \end{cases} \tag{12}$$

Higher values indicate greater visual salience. Additionally, let w_z denote the functional importance of module z. Then the VPI of the HMI layout is defined as:

$$VPI = \sum_{z=1}^{Z} \sum_{\tau=1}^{T} w_z q_\tau u_\tau^z \tag{13}$$

A higher VPI value indicates that functionally critical modules are preferentially positioned within regions of greater visual salience on the service robot HMI. This enhanced alignment between functional importance and perceptual prominence contributes to a more rational and user-centered HMI layout in service robot, supporting faster visual acquisition and reduced cognitive load during interaction.

3.3. Integrated Multi-Criteria Evaluations for Service Robot HMI Design Based on AD

The evaluation of service robot HMI layouts involves a multifaceted set of objective criteria. Key evaluation dimensions include the aesthetic assessment of layout composition, the analysis of color components, and the rationality of the layout based on visual perceptual intensity. Each of these dimensions contributes significantly to the overall usability, visual appeal, and cognitive efficiency of the service robot HMI. The integration of heterogeneous criteria—spanning aesthetic design, color psychology, and visual ergonomics—demands a systematic framework capable of unifying diverse metrics to support rational, data-informed decision-making in the service robot HMI design selection process.

AD, a framework introduced by Nam Suh, establishes a systematic and rigorous approach to engineering design. Its core principle asserts that the optimal design is the one with minimal information content [68]. Given its strong conceptual alignment with design evaluation [69], this study integrates axiomatic design into the selection and assessment of service robot HMI layouts.

According to the information axiom of AD, the optimal design solution is the one that minimizes the information content I, which corresponds to maximizing the probability of satisfying the functional requirements (FRs). The information content is defined as $I = -\log_2(p)$, where p is the probability that a given design fulfills the specified FRs. Thus, a higher success probability p results in lower information content, indicating a more robust and desirable design. In practice, p is determined by the overlap between the design range—the acceptable performance interval defined by decision-makers—and the system range—the actual distribution of a design's output or indicator values. The intersection of these two ranges defines the common range, representing the set of outcomes that satisfy the FRs. Assuming a uniform distribution of system performance within the system range, the information content can be expressed as: $I = \log_2^{\left(\frac{system\ range}{common\ range}\right)}$. This conceptual relationship is illustrated in Figure 4. In the context of service robot HMI layout design evaluation, the design range for a benefit criterion is set to the maximum evaluation value across all alternatives, and for cost-related criteria, to the minimum value [70].

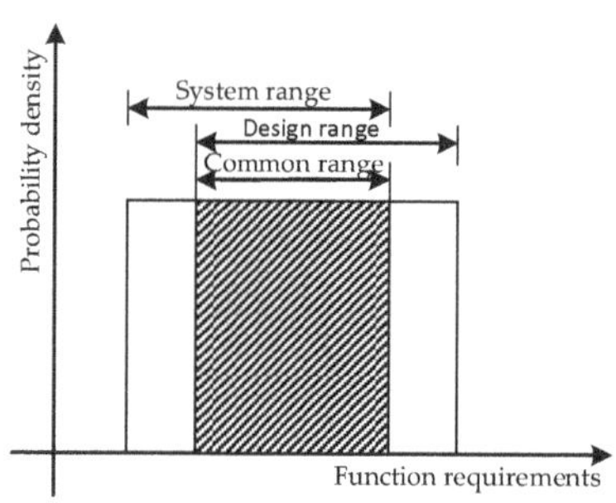

Figure 4. The relationship among design range, system range, and common range.

In this study, we adapt the AD framework to the domain of HMI evaluation by reinterpreting its structure: the evaluation criteria—including layout aesthetics, color aesthetics, and functional layout rationality—are treated as design-level FRs that the HMI must fulfill. For each criterion, specific design parameters are defined to quantify performance. The independence axiom guides the decoupling of these criteria during assessment, ensuring that, for instance, judgments of color harmony do not inadvertently conflate with layout density. The information axiom is then applied to compute an overall information content for each candidate HMI design, integrating both subjective (AHP-derived) and objective (EWM-derived) weights within the AD formalism. This enables a unified, multidimensional comparison of design alternatives. As illustrated in Figure 5, the resulting framework supports rational selection of HMIs for service robots.

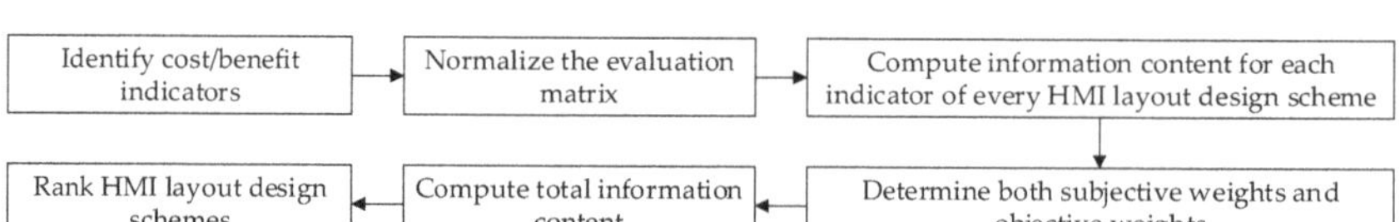

Figure 5. The AD framework for selection of HMI layout design schemes.

Let $X = (x_1, x_2, \ldots, x_m)$ denote the set of candidate service robot HMI layout design schemes, and $C = (c_1, c_2, \ldots, c_n)$ the set of evaluation indicators. The overall evaluation matrix is represented as $P_i = (p_{ij})_{m \times n}$, where p_{ij} denotes the value of indicator c_j of design scheme x_i. To eliminate the dimensional differences and enable comparison across heterogeneous indicators, the evaluation matrix P_i is standardized into a dimensionless form $P_i' = (p_{ij}')_{m \times n}$ using Equation (14), as follows:

$$p_{ij}' = \begin{cases} p_{ij} / \max\limits_{1 \le j \le n} p_{ij}, (c_j \in C^+) \\ 1 - p_{ij} / \max\limits_{1 \le j \le n} p_{ij}, (c_j \in C^-) \end{cases} \tag{14}$$

where C^+ represents the subset of benefit indicators; C^- represents the subset of cost indicators.

Let the indicator value of the ideal solution for criterion c_j be denoted as $B(p_{ij}')$, and the attribute value of the worst solution as $W(p_{ij}')$. These reference values represent the optimal and least desirable performance levels, respectively, across all service robot HMI design alternatives. The degree of correlation between each alternative and the ideal solution is measured using information content derived from the information axiom. A lower information content indicates greater proximity to the ideal solution, reflecting superior design performance and robustness. The information content for criterion c_j of HMI design scheme x_i is then expressed as:

$$I_{ij} = \frac{B(p_{ij}')}{B(p_{ij}') - W(p_{ij}')} \cdot \log_2^{\left(\frac{B(p_{ij}')}{p_{ij}'}\right)} \tag{15}$$

Considering that different evaluation indicators vary in their significance within service robot HMI design, we integrate AHP with EWM to determine the comprehensive weights of the indicators [71]. This hybrid approach combines subjective weights derived from expert judgments (via AHP) with objective weights calculated from the intrinsic information content of empirical HMI evaluation data (via EWM). By synthesizing both perspectives, the method achieves a more balanced and reliable weighting scheme, mitigating the biases associated with purely subjective or purely data-driven approaches.

Due to its ability to transform subjective expert judgments into quantifiable data, the AHP is employed to derive indicator weights for service robot HMI design schemes. Domain experts are invited to perform pairwise comparisons among the HMI evaluation criteria, assessing their relative importance using Saaty's 1–9 scale. These qualitative judgments are then converted into precise numerical weights through mathematical techniques. A widely used approach involves eigenvector computation [72], which synthesizes the complex network of pairwise comparisons into quantitative priority for each criterion. To ensure logical consistency in the experts' judgments, a critical quality control step is incorporated: the calculation of the consistency ratio (CR). If the CR exceeds the acceptance threshold of 0.1, the pairwise comparison matrix is deemed inconsistent, and experts are requested to revise their assessments to resolve contradictions. Once a consistent matrix is obtained, the normalized principal eigenvector is adopted as the priority vector, representing the relative weights of the indicators. The weight vector is denoted by $\varphi = \{\varphi_1, \varphi_2, \ldots, \varphi_n\}$, where φ_j denotes the AHP-derived weight of the j-th indicator, and $\sum\limits_{j=1}^{n} \varphi_j = 1$.

To mitigate the inherent subjectivity of AHP-based weighting, the EWM is employed as an objective weighting approach. When the variation range of an indicator parameter is large, it conveys more discriminative information, resulting in a lower entropy value and, consequently, a higher assigned weight. Conversely, indicators with smaller variations provide less information, leading to higher entropy values and lower weights [73]. The entropy value H_j of the j-th HMI layout evaluation indicator can be defined as:

$$\begin{cases} H_j = -\frac{1}{\ln m}\sum\limits_{i=1}^{m} f_{ij}\ln f_{ij} \\ f_{ij} = p'_{ij} / \sum\limits_{i=1}^{m} p'_{ij} \end{cases} \tag{16}$$

Then, the objective weight for each criterion, derived from its entropy value, can be determined as follows:

$$\psi_j = \frac{1 - H_j}{\sum\limits_{j=1}^{n} (1 - H_j)} \tag{17}$$

The AHP and the EWM offer complementary perspectives on criterion weighting, each with distinct strengths and limitations when applied in isolation. AHP captures expert knowledge and stakeholder preferences through structured pairwise comparisons, providing transparent and justifiable reasoning behind the assigned weights. However, its reliance on subjective judgment introduces the risk of cognitive bias, inconsistency, or personal preference distortion, potentially affecting the robustness of the results. In contrast, EWM derives weights purely from the intrinsic variability in the evaluation data through mathematical analysis, ensuring complete objectivity and reducing human bias. While this data-driven approach enhances reproducibility, it may produce weights that conflict with domain-specific priorities or practical design considerations—particularly when critical but less variable criteria are underweighted by the algorithm. To leverage the advantages of both methods while mitigating their respective drawbacks, we adopt a hybrid weighting framework that integrates subjective and objective perspectives. This combined approach ensures that both expert judgment and empirical data inform the final evaluation. The integrated weight for each indicator is calculated as:

$$\xi_j = \alpha\varphi_j + (1 - \alpha)\psi_j \tag{18}$$

where $\alpha \in [0, 1]$ is the balancing coefficient that determines the relative influence of subjective and objective weighting components. A higher value of α emphasizes expert judgment (AHP), while a lower value prioritizes data-driven objectivity (EWM), enabling flexible adaptation of the model to different design evaluation contexts.

Accordingly, the total information of HMI design scheme x_i can be calculated as follows:

$$I(x_i) = \sum_{j=1}^{n} \xi_j I_{ij} \tag{19}$$

According to axiomatic design, the smaller the information content, the better the HMI design scheme.

4. Case Study

Building on the proposed evaluation framework, this section presents the implementation and application of the method in assessing the HMI layout design of a medical service robot developed for a healthcare institution. The robot is designed to integrate advanced technologies—including artificial intelligence, voice recognition, and image recognition—while delivering core functionalities such as navigation, appointment registration, and patient guidance. Crucially, the HMI must accommodate a diverse user population, including elderly and first-time users, by ensuring intuitive operation, high usability, and a modern aesthetic, thereby enhancing the overall efficiency and accessibility of healthcare services.

Through a collaborative design process, five candidate HMI layout designs were developed under a unified design specification derived from both clinical requirements and user-centered design principles.

(1) Functional consistency: Each design incorporates the same six mandatory modules—(a) self-service guidance, (b) appointment registration, (c) intelligent inquiry, (d) location navigation, (e) department classification, and (f) user health education—as stipulated by the healthcare client. Additionally, the interface includes a top banner area that serves as a visual "business card" for the HMI's external display, helping to establish brand identity and communicate the interface's primary purpose.

(2) Visual and technical constraints: All interfaces are implemented at a fixed resolution of 1920 × 1080 pixels. The three light-mode designs share an identical color palette (based on institutional branding guidelines), while the two dark-mode variants use a consistent, accessibility-optimized dark theme. Main typography, iconography, and interactive element sizing were standardized across all schemes.

(3) Controlled variation: Differences among the five schemes are intentionally limited to layout structure, spatial grouping of modules, and navigation flow (linear vs. hub-and-spoke)—all of which are legitimate dimensions of HMI design exploration. Crucially, no scheme introduces additional functionality, novel interaction modes, or stylistic elements (e.g., animations, illustrations) absent in others.

(4) Design process: The candidates were co-developed by the same interdisciplinary team (HCI researchers, visual designers, and clinical stakeholders) over a three-week sprint, using shared wireframes and component libraries to enforce consistency.

Thus, while the schemes vary in compositional strategy—as needed to enable comparative evaluation—they are controlled for extraneous stylistic or implementation differences that could bias aesthetic or usability judgments. The main screen layouts of the five HMI design schemes are illustrated in Figure 6.

To evaluate the HMI design in Figure 6, ten domain experts in HMI design—comprising academic researchers, industry practitioners, and end users—were invited to assess the relative importance of the three primary evaluation dimensions and their associated secondary criteria for HMI applications in public environments. Academic researchers and industry professionals typically have between 3 and 20 years of experience. Academic researchers are primarily engaged in academia or research institutions, focusing on theoretical studies and innovations in HMI design. Their work includes HMI optimization, user experience research, and the application of new interactive technologies. Industry professionals, on the other hand, work as product designers, interaction designers, or similar roles in companies, where they are responsible for practical interface design and user experience optimization. They integrate market demands with technological advancements to implement the latest HMI design concepts. The end users were selected from a group with extensive experience in HMI user experience studies. These users possess unique insights into the intuitiveness and operability of HMI and are capable of providing valuable feedback on the design of public service robot HMI. By selecting experts from these diverse perspectives, the study ensures a comprehensive evaluation of the current state and future direction of HMI design, considering theoretical, technical, and user feedback aspects.

Figure 6. Service robot HMI design schemes: **(1)** x_1; **(2)** x_2; **(3)** x_3; **(4)** x_4; **(5)** x_5. (Each design scheme incorporates the same mandatory modules—(a) self-service guidance, (b) appointment registration, (c) intelligent inquiry, (d) location navigation, (e) department classification, (f) user health education, and (g) banner).

Manual marking is used to extract function module areas from the user interface. When an observer directly views the interface, the angle θ between the line of sight to a given point and the central visual axis, combined with the viewing distance l, can be used to define regions of varying perceptual intensity. Due to the circular symmetry of the distribution of cone cells, the visual perception field can be modeled as concentric areas with decreasing sensitivity. The radius r of the perceptual region corresponding to a specific angular eccentricity θ can be calculated using Equation (11). For a rectangular HMI, the perception level is divided using the smallest unit—a square with side length a—which is determined by visual intensity theory and user visual habits. Consequently, the visual field is discretized into a grid of these smallest square units, each with side length a. By defining the comfortable viewing distance l as 500 mm, the radius of the visual perception field at 1° from the user's viewpoint on the HMI is 8.73 mm. According to the formula, the side length of the quantized smallest unit on the interface is 15.47 mm. Therefore, the entire HMI interface is divided into multiple grid units of 15.47 mm × 15.47 mm. By manually marking the boundaries of each functional area, the number of grid cells occupied by each function module is determined, and the size and area of the function module regions are calculated, thereby allowing for the quantification of layout design metrics.

5. Results

5.1. Evaluation Results

Using Equations (1)–(13), the aesthetic qualities and VPI index of all five HMI design schemes are computed, with results presented in Table 2. In this process, the relative importance of the six function modules is determined through a separate AHP process. We constructed a pairwise comparison matrix and validated it through consistency testing (CR < 0.1), obtaining normalized weight vectors: w = {0.4435, 0.2334, 0.0936, 0.1294, 0.0599, 0.0402}, which were used to calculate VPI.

As shown in Table 2, each design alternative exhibits distinct strengths across the evaluation indicators: x_1 achieves the highest scores in Color Difference, Color Distribution, and VPI; x_2 excels in Balance, Color Difference, and Color Personality; x_3 performs best in Unity and Color Difference; x_4 ranks highest in Proportion and Color Harmony; and x_5 outperforms the others in Regularity, Density, and Color Harmony. Given that these indicators carry heterogeneous importance—reflected in their differing weights—a simple comparison of raw scores is insufficient for identifying the optimal solution. To account for this, we employed axiomatic design in conjunction with the derived indicator weights to systematically integrate both qualitative and quantitative criteria, thereby enabling a more robust and rational selection of the best-performing HMI design.

Table 2. Evaluation data of all five HMI layout design schemes.

Design Schemes	Indicators									
	Balance (c_1)	Proportion (c_2)	Unity (c_3)	Regularity (c_4)	Density (c_5)	Color Difference (c_6)	Color Distribution (c_7)	Color Harmony (c_8)	Color Personality (c_9)	Visual Perceptual Intensity (c_{10})
x_1	0.3968	0.4169	0.3693	0.3000	0.7189	1.3632	0.1633	0.3980	0.7030	64.4751
x_2	0.7283	0.9120	0.6249	0.2667	0.6986	1.3632	0.2472	0.3980	0.8327	33.4372
x_3	0.6915	0.5767	0.7364	0.3083	0.6190	1.3632	0.2313	0.3980	0.7476	37.2502
x_4	0.4724	0.9157	0.6162	0.1833	0.4988	1.8490	0.9991	0.0400	0.3596	19.3571
x_5	0.6623	0.7854	0.5124	0.4083	0.7754	1.8490	0.9822	0.0400	0.5543	44.4055

Using Saaty's 1–9 pairwise comparison scale, each expert independently constructed a judgment matrix to articulate their relative preferences among the evaluation criteria. These individual judgments were then aggregated through geometric mean averaging to ensure consistency and mitigate the influence of outliers. The resulting normalized subjective weight vector for the ten criteria is: $\varphi = \{0.0815, 0.0504, 0.1387, 0.2553, 0.0325, 0.1481, 0.1001, 0.0486, 0.0228, 0.1220\}$.

The entropy values for each evaluation indicator were computed using Equation (16), based on the normalized performance data presented in Table 1. Subsequently, the objective weights of the criteria were derived by applying Equation (17), which accounts for the degree of variation across design alternatives. The resulting EWM-based weights are summarized in Table 3.

Table 3. The EWM-based weights.

	Indicators									
	c_1	c_2	c_3	c_4	c_5	c_6	c_7	c_8	c_9	c_{10}
H_j	0.7924	0.7773	0.8301	0.7981	0.8366	0.4307	0.7034	0.4307	0.8335	0.7978
ψ_j	0.0749	0.0804	0.0614	0.0729	0.059	0.2056	0.1071	0.2056	0.0601	0.0730

The comprehensive evaluation score for each HMI design scheme was then calculated using Equations (18) and (19), which integrate both subjective and objective criterion weights through a weighted fusion mechanism. By varying the balancing coefficient $\alpha \in [0, 1]$, the influence of expert judgment and data-driven entropy weights is adjusted to reflect different prioritization strategies. The resulting total information content for the five design alternatives are presented in Table 4. As illustrated in Table 4, the optimal HMI design scheme varies with the balancing coefficient α, indicating a shift in preference based on the weighting strategy. When α = 0.1, 0.2, 0.3, and 0.4, the HMI design scheme x_2 ranks first, with x_3 as the secondary choice. However, when $\alpha \geq 0.5$, the ranking reverses: x_3 becomes the optimal design, while x_2 drops to second place. This transition suggests a sensitivity to the trade-off between subjective expert judgment and objective data-driven weights.

Table 4. Total information content of the HMI design schemes with different α.

X	α								
	0.1	**0.2**	**0.3**	**0.4**	**0.5**	**0.6**	**0.7**	**0.8**	**0.9**
x_1	0.5599	0.5826	0.6054	0.6280	0.6510	0.6737	0.6964	0.7191	0.7419
x_2	0.2991	0.3268	0.3543	0.3819	0.4095	0.4370	0.4646	0.4921	0.5198
x_3	0.3582	0.3685	0.3789	0.3893	0.3995	0.4099	0.4203	0.4306	0.4410
x_4	1.1389	1.1660	1.1931	1.2203	1.2473	1.2744	1.3017	1.3287	1.3558
x_5	0.6413	0.6330	0.6245	0.6162	0.6079	0.5995	0.5911	0.5827	0.5742

5.2. Sensitivity Analysis

By varying the value of the balancing coefficient α, we conducted a sensitivity analysis to evaluate the robustness of the results for the service robot HMI design. The variation in comprehensive scores and ranking stability across different α values are illustrated in Figure 7 and Figure 8, respectively.

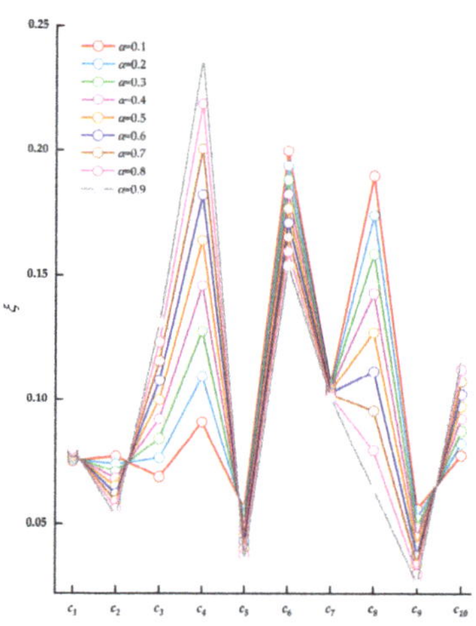

Figure 7. Indicator weight variation under different balance coefficients α.

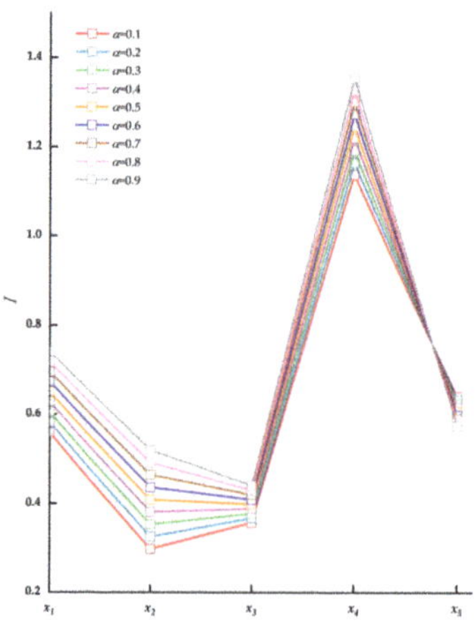

Figure 8. Ranking variation of HMI design schemes under different indicator weights.

As the balancing coefficient α increases, the weights assigned to the four criteria—balance, unity, regularity, and VPI—also increase. This indicates that, in subjective evaluations of the HMI, users place greater emphasis on these attributes when expert judgment is prioritized over data-driven objectivity. Among these, balance, unity, and regularity represent fundamental principles of interface layout design. They directly influence spatial organization, cognitive load, and operational efficiency, thereby playing a critical role in shaping the overall user experience. VPI, while serving as an auxiliary but essential factor, enhances interface usability by guiding visual attention and ensuring that key information is rapidly and accurately perceived. In contrast, criteria such as proportion and density contribute to maintaining a clean, uncluttered interface, further refining aesthetic quality and micro-level visual harmony. Meanwhile, color, though integrated within the broader layout structure, significantly influences both emotional appeal and functional clarity. Well-designed color schemes not only improve visual attractiveness but also enhance readability and interaction efficiency—such as through the differentiation of function modules or the highlighting of critical cues. However, from a subjective weighting perspective, Color tends to play a more supplementary and supportive role, ranking lower in priority compared to structural and perceptual dominance factors.

When the balancing coefficient α ranges from 0.1 to 0.4, the proposal ranking based on the information axiom is: $x_2 > x_3 > x_1 > x_5 > x_4$. As α increases, reflecting a greater emphasis on expert-derived subjective weights, the criterion importance distribution shifts accordingly. Specifically, when $\alpha \in [0.5, 0.9]$, the ranking changes to: $x_3 > x_2 > x_5 > x_1 > x_4$. This shift in ranking order indicates that the final evaluation outcome is sensitive to the trade-off between subjective judgment and objective data-driven weighting. The variation can be attributed to the following factors:

(1) Contextual dependence and domain expertise: HMI designs for public service robots operate in highly context-sensitive environments, where user interaction patterns, operational workflows, and environmental constraints introduce significant subjectivity. In such settings, expert knowledge plays a critical role in assigning meaningful weights to design criteria—particularly for attributes that are cognitively or perceptually salient but difficult to quantify purely through performance data.

(2) Functional prioritization in HMI decision-making: Effective registration and navigation support are primary objectives in public-facing HMIs. A moderate emphasis on subjective weighting allows designers to prioritize these functional goals, mitigating risks associated with overfitting to empirical data that may contain noise or reflect transient user behaviors rather than enduring usability principles.

(3) Limitations of EWM: While the EWM method assigns higher weights to criteria exhibiting greater data variability—thereby enhancing discriminative power—it may inadvertently undervalue key design attributes that show low variation due to technological optimization or standardized implementation. For instance, well-engineered color schemes or balanced layouts often exhibit minimal fluctuation across alternatives, not because they are unimportant, but because they have been consistently optimized. Overreliance on EWM in such cases can lead to weight distortion, where critical but stable criteria are downweighted.

Therefore, reducing the proportion of entropy weight (i.e., increasing α) in a controlled manner helps preserve the influence of expert judgment on these essential yet stable design elements, ensuring a more balanced and contextually appropriate evaluation.

5.3. Eye-Tracking Experiment Verification

To further validate the effectiveness and objectivity of the proposed multi-criteria evaluation method, an eye-tracking experiment was conducted as an objective, physiology-based assessment of the alternative HMI designs. Eye-tracking technology enables the precise monitoring and recording of participants' ocular movements, providing quantifiable insights into visual attention distribution, information acquisition patterns, and perceptual preferences across design alternatives. By incorporating this empirical approach, we mitigate potential subjective bias inherent in expert judgment, thereby enhancing the scientific rigor and reliability of the decision-making process.

The experiment aimed to evaluate key visual design dimensions—layout structure, color scheme, and VPI—across five distinct HMI design proposals for a medical guidance service robot. The primary objective was to identify the design that optimizes user visual experience and operational efficiency from a cognitive ergonomics perspective. A total of 15 participants took part in the study, comprising 10 domain experts in HCI from academic and industrial R&D backgrounds, and 5 general users aged 25–45 with no prior specialized training in interface design. All participants reported normal or corrected-to-normal vision, were free from color vision deficiencies (e.g., color blindness or weakness), and were right-handed. This mixed-participant design ensures a balance between professional insight and real-world user behavior. The experiment was conducted using the Tobii Pro Lab eye-tracking system, which operates at a sampling rate of 120 Hz and has an angular resolution of 0.5°, representing the smallest detectable change in gaze direction. Each stimulus was presented for 30 s per task. To ensure data quality, Tobii Pro Lab's built-in filtering algorithm was applied to automatically exclude outlier samples caused by pupil occlusion, signal loss, or instrumental artifacts. Participants stood during the session to simulate real-world interaction conditions, with their eye level aligned to the center of the display at a standardized viewing distance of 50 cm. Prior to each trial, a nine-point calibration procedure was performed to ensure data accuracy.

Participants were first briefed on the purpose and procedure of the experiment, including task expectations and ethical considerations. They were then presented with a single composite image containing all five HMI design proposals, displayed simultaneously to allow direct visual comparison. Each participant viewed the stimuli freely for approximately 30 s under a free-viewing paradigm, during which no specific task (e.g., search or selection) was imposed—allowing natural gaze behavior to emerge. The following objective oculomotor metrics were recorded for predefined areas of interest (AOIs) corresponding to each design proposal: (1) Total fixation duration (ms): cumulative time spent fixating on an AOI, indicating overall attentional engagement; (2) Fixation count: number of fixations, reflecting visual scrutiny and information processing intensity; (3) First fixation duration (ms): initial dwell time, indicating early visual attraction or salience; (4) Eye movement heatmaps: spatial visualization of gaze concentration, used to identify regions of high visual focus. These physiological indicators serve as objective benchmarks for evaluating the visual effectiveness and usability of each service robot HMI design.

In the eye tracking experiment, the five HMI schemes were divided into five Areas of Interest (AOI): AOI1-x_1, AOI2-x_2, AOI3-x_3, AOI4-x_4, and AOI5-x_5. As illustrated in Figure 9, the heatmap analysis reveals that HMI design scheme x_3 exhibits the largest and most intense red-colored region, indicating the highest level of visual attention and gaze concentration. This suggests that x_3 achieves superior visual salience and information hierarchy, guiding users' attention more effectively than the other designs.

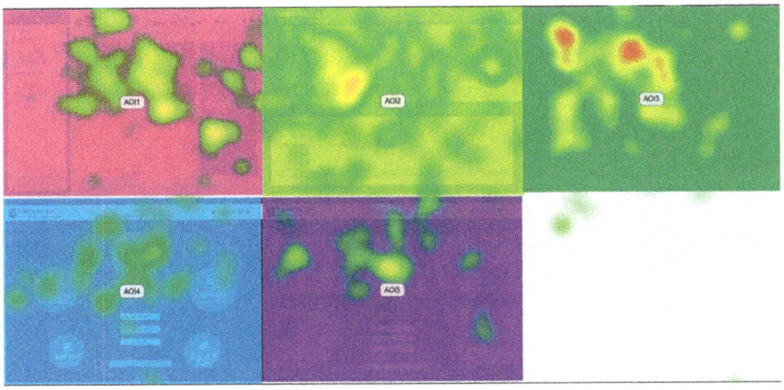

Figure 9. Eye movement heatmap for five HMI design schemes.

The quantitative eye-tracking data—total fixation duration, fixation count, and first fixation duration—are presented in Tables 5–7. These results provide empirical validation of the proposed evaluation framework, demonstrating strong alignment between the model's top-ranked design (x_3 at higher α values) and actual user attention patterns.

Table 5. Total fixation duration.

Participants	HMI Design Schemes				
	x_1	x_2	x_3	x_4	x_5
1	2.22	3.93	5.18	2.64	1.75
2	2.08	6.04	9.97	2.47	2.17
3	3.04	2.67	2.87	3.67	2.22
4	3.27	10.05	5.75	1.48	2.47
5	1.35	2.39	14.62	1.56	1.78
6	2.71	4.13	9.41	3.89	3.26
7	2.94	2.39	10.10	1.03	1.81
8	6.17	4.53	5.80	0.52	2.85
9	0.74	1.11	16.42	0.12	0.44
10	1.28	2.70	19.95	0.47	1.42
11	4.02	7.54	11.76	0.22	0.97
12	1.72	2.60	13.86	0.81	2.09
13	1.12	0.85	14.49	0.18	0.13
14	0.83	1.20	6.80	3.20	2.60
15	0.97	1.37	8.46	0.97	1.57
Average	2.29	3.57	10.36	1.55	1.84

Table 6. Fixation count.

Participants	HMI Design Schemes				
	x_1	x_2	x_3	x_4	x_5
1	12	20	22	9	8
2	9	19	42	10	11
3	19	14	14	19	15
4	18	32	18	7	8
5	6	13	49	7	10
6	4	9	32	7	8
7	17	19	55	5	12
8	33	22	35	5	16
9	2	5	74	1	2
10	5	14	57	2	6
11	8	26	26	1	3
12	9	11	56	4	12
13	7	5	51	1	1
14	6	5	21	3	5
15	5	5	32	3	9
Average	10.67	14.6	38.93	5.6	8.4

Table 7. First fixation duration.

Participants	HMI Design Schemes				
	x_1	x_2	x_3	x_4	x_5
1	x_1	x_2	x_3	x_4	x_5
2	7.88	10.85	4.18	0.02	0.62
3	1.37	0.27	3.33	0.37	0.5
4	2.34	20.23	16.68	0.51	0.35
5	3.13	13.43	24.09	0.13	5.41
6	7.65	0.48	2.73	0.34	1.92
7	18.14	9.49	4.41	0.36	1.2
8	2.61	0.16	16.82	0.49	1.16
9	0.46	1.28	25.01	2.88	2.47
10	1.08	0.25	17.56	0.8	3.48
11	4.12	1.91	5.52	0.12	0.82
12	1.12	2.66	3.01	0.51	0.26
13	1.65	0.56	1.3	2.98	0.87
14	1.71	6.29	6.66	0.21	0.92
15	1.58	1.21	0.68	0.35	0.76
Average	2.00	3.53	5.84	4.54	0.62

To ensure that the observed eye-tracking data accurately reflect participants' behavioral patterns and perceptual preferences—rather than random noise or incidental factors—a statistical significance analysis was conducted using SPSS Statistics 27.0. Prior to parametric testing, a Levene's test for homogeneity of variance was performed to assess the equality of variances across the five HMI design schemes. As shown in Table 8, the results indicated a significant violation of homogeneity ($p < 0.001$) for all three physiological metrics, suggesting unequal variances across groups. Given this violation, the non-parametric Kruskal–Wallis H test was employed to compare differences in eye-tracking responses across the five HMI design schemes. The results, presented in Table 9, reveal that all three measured metrics—total fixation duration, fixation count, and first fixation duration—exhibited statistically significant differences among the designs ($p < 0.05$). These findings indicate that the variations in visual attention and gaze behavior are not due to chance, but are instead systematically associated with differences in HMI design features. This supports the conclusion that the observed user responses reflect genuine design-induced cognitive and perceptual processes, such as visual salience, information hierarchy, and interface intuitiveness.

Table 8. Tests of homogeneity of variances.

Indicators	Based on Mean			
	Levene Statistic	Df 1	Df 2	Sig.
Total fixation duration	11.120	4	70	<0.001
Fixation count	12.258	4	70	<0.001
First fixation duration	13.520	4	70	<0.001

Table 9. Kruskal–Wallis H test.

Indicators	Kruskal–Wallis H Test Statistics	Df	Sig.
Total fixation duration	36.715	4	<0.001
Fixation count	39.063	4	<0.001
First fixation duration	25.756	4	<0.001

To explore the relationship between aesthetic evaluation metrics and visual attention patterns, we conducted Pearson correlation analyses between the ten HMI design indicators and three eye-tracking measures (see Table 10).

Table 10. Correlation analysis between evaluation indicators and eye movement indicators.

HMI Design Indicators	Total Fixation Duration		Fixation Count		First Fixation Duration	
	Pearson_r	*p_Value*	*Pearson_r*	*p_Value*	*Pearson_r*	*p_Value*
Balance	0.485	0.407	0.488	0.405	0.442	0.456
Proportion	−0.341	0.575	−0.380	0.528	−0.443	0.455
Unity	0.682	0.205	0.642	0.243	0.527	0.362
Regularity	0.097	0.876	0.141	0.821	0.085	0.892
Density	−0.147	0.814	−0.088	0.888	−0.002	0.998
Color difference	−0.553	0.334	−0.587	0.298	−0.788	0.114
Color distribution	−0.523	0.366	−0.560	0.327	−0.763	0.133
Color harmony	0.553	0.334	0.587	0.298	0.788	0.114
Color personality	0.498	0.393	0.543	0.345	0.724	0.167
VPI	−0.063	0.920	−0.004	0.995	0.120	0.847

The results reveal several notable directional trends, despite the absence of statistically significant correlations (all *p_value* > 0.05), which is likely attributable to the limited sample size ($N = 15$). Among all indicators, unity and color harmony consistently showed the largest effect sizes: (1) Unity exhibited positive correlations with total fixation duration (*Pearson_r* = 0.682), fixation count (*Pearson_r* = 0.642), and first fixation duration (*Pearson_r* = 0.527), suggesting that interfaces perceived as more cohesive tend to attract and sustain visual attention. (2) Color harmony demonstrated a similarly strong positive association with first fixation duration (*Pearson_r* = 0.788) and fixation count (*Pearson_r* = 0.587), indicating that color harmony may influence early and sustained visual engagement. Conversely, color difference and color distribution showed moderate-to-strong negative correlations with eye-tracking metrics—particularly first fixation duration (*Pearson_r* = −0.788 and *Pearson_r* = −0.763, respectively)—implying that HMI designs rated high on these attributes (e.g., high contrast or irregular color placement) were associated with shorter initial fixations, possibly reflecting visual discomfort or reduced perceptual fluency. In contrast, indicators such as regularity, density, and VPI showed negligible correlations (|*Pearson_r*| < 0.15), suggesting little to no linear relationship with the selected eye-tracking measures under the current experimental conditions.

Although none of these correlations reached conventional levels of statistical significance, the consistency in direction and magnitude across related constructs (e.g., unity/color harmony → increased attention; color difference/color distribution → decreased attention) provides preliminary empirical evidence that certain aesthetic dimensions do influence visual behavior. This supports the theoretical grounding of our evaluation framework while highlighting the need for larger-sample validation. Moreover, the pattern of results suggests that eye-tracking metrics may be more sensitive to holistic, integrative qualities (e.g., unity, color harmony) than to localized or structural features (e.g., density, regularity)—a finding that aligns with Gestalt principles of visual perception.

The experimental results demonstrate that participants exhibited significantly higher visual attention toward scheme x_3 when evaluating the alternative HMI designs. As illustrated in the eye movement heatmap (Figure 9), the most intense and densely concentrated red region—indicative of strong gaze fixation—is localized on x_3, reflecting its superior visual salience and perceptual dominance. This qualitative observation is further supported by quantitative AOI data: total fixation duration, fixation count, and first fixation duration for x_3 were all higher than those of the other four schemes, confirming that users not only attended to x_3 more frequently and for longer durations but also fixated on it earlier during visual exploration. These metrics collectively suggest that x_3 achieves greater visual attractiveness, faster information acquisition, and stronger attentional capture—key indicators of an effective and user-centered HMI design.

Critically, this empirical finding aligns closely with the outcomes of the proposed hybrid evaluation framework. As the balancing coefficient α increases—placing greater emphasis on expert-derived subjective weights—x_3 emerges as the top-ranked design (particularly when $\alpha \in [0.5, 0.9]$). The convergence between the objective physiological data from eye tracking and the subjectively informed decision model underscores the robustness and practical applicability of the method.

This consistency across independent assessment modalities—biometric measurement and structured multi-criteria decision analysis—validates the effectiveness, reliability, and objectivity of the proposed hybrid approach. It demonstrates that the method not only integrates domain expertise meaningfully but also reflects real-world user behavior in service robot HMI evaluation.

6. Discussion

To further validate the robustness of the proposed method, we introduced an alternative objective weighting approach—CRiteria Importance Through Intercriteria Correlation (CRITIC) [74]—and integrated it with AHP to examine potential shifts in the ranking of HMI design schemes. Using the AD framework, we compared the evaluation outcomes under two hybrid weighting strategies: AHP–EWM and AHP–CRITIC (see Table 11). The results show largely consistent trends across both methods. When the balancing coefficient $\alpha \in [0.1, 0.4]$ (emphasizing objective weights), the AHP–CRITIC ranking is $x_2 > x_3 > x_5 > x_1 > x_4$, which slightly differs from the AHP–EWM ranking ($x_2 > x_3 > x_1 > x_5 > x_4$) only in the relative order of x_1 and x_5. Notably, when $\alpha \in [0.5, 0.9]$ (favoring subjective judgment), both methods yield identical rankings: $x_3 > x_2 > x_5 > x_1 > x_4$. This high degree of consistency suggests that the proposed framework is robust to the choice of objective weighting method, reinforcing the reliability of the optimal design recommendations—particularly the superiority of x_3 under user-centered conditions ($\alpha \geq 0.5$).

Table 11. Information content comparison between AHP-EWM and AHP-CRITIC.

Weighting Scheme	X	α								
		0.1	0.2	0.3	0.4	0.5	0.6	0.7	0.8	0.9
AHP-EWM	x_1	0.5599	0.5826	0.6054	0.6280	0.6510	0.6737	0.6964	0.7191	0.7419
	x_2	0.2991	0.3268	0.3543	0.3819	0.4095	0.4370	0.4646	0.4921	0.5198
	x_3	0.3582	0.3685	0.3789	0.3893	0.3995	0.4099	0.4203	0.4306	0.4410
	x_4	1.1389	1.1660	1.1931	1.2203	1.2473	1.2744	1.3017	1.3287	1.3558
	x_5	0.6413	0.6330	0.6245	0.6162	0.6079	0.5995	0.5911	0.5827	0.5742
AHP-CRITIC	x_1	0.6807	0.6902	0.6995	0.7090	0.7179	0.7272	0.7366	0.7460	0.7555
	x_2	0.4374	0.4497	0.4619	0.4742	0.4862	0.4984	0.5107	0.5228	0.5352
	x_3	0.4981	0.4930	0.4878	0.4826	0.4771	0.4720	0.4668	0.4616	0.4566
	x_4	1.3308	1.3373	1.3434	1.3497	1.3553	1.3615	1.3679	1.3740	1.3805
	x_5	0.5532	0.5547	0.5561	0.5576	0.5587	0.5601	0.5616	0.5630	0.5645

The influence of α on decision outcomes is systematic and interpretable. At low α values (0.1–0.4), EWM-derived weights dominate, yet the resulting rankings exhibit limited sensitivity—likely because many design indicators (e.g., standardized color harmony or layout balance) display inherently low dispersion after optimization. This constraint may lead EWM to underrepresent the practical importance of key aesthetic criteria. In contrast, at higher α values (0.5–0.9), expert judgments exert greater influence, shifting preference toward x_3. While AHP is susceptible to variability in experts' experience and evaluative standards, its integration with EWM mitigates potential bias by anchoring subjective inputs in empirical data, thereby producing more stable and contextually grounded weight distributions.

Complementing this, our correlation analysis between HMI design indicators and eye-tracking metrics offers preliminary but meaningful insights into how aesthetic attributes map onto visual behavior [75]. Although none of the observed correlations reached conventional statistical significance ($p\_value > 0.05$)—likely due to the modest sample size

($N = 15$)—several effect sizes were moderate to large (e.g., *Pearson_r* = 0.682 for unity vs. total fixation duration; *Pearson_r* = 0.788 for color harmony vs. first fixation duration). Critically, the absence of statistical significance does not negate these patterns; rather, it reflects a broader limitation of physiological proxies: eye-tracking metrics are highly sensitive to visual saliency, task demands, and information complexity, but less attuned to subtle hedonic or aesthetic responses.

Consequently, our findings suggest that HMI layout design evaluation is a multidimensional construct that cannot be fully captured by gaze-based measures alone. Relying exclusively on physiological data risks overlooking the nuanced interplay between form, function, and user experience. In contrast, hybrid frameworks—such as the AHP–EWM integration proposed here—offer a more balanced and theoretically grounded approach by synthesizing expert judgment, objective performance data, and empirical validation. This synergy not only enhances decision robustness but also aligns technical evaluation with human-centered design principles.

7. Conclusions

This study proposes a multidimensional HMI evaluation framework designed to quantitatively assess key aspects of HMI design in service robots, specifically focusing on layout aesthetics, color aesthetics, and function layout rationality from the perspective of visual cognition. By systematically analyzing the core design elements and principles inherent in HMI development, and integrating the information axiom from axiomatic design theory, a hybrid multi-attribute evaluation system is established. This system combines subjective weights (derived from expert judgment via AHP) and objective weights (determined by EWM-based methods), thereby balancing domain expertise with data-driven insights. A case study on the HMI of a medical service robot demonstrates the feasibility and practical applicability of the proposed method in the preliminary screening and optimization of digital interface designs. The results, further validated through eye-tracking experiments, confirm that the method not only supports rational decision-making but also aligns with real user attention patterns. These findings underscore the method's theoretical significance in advancing HMI evaluation theory and its practical value in guiding the development of effective, user-centered interfaces for public service robots.

Despite these contributions, several limitations should be acknowledged. First, it focuses exclusively on HMIs for public service robots designed for group users, where interfaces prioritize intuitive navigation through visual cues (e.g., color and shape) while minimizing textual elements. The role of text and other domain-specific design factors remains unexplored, limiting generalizability to other HMI contexts (e.g., industrial or personal-use robots). Second, the eye-tracking validation was conducted with only 15 participants—a sample size insufficient to achieve statistical power for detecting moderate correlations. While observed effect sizes suggest meaningful relationships between evaluation attributes and visual attention, the lack of statistical significance underscores the preliminary nature of these findings and limits their reliability and generalizability. Third, subjective weights were derived via AHP under the assumption of equal expert influence, which may overlook differences in professional expertise and background. Meanwhile, objective weights were computed using EWM, which can underestimate the importance of design criteria with inherently low variability—such as standardized color schemes or balanced layouts—potentially skewing weight distributions across different HMI configurations. Future work will extend the framework to diverse application domains and validate it with larger, more representative user samples to improve robustness and external validity.

Author Contributions: Writing—review & editing, Writing—original draft, Validation, Supervision, Project administration, Investigation, Funding acquisition, Conceptualization, Y.Y.; Writing—original draft, Validation, Resources, Methodology, Data curation, Conceptualization, Y.Z.; Visualization, Validation, J.L., W.M. and Z.W. All authors have read and agreed to the published version of the manuscript.

Funding: This research was funded by the Humanities and Social Sciences Project of Ministry of Education of China (23YJC760141) and National Natural Science Foundation of China (51805043).

Data Availability Statement: The original contributions presented in this study are included in the article. Further inquiries can be directed to the corresponding author.

Conflicts of Interest: The authors declare no conflicts of interest.

Abbreviations

HMI	human–machine interface
VPI	visual perceptual intensity
AHP	analytic hierarchy process
EWM	entropy weighting method
AD	axiomatic design
MCDM	multi-criteria decision-making
CR	the consistency ratio
AOI	areas of interest
Variable definition	
BM	the overall balance of the HMI layout
BM_{v}	the vertical balance components
BM_{h}	the horizontal balance components
a_{ij}	the area of object i on side j
d_{ij}	the distance between the centerline of object i and the corresponding frame boundary
n_j	the total number of objects on side j
PM	the overall proportion of the HMI layout
PM_{o}	the deviation between the proportions of individual interface objects and the nearest established proportional shape
PM_{l}	the deviation between the overall layout proportion and its closest proportional shape
p_j	the referenced proportion of shape j with $p_j \in \{(1{:}1), (1{:}1.414), (1{:}1.618), (1{:}1.732), (1{:}2)\}$
p_i	$\min\{h_i/b_i, b_i/h_i\}$, where b_i and h_i denote the width and height of object i, respectively
p_{l}	$\min\{h_{\mathrm{l}}/b_{\mathrm{l}}, b_{\mathrm{l}}/h_{\mathrm{l}}\}$, with b_{l} and h_{l} representing the width and height of the entire layout
UM	the overall unity of the HMI layout
UM_{f}	the degree of size consistency among interface objects
UM_{s}	the spatial relationship between the margin area of the screen and the space between individual components
a_i	the area of object i
a_{l}	the layout area
a_{f}	the frame area
n	the number of distinct sizes used
RM	the overall regularity of the HMI layout
RM_{a}	the degree to which alignment points are minimized
RM_{s}	the consistency in spacing between the alignment points

n_t	the total number of objects within the frame
n_v	the number of vertical alignment references
n_h	the number of horizontal alignment references
n_s	the number of distinct distances between column and row starting points
DM	the overall density of the HMI layout
$D_{difference}$	the overall color difference between two colors
D_{hue}	the differences in hue between two colors
D_{chroma}	the differences in chroma between two colors
D_{value}	the differences in hue between two colors
$D_{distribution}$	the spatial distribution of colors across these quadrants
γ_k	the angular separation between colors x and y on the hue circle (in degrees)
C_x	the chroma of color x
V_x	the value of color x
$\max C_x$	the maximum chroma achievable for color x within the applicable color system
E_i	the entropy associated with the i-th color
A_{ij}	the area in the j-th quadrant of the HMI occupied by regions dominated by the i-th color
M	the overall color harmony
C_m	the total number of colors in the HMI design scheme
C_h	the counts of color pairs differing in hue
C_v	the counts of color pairs differing in value
C_c	the counts of color pairs differing in chroma
O_g	the order term for schemes composed exclusively of achromatic colors
O_h	the order terms derived from hue differences in chromatic color schemes
O_v	the order terms derived from value differences in chromatic color schemes
O_c	the order terms derived from chroma differences in chromatic color schemes
S_p	the score for personality impression p
$MCPI_p$	the MCPI for personality impression p
σ_i	the ratio of the number of pixels in the i-th bin to the total number of pixels in HMI layout
u_τ^z	the number of discrete units occupied by function module z in the τ-th visual perceptual region of a service robot HMI layout
q_τ	the VPI weight associated with τ-th region
w_z	the function importance of module z
VPI	the VPI of the HMI layout
X	the set of candidate service robot HMI layout design schemes
x_i	the i-th service robot HMI layout design scheme
C	the set of evaluation indicators
c_j	the j-th evaluation indicator
P_i	the overall evaluation matrix of x_i
p_{ij}	the value of indicator c_j of design scheme x_i
p'_{ij}	the standardized p_{ij}
$B(p'_{ij})$	the indicator value of the ideal solution for criterion c_j
$W(p'_{ij})$	the attribute value of the worst solution
I_{ij}	the information content for criterion c_j of HMI design scheme x_i
φ_j	the AHP-derived weight of the j-th indicator
H_j	the entropy value of the j-th indicator

ψ_j	the EWM-derived weight of the j-th indicator
ξ_j	the integrated weight for each criterion based on AHP-EWM
α	the balancing coefficient that determines the relative influence of subjective and objective weighting components
$I(x_i)$	the total information of HMI design scheme x_i

References

1. Makedon, V.; Mykhailenko, O.; Vazov, R. Dominants and features of growth of the world market of robotics. *Eur. J. Manag. Issues* **2021**, *29*, 133–141. [CrossRef]
2. Mende, M.; Scott, M.L.; van Doorn, J.; Grewal, D.; Shanks, I. Service Robots Rising: How Humanoid Robots Influence Service Experiences and Elicit Compensatory Consumer Responses. *J. Mark. Res.* **2019**, *56*, 535–556. [CrossRef]
3. Wirtz, J.; Patterson, P.G.; Kunz, W.H.; Gruber, T.; Lu, V.N.; Paluch, S.; Martins, A. Brave new world: Service robots in the frontline. *J. Serv. Manag.* **2018**, *29*, 907–931. [CrossRef]
4. Kim, C.; Kim, D.; Yuan, J.; Hill, R.B.; Doshi, P.; Thai, C.N. Robotics to promote elementary education pre-service teachers' STEM engagement, learning, and teaching. *Comput. Educ.* **2015**, *91*, 14–31. [CrossRef]
5. Chivarov, N.; Shivarov, N. Remote Control User Interfaces for Service Mobile Robots for Elderly Care. *IFAC-PapersOnLine* **2016**, *49*, 73–76. [CrossRef]
6. Xi, Y.-A.-M.; Li, Y.-Z.; Chen, Y.-H.; Jiang, H.-H.; Huang, Z.-B. Energy demand and carbon emission analyses of a solar-driven domestic regional environment mobile robot as household auxiliary heating and cooling method. *Appl. Energy* **2024**, *371*, 123743. [CrossRef]
7. Ivanova, L.; Kurkin, A.; Ivanov, S. Hybrid trajectory optimization method for service logistics robots. *Transp. Res. Procedia* **2022**, *63*, 2151–2157. [CrossRef]
8. Begum, N.; Faisal, M.N.; Sobh, R.; Nunkoo, R.; Rana, N.P. Consumers acceptance of service robots in hotels: A meta-analytic review. *Int. J. Hosp. Manag.* **2025**, *126*, 104052. [CrossRef]
9. Pustejovsky, J.; Krishnaswamy, N. Embodied human computer interaction. *Künstl. Intell.* **2021**, *35*, 307–327. [CrossRef]
10. Guo, L.; Lu, Z.; Yao, L. Human-Machine Interaction Sensing Technology Based on Hand Gesture Recognition: A Review. *IEEE Trans. Hum.-Mach. Syst.* **2021**, *51*, 300–309. [CrossRef]
11. Ma, Y.; Yao, H. Research on understandability & cognitive load equilibrium of human-machine interface under time pressure. *Displays* **2025**, *89*, 102891. [CrossRef]
12. Yang, G.-Z.; Bellingham, J.; Dupont, P.E.; Fischer, P.; Floridi, L.; Full, R.; Jacobstein, N.; Kumar, V.; McNutt, M.; Merrifield, R.; et al. The grand challenges of Science Robotics. *Sci. Robot.* **2018**, *3*, eaar7650. [CrossRef]
13. Guo, F.; Chen, J.; Li, M.; Lyu, W.; Zhang, J. Effects of visual complexity on user search behavior and satisfaction: An eye-tracking study of mobile news apps. *Univers. Access Inf. Soc.* **2021**, *21*, 795–808. [CrossRef]
14. Zhang, M.; Hou, G.; Chen, Y.-C. Effects of interface layout design on mobile learning efficiency: A comparison of interface layouts for mobile learning platform. *Libr. Hi Tech.* **2023**, *41*, 1420–1435. [CrossRef]
15. Todi, K.; Jokinen, J.; Luyten, K.; Oulasvirta, A. Individualising graphical layouts with predictive visual search models. *ACM Trans. Interact. Intell. Syst.* **2019**, *10*, 1–24. [CrossRef]
16. Li, X.; Cui, Y.; Jin, N.; Su, J. A bacterial foraging optimization algorithm for user interface layout design in complex human-computer interaction system. In Proceedings of the 2021 IEEE 24th International Conference on Computer Supported Cooperative Work in Design (CSCWD), Dalian, China, 5–7 May 2021; pp. 987–990. [CrossRef]
17. Yang, C.; Yuan, B.; Wu, K.; Ye, J. Aesthetic evaluation method for interactive interface layouts on the basis of visual cognitive multi-attribute fusion decision making. *Int. J. Ind. Ergon.* **2025**, *105*, 103673. [CrossRef]
18. Shao, J.; Wu, J.; Tang, W.; Xue, C. How dynamic information layout in GIS interface affects users' search performance: Integrating visual motion cognition into map information design. *Behav. Inf. Technol.* **2023**, *42*, 1686–1703. [CrossRef]
19. Wang, X.; Guo, F.; Li, M. Research on the neural mechanism of subconscious evaluation of mobile interfaces in smart apps. *Int. J. Hum.-Comput. Interact.* **2024**, *40*, 1012–1021. [CrossRef]
20. Chikhaoui, B.; Pigot, H. Towards analytical evaluation of human machine interfaces developed in the context of smart homes. *Interact. Comput.* **2010**, *22*, 449–464. [CrossRef]
21. Diego-Mas, J.A.; Garzon-Leal, D.; Poveda-Bautista, R.; Alcaide-Marzal, J. User-interfaces layout optimization using eye-tracking, mouse movements and genetic algorithms. *Appl. Ergon.* **2019**, *78*, 197–209. [CrossRef]
22. Wang, Z.; Zhang, X.; Li, L.; Zhou, Y.; Lu, Z.; Dai, Y.; Liu, C.; Su, Z.; Bai, X.; Billinghurst, M. Evaluating visual encoding quality of a mixed reality user interface for human-machine co-assembly in complex operational terrain. *Adv. Eng. Inf.* **2023**, *58*, 102171. [CrossRef]
23. Sonderegger, A.; Sauer, J. The influence of design aesthetics in usability testing: Effects on user performance and perceived usability. *Appl. Ergon.* **2009**, *41*, 403–410. [CrossRef] [PubMed]

24. Pombo, M.; Corradi, B.G.; Elliot, J.A.; Velasco, C. When and how visual aesthetic features influence approach-avoidance motivated behavior. *Q. J. Exp. Psychol.* **2025**, *18*, 1–71. [CrossRef]
25. Chen, X.; Lu, Y.; Hao, G. Balanced Aesthetics: How Shape, Contrast, and Visual Force Affect Interface Layout. *Int. J. Hum.-Comput. Interact.* **2024**, *40*, 8750–8763. [CrossRef]
26. Lazard, A.J.; King, A.J. Objective design to subjective evaluations: Connecting visual complexity to aesthetic and usability assessments of eHealth. *Int. J. Hum.-Comput. Interact.* **2020**, *36*, 95–104. [CrossRef]
27. Pengnate, S.; Sarathy, R.; Lee, J. The engagement of website initial aesthetic impressions: An experimental investigation. *Int. J. Hum.-Comput. Interact.* **2019**, *35*, 1517–1531. [CrossRef]
28. Dianat, I.; Adeli, P.; Jafarabadi, M.A.; Karimi, M.A. User-centred web design, usability and user satisfaction: The case of online banking websites in Iran. *Appl. Ergon.* **2019**, *81*, 102892. [CrossRef]
29. Ngo, D.C.L.; Teo, L.S.; Byrne, J.G. Modelling interface aesthetics. *Inf. Sci.* **2003**, *152*, 25–46. [CrossRef]
30. Ha, J.S. A human-machine interface evaluation method based on balancing principles. *Procedia Eng.* **2014**, *69*, 13–19. [CrossRef]
31. Reinecke, K.; Yeh, T.; Miratrix, L.; Mardiko, R.; Zhao, Y. Predicting users' first impressions of website aesthetics with a quantification of perceived visual complexity and colorfulness. In Proceedings of the SIGCHI Conference on Human Factors in Computing Systems, Paris, France, 27 April–2 May 2013; pp. 2049–2058. [CrossRef]
32. Wan, H.; Ji, W.; Wu, G.; Jia, X.; Zhan, X.; Yuan, M.; Wang, R. A novel webpage layout aesthetic evaluation model for quantifying webpage layout design. *Inf. Sci.* **2021**, *576*, 589–608. [CrossRef]
33. Bauerly, M.; Liu, Y. Computational modeling and experimental investigation of effects of compositional elements on interface and design aesthetics. *Int. J. Hum.-Comput. Stud.* **2006**, *64*, 670–682. [CrossRef]
34. Liu, Q.; Chen, J.; Yang, K.; Liu, D.; He, L.; Qin, Q.; Wang, Y. An integrating spherical fuzzy AHP and axiomatic design approach and its application in human-machine interface design evaluation. *Eng. Appl. Artif. Intell.* **2023**, *125*, 106746. [CrossRef]
35. Yang, H.; Zhao, Y.; Zhao, Y.; Chen, N. Drivers' visual interaction performance of on-board computer under different heat conditions: Based on ELM and entropy weight. *Sustain. Cities Soc.* **2022**, *81*, 103835. [CrossRef]
36. Pei, H.; Wang, Z.; Cao, J.; Chen, Y.; Bai, Z. A cognitive load assessment method for fighter cockpit human-machine interface based on integrated multi-criteria decision making. *Appl. Soft Comput.* **2024**, *167*, 112287. [CrossRef]
37. Zhang, X.; Wang, W.; Ma, L.; Wang, Z.; Hu, N. Cognitive evaluation of HUD interface layout for intelligent automotive based on bayesian BWM and gray-TOPSIS. *Adv. Mech. Eng.* **2024**, *16*, 16878132241230227. [CrossRef]
38. Li, J. Study on Evaluation Method of Human-Computer Interface Quality of Intelligent Products Based on Bayesian Classification. *Int. J. Prod. Dev.* **2024**, *28*, 24–34. [CrossRef]
39. Spratt, F. Art production in discipline-based art education. *J. Aesthetic Educ.* **1987**, *21*, 197–204. [CrossRef]
40. Kurosu, M.; Kashimura, K. Apparent usability vs. inherent usability: Experimental analysis on the determinants of the apparent usability. In Proceedings of the Conference Companion on Human Factors in Computing Systems, Denver, CO, USA, 7–11 May 1995; pp. 292–293. [CrossRef]
41. Miniukovich, A.; De Angeli, A. Computation of interface aesthetics. In Proceedings of the 33rd Annual ACM Conference on Human Factors in Computing Systems, Seoul, Republic of Korea, 18–23 April 2015; pp. 1163–1172. [CrossRef]
42. Liu, J.; Ang, M.C.; Chaw, J.K.; Kor, A.-L.; Ng, K.W. Emotion assessment and application in human-computer interaction interface based on backpropagation neural network and artificial bee colony algorithm. *Expert Syst. Appl.* **2023**, *232*, 120857. [CrossRef]
43. Tractinsky, N.; Cokhavi, A.; Kirschenbaum, M.; Sharfi, T. Evaluating the consistency of immediate aesthetic perceptions of web pages. *Int. J. Hum.-Comput. Stud.* **2006**, *64*, 1071–1083. [CrossRef]
44. Schenkman, B.N.; Jönsson, F.U. Aesthetics and preferences of web pages. *Behav. Inf. Technol.* **2000**, *19*, 367–377. [CrossRef]
45. Kang, E.; Kang, Y.A. Counseling chatbot design: The effect of anthropomorphic chatbot characteristics on user self-disclosure and companionship. *Int. J. Hum.-Comput. Interact.* **2024**, *40*, 2781–2795. [CrossRef]
46. Tullis, T.S. The formatting of alphanumeric displays: A review and analysis. *Hum. Factors* **1983**, *25*, 657–682. [CrossRef]
47. Poulin, R. *The Language of Graphic Design: An Illustrated Handbook for Understanding Fundamental Design Principles*; Choice Reviews Online: Middletown, CT, USA, 2011; Volume 49, pp. 49–1257. [CrossRef]
48. Bessghaier, N.; Soui, M.; Ghaibi, N. Towards the automatic restructuring of structural aesthetic design of Android user interfaces. *Comput. Stand. Inter.* **2022**, *81*, 103598. [CrossRef]
49. Hu, H.; Liu, Y.; Lu, W.F.; Guo, X. A quantitative aesthetic measurement method for product appearance design. *Adv. Eng. Inf.* **2022**, *53*, 101644. [CrossRef]
50. Marcus, A. *Graphic Design for Electronic Documents and User Interfaces*; ACM Press: New York, NY, USA, 1992. [CrossRef]
51. Zhou, L.; Xue, C.; Tang, W.; Li, J.; Niu, Y. Aesthetic evaluation method of interface elements layout design. *J. Comput.-Aided Des. Comput. Graph.* **2013**, *25*, 758–766. [CrossRef]
52. Ng, A.W.Y.; Chan, A.H.S. Color associations among designers and non-designers for common warning and operation concepts. *Appl. Ergon.* **2018**, *70*, 18–25. [CrossRef] [PubMed]

53. Munsell, H. *A Color Notation: A Measured Color System, Based on the Three Qualities Hue, Value and Chroma*; Good Press: Glasgow, UK, 2019.
54. Jing, L.; Xue, C. Color encoding research of digital display interface based on the visual perceptual layering. *J. Mech. Eng.* **2016**, *52*, 201–208. [CrossRef]
55. Wu, Z.; Lin, T. Investigating the personality associations evoked by single colors: An exploratory study. *Color Res. Appl.* **2017**, *42*, 388–396. [CrossRef]
56. Judd, D.B. The Munsell color system. *J. Opt. Soc. Am.* **1940**, *30*, 574. [CrossRef]
57. Jia, Q.Q.; Zhang, L. Quick assessment of human-machine interface complexity in digital nuclear power plant based on image entropy. *At. Energy Sci. Technol.* **2014**, *48*, 2370–2374. [CrossRef]
58. Moon, P.; Spencer, D.E. Aesthetic Measure Applied to Color Harmony. *J. Opt. Soc. Am.* **1944**, *34*, 234–242. [CrossRef]
59. Birkhoff, G.D. *Aesthetic Measure*; Harvard University Press: Cambridge, MA, USA, 1933. [CrossRef]
60. Hsiao, S.-W.; Chiu, F.-Y.; Chen, C.S. Applying aesthetics measurement to product design. *Int. J. Ind. Ergon.* **2008**, *38*, 910–920. [CrossRef]
61. Hsiao, S.; Yang, M.; Lee, C. An aesthetic measurement method for matching colours in product design. *Color Res. Appl.* **2017**, *42*, 664–683. [CrossRef]
62. Lu, P.; Hsiao, S.-W. A product design method for form and color matching based on aesthetic theory. *Adv. Eng. Inform.* **2022**, *53*, 101702. [CrossRef]
63. Chan, A.H.S.; Courtney, A.J. Color associations for Hong Kong Chinese. *Int. J. Ind. Ergon.* **2001**, *28*, 165–170. [CrossRef]
64. Wu, Z.; Lin, T.; Li, M. A computer-aided coloring method for virtual agents based on personality impression, color harmony, and designer preference. *Int. J. Ind. Ergon.* **2018**, *68*, 327–336. [CrossRef]
65. Zibulski, M.; Zeevi, Y.Y. The generalized Gabor scheme and its application in signal and image representation. In *Wavelet Analysis and Applications*; Academic Press: Cambridge, MA, USA, 1998; Volume 7, pp. 121–164. [CrossRef]
66. Zhang, B.; Ding, M.; Li, Y. Optimization design of human machine interaction interface based on visual perception. *China Mech. Eng.* **2016**, *27*, 2196–2202. [CrossRef]
67. Saaty, T.L. Decision making with the analytic hierarchy process. *Int. J. Serv. Sci.* **2008**, *1*, 83–98. [CrossRef]
68. Yang, Y.; Zuo, Q.; Zhang, K.; Li, X.; Yu, W.; Ji, L. Research on multistage heterogeneous information fusion of product design decision-making based on axiomatic design. *Systems* **2024**, *12*, 222. [CrossRef]
69. Li, X.; Qiu, S.; Ming, H.X.G. An integrated module-based reasoning and axiomatic design approach for new product design under incomplete information environment. *Comput. Ind. Eng.* **2018**, *127*, 63–73. [CrossRef]
70. Liu, A.H.; Wan, S.P.; Dong, J.Y. An axiomatic design-based mathematical programming method for heterogeneous multi-criteria group decision making with linguistic fuzzy truth degrees. *Inf. Sci.* **2021**, *571*, 649–675. [CrossRef]
71. Kalyan, S.; Bansal, P.; Kumar, S. A novel hybrid AHP-entropy weighted dynamic network DEA framework for comprehensive efficiency assessment. *Expert Syst. Appl.* **2026**, *296*, 129137. [CrossRef]
72. Saaty, T.L.; Hu, G. Ranking by eigenvector versus other methods in the analytic hierarchy process. *Appl. Math. Lett.* **1998**, *11*, 121–125. [CrossRef]
73. Zhu, Y.; Tian, D.; Yan, F. Effectiveness of entropy weight method in decision-making. *Math. Probl. Eng.* **2020**, *2020*, 3564835. [CrossRef]
74. Saxena, P.; Kumar, V.; Ram, M. A novel CRITIC-TOPSIS approach for optimal selection of software reliability growth model (SRGM). *Qual. Reliab. Eng. Int.* **2022**, *38*, 2501–2520. [CrossRef]
75. Liang, X.; Shu, W. Mobile marketing interface layout attributes that affect user aesthetic preference: An eye-tracking study. *Asia Pac. J. Mark. Logist.* **2023**, *35*, 472–492. [CrossRef]

symmetry

MDPI

Article

Integrating Kansei Engineering and AI-Generated Image for Commercial Vehicle Body Morphology Design

Bo Li [1,2,*], Zhen Hu [1,2], Yuhang Liu [3] and Zewei Wang [1,2]

1 Complex Mechanical Equipment Industrial Design Center, Xi'an University of Technology, Xi'an 710054, China
2 Faulty of Industrial Design, Xi'an University of Technology, Xi'an 710054, China
3 Dectron Future Automobile Technology Co., Ltd., Xi'an 713700, China
* Correspondence: libo1983@xaut.edu.cn; Tel.: +86-152-0295-5363

Abstract: Symmetry in vehicle body morphology is a crucial factor for achieving visual sensory balance in users, and it also serves as an important method for enhancing the efficiency of vehicle body research and development. This study proposes an AHP-SD-TOPSIS-AIGC integrated morphological design method to address multi-factorial design complexities in new energy commercial vehicle body styling under emotion-driven frameworks. Through literature retrieval and survey analysis, a Kansei evaluation system was constructed, with hierarchical design indicators established via Analytic Hierarchy Process (AHP) and weights determined through consistency matrices. Technique for Order Preference by Similarity to Ideal Solution (TOPSIS) identified optimal style forms exhibiting high emotional intention coupling, while edge detection algorithms extracted symmetrical spline features for body contour modeling. Artificial Intelligence Generated Content (AIGC) tools subsequently generated innovative solutions, validated through truck design applications to confirm method rationality and effectiveness. The results of the study show that the styling elements are accurately matched to user preferences and can identify target improvement points, and that the method can effectively achieve the output of the proposal for the design of commercial vehicle body morphology and is also applicable to passenger car-type vehicles to achieve the adaptation of multi-intentional emotional design.

Keywords: multi-factors-driven; Kansei engineering; commercial vehicles; body morphology; emotional design; AI image generation

1. Introduction

Symmetry is a fundamental characteristic of commercial vehicle body morphology and a crucial factor in users' visual perception of balance. Commercial vehicles are an important means of transportation in economic development activities, playing a key role in the transportation of consumer goods, infrastructure construction, and export cargo transportation. These vehicles are responsible for more than 70% of China's overland freight transportation and are a key pillar of China's economic and infrastructure development. In recent years, the continuous promotion of the national "dual-carbon" strategy has prompted the exploration and development of new energy sources for commercial vehicles [1]. Industry forecasts suggest China's new energy commercial vehicle market will hit around 76 billion Yuan by 2024, growing at an average annual rate of 19.5%. Benefiting from low operating costs, technological advancements, and policy support, its appeal to users is rising. Various indicators point to significant growth potential in this market.

Sustainable development, energy conservation and emission reduction, and environmental protection have always been the main themes of today's world development era. The trend of passenger carization of new energy commercial vehicles has become the mainstream development direction of major OEMs, and the design thinking focuses more and more on the comfort experience of drivers and passengers. Relevant research mainly focuses on technology development, optimization of the vehicle from the body parts materials, structure, technology, electronic control, and other directions, such as an aerodynamic design to reduce air resistance or being lightweight to improve the energy consumption, economy, and range [2]; comprehensive analysis and optimization of energy consumption [3]; driving mode control research to improve the comfort of handling [4]; drive train research to improve the performance of power [5]; and the design of the frame stress fatigue analysis to reduce costs and increase efficiency [6], etc. The above technology upgrades can highlight the brand power of commercial vehicles. However, the new energy commercial vehicle body morphology research of the major OEMs are the more neglected part because most OEMs imitate the existing foreign products or outsource design companies to complete the styling program, which causes a lack of uniqueness and creativity [7]. Therefore, there is a certain degree of homogenization of body shape design in the new energy vehicle market, and the styling differences between various family systems and brands are not obvious, and there is a lack of distinctive brand personality and labels.

The body shape is the most intuitive element of the user's perception of the car, which has a multifaceted impact on the image of the car company, cultural values, and product brand power. It is not only a direct reflection of the aesthetics of automobile design but also carries the positioning of the model and brand concept. In the new car launch or auto show, the body shape is the first impression of users' perceptual cognition of the vehicle, which is the unconscious reaction to the product body shape. For example, the streamlined body can give the vehicle dynamism and vitality, so that users feel its sense of speed and rhythm; while the stable body shape, which conveys a calm and luxurious atmosphere, highlights the owner's taste and status. This kind of unconscious reaction triggered by external stimuli is called "Kansei" in the academic world, which is the comprehensive performance of the user using all the senses, including vision, hearing, feeling, smell, taste, cognition, and other senses to things, the environment, and the state of the specific feeling and imagery held by the comprehensive performance. It belongs to the category of tacit knowledge that is not easy to verbalize, reflecting the user's deep-seated needs for the product [8].

Kansei engineering, as a discipline that studies how to transform the perceptual needs of target users into product design elements, is widely used to understand the emotional needs and preferences of users for product research. Therefore, Kansei engineering can provide new ideas and methods for commercial vehicle body design [9], and the research on vehicle perceptual cognition is mainly focused on the field of passenger cars in the following three aspects:

① Kansei studies of CMF for automotive interior and exterior trim, such as Su Jianning et al. [10] studied the coupling characteristics of automotive body CMF to meet users' perceptual needs for automotive exterior design; QI et al. [11] compared user preferences and coupling degree of design samples to explore the synergistic characteristics of CMF design and people's cognitive process; and Shi Xiaotao et al. [12] combined Kansei engineering and an oculomotor experiment for interior seating for optimization.

② In their research on automobile styling feature lines, Hu Weifeng et al. [13] extracted the feature lines of the benchmark car, quantitatively described them using Bessel curves, and genotyped them based on genetic algorithms, reaching the goal of evolving styling genes through the image driven by user expectations, and leading the subsequent automobile styling design work accordingly; Ma Liza et al. [14] obtained the user's invisible intention based on eye movement experiments, combined with the eye movement index on the benchmark car for automotive styling feature line saliency analysis and feature line extraction, using shape grammar, to realize the inheritance and mutation of automotive styling features, combined with the case, to arrive at the final design scheme.

③ In his research on automotive interior and exterior styling design methods, Fu Lu [15] from Jilin University mentioned in his thesis that symmetry is the simplest form of equilibrium. At the same time, it is also a kind of law of car body modeling that the symmetrical balance pattern creates the overall body to give a person a sense of organization, order, and stability, with a majestic, dignified, and peaceful effect. Li Yu [16] implemented design parameters and imagery goals as nodes and identified the correlation between nodes as edges to establish a gene network model of the automobile shape for analysis and to guide the design of automobiles. G. Zacharewicz [17] proposed a method for service engineering that utilizes mathematical techniques to quickly eliminate incompatible solutions. Advanced mathematical methods such as fuzzy set theory or simulated time management are used to evaluate and rank the remaining solutions, reduce the number of candidate patterns, and select the optimal solution for use in correcting deviation processes.

Although the Kansei research on automobiles has achieved stage-by-stage results, the individual studies are relatively one-sided. The design factors affecting new energy commercial vehicles are diversified, and the selected perceptual vocabulary is difficult to meet the needs of multi-factorial evaluation. Some designs pursue high aesthetics while neglecting their practicability and a lack of reasonable technology and man–machine layout; or some models are too complex in appearance design, resulting in an increased wind resistance coefficient, which in turn affects the vehicle's range capability and energy consumption performance. In summary, the design elements of body shape are multifaceted and are the products of man–machine and aerodynamic layout, color and material selection, style and operation experience, etc., which need to be considered as a balance between practicality, aesthetics, comfort, and other elements of the vehicle. Kansei engineering may not be able to cover all the existing perceptual factors and potential user needs, and it is difficult to judge the importance of perceptual terms. Therefore, in this study, through the pre-AHP hierarchical analysis and Delphi expert group analysis, multi-dimensional, multi-angle, and multi-attribute body shape driving elements of commercial vehicles are summarized, and more levels of user needs as well as potential perceptual factors are excavated. The perceptual semantics condensed through hierarchy is more subdivided and accurate, and it will express the whole product's intrinsic elements more comprehensively. The weight relationship between different perceptual semantics is obtained by using the consistency matrix method. The user's subjective intention for different driving elements of the product is quantified by the Osgood semantic differentiation method (SD method) [18]. And finally, the positive and negative ideal solutions and relative proximity of each perceptual data index are determined using the TOPSIS multi-attribute decision-making method [19,20], which is used to assess the perceptual coupling of the solution and the computational solution [21,22].

The integration of AHP-SD-TOPSIS-AIGC new energy commercial vehicle design and Kansei evaluation methods will be examined to solve the problem of perceptual coupling between new energy commercial vehicles with multiple elements, categories, and forms, to quickly obtain users' comprehensive evaluation of multiple elements of new energy commercial vehicles, to determine the most suitable research direction, to generate multiple sets of solutions, and to guide new energy commercial vehicles to optimize in the direction of conforming to the Kansei preference of the majority of users.

2. Materials and Methods

The specific steps are shown in Figure 1, including five main steps:

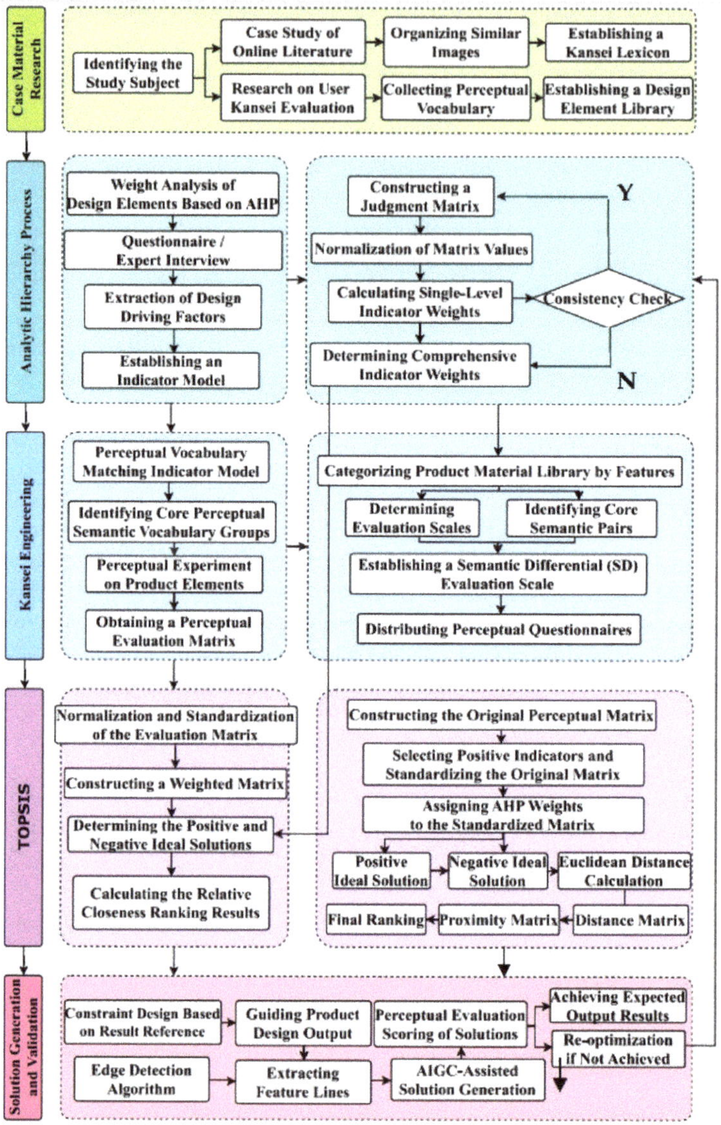

Figure 1. Technology roadmap.

In the first step, commercial vehicle materials were widely collected through the Internet, the literature, and case studies; semantic vocabulary of commercial vehicle features was collected through online user evaluation, and a Kansei imagery vocabulary was established.

In step 2, the AHP hierarchical analysis model was established, industry experts were invited to score, a complementary judgment matrix was constructed, the weights of each index were calculated using the consistent matrix method, the Kansei intention words were matched and summarized, the core perceptual semantic words were condensed, and the weights were assigned with the comprehensive weights of each level.

In step 3, the sample material was extracted from the design elements, processed, and generalized to identify representative models as test samples, and the core perceptual semantic words that were condensed were used as perceptual vocabulary to implement Kansei experiments.

In step 4, the Euclidean distance and relative proximity were calculated using the TOPSIS multi-attribute decision-making method. The smaller the value of the distance from the positive ideal solution, the higher the coupling of body styling intentions.

In step 5, the above information and data are summarized and aggregated, and the appropriate overall and local body shape was selected to guide the generation of the body design scheme in combination with the AIGC technology.

2.1. Construction of the Design Element System for New Energy Commercial Vehicle Body

2.1.1. Building Driving Elements

Compared with new energy passenger cars and traditional commercial vehicles, new energy commercial vehicles show significant differences in demand characteristics and purpose of use. Due to the lower cost of electricity compared to fuel costs, new energy commercial vehicles show a lower cost advantage in long-term operation. A series of policy support and subsidy measures have reduced initial investment costs, providing strong support for their market promotion.

This study is aimed at the relevant needs of domestic commercial vehicle consumers in China, and the research samples are selected for the relevant industry practitioners and experts in mainland China, which are the limitations of this paper's current sample research. For the study to be more comprehensive, it would be necessary to further expand the research sample through the network form of research to outside of the country and region.

A total of 152 questionnaires were distributed in this study, targeting commercial vehicle drivers in different capacities, ranging from shared van drivers, moving companies, logistics companies, and freelance freight drivers. Ninety-two questionnaires were collected from the working environment of the driver groups participating in the study for those who traveled in the city, sixty questionnaires were collected for those who traveled on long-distance and high-speed journeys, and the data were analyzed to summarize the key elements that were in line with the theme of the study. From the results of the research data, it can be seen that the core concerns of commercial vehicle consumers are product price, range, and reliability, followed by driving comfort, performance and safety, novelty of styling, loading capacity, after-sales experience, brand influence, and other elements. Through the Delphi method, relying on the results of the expert group discussion, we clarify the corresponding level contents of the first-level driving elements and the second-level elements from the subjective and objective "performance layer, perception layer, and technology layer" indicators of the new energy commercial vehicle body shape design.

There are three guideline layers (B_1,C_2,D_3) for the first-level driving factors, including styling factors, experience factors, and engineering factors. The performance layer mainly reflects the external characteristics of the commercial vehicle form, the perception layer mainly reflects the multi-sensory experience of the vehicle user, and the technology layer mainly reflects the objective technical points that need to be considered for the form. There are 10 indicator layers (B_{11}–B_{14}, C_{21}–C_{23}, D_{31}–$_{33}$) for the second-level driving factors, including color and material, styling features, brand characteristics, level of customization, operational experience, affective experience, technological experience, man–machine layout, aerodynamics, and manufacturing cost. The hierarchical model of the driving elements for the design of a new energy commercial vehicle body shape is shown in Figure 2. These 10 elements extensively cover the core key elements to be considered in the design of a new energy commercial vehicle body shape from both subjective and objective perspectives, and constitute the main guidance in the design process.

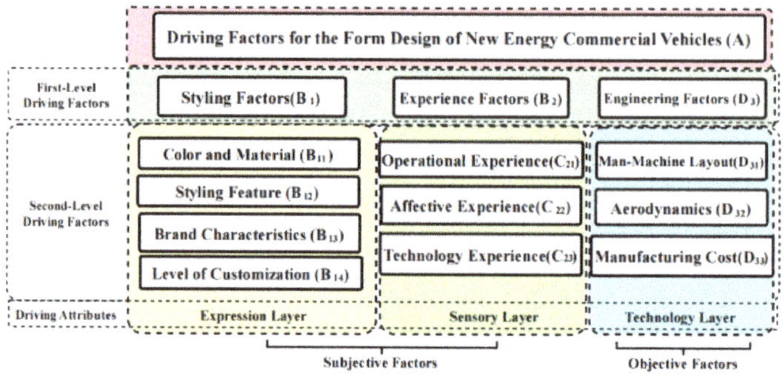

Figure 2. Hierarchical model diagram of driving elements for body shape design of new energy commercial vehicles.

2.1.2. Determining Indicator Weights

By establishing a hierarchical model, the elements of the product are deconstructed into the levels of objectives, guidelines, and programs to more comprehensively reflect the subjective and objective driving elements of the new energy commercial vehicle form design. In order to understand the relationship and importance of the elements, an expert focus group was set up to discuss and construct a judgment matrix, in which Santy's 1–9 scaling method was used, the meaning of which is shown in Table 1. $A = (aij)n{\cdot}n$, a_{ij} represents the first row and column of the indicators, and its complementary value is $a_{ij} = 1/a_{ij}$; n is the number of indicators.

$$A = \begin{bmatrix} a_{11} & a_{12} & \cdots & a_{1n} \\ a_{21} & a_{22} & \cdots & a_{2n} \\ \cdots & \cdots & \ddots & \cdots \\ a_{n1} & a_{n2} & \cdots & a_{nn} \end{bmatrix} \tag{1}$$

Table 1. Judgment matrix scale evaluation scale definition.

Numerical Scale	Meaning (Degree of Importance)
1	Both elements are equally important
3	The former is slightly more important than the latter
5	The former is significantly more important than the latter
7	The former is much more important than the latter
9	The former is extremely more important than the latter
1/3	The former is slightly less important than the latter
1/5	The former is significantly less important than the latter
1/7	The former is much less important than the latter
1/9	The former is extremely less important than the latter
2, 4, 6, 8	Intermediate values between the above

Normalize the matrix values by linearly mapping the data within the range of [0, 1], the sum of each row in the judgment matrix is calculated, and the normalized eigenvectors, i.e., the weight vectors of the hierarchical levels of the judgment matrix, are calculated by using the summation method of Equation (2).

$$W_i = \frac{\sum_{j=1}^{n} a_{ij}}{\sum_{i=1}^{n} \sum_{j=1}^{n} a_{ij}} \quad (2)$$

To determine whether the matrix passes the consistency test, the CR value is the basis of whether the consistency test passes or not, the largest characteristic root is obtained through Equation (3), the consistency index CI is obtained through Equation (4), and the consistency ratio CR is obtained through Equation (5), the CR value is the basis of whether the consistency test passes or not, and the RI is the average stochastic consistency index, when the $CR < 0.1$, it indicates that the judgment matrix A passes the consistency test, on the contrary, if it does not pass, then the matrix needs to be trimmed.

$$\lambda_{max} = \frac{1}{n} \sum_{i=1}^{n} \frac{(AW)i}{W_i} \quad (3)$$

$$CI = \frac{\lambda_{max} - n}{n - 1} \quad (4)$$

$$CR = \frac{CI}{RI} \quad (5)$$

2.2. Construction and Categorization of a Sample Library of Morphological and Local Features of New Energy Commercial Vehicle Bodies

Through in-depth excavation of diversified information channels such as the official websites of various enterprises and commercial vehicle platforms, and with "new energy heavy-duty truck" as the keyword, we have carefully collected and organized a total of 94 related vehicle modeling pictures, which require high clarity, a positive 45° body angle, the same front direction, and other local materials with a uniform perspective and scale. Photoshop 2025 image processing software was used for image segmentation, to adjust the contrast between light and dark, and other methods to highlight the main part. The body shapes with high similarity, strong redundancy, and weak brand influence were eliminated, and 20 brands with 48 models were initially filtered out.

Inviting five corporate professionals and eight automotive stylists to set up a panel of experts, the car's modeling line features were finally divided into five categories: ① Flat and slightly curved models are characterized by their overall shape being close to a cube, but the corners are rounded and chamfered, making the sense of unity stronger. The upper part of the chassis and the chassis are closely integrated on such models and did not form a clear separation, presenting a unified and harmonious aesthetic. ② Streamlined surface type body models are characterized by the integration of streamlined design elements and smooth body lines, showing a clear large-scale curve; similar to the flat type, the upper and lower parts show no obvious dividing line, and the style modeling is more coherent and unified, showing a dynamic sense of aesthetics. ③ Flat split type and ④ streamline split type are based on the above forms, with obvious split lines on the upper part of the front end and the chassis, which are not integrated, and the style and local details are richer. ⑤ The straight line cut model is known for its unique sense of cutting lines, the most representative of which is the Tesla Cyber pickup truck. The entire body of this model is made of an aluminum alloy steel plate without chamfering treatment, presenting an angular appearance.

Given the inherent bilateral symmetry of automotive body structures, parametric modeling can be optimally executed by unilateral contour generation followed by axial mirror transformations to ensure geometric integrity and reduce computational redundancy.

Using the inherent symmetry of the vehicle body shape, a multi-ridge feature extraction method was implemented by an advanced edge detection algorithm, which achieves the accurate capture of local style contours and maintains the geometric consistency of the bilateral parts [23]. By applying the Roberts operator [24] in MatLab 2023, the edge information in the car image, including contour lines and feature lines, can be accurately detected. Ten models were selected according to the line features, which were screened by a panel of experts, and the styling lines were extracted, analyzed, and categorized. The models with novel styling, obvious brand features, and representative styling were finally selected and classified into five categories. These models not only cover the mainstream new energy heavy-duty truck designs in the market, but also include some cutting-edge concept models, and an excerpt of the classified content is shown in Table 2.

Table 2. Example of classification and numbering of body shape characteristic lines.

Vehicle Body Form Types	Vehicle Body Images	Vehicle Body Contour Feature Lines	Description of Morphological Features
Flat with Slight Curvature Type (S_1)	 		Rectangular Overall Shape
Streamlined Curved Surface Type: (S_2)	 		Streamlined Overall Shape with Integrity
Flat and Segmented Type: (S_3)	 		Vertical Segmentation
Streamlined and Segmented Type: (S_4)	 		Vertical Segmentation
Straight Cut Type: (S_5)	 		Sharp Straight Lines

2.3. The Perceptual Evaluation Process of Vehicle Body Shapes and Local Features

2.3.1. Vocabulary Extraction of Kansei Imagery

Design imagery is the process by which designers give life and meaning to a product through its form, a process that prompts users to personalize and recreate the aesthetic value of the product through imagining, analyzing, and other mental activities. When this concept is applied to automobile styling, it means that people recognize and understand the appearance of an automobile not only by simply receiving information about its external shape, but also by deeply analyzing and understanding the design features, aesthetic principles, and overall styling concepts behind such information. This process covers both the specific features of the car's appearance, the norms or trends followed in the design, and the individual's subjective experience and understanding of the unique aesthetics of the car's shape [13], with the help of the emotional vocabulary of the secondary driving elements of the emotional expression of the user population to facilitate the user population's subjective understanding of the shape of the car body and the real emotional perception [25].

In order to establish a multi-dimensional vocabulary of Kansei imagery to accurately reflect the styling characteristics of the target product of new energy heavy-duty trucks, a wide range of resources have been collected, including, but not limited to, automotive professional magazines, relevant academic literature, and designers' professional evaluations. A total of 90 words closely related to the brand styling of heavy-duty trucks were summarized (see Table 3). And the Kansei intention vocabulary in the summary table of characteristic semantic words is categorized to each index layer, and the corresponding 10 core semantic words are condensed to represent the intention preference vocabulary for the index layer (see Table 4), thus pairing up the ten sets of perceptual semantic word groups here. This method not only effectively avoids the redundant overlapping of lexical meanings and promotes the accurate mapping of perceptual language to design elements, but also greatly enriches the expression dimension of product design features, thus ensuring the scientific nature of the assessment process and the effectiveness of the results [26].

Table 3. Summary table of feature semantic word extraction (excerpt).

Kansei Imagery Vocabulary				
Smooth	Dynamic	Elegant	Exquisite	Robust
Restrained	Mysterious	Technological	Intelligent	Steady
Luxurious	Light	Textured	Masculine	Professional
Energetic	Passionate	Enthusiastic	Compact	Flexible
Sharp	Bold	Serious	Fashionable	Cool
Delicate	Calm	Radical	Sci-fi	Warm
Dominant	Harmonious	Harmonious	Rustic	Cosmic
Dreamy	Feminine	Freehand	Shocking	Rhythmic
Safe	Fierce	Futuristic	Daring	Classic
Antique	High-end	Reasonable	Soft	Sturdy

Table 4. Hierarchical system of design elements for commercial vehicles.

Categorization by Driving Factors (A) and Related Feature Vocabulary (F)				
First-Level Driving Factors	**Second-Level Driving Factors**	**Primary Kansei Vocabulary for Commercial Vehicles**	**Key Semantic Words**	**Kansei Word Pairing**
Styling Factors (B_1)	Color and Material (B_{11})	Passionate, textured, vivid, eco-friendly, fresh	Texture (F_{11})	Texture-Dull
	Styling Feature (B_{12})	Avant-garde, dynamic, novel, dominant, robust	Aesthetic (F_{12})	Aesthetic-Ugly
	Brand Characteristics (B_{13})	High-end, classic, luxurious, grandeur	High-end (F_{13})	High-end-Low-end
	Level of Customization (B_{14})	Familial, recognizable, unique, innovative, novel	Innovative (F_{14})	Innovative-Ordinary
Experience Factors (C_2)	Operational Experience (C_{21})	Unrestrained, speed, sporty, flexible, steady	Flexible (F_{21})	Flexible-Cumbersome
	Affective Experience (C_{22})	Energetic, warm, cozy, passionate, enthusiastic	Emotion (F_{22})	Emotion-Unimpressed
	Technology Experience (C_{23})	Modern, futuristic, with a sense of technology, innovative, intelligent	Technology (F_{23})	Technology-Primitive
Engineering Factors (D_3)	Man-Machine Layout (D_{31})	Scientific, comfortable, spacious, clean, elegant	Comfortable (F_{31})	Comfortable-Uncomfortable
	Aerodynamics (D_{32})	Streamlined, curved, speed-oriented, rhythmic, dynamically beautiful	Aerodynamic (F_{33})	Aerodynamic-Non-aerodynamic
	Manufacturing Cos (D_{33})	Safe, durable, achievable, eco-friendly, professional	Reasonable (F_{33})	Reasonable-Unreasonable

2.3.2. Determining the Evaluation Sample

The expert team carried out systematic classification and selection in the sample database and extracted representative body shape samples from the five classification categories. On this basis, the local features of commercial vehicles were further disassembled and categorized, initially focusing on the five core modules of lights, grille, windows, roof, and hubcaps. Subsequently, for the specific categories under these modules, the expert team carried out in-depth segmentation and selected the representative component forms, so as to construct a set of samples for evaluation, as shown in Table 5.

2.3.3. Data Acquisition

In order to construct the evaluation system of Kansei imagery, this study takes semantic differential method (SD) as the theoretical basis, analyzes the carefully collected and organized materials in depth, and then constructs an evaluation matrix, the specific form of which is shown in Equation (6). This matrix is presented as an n × m dimension, where n represents the number of evaluated objects and m represents the number of evaluation indicators. In order to obtain Kansei-perceptual evaluations about the sample, a set of Kansei imagery questionnaires were carefully designed and distributed, and respondents were invited to score the sample based on their personal perceptions. Subsequently, the collected Kansei evaluation data were subjected to rigorous data processing using homogenization to ensure the objectivity and accuracy of the evaluation results, and to systematically explore and analyze the intrinsic connection between Kansei imagery and the characteristics of the sample.

$$X = \begin{bmatrix} x_{11} & x_{12} & \cdots & x_{1m} \\ x_{21} & x_{22} & \cdots & x_{2m} \\ \vdots & \vdots & \ddots & \vdots \\ x_{n1} & x_{n2} & \cdots & x_{nm} \end{bmatrix} \quad (6)$$

Table 5. Vehicle feature classification.

Vehicle Body Elements	Features and Codes of Styling Form Elements				
Vehicle Body	 Flat with Slight Curvature Type(S_1)	 Streamlined Curved Surface Type: (S_2)	 Flat and Segmented Type: (S_3)	 Streamlined and Segmented Type: (S_4)	 Straight Cut Type: (S_5)
Vehicle Lights	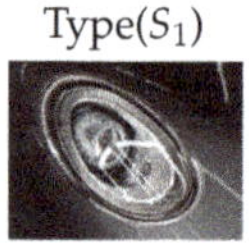 Rounded Type(S_6)	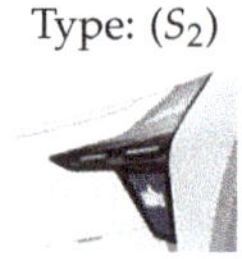 Irregular Shape Type(S_7)	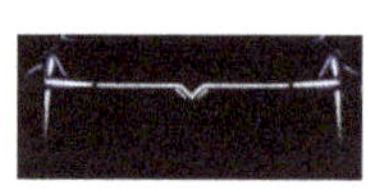 Linear Type(S_8)	 Matrix Type(S_9)	 Biomorphic Type(S_{10})
Grille	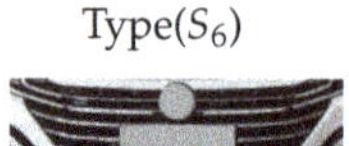 Horizontal Banner Type(S_{11})	 Vertical Waterfall Type(S_{12})	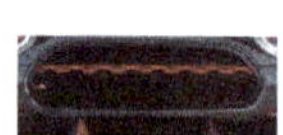 Honeycomb Type(S_{13})	 Parametric Grid Type(S_{14})	 Grille-less Type(S_{15})

Table 5. *Cont.*

Vehicle Body Elements	Features and Codes of Styling Form Elements			
Vehicle Roof	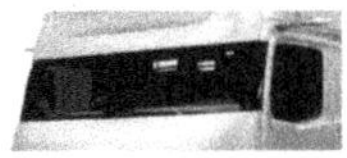 Non-continuous Type(S_{16})	 Integrated Top-Bottom Type(S_{17})	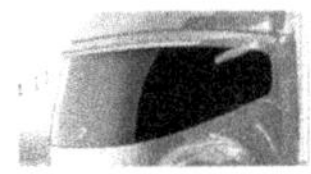 Integrated Left-Right Type(S_{18})	 Irregular Type(S_{19})
Vehicle Roof	 Integrated Curved Type(S_{20})	 Streamlined Flat-top Type(S_{21})	 Slanted Type(S_{22})	
Wheel Hub Cover	 Curved Circular Type(S_{23})	 Straight Cut Type(S_{24})	 Flat and Minimalist Type(S_{25})	

2.4. *TOPSIS-Based Scheme Ranking Preference*

TOPSIS is a multi-attribute decision-making method for evaluating and selecting the best decision-making solution. Its central idea lies in first determining the positive ideal solution (optimal solution) and negative ideal solution (worst solution) of each index. The positive ideal solution is the best value of each candidate solution, and the negative ideal solution is the worst value of each candidate solution. Then the Euclidean distance between each solution and the positive ideal solution and the negative ideal solution is calculated, and the proximity of each solution to the optimal solution is thus obtained as a criterion for evaluating the advantages and disadvantages of the solutions. If a scheme is closer to the positive ideal solution and farther away from the negative ideal solution, it is considered to be closer to the ideal scheme [27].

2.4.1. Matrix Normalization

The obtained evaluation matrices of each form of new energy commercial vehicles are normalized and standardized to eliminate the differences in scale and numerical range between different attributes. Here, the polar deviation method is used to obtain the normalized matrix Z. Where a and b are unequal, it can be called a range indicator, and when a and b are equal, it can be called an intermediate indicator.

(1) Positive indicators:

$$z_{ij} = \frac{x_{ij} - x_j^{\min}}{x_j^{\max} - x_j^{\min}} \tag{7}$$

(2) Negative indicators:

$$z_{ij} = \frac{x_j^{\max} - x_{ij}}{x_j^{\max} - x_j^{\min}} \tag{8}$$

(3) Moderate indicators:

$$z_{ij} = \begin{cases} 1 - \frac{a - x_{ij}}{\max\left(a - x_j^{\min},\ x_j^{\max} - b\right)}, & x_{ij} < a \\ 1, & a \leq x_{ij} \leq b \\ 1 - \frac{x_{ij} - b}{\max\left(a - x_j^{\min},\ x_j^{\max} - b\right)}, & x_{ij} > b \end{cases} \tag{9}$$

A weighting matrix was constructed by combining the AHP second-level driver element weights. In the normalized matrix, each column is multiplied with the corresponding AHP weights for each class to weight the raw data.

$$Z = \begin{bmatrix} \omega_1 \times z_{11} & \omega_2 \times z_{12} & \cdots & \omega_m \times z_{1m} \\ \omega_1 \times z_{21} & \omega_2 \times z_{22} & \cdots & \omega_m \times z_{2m} \\ \vdots & \vdots & \ddots & \vdots \\ \omega_1 \times z_{n1} & \omega_2 \times z_{n2} & \cdots & \omega_m \times z_{nm} \end{bmatrix} \tag{10}$$

2.4.2. Positive and Negative Ideal Solutions Euclidean Distance and Relative Proximity Solving

The processed matrix needs to determine the positive and negative ideal solutions. The positive ideal solution is the solution that is desired to achieve the maximum value on multiple attributes in optimal decision making, i.e., the solution that achieves the optimal level on all attributes. In general, the smaller the positive ideal value, the higher the evaluation, and the higher the coupling with Kansei intention; the negative ideal solution is the opposite of this. The positive ideal solution consists of the maximum value of each column element in the weighted normalized matrix, and the negative ideal solution consists of the minimum value of each column element. The weighted normalization matrix at this point is:

$$Z = \begin{bmatrix} z_{11} & z_{12} & \cdots & z_{1m} \\ z_{21} & z_{22} & \cdots & z_{2m} \\ \vdots & \vdots & \ddots & \vdots \\ z_{n1} & z_{n2} & \cdots & z_{nm} \end{bmatrix} \tag{11}$$

Positive Ideal Solution:

$$Z^+ = \left(Z_1^+, Z_2^+, \cdots, Z_m^+\right) \tag{12}$$

Negative Ideal Solution:

$$Z^- = \left(Z_1^-, Z_2^-, \cdots, Z_m^-\right) \tag{13}$$

This ranking uses the Euclidean distance to calculate the distance between the object and the positive ideal solution and the negative ideal solution, which provides the basis for the subsequent evaluation and ranking, and by comparing the distance between the evaluation object and the positive ideal solution and the negative ideal solution, the degree of proximity of the evaluation object to the optimal solution and the worst solution can be judged. This experiment uses a positive indicator, and the closer the distance to the positive ideal solution and the farther the distance to the negative ideal solution, the better the evaluation object is.

$$D_i^+ = \sqrt{\sum_{j=1}^{m} \left(Z_j^+ - z_{ij}\right)^2} \tag{14}$$

$$D_i^- = \sqrt{\sum_{j=1}^{m} \left(Z_j^- - z_{ij}\right)^2} \tag{15}$$

Relative closeness was calculated and ranked using the negative ideal solution distance. Relative proximity ranges from 0 to 1, where a larger number means that the further away from the negative ideal solution, the higher the Kansei-intentional coupling, and the better the result.

$$S_i = \frac{D_i^-}{D_i^+ + D_i^-} \tag{16}$$

3. Results

New energy heavy-duty trucks in the new energy commercial vehicle sector occupy a pivotal position. In this sector, the new energy tractor is very representative in comparison to new energy heavy trucks, with a proportion that has increased from 26.42% to more than 75%. This vehicle is therefore the dominant force in the long-distance bulk cargo transportation industry, and its power, range, speed, and other requirements are also higher, so the example of a new energy tractor is the object of study.

3.1. Determination of Driver Weights

Experts from various departments of the enterprise were organized, and six enterprise personnel were invited and formed a focus group. Based on their knowledge and experience of the work, they adopted a comparison level of 1–9 to quantitatively assign values to the driving elements required for the design of new energy commercial vehicle body forms, statistically organized the scalar values of each index, and combined that with the Formula (1) to construct a judgment matrix for the driving elements at each level, as follows:

$$A = \begin{bmatrix} 1 & 3 & 1 \\ \frac{1}{3} & 1 & \frac{1}{5} \\ 1 & 5 & 1 \end{bmatrix} B = \begin{bmatrix} 1 & \frac{1}{3} & 1 & 3 \\ 3 & 1 & 3 & 3 \\ 1 & \frac{1}{3} & 1 & 3 \\ \frac{1}{3} & \frac{1}{3} & \frac{1}{3} & 1 \end{bmatrix}$$

$$C = \begin{bmatrix} 1 & 5 & 1 \\ \frac{1}{5} & 1 & \frac{1}{3} \\ 1 & 3 & 1 \end{bmatrix} \mathrm{D} = \begin{bmatrix} 1 & 3 & \frac{1}{3} \\ \frac{1}{3} & 1 & \frac{1}{5} \\ 3 & 5 & 1 \end{bmatrix}$$

For the judgment matrix, after normalization, WA = (0.4055, 0.1150, 0.4796), the largest characteristic root $\lambda_{\max}$= 3.029, CI_A = 0.015, CR_A = 0.02511, $CR_A < 0.1$ passes the consistency test, and if it does not pass, the matrix needs to be trimmed. Similarly, other index weights can be obtained, the specific values are shown in Table 6.

3.2. A Kansei Experiment Based on the Semantic Differential Approach

The Kansei evaluation will be conducted with the help of questionnaire instruments, aiming to explore the subjective preference of participants for the market style and design element samples. The semantic difference method (SD) is used to construct a Kansei imagery evaluation scale, with Table 5 as the experimental sample. Listed in Table 4 are the 10 perceptual adjective groups, and examples can be referred to in Table 7. The larger the value, the higher the semantic word coupling. Through the statistical analysis of the questionnaire data and calculation of the average value, it can be simple and fast to collect and understand the user's subjective feelings and quantify them. Sixty-three copies of this questionnaire were issued. After the questionnaire reliability analysis, the Clonbach coefficients are all around 0.87 and greater than 0.8. The reliability of the quiz or scale meets the requirements, and the results have a reference value. The results of the experiment were obtained and are shown in Table 8 (body shape Kansei data) and Table 9 (car local shape Kansei data).

Table 6. Calculation results of design element hierarchy for commercial vehicles.

Weight of Each Indicator						
First-Level Driving Factors	**First-Level Weight**	**Second-Level Driving Factors**	**Key Semantic Words**	**Comprehensive Weight**	**Consistency Check**	**Rank**
Styling Factors (B_1)	0.4055	Color and Material (B_{11})	Texture (F_{11})	0.0853	$\lambda_{max} = 4.155$	4
		Styling Feature (B_{12})	Aesthetic (F_{12})	0.1951		2
		Brand Characteristics (B_{13})	High-end (F_{13})	0.0853	$CI_B = 0.05179$	4
		Level of Customization (B_{14})	Innovative (F_{14})	0.0397	$CR_B = 0.05819$	9
Experience Factors (C_2)	0.1150	Operational Experience (C_{21})	Flexible (F_{21})	0.0551	$\lambda_{max} = 3.029$	6
		Affective Experience (C_{22})	Emotion (F_{22})	0.0132	$CI_C = 0.01456$	10
		Technology Experience (C_{23})	Technology (F_{23})	0.0466	$CR_C = 0.02511$	8
Engineering Factors (D_3)	0.4796	Man-Machine Layout (D_{31})	Comfortable (F_{31})	0.1249	$\lambda_{max} = 3.039$	3
		Aerodynamics (D_{32})	Aerodynamic (F_{33})	0.0509	$CI_D = 0.01935$	7
		Manufacturing Cos (D_{33})	Reasonable (F_{33})	0.3037	$CR_D = 0.03337$	1

Table 7. Example of questionnaire survey.

Images	**Evaluation of Design-Related Adjectives**								
	Aesthetic	−3	−2	−1	0	1	2	3	Not aesthetic

Table 8. Statistics on the average sensory data of commercial vehicle body shape.

	F_{11}	F_{12}	F_{13}	F_{14}	F_{21}	F_{21}	F_{23}	F_{31}	F_{32}	F_{33}
S_1	1.03	0.21	1.10	1.21	0.40	−0.22	1.24	0.68	1.24	0.60
S_2	1.33	1.13	1.22	1.40	0.98	0.44	1.38	1.03	1.65	1.11
S_3	1.35	1.30	1.52	1.35	0.76	0.95	1.29	1.33	0.89	1.33
S_4	1.46	0.75	1.24	1.78	1.49	0.59	1.75	0.30	1.75	0.32
S_5	0.52	0.44	1.08	1.75	0.78	0.19	1.32	−0.03	−0.13	0.08

3.3. TOPSIS Kansei Coupling Calculation

The results obtained by the semantic difference method cannot be used directly, as it is difficult to make a decision in the number of items and many attributes of the data. In Tables 8 and 9 it can be seen that the data have negative values, so there is a need to standardize them. Here the use of the polar deviation method is used to normalize the matrix. The use of positive indicators, i.e., the larger the value of the indicator, the better the indicator, and attached to the weighting value after the weighting standardization matrix, as shown in Table 10.

Table 9. Statistics on the average results of sensory data of local morphology of commercial vehicles.

	F_{11}	F_{12}	F_{13}	F_{14}	F_{21}	F_{21}	F_{23}	F_{31}	F_{32}	F_{33}
S_6	1.22	1.33	1.30	0.73	1.11	0.86	1.08	1.21	1.44	1.67
S_7	1.40	1.32	1.54	1.63	1.22	1.10	1.70	1.02	0.76	1.29
S_8	1.94	2.00	2.00	1.84	1.79	1.52	2.03	1.71	1.63	1.75
S_9	1.52	1.19	1.33	1.37	1.27	1.13	1.17	1.29	0.90	1.62
S_{10}	1.71	1.83	1.68	1.25	1.41	1.32	1.46	1.54	1.79	1.75
S_{11}	0.51	0.49	0.21	−0.32	0.24	0.00	0.08	0.52	0.41	1.08
S_{12}	0.59	0.48	0.63	0.89	0.27	0.32	0.89	0.52	0.51	0.67
S_{13}	1.30	1.41	1.46	1.14	0.97	1.08	1.17	1.08	1.03	1.43
S_{14}	1.17	1.06	1.33	1.59	1.10	0.62	1.60	0.89	1.10	0.98
S_{15}	0.60	0.19	0.54	1.02	0.24	0.02	0.62	0.21	0.49	−0.13
S_{16}	0.81	0.90	0.92	0.65	0.32	0.49	0.75	0.71	0.63	1.17
S_{17}	1.32	1.21	1.70	1.41	1.37	1.05	1.59	0.98	1.40	1.02
S_{18}	1.43	1.71	1.60	1.52	1.49	1.14	1.60	1.57	1.83	1.44
S_{19}	1.57	1.22	1.62	1.78	1.30	1.25	1.79	1.29	1.67	0.90
S_{20}	1.38	1.44	1.46	1.29	1.30	1.22	1.51	1.33	1.86	1.19
S_{21}	0.81	0.68	0.59	0.38	0.54	0.52	0.73	0.94	0.67	1.22
S_{22}	1.13	0.97	0.98	0.83	0.89	0.63	0.75	1.06	1.32	1.33
S_{23}	1.46	1.44	1.56	1.10	1.32	1.14	1.30	1.43	1.24	1.62
S_{24}	2.05	2.06	2.03	1.97	1.89	1.81	2.14	1.84	1.65	2.00
S_{25}	1.29	1.03	1.33	1.49	0.87	0.86	1.33	0.97	1.35	1.02

Table 10. Weighted standardization matrix (vehicle form).

	F_{11}	F_{12}	F_{13}	F_{14}	F_{21}	F_{21}	F_{23}	F_{31}	F_{32}	F_{33}
S_1	0.029	0.002	0.042	0.027	0.005	0.000	0.026	0.047	0.035	0.104
S_2	0.045	0.098	0.047	0.030	0.025	0.004	0.029	0.071	0.046	0.177
S_3	0.047	0.116	0.061	0.029	0.017	0.008	0.027	0.091	0.026	0.208
S_4	0.053	0.058	0.048	0.036	0.042	0.005	0.038	0.022	0.048	0.064
S_5	0.001	0.026	0.041	0.036	0.018	0.003	0.028	0.000	0.000	0.030

Based on the results obtained from normalization, the Euclidean distance and relative proximity of the positive and negative ideal solutions are calculated. Among them, the positive ideal solution refers to the program that obtains the maximum value in each evaluation index, and the negative ideal solution is the program that reaches the minimum value in each evaluation index. Euclidean distance is used to measure the distance between each indicator and the positive ideal solution and the negative ideal solution. Based on the distance between each indicator and the positive ideal solution and the negative ideal solution, we can obtain the relative proximity of each indicator and the optimal indicator, so as to evaluate the advantages and disadvantages of each indicator. If the evaluation index value is closest to the positive ideal solution, it is the optimal solution, and vice versa, it is the worst solution. The relative proximity belongs to another evaluation process of the distance between the reference points of the positive and negative ideal solutions, and the smaller the value of the distance from the positive ideal solution, the better the indicator is. The results are calculated and shown in Figure 3, which clearly reflects the proximity comparison relationship between different styles of each part of the body shape. This study innovatively integrates scientific methods such as Kansei Engineering, Analytic Hierarchy Process (AHP), Semantic Difference Method (SD), and TOPSIS into the body design process to compensate for the shortcomings of AI generated content (AIGC). At the same time, AIGC also compensates for the low efficiency problem of traditional sensory engineering in transforming product images. Through AIGC, multiple sets of body shape schemes can be quickly generated for further screening, providing more choices for the generation of schemes guided by sensory engineering, as shown in Figure 4.

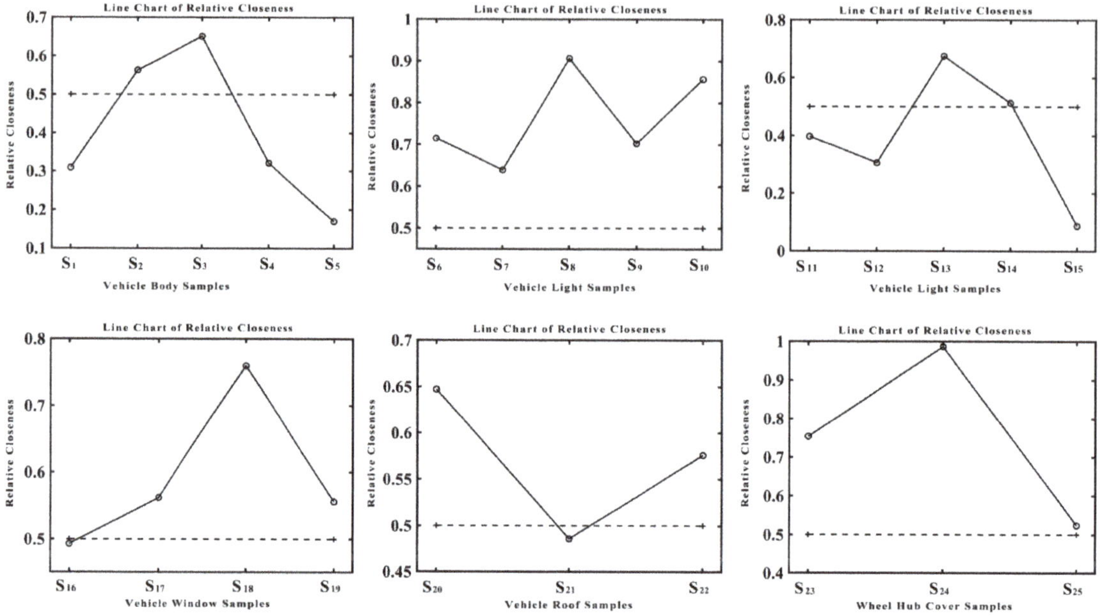

Figure 3. TOPSIS body shape evaluation calculation results.

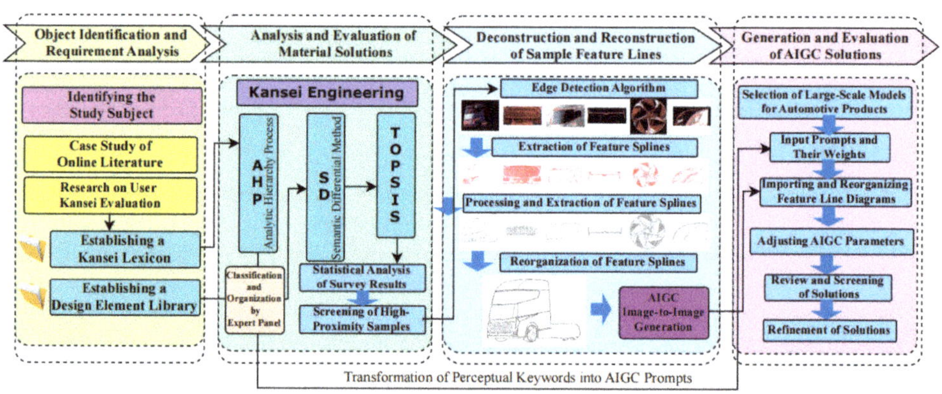

Figure 4. Flowchart for AIGC Scheme Design.

3.4. Analysis and Generation of AIGC Design Schemes

The results of the above experiments were summarized, analyzed, and processed, and are shown in Table 11. The body shape with the highest overall score is "S10", a flat segmented model represented by Geely Remote Star Han, which scores evenly, as can be seen from the data table. Its exterior design may adopt smooth lines and unique geometric shapes, the body is flat and at the same time the contours are rounded and full, and the aerodynamics are optimized to reduce wind resistance and improve energy efficiency and driving performance. Cutting waistline divides the top and bottom, rich in style and unity, and all parts of the vehicle echo each other in shape to form an overall coordinated and beautiful exterior image, with a well-proportioned body and a spacious and comfortable interior. Although the grille of the front face of the new energy commercial vehicle attracts users' attention visually, it has lost its actual function as a product and is mostly a decorative piece to balance the spatial layout of the front face, and will try to weaken the proportion of the grille's dimensions in the subsequent study.

Table 11. Intentional coupling degree ranking results.

Ranking Results	**Vehicle Body**	**Grille**	**Vehicle Window**	**Vehicle Lights**	**Wheel Hub Cover**	**Vehicle Roof**
Vehicle Model	Flat and Segmented Type: (S_3)	Honeycomb Type (S_{13})	Integrated Left-Right Type (S_{18})	Linear Type (S_8)	Straight Cut Type (S_{24})	Integrated Curved Type (S_{20})
Case Study Images			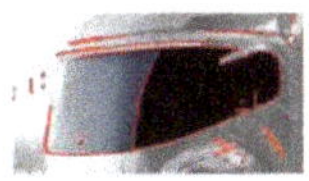	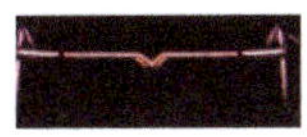		
Feature Line Extraction	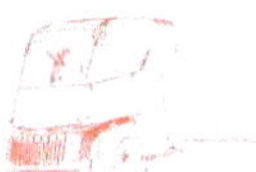		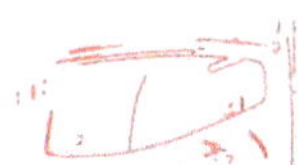		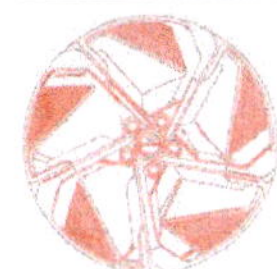	
Feature Line Deconstruction					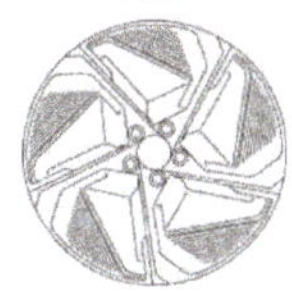	

In the body section, the lamps part of the intention coupling degree are overall high. The S8 linear lamps intention coupling degree is very high, and linear lamps are often fused with the body lines, forming a whole design language that enhances the overall sense of the vehicle. Next is the S10 bionic type. The intentional coupling is relatively high, the S13 honeycomb grid-like grille is selected, which implies strong power and solid performance, so that the vehicle has a more solid foundation and strong driving force. Because the new energy commercial vehicle does not need an air intake grille, the lighting grille texture is used to reflect the method. The windows use the left and right one-piece type, which scores much higher than other types and has a stronger sense of wholeness. The S20 roof curved one-piece type has a strong sense of overall curves, so the curves of the roof have a rounded transition with the curves of the front face. The S24 straight line cutting type has the highest coupling of the hubcaps, but the score of this style is the lowest when put on a whole vehicle, so it maintains the overall simple and smooth style, and locally adopts the delicate and unique style to show the character. The S24 linear cut wheel covers are the most popular style in the whole car, so to keep the simple and smooth style on the whole, use the exquisite and unique style on the local shape to show the individuality.

The final sorting will filter out the highest intentional coupling of the form, through the edge detection algorithms (such as the Canny operator or Roberts operator). To extract the parts of the form feature line, the Canny operator detects more details for the grille and hubcap. The rich details of the form can be used in this tool. These feature lines are processed using the Bezier curve drawing tool in the CorelDraw 2023 vector drawing software. With the help of AIGC technology, a variety of conceptual sketches and creative directions can be generated quickly to stimulate the creative inspirations of the design workers, greatly improve the efficiency of the creation, shorten the time required for the creation of the image, and provide a wealth of choices for the user [28–31]. This time, Stable Diffusion 3 software is used, mainly using the principle of Generative Adversarial Networks (GANs) to generate real images, and the low-dimensional feature vectors are converted into high-dimensional image data according to the analysis of the shape of the splines, line thickness, color, and other information.

3.5. Design Solution Selection and Verification

After the extracted spline is broken up and reorganized, the commands are input as required to transform the perceptual words into cue words recognizable by the AI, and the weight values are derived through AHP analysis and assigned to the cue words. For example, beautiful: 1.6 represents that the weight of the cue word is increased by 1.6 times, and the value is kept between 1 and 2 as much as possible for the best effect, as shown in Table 12.

Table 12. AIGC prompt word conversion and weighting.

Item	Kansei Words	Weight Value	Rank	AI Prompt Conversion: Weight
F_{11}	Texture (F_{11})	0.0853	4	High-Quality Texture:1.3
F_{12}	Aesthetic (F_{12})	0.1951	2	Aesthetically Pleasing:1.6
F_{13}	High-end (F_{13})	0.0853	4	High-End:1.3
F_{14}	Innovative (F_{14})	0.0397	9	Innovative:1.1
F_{21}	Flexible (F_{21})	0.0551	6	Versatile:1.2
F_{22}	Emotion (F_{22})	0.0132	10	Emotion-Rich:1
F_{23}	Technology (F_{23})	0.0466	8	Technological:1.1
F_{31}	Comfortable (F_{31})	0.1249	3	Comforting:1.4
F_{33}	Aerodynamic (F_{33})	0.0509	7	Streamlined Shape:1.2
F_{33}	Reasonable (F_{33})	0.3037	1	Well-Structured:1.7

In this paper, we first selected images for the S3 flat style model. Secondly, the local Lora model training environment was debugged, and an N-card RTX 4070 super graphics card was used for training. Then the selected images were preprocessed in high definition to unify their resolution as the base environment for training the model. Finally, the perceptual vocabulary was converted into AI-identified cue words for image generation to achieve the product effect image. For AIGC-generated solutions, eight designers were invited to screen the logical soundness of the solutions after the design was completed, and obvious errors due to AI operation logic were eliminated.

According to the weight ranking, the parameter values, such as its relevance and re-entry magnitude, were gradually reduced. The middle parameter values were selected and fine-tuned left and right, 200 effect diagrams were generated, and finally four new energy commercial heavy-duty trucks were selected, as shown in Figures 5–8. Seventy-five Kansei questionnaires were issued, with a result of seventy-one valid questionnaires which underwent evaluation screening. Questionnaire results data of the Clonbach coefficient are around 0.89, greater than 0.8, indicating that the results are valid. TOPSIS proximity is generally greater than 0.5, according to the questionnaire evaluation results sorting, and finally the program with the highest perceptual coupling as T3 was selected, as shown in Table 13.

Figure 5. Rendering T1.

Figure 6. Rendering T2.

Figure 7. Rendering T3.

Figure 8. Rendering T4.

Table 13. Scheme evaluation.

Item	Distance to Positive Ideal Solution ($D+$)	Distance to Negative Ideal Solution ($D-$)	Relative Closeness (C)	Rank
T_1	0.181	0.234	0.563	4
T_2	0.204	0.274	0.573	3
T_3	0.053	0.390	0.881	1
T_4	0.177	0.265	0.599	2

4. Discussion

This study is grounded in the solid theoretical foundation of Kansei engineering, skillfully integrating cutting-edge methodologies such as Artificial Intelligence (AI) image generation technology, with new energy commercial vehicles serving as the focus of in-depth research. Its core focus lies in leveraging scientific and advanced research techniques to efficiently and rationally uncover users' emotional resonance and aesthetic preferences towards the exterior design of new energy commercial vehicles. It is dedicated to exploring a pathway that precisely translates these deep-seated user needs into key elements of product exterior design, thereby giving rise to innovative design solutions that not only meet user expectations but also exhibit creativity.

Addressing the multifaceted complexity of emotion-driven design in the body shape design of new energy commercial vehicles, this study firstly proposes an innovative method integrating AHP (Analytic Hierarchy Process)-SD (Semantic Differential Method)-TOPSIS (Technique for Order Preference by Similarity to Ideal Solution)-AIGC (Artificial Intelligence Generated Content) for morphological design. This method aims to scientifically and precisely translate users' emotional needs into design elements for vehicle body shapes. Secondly, we extensively collect relevant information through mainstream search engines and literature searches, conducting thorough and detailed investigations and analyses to establish a sentiment evaluation sample library. This step provides abundant materials and references for subsequent morphological design. Then, based on the AHP method, we establish an index system of driving factors for the body shape design of new energy commercial vehicles. By classifying emotional vocabulary according to various levels of indicators and refining core semantic words, we further use the consistent matrix method to determine the weights of multi-dimensional factor indicators for body shape design. This process ensures that the selection of design elements not only aligns with users' emotional needs but also embodies scientific and rational design principles. Subsequently, based on the closeness values in TOPSIS, we prioritize the design schemes and derive the style morphology with the highest coupling degree to the emotional intentions of commercial vehicle users. This step effectively enhances the pertinence and effectiveness of the design, ensuring that the design scheme precisely meets users' aesthetic preferences. Finally, based on the symmetry of the vehicle body shape, we use edge detection algorithms to extract multiple local morphological style feature sample curves and fit their line shapes into the commercial vehicle body contours. On this basis, we utilize AIGC tools to generate innovative schemes and validate them through a case study of heavy-duty truck body shape design. The results indicate that this method can quickly generate multiple sets of design schemes that meet users' emotional needs and complete sentiment evaluations, thereby verifying the rationality and effectiveness of the research.

This study proposes a design process for the exterior of new energy commercial vehicles that integrates the concept of Kansei engineering with AHP (Analytic Hierarchy Process), SD (Semantic Differential Analysis), TOPSIS (Technique for Order of Preference by Similarity to Ideal Solution), and AIGC (Artificial Intelligence Generated Content) technologies. It achieves precision and objectivity in demand mining. We delve into how to scientifically and reasonably incorporate control conditions such as user needs, functional practicability, and market orientation into the AI image generation process, thereby efficiently producing a large number of conceptual sketches for new energy commercial vehicle body shapes that meet user expectations. Compared with AI-generated schemes that rely entirely on designers' individual creativity or lack refined conditional control, the method proposed in this study demonstrates significant advantages in objectivity, rigor, and accuracy. It not only substantially improves the overall efficiency and rationality of vehicle body exterior analysis and design but also effectively overcomes the limitations of traditional Kansei engineering methods in directly generating concrete product images. Meanwhile, this method addresses issues such as vague objectives and lack of theoretical support that may arise in the scheme generation process using a single AI tool, providing more reliable and objective guidance for final decisions in vehicle body design. Furthermore, the application of this process significantly shortens the cycle from conceptual design to mass production for automakers, bringing revolutionary changes to the design and development of new energy commercial vehicles. It not only provides automakers with more efficient and precise design tools but also points the way forward for the intelligent and personalized development of future automotive design.

5. Conclusions

This paper proposes a design approach for rapidly generating new energy commercial vehicle body shapes that align with market and user demands. This approach aids enterprises in swiftly and scientifically matching body shapes that conform to users' aesthetics and complete the design scheme for vehicle body shapes. The contributions and guiding significance are summarized as follows:

(1) This paper integrates the AHP-SD-TOPSIS method, firstly, through the pre-AHP hierarchical analysis method and Delphi expert group analysis method. The multi-dimensional, multi-angle, and multi-attribute commercial vehicle body shape driving elements are summarized. The whole product's intrinsic elements are more comprehensively expressed through the more accurately subdivided layered and condensed perpetual semantics. The consistency matrix is used to obtain the different perceptual semantic words between the weight relationship. By analyzing this data, the design of the body form can become more in line with the user's perceptual needs, making the design more scientific and with a greatly improved efficiency.

(2) This paper integrates the edge detection algorithm and the expert group method for cooperation, relying on the expert group to summarize the basic form of the product, and adopting the edge detection algorithm to classify the summarized product form. Compared with relying on the experience of individual experts, the lines extracted by the algorithm are more representative. The obtained classification of product outline features can effectively summarize the subjective preference of the expert panel for market style and design element samples.

(3) To simply and quickly obtain the user's perceptual evaluations of the product component styles, split the product structural components and conduct user questionnaire research on product component styles. After extracting the research data, collect the questionnaires and calculate their average values through the semantic difference scale (SD). Construct the evaluation data matrix and construct the weighting matrix by combining the AHP weights after the normalization of the matrix data.

(4) The TOPSIS method can be a good way to face this complex multi-factor evaluation decision-making system, and its proximity calculation can be a good response to the user's perceptual imagery of modeling coupling, which demonstrates that the higher

the value, the closer the user's imagery. The optimal solution that meets the user's expected preference can be derived after the screening of the solutions.

(5) Choosing the new energy commercial vehicle, an emerging transport product with user demand as the dominant consumer, as the research object not only verifies the reasonableness of the morphological design process in the paper but also fills the gap in the field of appearance design of this product, which will help its comprehensive development in the future.

The follow-up study will combine the complex network analysis method or introduce the fuzzy evaluation theory to study the relationship between the driving factors. In addition, the perceptual experiment will combine the most advanced design concepts at home and abroad, continue to enrich the local component elements, screen better experimental samples, and make the results more objective based on eye movement and EEG multimodal analysis. Although this study is based on the design and development background of Chinese commercial vehicles, the data collection and analysis involved in using this method are objective and universal, and therefore applicable to other cultural or regional backgrounds as well.

This research currently does not comprehensively cover the selection of local styling features for new energy commercial vehicles, such as not considered components like LiDAR and electronic rearview mirrors, and profit models. In the future, the Analytic Network Process (ANP) or the introduction of fuzzy evaluation theory will be combined to study the relationships among the driving elements of styling design. In terms of styling features, more local component elements can be adopted and combined with multimodal elements such as eye movement and electroencephalogram (EEG) analysis to further improve this design method.

Author Contributions: Conceptualization, B.L. and Z.H.; methodology, B.L.; software, B.L. and Z.H.; validation, B.L., Z.H., Y.L. and Z.W.; formal analysis, B.L.; investigation, B.L., Z.H., Y.L. and Z.W.; resources, B.L.; data curation, B.L.; writing—original draft preparation, investigation, B.L., Z.H., Y.L. and Z.W.; writing—review and editing, B.L. and Y.L.; visualization, B.L.; supervision, B.L., Z.H., Y.L. and Z.W.; project administration, B.L.; funding acquisition, B.L. All authors have read and agreed to the published version of the manuscript.

Funding: This research was funded by the National Social Science Fund of China (grant number: NO. 22BSH122),the Key R&D Project in Shaanxi Province (grant number: NO. 2022ZDLSF07-07), the Special Fund for Natural Sciences of Shaanxi Provincial Department of Education (grant number: NO. 23JK0567), and the Key R&D Project in Shaanxi Province (grant number: NO. 2025SF-YBXM-231).

Data Availability Statement: The datasets used during the current study are available from the corresponding author upon reasonable request.

Conflicts of Interest: Author Yuhang Liu was employed by the Dectron Future Automobile Technology Co., Ltd. The remaining authors declare that the research was conducted in the absence of any commercial or financial relationships that could be construed as a potential conflict of interest.

References

1. Liu, F. The Development Trend of Commercial Vehicles under Carbon Neutrality. *Auto Time* **2024**, *1*, 22–24.
2. Meng, Z.; Wang, D.; Zhang, X.; Zhang, Z.; Lian, F.; Chen, J. Integrated optimization design of lightweight and fatigue life for the integrated structure of cell-to-frame. *Automot. Eng.* **2024**, *46*, 2143–2153+2219.
3. Liu, Y.; Cao, Y.; Liu, C.; Zhang, D.; Liu, X.; Qiao, J.; Luo, G. Progress of energy and power system technologies for commercial vehicles under china's carbon peaking and carbon neutrality goals. *Chin. J. Automot. Eng.* **2022**, *12*, 478–494.
4. Zhang, X.; Yang, L.; Yang, Z.; Zhang, N. Research on driving mode control of new energy commercial vehicles. *Auto Electr. Parts* **2023**, 40–42. [CrossRef]
5. Gao, Y.; Qiao, H.; Chen, J.; Zhang, C.; Wang, D.; Sun, X. Design of the high-torque density permanent magnet synchronous motor used in nesw energy commercial vehicles. *Electr. Mach. Technol.* **2024**, *1*, 1–6.

6. Guo, H.; Li, Q.; Han, Y.; Zhao, W. Improvement analysis on the braking weakness of a new energy commercial vehicle. *Automob. Appl. Technol.* **2022**, *47*, 109–113.
7. Qin, G. New Energy Heavy-Duty Truck Styling Design Research and Application. Master's Thesis, Henan University of Technology, Zhengzhou, China, 2023.
8. Carreira, R.; Patrício, L.; Jorge, R.N.; Magee, C.L. Development of an extended Kansei engineering method to incorporate experience requirements in product–service system design. *J. Eng. Des.* **2013**, *24*, 738–764. [CrossRef]
9. Lu, W.; Ye, C.; Fang, Y.; Čok, V. A systematic review of Kansei engineering in vehicle design. *Digit. Eng.* **2024**, *3*, 100022. [CrossRef]
10. Su, J.; Hu, Q.; Zhang, S.; Yang, W.; Li, X. Research on coupling design characteristics for color-material-finishing of car body. *J. Mach. Des.* **2020**, *37*, 119–125.
11. Tian, Q.H.; Zhang, C.; Zhu, W.; Huang, J.K.; Zhang, Y.R.; Zhou, X.M. Study on fuzzy duration of serial coupled iterative design tasks in product development. *IOP Conf. Ser. Mater. Sci. Eng.* **2020**, *892*, 012080. [CrossRef]
12. Shi, X.; Guo, X.; Lu, Z.; Cheng, Y.; Wang, W.; Shen, H. CMF Design and Application of Chinese Elements in Cockpit Seat Based on Kansei Engineering. *Packag. Eng.* **2023**, *44*, 441–448.
13. Hu, W.; Zhao, J. Automobile styling gene evolution driven by users' expectation image. *J. Mech. Eng.* **2011**, *47*, 176–181. [CrossRef]
14. Ma, L.; Lu, J.; Shan, J.; Pan, W. Design method of automobile modeling feature line based on eye movement tracking. *Packag. Eng.* **2019**, *40*, 234–241.
15. Fu, L. Research on the Aesthetics of Automobile Body Modelling Design. Ph.D. Thesis, Jilin University, Changchun, China, 2009.
16. Li, Y.; Lu, C.; Liu, X.; Sheng, Z.; Cai, G. Gene network model of automobile styling design. *Comput. Integr. Manuf. Syst.* **2018**, *24*, 1249–1260.
17. Kady, C.; Jalloul, K.; Trousset, F.; Yaacoub, C.; Akl, A.; Daclin, N.; Zacharewicz, G. Addressing Business Process Deviations through the Evaluation of Alternative Pattern-Based Models. *Appl. Sci.* **2023**, *13*, 7722. [CrossRef]
18. Osgood, C.E.; Suci, G.J.; Tannenbaum, P.H. *The Measurement of Meaning*; University of Illinois Press: Chicago, IL, USA, 1957.
19. Raja, S.; Praveenkumar, V. Optimizing additive manufacturing parameters for graphene-reinforced PETG impeller production: A fuzzy AHP-TOPSIS approach. *Results Eng.* **2024**, *24*, 103018.
20. Tianxiong, W. A Novel Approach of Integrating Natural Language Processing Techniques with Fuzzy TOPSIS for Product Evaluation. *Symmetry* **2022**, *14*, 120. [CrossRef]
21. Su, J.; Chen, Y.; Jing, N.; Zhang, X. Coupling characteristics study in product image modeling design. *J. Mach. Des.* **2017**, *34*, 105–109.
22. Liu, L.; Zhen, G. Design of Portable Oxygen Concentrator Based on Kj-Ahp Method. *Design* **2023**, *36*, 112–115.
23. Lu, W.; Jiang, G.; Liu, Y.; Zhang, Y.; Zhang, Z. Kansei evaluation of interior layout design of business jet cockpit. *Comput. Integr. Manuf. Syst.* **2024**, *30*, 28–41.
24. Bi, Z.; Han, B. Anti-noise roberts edge detector. *Comput. Technol. Dev.* **2013**, *23*, 258–261.
25. Yoshihisa, S.; Hideki, A. Design System for Basic Shapes of Automatic Vehicles Using Sensory Language. *Proc. Acad. Lect. Precis. Eng. Soc.* **2003**, *2003*, 13.
26. Yang, L.; Xiang, Z.; Zhao, C.; Xu, J.; Gao, P. Exterior design for air rail train based on feature semantics and fuzzy analytic hierarchy process. *Packag. Eng.* **2024**, *45*, 150–157+167.
27. Liu, A.; Cheng, X.; Wang, M. Multiple affective responses design method of product based on kansei engineering and topsis-aism. *Packag. Eng.* **2024**, *45*, 183–193.
28. Du, Y.; Liu, X.; Cai, M.; Park, K. A Product's Kansei Appearance Design Method Based on Conditional-Controlled AI Image Generation. *Sustainability* **2024**, *16*, 8837. [CrossRef]
29. Wang, C.; Chung, J. Research on AI Painting Generation Technology Based on the [Stable Diffusion]. *Int. J. Adv. Smart Converg.* **2023**, *12*, 90–95.
30. Zhu, B.; Yang, C.; Yu, C.; An, F. Product image recognition based on deep learning. *J. Comput.-Aided Des. Comput. Graph.* **2018**, *30*, 1778–1784. [CrossRef]
31. Lai, X.; Zhang, S.; Mao, N.; Liu, J.; Chen, Q. Kansei engineering for new energy vehicle exterior design: An internet big data mining approach. *Comput. Ind. Eng.* **2022**, *165*, 107913. [CrossRef]

symmetry

MDPI

Article

An Intelligent Optimization Design Method for Furniture Form Considering Multi-Dimensional User Affective Requirements

Lei Fu [1], Xinyan Yang [1], Ling Zhu [1] and Jiufang Lv [1,2,*]

[1] College of Furnishings and Industrial Design, Nanjing Forestry University, Nanjing 210037, China; fu1181149050@163.com (L.F.)
[2] Co-Innovation Center of Efficient Processing and Utilization of Forest Resources, Nanjing Forestry University, Nanjing 210037, China
* Correspondence: lvjiufang8189@njfu.edu.cn

Abstract: A pervasive cognitive asymmetry exists between designers and users, and contemporary furniture form design often struggles to accommodate and balance multi-dimensional user affective requirements. To address these challenges, this study proposes an intelligent optimization design method for furniture form that enhances the universality of user research and the balance of design decision-making. First, representative URs are extracted from online user review texts collected through web crawling. These URs are then classified into three-dimensional quality attributes using the refined Kano's model, thereby identifying the key URs. Second, a decomposition table of furniture design characteristics (DCs) is constructed. Third, the multi-objective red-billed blue magpie optimizer (MORBMO) is employed to automatically generate a Pareto solution set that satisfies the multi-dimensional key URs, from which the final optimal solution is determined. The proposed method improves the objectivity and granularity of user research, assists furniture enterprises in prioritizing product development, and enhances user satisfaction across multiple affective dimensions. Furthermore, it provides enterprises with flexible choices among diverse alternatives, thereby mitigating the asymmetry inherent in furniture form design.

Keywords: multi-dimensional user affective requirements; furniture form design; the refined Kano's model; multi-objective red-billed blue magpie optimizer (MORBMO); Ming-style furniture

1. Introduction

In today's highly competitive market environment, most product companies place great emphasis on satisfying consumer needs [1], including both functional and emotional demands. When consumers perceive that their needs are reflected in new products, their satisfaction levels tend to increase [2]. With the widespread adoption of modern mechanized and intelligent manufacturing technologies [3], the differences in quality, structure, and functionality among furniture products have gradually diminished. As a result, traditional approaches such as structural design [4], functional improvement [5], and ergonomic studies [6] are no longer sufficient to ensure a competitive advantage in the consumer market. Increasingly, scholars are turning their attention to optimizing furniture form [7] to meet users' higher-level affective requirements. On the other hand, in the era of the experience economy, consumers, having met their basic material needs, now demand enhanced emotional experiences from products [8]. The sensory characteristics

https://doi.org/10.3390/sym17091406

of a product play a critical role in consumer acceptance and decision-making [9]. Human beings predominantly acquire information from the external world through visual perception [10]. The explicit form of a product creates a first impression by stimulating visual senses, which in turn shapes users' perceptual experiences and influences their purchasing behavior. Therefore, product manufacturers must consider leveraging form innovation to meet emotional demands, launch emotionally resonant products, enhance user satisfaction, and ultimately gain substantial market returns [11]. However, there are significant challenges. On one hand, current product form development is overly reliant on the experience and personal judgment of designers. Design departments often spend excessive time on repeated modifications, leading to inefficiency. On the other hand, cognitive asymmetries between designers and users often hinder products from meeting consumer expectations. These asymmetries arise from differences in knowledge, education, and product understanding. As a result, enterprises struggle to identify key affective requirements and translate them into design elements. The subjective nature of design intensifies this problem. It causes repeated trial-and-error cycles, which extend development time and increase costs. Therefore, design decision-making is critical to business strategy and performance [12,13]. To address these issues, this study proposes a consumer-centered approach. The method integrates Kansei engineering (KE), big data analytics, and artificial intelligence. KE provides a framework to link user perceptions with design elements. Big data extracts authentic consumer insights and reduces the cognitive gap between designers and users. Intelligent optimization techniques satisfy multi-dimensional emotional needs and improve the efficiency of product development.

KE is defined as a methodology that translates consumers' feelings and impressions of a product into design elements [14]. This approach aligns with the current trend of consumer-centered product development and aims to provide product functions and design features that embody and respond to users' affective perceptions [2]. However, traditional KE approaches still exhibit certain limitations.

First, the identification of key URs and the determination of their corresponding weights are foundational to bridging the gap between the user and design domains. They also play a critical role in setting priorities for product development. Currently, traditional KE methods collect Kansei-related terms through two main channels to identify URs: (1) prior research findings documented in the academic literature or professional publications [15], and (2) direct user interviews. These methods often fall short in terms of timeliness, objectivity, and efficiency. Online review data, by contrast, have become one of the most influential sources of information affecting consumer decisions. They provide a direct link between products and real user experiences [16]. While online reviews are commonly used in sentiment analysis and feature extraction research [17], they have been infrequently applied within KE frameworks. On the other hand, user requirements often exhibit qualitative characteristics. After gathering user needs, Kano's model [18] is commonly used to analyze the implicit relationship between product attributes and consumer satisfaction. It enables the classification of quality attributes into four types: "attractive quality", "one-dimensional quality", "must-be quality", and "indifferent quality". However, Kano's model only supports coarse-grained classification of URs and lacks the capacity to determine their relative importance or weights in a detailed manner. To date, there is limited research that leverages online review data to perform both fine-grained classification and weighting of user requirements within a KE framework.

Second, once the key URs have been identified, constructing a mapping model between URs and DCs to determine the optimal design solution is a core component of KE. In addition to traditional linear models—such as Multiple Linear Regression and Quantification Theory Type I—many advanced algorithms have been introduced in recent years to build nonlinear models, thanks to the rapid advancement of artificial intelligence technologies. These include BackPropagation Neural Networks (BPNNs), Support Vector Regression (SVR), and Long Short-Term Memory (LSTM) networks. By learning from user evaluation data, such models can predict the effectiveness of furniture features and help generate optimized design solutions that meet specific URs. While these studies have advanced the automation of furniture development and improved the precision of design decision-making, they predominantly focus on single-objective optimization, i.e., optimizing product forms for a single user requirement. The need to simultaneously address multiple dimensions of emotional user needs has not been adequately emphasized. In reality, engineering design problems are typically multi-objective in nature [19]. Human emotional responses to products are likewise multifaceted [20]. Specifically, users often present complex and diverse requirements, and in real-world scenarios—such as product usage or purchasing decisions—they expect products to satisfy multiple needs concurrently, rather than just a single aspect.

In summary, the asymmetry commonly observed in user research and optimization design processes often results in final products that fail to meet the genuine requirements of users. This, in turn, hinders furniture enterprises—despite significant resource investment—from gaining a competitive edge in the consumer market. In the design framework proposed by this study, user elements and furniture elements together form an integrated design system. User elements encompass actual URs from various sources and levels of granularity, while furniture elements include deconstructed DCs and form components. In this study, "symmetry" is defined as the internal equilibrium of a design system that integrates both elements, which is achieved through furniture forms that effectively fulfill users' affective requirements. Specifically, at the user research level, large volumes of authentic online user reviews from diverse sources are employed to address cognitive and preference asymmetries between designers and users. At the optimization design level, multi-objective optimization is used to overcome the limitations of single-objective approaches, which often fail to balance and fulfill users' multi-dimensional affective requirements. Thus, this study aims to explore the phenomena of symmetry and asymmetry in the field of morphological design and proposes an intelligent optimization design method for furniture forms that considers users' multi-dimensional affective requirements.

Accordingly, this study identifies two key research questions (RQs) that require urgent attention. RQ1: how can authentic URs be extracted from widely sourced online consumer reviews, and how can the key requirements that contribute most to enhancing user satisfaction be identified? RQ2: once the key URs are determined, how can a multi-objective optimization approach be constructed to ensure that new product forms simultaneously accommodate these multi-dimensional affective requirements?

To address these RQs, this study proposes two main solutions:

(1) For RQ1, this study integrates online review data and the refined Kano's model to develop a big-data-driven approach to user research. In the field of product form design, few researchers have applied this enhanced Kano's model. The method begins by crawling massive amounts of online user reviews as data sources, which are then automatically processed using NLP techniques. Online review data are voluntarily generated by real consumers [21,22], and compared to traditional surveys or interviews, such publicly available data reduce the subjectivity and cost of user research. The improved Kano model overcomes the limitations of the traditional model by enabling fine-grained quality classification and importance weighting of URs. This provides valuable insights into the nuanced and dynamic needs of consumers and effectively bridges the cognitive gap between designers and users.

(2) For RQ2, an integrated design method combining MORBMO and VIKOR is introduced. Specifically, MORBMO is employed to solve the multi-objective optimization problem of furniture form design, thereby enabling product solutions to balance multiple affective requirements of users. The MORBMO algorithm [23] simulates the magpie's food storage behavior to retain superior solutions and balances exploration and exploitation through food searching and attacking strategies, effectively avoiding local optima. In addition, the multi-criteria decision-making method VIKOR [24] is employed to assist the design team in selecting the optimal solution from the Pareto front. Compared to traditional design methods that generate only a single optimized solution for a single user requirement, the integrated approach of multi-objective optimization and multi-attribute decision-making offers greater flexibility and realism. It supports the development of multiple candidate solutions, each balancing different user demands, thereby ensuring the final product aligns with various consumer expectations. This not only reduces the trial-and-error cost for design teams but also helps companies gain a competitive edge in the market at a lower cost.

The structure of this paper is organized as follows: Section 2 presents a comprehensive review of the relevant theories and methods. Section 3 introduces the methodologies employed in this study. Section 4 validates the proposed model using a real-world case study. Section 5 discusses the results and implications of the case. Section 6 concludes this paper by summarizing its contributions and limitations.

2. Literature Review

2.1. Kansei Engineering

Kansei engineering is a methodology proposed by Nagamachi from the Faculty of Engineering at Hiroshima University in Japan in the late 20th century, aimed at addressing users' affective requirements by exploring the relationship between users' Kansei (affective impressions) and the physical characteristics of products. This approach opened up a new field within human factors engineering and aligned with the evolving trends in modern product design. Its effectiveness has been demonstrated through successful applications in companies such as Mazda, Samsung, and Matsushita Electric Works [14], and an increasing number of academic studies on KE have since been published. KE typically comprises three core stages: construction of the Kansei semantic space, construction of the design element space, and development of the correlation model. Traditional KE relies on statistical analysis methods to establish relationships between psychological and physical variables. For example, Kittidecha and Marasinghe [25] applied the Response Surface Methodology (RSM) to determine optimal design parameters of wine glass under different emotional demands. Smith and Fu [26] combined factor analysis and cluster analysis to construct a semantic space, and then used Quantification Theory Type I to build associations between representative Kansei factors and the design attributes of an automobile head-up display (HUD). In recent years, KE has actively incorporated various interdisciplinary methods to form novel methodological models, thus expanding its capabilities. For instance, Hartono et al. [27] applied Kano's model to classify logistics service attributes in service design, and then used QFD to construct a correlation matrix between important attributes and modular systems. Zhou et al. [28] integrated fuzzy logic models based on Grey Relational Analysis (GRA) within the KE framework and achieved high prediction accuracy in the morphological design of electric recliner chairs. Woo et al. [29] employed natural language processing (NLP) to extract product review texts, used factor analysis and cluster analysis to identify perceptual impressions, and then applied an artificial intelligence technique—BPNN—to map semantic data to product design elements, thereby enabling an electric toothbrush design. Fu et al. [30] used game theory to identify key URs and then applied

PSO-SVR to establish a predictive model linking these key URs to the morphology of Ming-style chairs. Cai et al. [31] employed a GWO-BPNN to model the mathematical relationship between wheelchair form elements and user emotions. Wang et al. [32] first used factor analysis to identify key Kansei factors and then combined eye-tracking data from users with expert evaluation to determine critical design features. Finally, they proposed an enhanced algorithm that integrates the Sparrow Search Algorithm (SSA), Long Short-Term Memory (LSTM) networks, and an attention mechanism (SSA-LSTM-Attention) to construct a correlation model between user emotion and design features, significantly enhancing the emotional experience of users in the intelligent cockpit of new energy vehicles (NEVICs). The methodological comparison between this study and previous research is presented in Table 1.

Table 1. The methodological comparison between this study and previous research.

Publication	Research Filed	Main Methods	Main Contributions
This study (2025)	Ming-style square stool	The refined Kano's model, MORBMO	An intelligent optimization design method that considers multi-dimensional user affective requirements was constructed
Kittidecha and Marasinghe [25] (2015)	Wine glass	RSM, Multiple Regression Analysis	A morphological design model was constructed to interpret user emotional responses
Smith and Fu [26] (2011)	Automobile head-up display	FA, CA, QT1	A statistical prediction model was created to link representative affective elements with product physical attributes
Hartono et al. [27] (2017)	Logistics service	Kano's model, QFD	A composite model was proposed to enhance user emotional satisfaction
Zhou et al. [28] (2023)	Electric recliner chair	GRA	A fuzzy logic model integrated with GRA was established
Woo et al. [29] (2022)	Electric toothbrush	BPNN	Intelligent prediction of product form was achieved using machine learning algorithms
Fu et al. [30] (2024)	Ming-style armchair	GT, PSO-SVR	An evaluation and design method based on GT and PSO-SVR was constructed
Wang et al. [32] (2024)	Intelligent cockpit	SSA-LSTM-Attention	A product form prediction model based on an improved LSTM was constructed

RSM: Response Surface Methodology; FA: Factor Analysis; CA: Cluster Analysis; QT1: Quantification Theory Type I; QFD: Quality Function Deployment; GRA: Grey Relational Analysis; BPNN: Back Propagation Neural Network; GT: Game Theory; PSO-SVR: Particle Swarm Optimization–Support Vector Regression; SSA: Sparrow Search Algorithm; LSTM: Long Short-Term Memory.

2.2. The Refined Kano's Model

Kano's model [18], proposed by Japanese scholar Noriaki Kano in 1984, is a two-dimensional quality classification model designed to analyze the relationship between customer requirements and satisfaction. This model overcomes the limitations of traditional one-dimensional quality analysis, which assumes that customer satisfaction always increases with the degree of quality fulfillment—a premise that does not always hold true [33]. Instead, the Kano model considers both the degree of quality and the corresponding level of customer satisfaction, classifying quality attributes into five categories: attractive quality, one-dimensional quality, must-be quality, indifferent quality, and reverse quality. The model has been widely applied across fields such as product design, service industries, and real estate. For instance, Yang et al. [34] applied Kano's model in drone design to classify design elements, helping designers identify key influencing factors. Qu et al. [35] applied the fuzzy Kano's model to classify a large number of user requirements, providing design direction for a smart blood pressure monitor.

However, the traditional Kano's model does not incorporate attribute weighting and fails to reflect the relative importance of individual quality indicators within each category [36]. The extent to which quality attributes influence consumers is strongly associated with the level of importance that consumers assign to them [37]. To address this issue, Yang [36] proposed a refined version of Kano's model by extending the original four quality types into eight subcategories: highly attractive and less attractive, high value-added and low value-added, critical and necessary, and potential and care-free. This refined model offers a higher level of granularity and includes attribute weights, thereby enabling businesses and designers to better understand and prioritize user needs. Chen et al. [38], for example, employed the refined Kano's model to classify and evaluate the quality of pharmaceutical logistics services, providing strategic insights for suppliers. However, despite its potential, this refined model has been rarely applied in the field of product design and Kansei engineering to date.

2.3. Multi-Objective Red-Billed Blue Magpie Optimizer

The red-billed blue magpie optimizer (RBMO) is a novel metaheuristic algorithm proposed by Fu et al. [23] in 2024. Inspired by the intelligent behavior of birds, this algorithm mimics the way individuals in a red-billed blue magpie flock share information and collaborate to find optimal solutions. It effectively avoids getting trapped in local optima by combining small-group cooperation with global population-level searches. Its food-storing mechanism allows the algorithm to retain high-quality solutions, contributing to its stable performance in both benchmark tests and real-world engineering problems. For example, Sivabalan and Minu [39] employed RBMO to enhance the weight parameters of an MSTCNN classifier in order to improve the accuracy of automobile sales prediction. The multi-objective red-billed blue magpie optimizer (MORBMO) is a further extension of the RBMO, designed specifically to address multi-objective engineering optimization problems. For instance, Wang et al. [40] applied the MORBMO to optimize the configuration of photovoltaic energy storage systems in power grids, achieving significant improvements in overall grid performance.

In the field of industrial design, machine learning algorithms are commonly used to optimize product forms [29,41]. However, to date, few studies have applied metaheuristic algorithms like the MORBMO to the multi-objective optimization of furniture form. This gap in research undoubtedly limits the potential for further innovation and market competitiveness in the furniture industry.

3. Methods

The framework of the intelligent optimization design method for furniture form proposed in this study is illustrated in Figure 1 and consists of the following stages:

Phase 1: Identification of key user requirements. Consumer online reviews are collected using the Octopus web crawler, and the textual data are preprocessed accordingly. The Jieba tool is employed for word segmentation and part-of-speech tagging to extract Kansei words that represent consumers' affective requirements. Then, the semantic similarity between these requirements is calculated using cosine similarity based on the Word2Vec model. Finally, the refined Kano's model is applied to perform fine-grained classification and weighting of the representative user requirements, resulting in the identification of key user requirements.

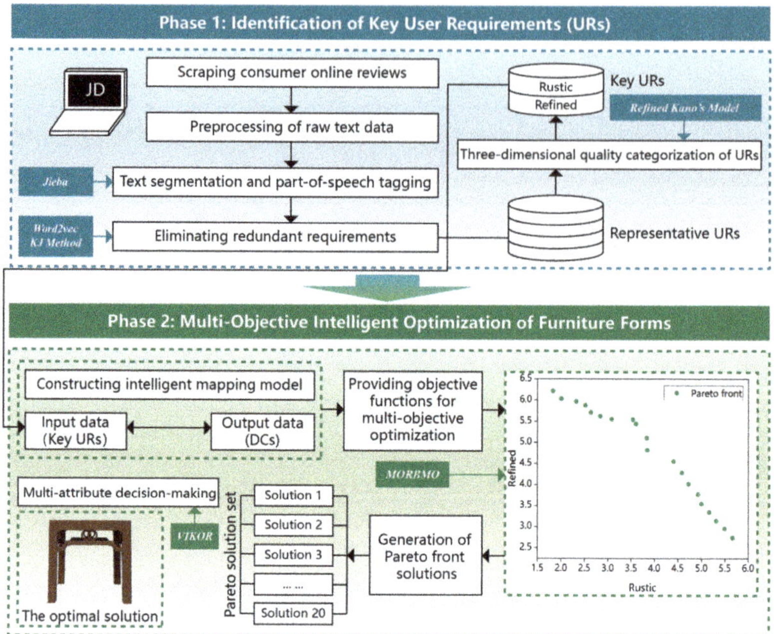

Figure 1. The framework of the intelligent optimization design method for furniture form.

Phase 2: Multi-objective intelligent optimization of furniture form. A mapping model constructed using Support Vector Regression (SVR) provides the objective functions for multi-objective optimization. Subsequently, the MORBMO algorithm is used to generate a Pareto front of optimal solutions, and its performance is compared with two other multi-objective optimization algorithms—MOSSA and MOPSO. The final optimal solution is determined using the VIKOR method.

3.1. Determination of Key User Requirements (URs)

3.1.1. Data Acquisition and Preprocessing

User research begins with the acquisition and preprocessing of user review data. Online consumer reviews are collected using web scraping technology and saved in .txt files (UTF-8 format), which are easily processed by Python 3.7.0. After reading the raw dataset, text cleaning is conducted, including the removal of special characters and punctuation marks, elimination of overly short texts, and deletion of duplicate comments. The Jieba tool is used for word segmentation, stop word removal, and part-of-speech tagging. Adjectives are extracted from the texts to build an adjective corpus.

3.1.2. Screening of Representative URs Utilizing Word2vec and KJ Method

Semantic similarity of Kansei words in terms of emotional orientation is preferably assessed using cosine similarity, as it focuses more on the directional difference between vectors compared to Euclidean distance, which emphasizes magnitude. The Word2Vec model evaluates the semantic relationships between words by analyzing their vector representations, and cosine similarity is employed to compute the angular distance between word vectors in the semantic space. The similarity between two Kansei words and y is calculated using the cosine similarity formula, as shown in Equation (1):

$$Similarity(\theta, y) = \frac{\sum_{t=1}^{q} (\theta_t \times y_t)}{\sqrt{\sum_{t=1}^{q} (\theta_t)^2} \times \sqrt{\sum_{t=1}^{q} (y_t)^2}}. \quad (1)$$

After calculating semantic similarities, a focus group uses the KJ method to manually cluster and organize the vocabulary, eliminating semantically redundant or highly similar words. These two methods complement each other to filter out the most representative user requirements. Through this process, the Kansei vocabulary dictionary is successfully constructed.

3.1.3. Classification and Weights Calculation for Representative URs Utilizing the Refined Kano's Model

The refined Kano's model is used to perform three-dimensional quality classification and importance weighting of representative URs. It assists designers in clarifying the hierarchical relationships among URs, identifying key requirements, and defining the direction for product development. The refined Kano questionnaire is shown in Figure 2. Building on the original Kano's model, the refined Kano's model introduces an importance evaluation system, addressing the traditional model's limitation in precisely measuring quality attributes. The implementation steps of the refined Kano's model proposed in this study are as follows:

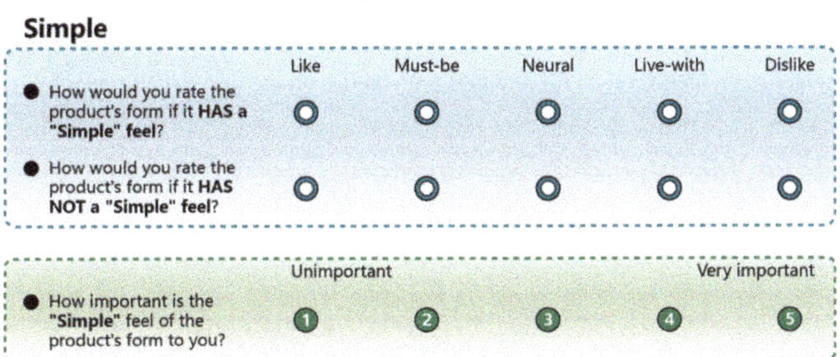

Figure 2. The refined Kano's model questionnaire.

Step 1: The quality classification module of the refined Kano's model consists of a pair of bidirectional qualitative questions. After collecting the responses, the most frequent classification result is determined using the Kano evaluation table. The quality attributes include attractive quality, one-dimensional quality, must-be quality, indifferent quality, reverse quality, and questionable quality. The better–worse calculation divides the results into four quadrants. Satisfaction and dissatisfaction coefficients are calculated using Equations (2) and (3), respectively:

$$SI_i = \frac{A_i + O_i}{A_i + O_i + M_i + I_i} \quad (2)$$

$$DSI_i = -1\frac{M_i + O_i}{A_i + O_i + M_i + I_i}, \quad (3)$$

where A_i, O_i, M_i, and I_i represent the proportions of the i-th user requirement in each quality classification category.

Step 2: The importance evaluation module uses a 5-point Likert scale, ranging from not important, less important, moderately important, important, to very important. The average importance score for each requirement is computed using Equation (4).

$$ID_i = \overline{X} = \frac{1}{N}\sum_{j=1}^{N} X_{ij}, \quad (4)$$

where X_{ij} represents the evaluation score given by the j-th user for the i-th user requirement, and N denotes the total number of users.

Step 3: By integrating the results from Steps 1 and 2, each user requirement is classified into a three-dimensional quality category, as shown in Table 2, which provides finer granularity compared to traditional two-dimensional classification. A visualization of the refined Kano's model is presented in Figure 3.

Table 2. Three-dimensional quality category.

Categories of Quality Attributes in Traditional Kano's Model	Categories of Quality Attributes with High Importance in the Refined Kano's Model	Categories of Quality Attributes with Low Importance in the Refined Kano's Model
Attractive	Highly Attractive	Less Attractive
One-dimensional	High value-added	Low value-added
Must-be	Critical	Necessary
Indifferent	Potential	Care-free

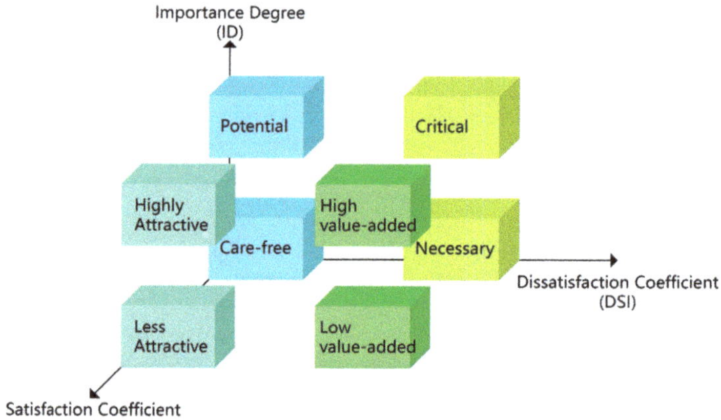

Figure 3. The refined Kano's model.

3.2. Multi-Objective Optimization and Decision-Making for Furniture Form

3.2.1. Multi-Objective Optimization of Furniture Form Utilizing MORBMO

This novel metaheuristic algorithm performs the optimization task by simulating the biological behaviors of red-billed blue magpies, such as searching, chasing, attacking prey, and food storage.

(1) Population Initialization: candidate solutions are initialized using Equation (5).

$$X = \begin{bmatrix} x_{1,1} & \cdots & x_{1,j} & x_{1,\dim-1} & x_{1,\dim} \\ x_{2,1} & \cdots & x_{2,j} & \cdots & x_{2,\dim} \\ \cdots & \cdots & x_{i,j} & \cdots & \cdots \\ \vdots & \vdots & \vdots & \vdots & \vdots \\ x_{n-1,1} & \cdots & x_{n-1,j} & \cdots & x_{n-1,\dim} \\ x_{n,1} & \cdots & x_{n,j} & x_{n,\dim-1} & x_{n,\dim} \end{bmatrix}, \quad (5)$$

where X represents the search agent positions generated by Equation (6), n denotes the population size, and dim is the dimensionality of the problem.

$$x_{i,j} = (ub - lb) \times Rand_1 + lb, \quad (6)$$

where ub and lb refer to the upper and lower bounds of the problem, respectively, and $Rand$ is a random number in the range [0, 1].

(2) Food Searching: In this phase, several red-billed blue magpies adopt different strategies to search for prey. Individuals in small groups use Equation (7), while those in larger groups utilize Equation (8) to complete the search task.

$$X^i(t+1) = X^i(t) + (\frac{1}{p} \times \sum_{m=1}^{p} X^m(t) - X^{rs}(t)) \times Rand_2 \quad (7)$$

$$X^i(t+1) = X^i(t) + (\frac{1}{q} \times \sum_{m=1}^{q} X^m(t) - X^{rs}(t)) \times Rand_3, \quad (8)$$

where t denotes the current iteration number, p represents the number of individuals in the small group, and q refers to the number of individuals in the large group. $X^i(t+1)$ indicates the new position of the i-th search agent, X_i is the current position of the i-th individual, X^m represents a randomly selected individual from the population, and $X^{rs}(t)$ refers to a randomly chosen search agent during the current iteration.

(3) Attacking Food: Once food is located, the red-billed blue magpies initiate their attack behavior. Small groups target smaller prey, as described in Equation (9), while larger groups attack larger prey, as shown in Equation (10).

$$X^i(t+1) = X^{food}(t) + CF \times (\frac{1}{p} \times \sum_{m=1}^{p} X^m(t) - X^i(t)) \times Randn_1 \quad (9)$$

$$X^i(t+1) = X^i(t) + (\frac{1}{q} \times \sum_{m=1}^{q} X^m(t) - X^{rs}(t)) \times Rand_3, \quad (10)$$

where $X^{food}(t)$ denotes the position of the food, and $Randn$ represents a random number drawn from a standard normal distribution (with a mean of 0 and a standard deviation of 1). $CF = (1 - (\frac{t}{T}))^{(2 \times \frac{t}{T})}$.

(4) Storing Food: After attacking the food, the red-billed blue magpies store it for future use. This behavior is analogous to preserving solution information to help individuals locate the global optimum. The food storage mechanism is described in Equation (11).

$$X^i(t+1) = \begin{cases} X^i(t) & if\ fitness^i_{old} > fitness^i_{new} \\ X^i(t+1) & else \end{cases}, \quad (11)$$

where $fitness^i_{old}$ denotes the fitness value of the i-th individual before the update, and $fitness^i_{new}$ represents the fitness value after the update.

In addition, this study introduces four metrics—inverted generational distance (IGD), generational distance (GD), hypervolume (HV), and spacing metric (Spacing)—to comprehensively evaluate the algorithm's performance.

The IGD measures the extent to which the obtained solution set covers the reference Pareto front. A smaller IGD value indicates better convergence and diversity. For each solution in the reference Pareto front, the closest solution in the obtained set is identified, and the Euclidean distance is calculated.

$$IGD = \frac{\sum_{i=1}^{|P^*|} \min_{x \in P} dis(y,x)}{|P^*|}, \tag{12}$$

where $dis(y, x)$ denotes the Euclidean distance between a point in the reference set P^* and a point in the obtained solution set P.

The GD evaluates the proximity of the obtained solution set to the reference Pareto front (RPF). This metric calculates the average distance from each point in the obtained solution set to the RPF. A smaller GD value indicates better convergence; a GD value of zero means that all solutions lie exactly on the RPF.

$$GD = \sqrt{\frac{\sum_{i=1}^{|P|} \min_{x^* \in P^*} dis(x,y)^2}{|P|}}. \tag{13}$$

The HV measures the volume of the objective space covered by the obtained solution set with respect to a reference point. This metric simultaneously assesses both the spread and quality of the solution set.

$$HV = Volume\left(\bigcup_{i=1}^{|S|} v_i\right), \tag{14}$$

where $|S|$ represents the number of non-dominated solutions, and v_i denotes the hypervolume formed between the reference point and the i-th solution in the set. A larger HV value indicates better diversity and convergence of the solution set.

Spacing evaluates the uniformity of the distribution of solutions within the set. A smaller spacing value indicates a more evenly distributed solution set. This metric calculates the standard deviation of the distances between adjacent solutions.

$$Spacing = \sqrt{\frac{1}{|P|-1}\sum_{i=1}^{|P|} \left(\bar{d} - d_i\right)^2}, \tag{15}$$

where $\bar{d}$ represents the mean of all d_i values.

3.2.2. Multi-Criteria Decision-Making of Pareto Solutions Utilizing the VIKOR Method

(1) The decision matrix X is normalized, as all the criteria in this study are benefit-type indicators. The normalization process is carried out using Equation (16). Assuming there are n alternatives and m evaluation criteria, the normalized matrix X' is obtained as shown in Equation (17).

$$x'_{ij} = x_{ij} / \sqrt{\sum_{i=1}^{n} x_{ij}^2} \tag{16}$$

$$X' = \begin{bmatrix} x'_{11} & x'_{12} & \cdots & x'_{1m} \\ x'_{21} & x'_{22} & \cdots & x'_{2m} \\ \vdots & \vdots & \ddots & \vdots \\ x'_{n1} & x'_{n2} & \cdots & x'_{nm} \end{bmatrix}. \tag{17}$$

(2) Based on the normalized matrix X' obtained in the previous step, the positive ideal solution and negative ideal solution are determined, as shown in Equation (18).

$$\begin{cases} x_i^+ = (\max\{x'_{11}, x'_{21}, \ldots, x'_{n1}\}, \max\{x'_{12}, x'_{22}, \ldots, x'_{n2}\}, \ldots, \max\{x'_{1m}, x'_{2m}, \ldots, x'_{nm}\}) \\ x_i^- = (\min\{x'_{11}, x'_{21}, \ldots, x'_{n1}\}, \min\{x'_{12}, x'_{22}, \ldots, x'_{n2}\}, \ldots, \min\{x'_{1m}, x'_{2m}, \ldots, x'_{nm}\}) \end{cases}. \tag{18}$$

(3) Using Equations (19) and (20), the group utility value S_i and individual regret value R_i for each alternative are calculated.

$$S_i = \sum_{j=1}^{m} w_j \frac{x_j^+ - x'_{ij}}{x_j^+ - x_j^-} \tag{19}$$

$$R_i = \max_i w_j \frac{x_j^+ - x'_{ij}}{x_j^+ - x_j^-}. \tag{20}$$

(4) Based on the group utility value S_i and individual regret value R_i of each alternative, a compromise solution value Q_i is determined using a weighted method, as shown in Equation (21).

$$Q_i = v\frac{S_i - S^-}{S^+ - S^-} + (1 - v)\frac{R_i - R^-}{R^+ - R^-} \tag{21}$$

In Equation (21), v is the weight of the decision-making strategy, where $v \in [0, 1]$. When $v = 0.5$, it indicates a decision-making mechanism based on consensus. When $v < 0.5$, the decision favors the strategy that minimizes individual regret. When $v > 0.5$, the decision favors the strategy that maximizes group utility. In general, v is set to the neutral value (0.5).

4. Empirical Study

4.1. Determination of Key User Requirements

4.1.1. Data Acquisition and Preprocessing

The identification of key URs is essential for guiding subsequent product development strategies, as Kansei words directly reflects users' affective requirements. JD.com, one of the largest e-commerce platforms in China, offers a vast variety of products and a large consumer base, while actively encouraging customers to share their opinions. The massive volume of user reviews available on this platform provides researchers with authentic, objective, and representative data for conducting user studies—offering a clear advantage over traditional sources such as literature reviews, user reports, or expert interviews.

Accordingly, this study takes Ming-style furniture as a research case. Fourteen representative products from different brands—selected based on high sales and review counts—were chosen as the data source. Using the BAZHUAYU web scraping tool, a total of 143,524 characters of raw user reviews were collected and saved in UTF-8 encoded.txt files. Subsequently, the raw text data underwent preprocessing using Python 3.7.0. First, special characters and punctuation marks were removed from the review texts. Then, invalid reviews were filtered out by removing entries that were too short (fewer than five characters) or duplicated.

After text cleaning, the Jieba package was used for Chinese word segmentation, stop word removal, and part-of-speech tagging. A stop word list developed by Harbin Institute of Technology was used to eliminate non-informative words, and adjectives within the reviews were finally tagged for further analysis.

4.1.2. Screening of Representative URs Utilizing Word2vec and KJ Method

A combined approach of semantic similarity computation and focus group discussion was employed to filter out representative URs and avoid redundant entries with similar meanings. First, to enhance model performance, the study utilized the gensim package to load a pre-trained Word2Vec model based on a Chinese Wikipedia corpus. This model was used to obtain vector representations of 18 initial URs and to compute the cosine similarity between them. Next, a cosine similarity heatmap of these URs was generated using the matplotlib package, as shown in Figure 4. A similarity threshold of 0.7 was set, and pairwise comparisons were conducted to identify semantically redundant terms. Specifically, it was found that the similarity between "refined" and terms such as "exquisite", "meticulous", and "ornate" exceeded the threshold of 0.7, indicating that these requirements convey highly overlapping meanings. In addition, the similarity between "exquisite" and "delicate", "ornate", and "tasteful" was also above the threshold; between "substantial" and "weighty" above the threshold; between "towering" and "robust" above the threshold; between "meticulous" and "delicate" above the threshold; between "delicate" and "graceful" above the threshold; between "ornate" and "tasteful" and "rustic" above the threshold; between "weighty" and "rustic" above the threshold; between "excellent" and "superb" above the threshold; between "elegant" and "tasteful" and "graceful" above the threshold; between "dignified" and "composed" above the threshold; between "tasteful" and "rustic" and "understated" above the threshold; between "radiant" and "graceful" and "vibrant" above the threshold; and between "vibrant" and "understated" above the threshold. Subsequently, redundant requirements with high similarity were removed. Finally, a focus group applied the KJ method to manually classify and analyze the filtered URs, verifying and eliminating entries with overlapping meanings. Through this two-step screening process, a final set of 11 representative URs was retained: "refined", "comfortable", "sturdy", "substantial", "towering", "simple", "uniform", "elegant", "luxurious", "rustic", and "vibrant". These representative URs collectively formed the Kansei dictionary.

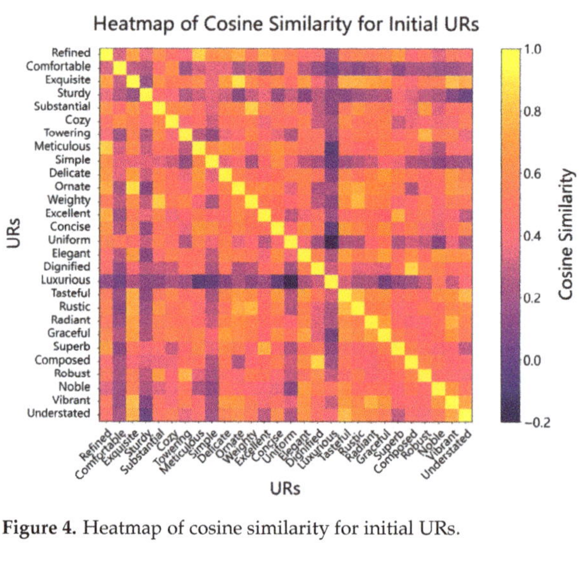

Figure 4. Heatmap of cosine similarity for initial URs.

4.1.3. Classification and Wights Calculation for Representative URs Utilizing the Refined Kano's Model

After obtaining the representative URs, the refined Kano's model proposed in this study was applied to perform three-dimensional quality classification and weight calculation of the representative URs, in order to further identify the key URs. First, the refined Kano's model questionnaire, as described in Section 3.1.3, was distributed to 88 participants with prior experience using Ming-style furniture. After collecting the responses, the data were verified for validity, and responses with excessively short completion times or illogical answers were removed. A total of 73 valid questionnaires were retained.

Using Equations (2) and (3), the Satisfaction Index (SI) and Dissatisfaction Index (DSI) for the 11 representative URs were calculated. Subsequently, Equation (4) was used to compute the perceived importance of each requirement. Reliability analysis showed a Cronbach's Alpha coefficient of 0.743, indicating a good level of internal consistency for the Likert scale data. A three-dimensional scatter plot was then generated to visualize the representative URs based on their SI, DSI, and importance scores (see Figure 5).

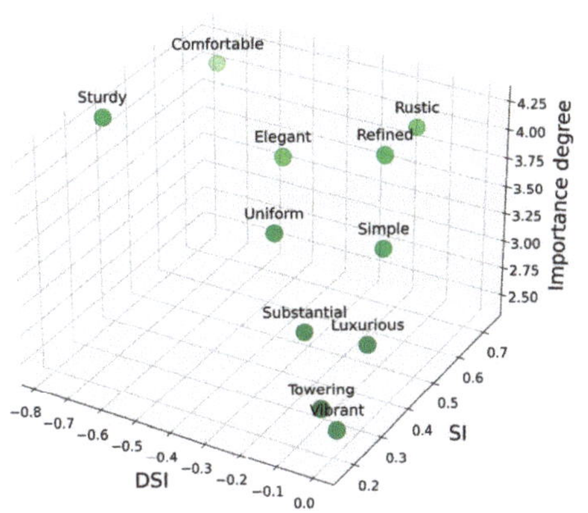

Figure 5. 3D scatter diagram of representative URs.

A closer analysis of Figure 5 showed that "rustic" and "refined" not only had higher SI values and lower DSI values but also carried relatively high weights, 3.92 and 3.89, both significantly above the mean (3.465). This indicated that these two requirements were not only conducive to enhancing customer satisfaction but were also of critical importance. Accordingly, they were classified as highly attractive (HA) attributes within the attractive category. In other words, providing these two qualities in a product could effectively assist firms in attracting potential customers and improving user satisfaction, making them strategic quality attributes that products should possess. By contrast, although "simple" also had a higher SI and lower DSI value, its perceived importance (3.36) was below the mean, thus classifying it as a less attractive (LA) attribute, which could be discarded under cost constraints. "Comfortable" and "elegant" were high value-added (HV) quality attributes, which contributed considerably to customer satisfaction but showed relatively high DSI values. "Sturdy" was identified as a critical (C) attribute within must-be attributes. "Uniform" was categorized as a potential (P) attribute within indifferent attributes, suggesting potential to become attractive to consumers. Finally, "substantial", "luxurious", "towering", and "vibrant" all had importance scores significantly below the mean and exerted little influence on customer satisfaction, thus falling under care-free (CF) attributes in the ondifferent category, which firms did not need to consider when resources were limited. As argued by Tan et al. [42], designers should prioritize attractive attributes first, followed by one-dimensional and must-be attributes, while indifferent attributes may be disregarded due to their negligible contribution to customer satisfaction.

Therefore, in order to guide firms in concentrating limited resources on critical issues and maximizing overall benefits, this study first identified HA attributes—namely "rustic" and "refined"—as the key user requirements (URs). These were regarded as strategic quality attributes for enhancing customer satisfaction and were subsequently applied in the product case development. The quality classifications of the representative URs are summarized in Table 3.

Table 3. Quality attributes classification of representative URs.

Representative URs	Importance Degree	2-Dimensional Category in Traditional Kano's Model	3-Dimensional Category in the Refined Kano's Model
Rustic	3.92	Attractive (A)	Highly Attractive (HA)
Refined	3.89	Attractive (A)	Highly Attractive (HA)
Simple	3.36	Attractive (A)	Less Attractive (LA)
Comfortable	4.11	One-dimensional (O)	High value-added (HV)
Elegant	3.74	One-dimensional (O)	High value-added (HV)
Sturdy	4.25	Must-be (M)	Critical (C)
Uniform	3.51	Indifferent (I)	Potential (P)
Substantial	3.07	Indifferent (I)	Care-free (CF)
Luxurious	3.03	Indifferent (I)	Care-free (CF)
Towering	2.81	Indifferent (I)	Care-free (CF)
Vibrant	2.44	Indifferent (I)	Care-free (CF)
Mean	3.465		

4.2. Morphological Decomposition of Furniture Forms

This section selects the square stool from Ming-style furniture as the analysis subject for design characteristics (DCs), as it not only represents a fundamental functional category of furniture but is also widely used in both commercial and residential spaces. With its strong connection to users and diverse range of styles, it serves as a highly representative example.

Through morphological analysis, the furniture was classified into six distinct DCs, each of which was systematically coded, as illustrated in Figure 6. These characteristics were identified as the seat rim (A), apron (B), decorative strut (C), stretcher (D), leg (E), and decorative pattern (F).

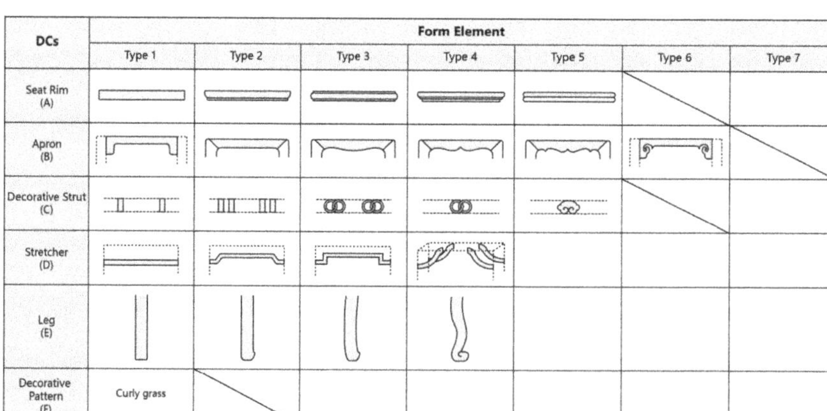

Figure 6. Morphological deconstruction table for Ming-style square stool.

The seat rim, positioned along the perimeter of the square stool's seat, secures the surface structurally and contributes to its aesthetic appeal through variations in linear form; in this study, it was further subdivided into six categories. The apron, situated directly beneath the seat rim and joined to the legs on all four sides, transfers structural loads from the rim to the legs. Functionally analogous to beams in architectural structures, it was categorized into seven types. The decorative strut, serving primarily ornamental purposes, extends downward to connect with the stretcher and consists of six types. The stretcher, a horizontal member linking the legs at their midsection, reinforces overall stability and appears in four common configurations. The leg, as a fundamental load-bearing element comparable to architectural columns, was classified into four categories. Finally, the decorative pattern, which has no structural function, is mainly applied to the apron's surface, where it enriches the visual hierarchy and enhances artistic expression.

A total of 150 sample images were collected from books and websites, from which 80 high-resolution images with clear morphological differences and strong representativeness were selected as experimental samples. After selecting the samples, standardized image processing was conducted. First, irrelevant elements such as backgrounds and shadows were removed. Next, the color saturation of all images was reduced to -100 to achieve grayscale processing. Finally, the images were uniformly output as JPG files with dimensions of 100×100 mm, a resolution of 150 ppi, and a white background. These preprocessing steps eliminated confounding variables unrelated to the independent variables—such as color, size, background, and lighting—ensuring the validity of the experimental conditions. Following preprocessing, a 7-point Likert scale questionnaire was designed to collect users' emotional evaluations of the 80 stool samples. After excluding responses with extremely short completion times or illogical patterns, a total of 70 valid questionnaires were retained. The morphological elements of the DCs were used as input characteristics, while the users' affective evaluations served as output characteristics. In this way, a Kansei evaluation matrix under two requirement objectives was constructed, providing a foundational dataset for subsequent multi-objective optimization.

4.3. Multi-Objective Intelligent Optimization of Furniture Forms

4.3.1. Generation of Pareto Solutions

Based on Figure 6, the independent variables of the 80 samples were encoded using a discrete feature representation, ensuring that the data could be correctly recognized within the MATLAB R2017b environment. The resulting Kansei evaluation matrix is shown in Table A1 of Appendix A.

Both surrogate model training and multi-objective optimization were conducted in the MATLAB R2017b environment. First, the dataset was partitioned. The first six columns, corresponding to the DCs (categorical variables), were treated as input features, while the final two columns, representing user Kansei evaluation values (continuous variables), were used as output features. The sampling size was configured as follows: the first 90% of the dataset (seventy-two samples) was allocated to the training set, and the remaining 10% (eight samples) was used as the test set. Next, in order to optimize the hyperparameters of the Support Vector Regression (SVR) surrogate model, Particle Swarm Optimization (PSO) was applied to globally search for the optimal combination of two hyperparameters: the penalty factor and the kernel function parameter. The optimal hyperparameter combination for Objective 1 ("rustic") was determined as (30.6259, 0.73224), and for Objective 2 ("refined") as (16.7981, 0.68201).

After the optimal parameters were identified, the SVR model was trained and used to construct the objective functions for subsequent multi-objective optimization. With the objective functions established, the MORBMO algorithm was implemented for multi-objective optimization. The repository size was set to 20, meaning the algorithm outputs 20 solutions per run. The population size was set to 100, and the maximum number of iterations was 200. Table 4 provides the details of the hyperparameter settings and experimental environment configuration. The Pareto front solutions generated by the MORBMO algorithm are illustrated in Figure 7. The 20 solutions are evenly distributed across the two-dimensional space. All points on the Pareto front are optimal solutions, offering the design team a diverse set of alternatives rather than a single solution. By examining the overall trend of the Pareto front solutions, it was observed that an increase in the "rustic" value was accompanied by a decrease in the "refined" value, and vice versa. This finding indicates that the optimization of one requirement is typically associated with the deterioration of another, as different objectives are inherently in conflict and coupled through shared resources. In this study, both objectives shared the same set of input variable resources—namely, the six DCs illustrated in Figure 6. As a result, the optimization of one objective occupied resources that could otherwise have been allocated to the other. Traditional morphology-based optimization methods that focused solely on a single objective often led to products incapable of simultaneously satisfying multi-dimensional user affective requirements. By contrast, the Pareto front represents the essence of balance, as it enables simultaneous improvements across multiple objectives through holistic optimization, thereby maximizing overall benefits in engineering tasks.

Table 4. Parameters settings and experimental configuration.

Parameters Setting		Environment Configuration	
Sampling size of training set	72	Operating system	Windows 11
Sampling size of test set	8	CPU	AMD Ryzen 9 6900HX
Population size	100	GPU	RTX 3060
Repository size	20	Memory capacity	16 GB
Maximum number of generations	200	Environment	Matlab R2017b

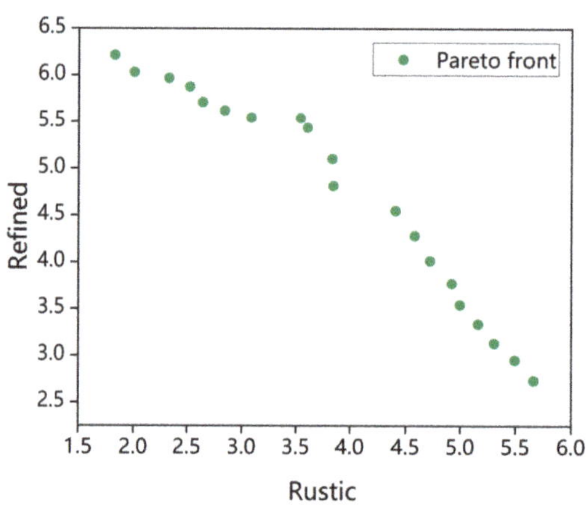

Figure 7. The Pareto front solutions generated by the MORBMO algorithm.

4.3.2. Comparative Experiment on Algorithm Performance

In addition to the MORBMO algorithm, two other classical optimization algorithms—Multi-Objective Sparrow Search Algorithm (MOSSA) [43] and Multi-Objective Particle Swarm Optimization (MOPSO) [44]—were employed for performance comparison. In the comparative experiments, all three algorithms were configured with identical parameter settings. Each algorithm was independently executed 20 times, and all the resulting solutions were subjected to non-dominated sorting to construct a reference Pareto front (RPF) [19]. To systematically and comprehensively evaluate the performance of the three algorithms, four indicators—IGD, GD, HV, and spacing—were introduced. The evaluation results are summarized in Table 5. Pairwise comparisons of the algorithms were conducted using the Wilcoxon rank sum test to assess performance differences [45]. For the IGD metric, MORBMO significantly outperformed MOPSO ($p < 0.05$), whereas no statistically significant difference was observed between MORBMO and MOSSA. For the GD metric, none of the algorithm pairs exhibited statistically significant differences. Regarding the HV metric, MORBMO performed significantly better than both MOSSA and MOPSO ($p < 0.05$), while the difference between MOSSA and MOPSO was not statistically significant. For the spacing metric, both MORBMO and MOSSA significantly outperformed MOPSO ($p < 0.05$), but no statistically significant difference was found between MORBMO and MOSSA. Furthermore, Figure 8 presents boxplots for a more intuitive comparison of the algorithms' performance across the different metrics. Overall, the MORBMO algorithm demonstrated superior performance, with smaller standard deviations. Specifically, it achieved the lowest IGD and GD values, indicating that the solution set generated by MORBMO is closer to the theoretical optimal front. In addition, its significantly lower spacing value suggests better distribution uniformity and greater solution diversity. Finally, the MORBMO algorithm attained a comparatively higher HV value, which demonstrates that its solution set encompassed a larger and more extensive coverage of the objective space, thereby yielding a Pareto front with superior diversity.

Table 5. The evaluation results.

Algorithm		IGD	GD	HV	Spacing
MORBMO	Mean	9.4467×10^{-2}	1.4438×10^{-2}	2.2438×10^{-1}	1.0261×10^{-1}
	Std	5.6427×10^{-3}	2.4039×10^{-3}	1.4892×10^{-3}	2.2994×10^{-2}
MOSSA	Mean	9.8337×10^{-2}	1.4864×10^{-2}	2.2282×10^{-1}	1.1182×10^{-1}
	Std	1.0218×10^{-2}	4.4025×10^{-3}	1.8205×10^{-3}	2.3288×10^{-2}
MOPSO	Mean	1.0552×10^{-1}	1.5187×10^{-2}	2.2244×10^{-1}	1.4073×10^{-1}
	Std	1.4049×10^{-2}	3.3289×10^{-3}	1.4216×10^{-3}	4.7837×10^{-2}

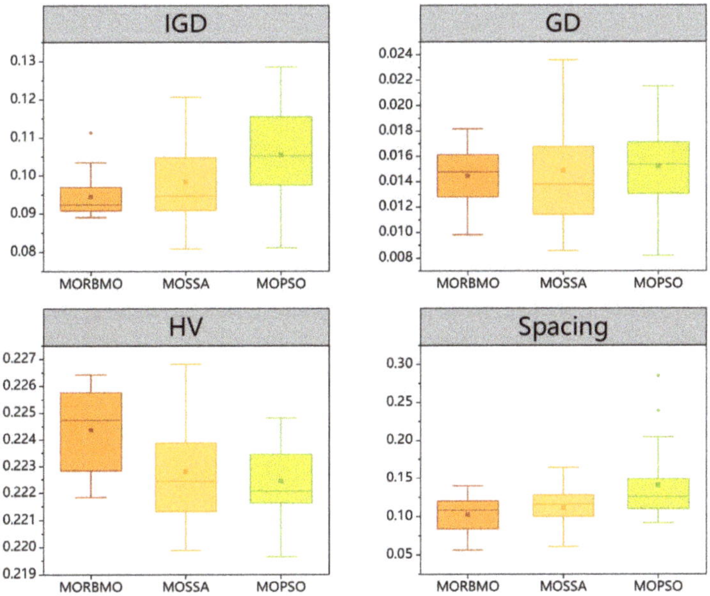

Figure 8. Boxplots of the four evaluation metrics.

4.3.3. Multi-Criteria Decision-Making for Pareto Solutions

The VIKOR method was applied to identify the optimal solution among the 20 Pareto front solutions presented in Figure 7. After normalizing the 20 solutions, the group utility values and individual regret values for each solution were calculated using Equations (19) and (20), respectively. The compromise values were then determined using Equation (21). Table 6 presents the overall decision results for all 20 solutions. For Solution 4, the group utility value (0.3739) and the individual regret value (0.2769) were both markedly lower than those of the other solutions, indicating that this solution not only performed well in terms of overall performance across the two objectives but also maintained satisfactory performance on individual criteria. When these two measures were combined, the resulting compromise value (0.0761) was the smallest among the 20 solutions. This demonstrates that Solution 4 simultaneously maximized the overall benefit and avoided severe underperformance on any single criterion and was therefore identified as the final optimal solution. The characteristic combination for Solution 4 is (A6, B2, C4, D2, E1, F2), and its output values for the two objectives are (3.5383, 5.5420).

Table 6. Decision-making results.

NO.	Group Utility Values (S_i)	Individual Regret Values (R_i)	Compromise Values (Q_i)	Ranking
Solution 1	0.5000	0.5000	0.9887	20
Solution 2	0.5000	0.5000	0.9887	20
Solution 3	0.4582	0.4096	0.6550	11
Solution 4	0.3739	0.2769	0.0761	1
Solution 5	0.4323	0.3364	0.4158	8
Solution 6	0.4708	0.4353	0.7525	15
Solution 7	0.4384	0.3159	0.4004	7
Solution 8	0.4534	0.3680	0.5575	10
Solution 9	0.4471	0.3509	0.5004	9
Solution 10	0.3798	0.2682	0.0825	2
Solution 11	0.5029	0.4767	0.9557	18
Solution 12	0.4911	0.4691	0.8957	17
Solution 13	0.4710	0.3844	0.6569	12
Solution 14	0.4786	0.4135	0.7416	14
Solution 15	0.4667	0.3941	0.6584	13
Solution 16	0.4186	0.2777	0.2508	6
Solution 17	0.4892	0.4431	0.8386	16
Solution 18	0.4381	0.2369	0.2491	5
Solution 19	0.3979	0.2381	0.0958	3
Solution 20	0.4031	0.2394	0.1182	4

4.4. Design Practice

This section focuses on product line planning and development based on the final solution. After completing the conceptual design through hand-drawn sketches, the selected scheme underwent detailed design, modeling, and rendering. Modeling was carried out using AutoCAD 2019 in conjunction with Rhino 6. To ensure ergonomic suitability, the stool was designed with a seat height of 430 mm and a length and width of 420 mm. In addition, an experienced professional furniture designer oversaw the proportion of the contours and the curvature of the lines to enhance the overall harmony and elegance of the product form. The 3D model was then imported into KeyShot 2023 for rendering. The final product was successfully developed, as shown in Figure 9.

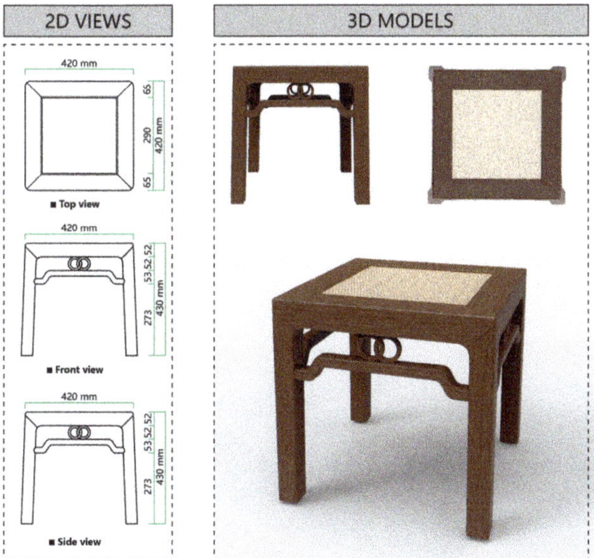

Figure 9. The final solution.

In terms of styling, the stool inherits the understated elegance and refined simplicity typical of Ming-style furniture. The form is clean and fluid, with the stool legs angled outward by 2 degrees. As a result, both the side and front views reveal a trapezoidal rather than rectangular silhouette, conveying a sense of stability. In terms of decoration, a decorative strut with a patterned element is added between the apron and the stretcher. This feature not only enhances the piece's visual refinement but also serves a structural role in reinforcing the frame. Apart from this, no excessive ornamental carvings are used, allowing the piece to stand out through its proportion and linework alone. The main structure is crafted from black walnut heartwood, featuring a natural chocolate hue and a fine, elegant grain. A transparent water-based lacquer is applied to the wood surface, serving as a protective layer to minimize damage from wear and environmental factors while also adding a soft sheen that accentuates the wood's natural texture. The seat surface is woven using a traditional cane technique, providing elasticity and enhanced seating comfort.

5. Discussion

On the one hand, in today's user-centered consumer market, the extraction of key URs directly shapes the direction of new product development. In KE research, Kansei words serve as an important medium for expressing users' affective requirements. Previous studies have often relied on sources such as magazines and journals, supplemented by the KJ method to mine Kansei words, and then employed multi-criteria decision analysis to determine the priority of URs. While such methods are classical and easy to implement, they are constrained by limited sample sizes, which restrict their ability to represent the overall characteristics of user groups and to capture the dynamic and quality-oriented nature of consumer preferences. To address this issue, this study proposed a big-data-driven refined Kano's model for the three-dimensional classification of URs. Online user reviews were collected to capture authentic needs in a more objective and comprehensive way. Eleven representative requirements were then extracted using natural language processing techniques. These requirements were classified through the refined Kano's model with greater granularity, and categories such as HA, LA, and HV attributes were identified. Two HA requirements—"rustic" and "refined"—emerged as the key URs. Under resource constraints, this approach enabled furniture enterprises to prioritize product development more effectively. The results showed that the refined Kano's model reduced cognitive asymmetry between designers and users. It also revealed multi-layered requirements with higher depth and granularity, reflecting the model's inherent symmetry and resolution.

On the other hand, earlier KE studies predominantly employed statistical models to establish associations; however, these approaches are inherently linear, with limited scalability and weak robustness to noise. Consequently, in recent years, machine learning algorithms have increasingly been introduced into the domain of furniture form design, achieving a series of promising outcomes. Such algorithms offer greater scalability, higher predictive accuracy, and the ability to model more complex nonlinear relationships. Nevertheless, their limitation lies in their narrow focus: they typically optimize only a single requirement, thereby neglecting or even worsening other objectives, and they generally yield only a single optimal solution. In contrast, real-world furniture design invariably involves multiple objectives that must be simultaneously considered and optimized. Compared with prior studies, this research innovatively employed the multi-objective optimization algorithm MORBMO to automatically generate a set of non-dominated solutions, thereby revealing the balance among conflicting objectives and covering diverse requirements. The results indicated that MORBMO achieved strong overall performance, producing a solution set with greater diversity and closer approximation to the RPF. Subsequently, the multi-criteria decision-making method VIKOR was applied to identify the final solution from the Pareto set. Among the alternatives, Solution 4 was distinguished by its relatively low group utility value (0.3739) and individual regret value (0.2769), as well as the smallest compromise value (0.0761), and was therefore determined to be the final optimal solution. This outcome highlights the methodological innovation of this study: rather than providing enterprises or researchers with a single prescriptive solution, the proposed approach offers a diverse set of alternatives. In summary, the integrated methodology proposed in this research—combining MORBMO and VIKOR—achieved both global balance and diversified choices in the optimization design process, thereby addressing the multi-dimensional expectations of the market and users. Such multi-dimensional trade-offs not only prevent "one-sided optimization" but also offer new insights for related studies in furniture form design.

6. Conclusions

In the era of emotional experience, product forms that align with users' affective requirements can effectively stimulate purchasing and usage behaviors. However, key challenges remain in this field—namely, how to more comprehensively and objectively extract key URs to bridge the cognitive gap between designers and users, and how to develop innovative furniture that balances users' multi-dimensional affective requirements. In response to the asymmetries observed in the field of form design, this study, grounded in KE, proposes an intelligent optimization method for furniture form design that takes into account users' multi-dimensional affective requirements. This approach effectively restores symmetry between user-related factors and product-related factors within the design system. First, natural language processing techniques were employed to extract online user reviews. After identifying representative URs using Word2Vec and the KJ method, the refined Kano's model was applied to perform three-dimensional quality classification and weight calculation, ultimately identifying "rustic" and "refined" as the two key URs. Next, morphological analysis was used to deconstruct the product into six DCs: seat rim (A), apron (B), decorative strut (C), stretcher (D), leg (E), and decorative pattern (F). A surrogate model was then built using SVR, and a set of Pareto-optimal solutions was generated using the proposed MORBMO algorithm. A comparative experiment on algorithm performance showed that the MORBMO algorithm outperformed other algorithms. Solution 4 was identified as the final optimal solution using the VIKOR method. Finally, the selected design was refined and evaluated. Compared with previous studies, this research makes the following three key contributions:

(1) This study proposes an intelligent optimization design method for furniture form that integrates big data and artificial intelligence technologies into the design domain. This approach enhances the universality and objectivity of user requirement data sources while improving design efficiency.

(2) A big-data-driven refined Kano's model is introduced to enable both fine-grained classification of URs and the identification of key URs. This assists design teams in prioritizing product line planning based on URs.

(3) An automated solution generation model is constructed using the MORBMO algorithm, which outputs a set of solutions that satisfy users' multi-dimensional affective requirements rather than a single optimal solution. The final solution is then selected using the VIKOR method. This combination of multi-objective optimization and multi-criteria decision-making provides design departments with more diverse and flexible pathways for new product development.

Admittedly, this study has the following three limitations that warrant further improvement in future work:

(1) This study applies morphological analysis to deconstruct product characteristics, which limits the granularity of the morphological breakdown. As a result, some design details may not have been fully considered. Future research will explore more nuanced and multi-layered morphological deconstruction, potentially using CAD tools to quantitatively describe product forms.

(2) This study focuses on a single visual design attribute—furniture form. Due to experimental constraints, it does not account for other multi-dimensional design features such as color, material, and surface finishing. However, in real-world purchasing and usage contexts, consumers perceive products through multiple senses, such as vision and touch. Future research will expand on this work by examining how multi-dimensional design attributes influence consumer preferences.

(3) This study employs the square stool from Ming-style furniture as a specific case to validate the feasibility of the proposed method. In fact, the method demonstrates both extensibility and generalizability. When applied to other product categories, it requires case-specific analysis to identify emerging market trends and accurately capture product characteristics. Future work may further extend this method and apply it to diverse product types, thereby broadening its practical significance.

Author Contributions: Conceptualization, L.F. and X.Y.; methodology, L.F.; software, X.Y. and L.Z.; validation, L.F.; formal analysis, L.F.; investigation, L.Z.; resources, J.L.; data curation, L.F.; writing—original draft preparation, L.F.; writing—review and editing, L.F. and X.Y.; visualization, X.Y.; supervision, J.L.; project administration, J.L. All authors have read and agreed to the published version of the manuscript.

Funding: This research received no external funding.

Data Availability Statement: The original contributions presented in this study are included in the article. Further inquiries can be directed to the corresponding author(s).

Conflicts of Interest: The authors declare no conflicts of interest.

Abbreviations

The following abbreviations are used in this manuscript:

KE	Kansei Engineering
URs	User requirements
DCs	Design characteristics
MORBMO	Multi-Objective Red-Billed Blue Magpie Optimizer
VIKOR	VIseKriterijumska Optimizacija I Kompromisno Resenje

Appendix A

Table A1. Kansei evaluation matrix.

Sample Number	DCs						URs	
	A	B	C	D	E	F	Rustic	Refined
NO. 1	2	2	6	5	2	2	5.04	3.25
NO. 2	5	7	3	1	1	2	4.42	4.14
NO. 3	2	2	6	2	3	1	3.29	5.33
NO. 4	6	2	1	3	1	2	4.3	4.17
NO. 5	1	1	6	1	1	2	5.23	2.75
NO. 6	6	2	5	3	1	2	4.23	4.35
NO. 7	1	6	6	2	1	2	4.16	4.45
NO. 8	1	2	6	5	1	2	5.25	3.45
NO. 9	4	4	6	2	4	1	3.01	5.41
NO. 10	4	2	6	2	2	2	4.57	3.88
NO. 11	6	7	4	1	2	2	4.42	4.42
NO. 12	4	4	6	2	2	2	4.54	4.28
NO. 13	6	2	6	1	2	2	5.49	2.87
NO. 14	1	7	1	2	1	2	4.94	3.2
NO. 15	5	7	1	1	1	2	4.93	3.35
NO. 16	4	5	6	2	2	2	3.16	5.36
NO. 17	2	4	6	2	4	2	3.65	5.09
NO. 18	2	4	6	5	3	1	4.14	4.48
NO. 19	2	2	6	4	2	2	4.78	3.74
NO. 20	1	2	6	2	2	2	5.32	2.97
NO. 21	2	1	6	1	1	2	5.46	2.91
NO. 22	5	7	6	2	1	2	4.74	3.68
NO. 23	6	3	6	2	2	2	5	3.48
NO. 24	1	2	6	5	1	2	5.33	2.97
NO. 25	2	5	6	5	4	2	3.99	4.62
NO. 26	2	2	6	2	3	2	4.46	4.03
NO. 27	6	2	1	3	1	2	4.32	4.26
NO. 28	6	2	5	2	2	2	3.9	4.99
NO. 29	2	5	6	4	4	2	3.86	4.72
NO. 30	6	2	6	5	2	2	4.91	3.2
NO. 31	6	2	6	6	1	2	5.09	3.12
NO. 32	6	2	5	2	1	2	3.83	4.94
NO. 33	2	5	6	2	2	2	3.97	4.51
NO. 34	3	1	6	1	1	2	4.81	3.42
NO. 35	4	5	6	4	4	2	4.04	4.62
NO. 36	3	5	6	5	3	1	3.67	5.1
NO. 37	4	6	6	2	1	2	3.81	4.97
NO. 38	2	2	6	4	3	2	4.52	3.87
NO. 39	1	2	6	4	1	2	4.61	3.54
NO. 40	1	2	6	5	2	2	5.39	2.58

Table A1. *Cont.*

Sample Number	DCs						URs	
	A	B	C	D	E	F	Rustic	Refined
NO. 41	4	3	6	5	2	2	4.8	3.59
NO. 42	1	2	6	5	3	2	4.72	4.14
NO. 43	6	2	6	2	2	2	4.52	3.94
NO. 44	4	3	6	2	2	2	4.62	4.04
NO. 45	6	2	6	2	1	2	4.59	3.52
NO. 46	4	7	2	2	1	2	4.52	4.07
NO. 47	2	7	1	1	1	2	4.97	3.13
NO. 48	2	2	1	2	2	2	4.55	3.88
NO. 49	2	4	6	5	2	2	4.52	4.23
NO. 50	1	2	6	2	1	2	4.71	3.61
NO. 51	2	6	6	1	1	2	4.25	4.45
NO. 52	2	2	6	5	2	2	4.67	3.84
NO. 53	1	5	6	2	4	1	3.09	5.23
NO. 54	2	3	6	5	2	2	4.51	4.13
NO. 55	4	2	1	2	1	2	4.67	3.93
NO. 56	1	2	6	2	1	2	4.93	3.23
NO. 57	2	2	6	2	2	2	4.93	3.52
NO. 58	2	2	6	1	2	2	4.9	3.42
NO. 59	2	2	5	2	2	2	3.94	4.75
NO. 60	2	7	1	1	1	2	5.26	2.93
NO. 61	4	2	6	4	2	2	4.77	3.91
NO. 62	2	6	6	2	1	2	4.59	3.91
NO. 63	6	2	1	3	2	2	4.28	4.13
NO. 64	2	2	6	4	3	1	3.12	5.35
NO. 65	6	2	6	4	2	2	5.01	3.04
NO. 66	2	2	4	2	2	2	4.16	4.52
NO. 67	5	7	4	1	1	2	4.22	4.28
NO. 68	5	7	1	2	1	2	4.43	3.86
NO. 69	6	2	6	5	2	2	5.25	3.09
NO. 70	4	5	1	2	4	1	3	5.49
NO. 71	5	7	2	2	1	2	4.51	3.81
NO. 72	2	7	1	1	2	2	4.96	3.25
NO. 73	2	2	1	1	2	2	4.58	3.7
NO. 74	6	7	2	2	2	2	4.49	3.75
NO. 75	2	3	6	5	3	2	4.33	4.14
NO. 76	2	2	2	2	2	2	4.64	3.68
NO. 77	1	2	6	1	1	2	5.04	3.22
NO. 78	2	5	6	2	2	1	3.59	4.91
NO. 79	1	2	6	2	2	2	5.23	3.07
NO. 80	2	5	6	5	4	1	3.59	4.87

References

1. Yang, C.X.; Liu, F.; Ye, J.N. A product form design method integrating Kansei engineering and diffusion model. *Adv. Eng. Inform.* **2023**, *57*, 14. [CrossRef]
2. Nagamachi, M. Kansei engineering as a powerful consumer-oriented technology for product development. *Appl. Ergon.* **2002**, *33*, 289–294. [CrossRef] [PubMed]
3. Yue, X.Y.; Xiong, X.Q.; Xu, X.T.; Zhang, M. Big data for furniture intelligent manufacturing: Conceptual framework, technologies, applications, and challenges. *Int. J. Adv. Manuf. Technol.* **2024**, *132*, 5231–5247. [CrossRef]
4. Xu, X.T.; Zhang, M.; Yue, X.Y.; Xiong, X.Q. Design of furniture mortise-and-tenon joints: A review of mechanical properties and design recommendations. *Wood Mater. Sci. Eng.* **2025**, *20*, 1–15. [CrossRef]
5. Miao, Y.F.; Gao, X.F.; Jiang, W.Y.; Xu, W. An evaluation model for interactive gaming furniture design based on parent-child behavior. *PLoS ONE* **2024**, *19*, 23. [CrossRef]

6. Zhang, H.Y.; Shen, L.M. Thermal preference effects on physiological responses and bedding system insulation selection during good quality sleep in the transitional season. *Build. Environ.* **2024**, *253*, 12. [CrossRef]
7. Hao, K.Q.; Guan, H.Y. Children's Preferences for the Styling of Consultation Room Furniture Based on Scenic Beauty Estimation and Kansei Engineering. *BioResources* **2025**, *20*, 2711–2727. [CrossRef]
8. Demirbilek, O.; Sener, B. Product design, semantics and emotional response. *Ergonomics* **2003**, *46*, 1346–1360. [CrossRef]
9. Miao, Y.F.; Gao, X.F.; Miao, T.M.; Xu, W. A Study on the Visual and Tactile Perception of Oriented Strand Board Combined with Consumer-Preference Analysis. *Coatings* **2024**, *14*, 24. [CrossRef]
10. Ilhan, A.E.; Togay, A. Pursuit of methodology for data input related to taste in design: Using eye tracking technology. *Displays* **2023**, *76*, 14. [CrossRef]
11. Kwong, C.K.; Fung, K.Y.; Jiang, H.M.; Chan, K.Y.; Siu, K.W.M. A Modified Dynamic Evolving Neural-Fuzzy Approach to Modeling Customer Satisfaction for Affective Design. *Sci. World J.* **2013**, *1*, 636948. [CrossRef] [PubMed]
12. Barnes, C.; Lillford, S. Affective design decision-making—Issues and opportunities. *CoDesign* **2007**, *3*, 135–146. [CrossRef]
13. Wang, Y.H.; Yu, S.H.; Ma, N.; Wang, J.L.; Hu, Z.G.; Liu, Z.; He, J.B. Prediction of product design decision Making: An investigation of eye movements and EEG features. *Adv. Eng. Inform.* **2020**, *45*, 10. [CrossRef]
14. Nagamachi, M. Kansei engineering: A new ergonomic consumer-oriented technology for product development. *Int. J. Ind. Ergon.* **1995**, *15*, 3–11. [CrossRef]
15. Wang, N.; Kang, X.; Wang, Q.; Shi, C. Using grey-quality function deployment to construct an aesthetic product design matrix. *Concurr. Eng.* **2023**, *31*, 49–63. [CrossRef]
16. Zhang, L.; Wu, L.R.; Mattila, A.S. Online Reviews: The Role of Information Load and Peripheral Factors. *J. Travel Res.* **2016**, *55*, 299–310. [CrossRef]
17. Wang, Z.; Hu, S.J.; Liu, W.D. Product feature sentiment analysis based on GRU-CAP considering Chinese sarcasm recognition. *Expert Syst. Appl.* **2024**, *241*, 17. [CrossRef]
18. Xu, Q.; Jiao, R.J.; Yang, X.; Helander, M.; Khalid, H.M.; Opperud, A. An analytical Kano model for customer need analysis. *Des. Stud.* **2009**, *30*, 87–110. [CrossRef]
19. Tang, W.Y.; Xiang, Z.R.; Ding, T.C.; Zhao, X.; Zhang, Q.; Zou, R. Research on multi-objective optimisation of product form design based on kansei engineering. *J. Eng. Des.* **2024**, *35*, 1023–1048. [CrossRef]
20. Li, Y.F.; Zhu, L.P. Extracting knowledge for product form design by using multiobjective optimisation and rough sets. *J. Adv. Mech. Des. Syst. Manuf.* **2020**, *14*, 16. [CrossRef]
21. Decker, R.; Trusov, M. Estimating aggregate consumer preferences from online product reviews. *Int. J. Res. Mark.* **2010**, *27*, 293–307. [CrossRef]
22. Xiao, S.S.; Wei, C.P.; Dong, M. Crowd intelligence: Analyzing online product reviews for preference measurement. *Inf. Manag.* **2016**, *53*, 169–182. [CrossRef]
23. Fu, S.W.; Li, K.; Huang, H.S.; Ma, C.; Fan, Q.S.; Zhu, Y.W. Red-billed blue magpie optimizer: A novel metaheuristic algorithm for 2D/3D UAV path planning and engineering design problems. *Artif. Intell. Rev.* **2024**, *57*, 89. [CrossRef]
24. Opricovic, S.; Tzeng, G.H. Compromise solution by MCDM methods: A comparative analysis of VIKOR and TOPSIS. *Eur. J. Oper. Res.* **2004**, *156*, 445–455. [CrossRef]
25. Kittidecha, C.; Marasinghe, A.C. Application of Kansei Engineering and Box-Behnken response surface methodology for shape parameter design: A case study of wine glass. *J. Adv. Mech. Des. Syst. Manuf.* **2015**, *9*, 12. [CrossRef]
26. Smith, S.; Fu, S.H. The relationships between automobile head-up display presentation images and drivers' Kansei. *Displays* **2011**, *32*, 58–68. [CrossRef]
27. Hartono, M.; Santoso, A.; Prayogo, D.N. How Kansei Engineering, Kano and QFD can improve logistics services. *Int. J. Technol.* **2017**, *8*, 1070–1081. [CrossRef]
28. Zhou, C.M.; Jiang, L.S.; Kaner, J. Study on Imagery Modeling of Electric Recliner Chair: Based on Combined GRA and Kansei Engineering. *Appl. Sci.* **2023**, *13*, 20. [CrossRef]
29. Woo, J.C.; Luo, F.; Lin, Z.H.; Chen, Y.T. Research on the Sensory Feeling of Product Design for Electric Toothbrush Based on Kansei Engineering and Back Propagation Neural Network. *J. Internet Technol.* **2022**, *23*, 863–871. [CrossRef]
30. Fu, L.; Lei, Y.L.; Zhu, L.; Lv, J.F. An evaluation and design method for Ming-style furniture integrating Kansei engineering with particle swarm optimization-support vector regression. *Adv. Eng. Inform.* **2024**, *62*, 14. [CrossRef]
31. Cai, W.L.; Wang, Z.Y.; Wang, Y.; Zhou, M.Y. Research on wheelchair form design based on Kansei engineering and GWO-BP neural network. *Sci. Rep.* **2025**, *15*, 25. [CrossRef]
32. Wang, N.Y.; Shi, D.; Li, Z.R.; Chen, P.T.; Ren, X.P. Investigating emotional design of the intelligent cockpit based on visual sequence data and improved LSTM. *Adv. Eng. Inform.* **2024**, *61*, 24. [CrossRef]
33. Matzler, K.; Hinterhuber, H.H. How to make product development projects more successful by integrating Kano's model of customer satisfaction into quality function deployment. *Technovation* **1998**, *18*, 25–38. [CrossRef]

34. Yang, H.; Huo, Y.X.; Jia, R.Y.; Sha, F.; Hu, N.Q.; Yu, L.L.; Wang, Y.R. Sustainable Recognition Methods of Modeling Design Features of Light and Micro Vehicle-Mounted UAV: Based on Support Vector Regression and Kano Model. *Sustainability* **2022**, *14*, 18. [CrossRef]
35. Qu, M.; Ren, Z.X.; Wu, J. Design and evaluation of smart blood pressure monitor oriented to user needs. *J. Eng. Des.* **2024**, *35*, 290–319. [CrossRef]
36. Yang, C.-C. The refined Kano's model and its application. *Total Qual. Manag. Bus. Excell.* **2005**, *16*, 1127–1137. [CrossRef]
37. Kristensen, K.; Kanji, G.K.; Dahlgaard, J.J. On measurement of customer satisfaction. *Total Qual. Manag.* **1992**, *3*, 123–128. [CrossRef]
38. Chen, M.C.; Hsu, C.L.; Lee, L.H. Investigating pharmaceutical logistics service quality with refined Kano's model. *J. Retail. Consum. Serv.* **2020**, *57*, 12. [CrossRef]
39. Sivabalan, S.; Minu, R. Optimized multi-anchor space-aware temporal convolutional neural network for automobile sales prediction. *Knowl. Based Syst.* **2025**, *311*, 12. [CrossRef]
40. Wang, Q.; Zhang, M.; Li, L.; Yan, W.; Liu, B.; Xia, Z.; Tseng, M.-L. Optimal capacity configuration of coupled photovoltaic and energy storage system: Multi-objective red-billed blue-magpie optimizer. *J. Ind. Prod. Eng.* **2025**, *42*, 1–21. [CrossRef]
41. Kang, X.H.; Wan, H.Q.; Li, S.Y. Combining Kansei Engineering and SSA-XGBoost for new energy vehicle front-face form design. *J. Eng. Des.* **2025**, 39. [CrossRef]
42. Tan, K.C.; Pawitra, T.A. Integrating SERVQUAL and Kano's model into QFD for service excellence development. *Manag. Serv. Qual. An. Int. J.* **2001**, *11*, 418–430. [CrossRef]
43. Li, B.; Wang, H.L. Multi-objective sparrow search algorithm: A novel algorithm for solving complex multi-objective optimisation problems. *Expert Syst. Appl.* **2022**, *210*, 19. [CrossRef]
44. Mostaghim, S.; Teich, J. Strategies for finding good local guides in multi-objective particle swarm optimization (MOPSO). In Proceedings of the 2003 IEEE Swarm Intelligence Symposium, SIS'03, Indianapolis, IN, USA, 26 April 2003; pp. 26–33.
45. Shieh, M.D.; Li, Y.F.; Yang, C.C. Comparison of multi-objective evolutionary algorithms in hybrid Kansei engineering system for product form design. *Adv. Eng. Inform.* **2018**, *36*, 31–42. [CrossRef]

symmetry MDPI

Article

Symmetrical Traditional Patterns and User Perception: A Study on Innovation in Home Textile Design

Mengqi Qin, Jianfang Wang *, Xueying Ding and Haihong Zhang

School of Fashion Design, Zhejiang Sci-Tech University, Hangzhou 311103, China; 2023220404068@mails.zstu.edu.cn (M.Q.); 2024220403015@mails.zstu.edu.cn (X.D.); zhanghaihong@zstu.edu.cn (H.Z.)
* Correspondence: wangjianfang1231@163.com

Abstract: With the increasing diversification of modern home textile design (HTD), the integration of traditional cultural elements has become an important trend. This study investigates the impact of symmetry in traditional patterns on the optimization of home textile product design and examines its role in consumer acceptance. First, the affinity diagram method was employed to collect core affective vocabularies. Based on a selection of home textile products incorporating traditional patterns available in the market, a questionnaire was developed to solicit consumers' evaluations of these affective descriptors. Principal component analysis (PCA) was conducted to extract key perceptual dimensions, with particular emphasis on the influence of pattern symmetry on consumer perception. Subsequently, the Fuzzy Analytic Hierarchy Process (FAHP) was applied to determine the relative weights of the affective terms. Incorporating expert input, five representative traditional patterns from the Homespun Fabric of Jiangnan (HFoJ) were selected and reinterpreted with a focus on symmetrical design. Through the Quality Function Deployment (QFD) method, the effective vocabularies were mapped to the redesigned patterns, leading to the identification of the scheme that most effectively embodied the symmetrical principle for integration into HTD. Finally, the Grey Relation Analysis (GRA) was used to conduct a comprehensive evaluation of multiple design alternatives. The optimal design was selected and subsequently validated through consumer feedback to assess its market feasibility. This study contributes a symmetric approach to the application of symmetry in traditional pattern design, offering both traditional insights and practical guidance for the modernization and innovative transformation of cultural elements in HTD.

Keywords: traditional patterns; user perception; innovation in home textile design; design innovation; symmetry optimization

1. Introduction

Traditional patterns (TPs) not only carry rich cultural connotations but also endow products with distinctive visual characteristics and emotional values, thereby enhancing their appeal in a competitive market. In contemporary home textile design (HTD), a central challenge lies in accurately interpreting traditional cultural symbols while fostering emotional resonance and improving consumer acceptance [1]. This study aims to investigate the interplay between the symmetry of TPs and user perception, with the goal of optimizing their application pathways in HTD.

In recent years, increasing academic attention has been directed toward the integration of traditional cultural elements into modern design. Several studies have emphasized the application of cultural motifs in home textiles, arguing that traditional elements not only enrich product aesthetics but also strengthen emotional and cultural identification. For instance, Jowers et al. [2] analyzed fixed structural forms using shape grammars theory, revealing limitations in their variation capabilities and demonstrating how structural formalization can enhance user acceptance. Similarly, Zou et al. [3] employed the Analytic Hierarchy Process (AHP) to explore cross-cultural design strategies involving Chinese dragon and Thai Naga motifs, concluding that cultural meaning can be effectively communicated through a structured four-stage design model. However, while these studies highlight the symbolic and aesthetic functions of TPs, they often overlook the perceptual and emotional needs of users.

In parallel, Kansei Engineering (KE) has been widely adopted to bridge product features with user perception across design fields, such as furniture, apparel, and home textiles. KE enables the quantification of emotional responses, thereby optimizing both visual and tactile product experiences. Miao et al. [4] applied traditional Chinese auspicious motifs to modern wedding bedding design, reconstructing pattern forms using contemporary aesthetics to enhance cultural resonance and market potential. Yang et al. [5] combined the AHP and Grey Relational Analysis (GRA) to reduce subjectivity in evaluating campus cultural and creative products and to identify an optimal design scheme. Despite the effectiveness of such approaches, most prior studies rely on a single-dimensional KE evaluation, lacking a multi-faceted cognitive framework. Moreover, the specific impact of symmetry in TPs on user perception remains underexplored.

To address these limitations, this study proposes a comprehensive and data-driven design framework, recognizing that optimizing traditional pattern design requires a complete logical chain from quantifying user perception and extracting key factors to assigning scientific weights and evaluating design schemes. The key contributions of this study are threefold: (i) it conducts an in-depth analysis of how symmetry of TPs influences user perception and develops a multi-dimensional cognitive evaluation system; (ii) it proposes an integrated optimization approach combining KE with quantitative analysis to improve alignment with user preferences and enhance market acceptance; (iii) it presents a practical framework for the innovative transformation and sustainable modernization of traditional cultural elements in contemporary HTD.

Subsequent sections of this paper are structured as follows: Section 2 reviews the interdisciplinary literature on TP symbolism, user cognitive preference, and design strategies; Section 3 introduces the research methodology and proposes an optimization model for reinterpreting the HFoJ; Section 4 analyzes the morphological evolution and cultural background of the HFoJ pattern, integrating these insights with the user perception data, to inform innovative design iterations; Section 5 identifies the optimal HFoJ-based HTD through sensitivity analysis and validates the feasibility via consumer feedback; Section 6 concludes this study by summarizing key findings, addressing limitations, and outlining future research directions.

2. Literature Review

2.1. Traditional Pattern and Textile Design

TPs hold profound cultural significance and occupy a unique position in Chinese visual heritage. For instance, Chen et al. [6] employed KE to explore how consumers of different age groups emotionally perceive the lotus motif from the Tang Dynasty's Mogao Grottoes. By constructing a predictive model of user emotion, their research enabled designers to reconfigure traditional motifs to align with contemporary user preferences. Similarly, Chen et al. [7] addressed the gap between consumers' individualized aesthetic demands and pattern design by analyzing perceptual adjectives and developing a regression model linking visual design elements with emotional responses. This model provided actionable insights into tailoring designs for targeted emotional effects. An et al. [8] used semantic differential analysis and Quantification Theory I to identify the modern aesthetic potential embedded in the linear structures of traditional screen designs. Their results revealed that specific linear features, such as carved bases, contributed significantly to a sense of modernity and lightness, offering practical guidance for updating traditional aesthetics. In a related study, Song et al. [9] applied factor analysis to investigate how geometric patterns and dress silhouettes influenced users' sensory impressions. They identified three key perceptual dimensions that interact differently depending on pattern-silhouette combinations, providing refined design strategies for summer dresses using KE.

While existing studies have successfully linked traditional motifs to perceptual evaluation and aesthetic innovation, they often overlook individual variance and group diversity in sample selection. Additionally, traditional analytical methods may fail to uncover deeper latent patterns or adapt well to complex real-world contexts. This study responds to these gaps by integrating perceptual vocabularies analysis, expert scoring, and design optimization techniques to systematically examine the role of symmetry in TP-based HTD and its acceptance in the market. The proposed framework aims to enhance the cultural inheritance and innovation of traditional patterns while improving the practical efficacy of design outcomes.

2.2. User Perception and Innovation in Home Textile Design

In textile design, the application of TPs is not a matter of mere recreation but a complex process of reinterpretation and cultural replication. Quan et al. [10] proposed a hybrid method combining deep learning and KE to derive user preferences and generate novel design schemes through a style transfer model. Their method was validated using a women's coat design as an example, though they acknowledged persisting subjectivity in style image evaluations. Gao et al. [11] findings underscored the significant influence of elements such as color and lines on users' visual impressions, offering valuable insights for applying traditional motifs in contemporary product design. Cui et al. [12] used shape grammar to systematize the design rules for Zhuang embroidery, generating outputs at two levels of abstraction. By combining algorithmic modeling and design exploration, they demonstrated the method's capacity to inspire innovation, validating its potential for wider design applications. Fu et al. [13] integrated KE and a genetic algorithm to correlate consumer emotions with design parameters. Through a multiphase modeling approach applied to a mini digital camera design, they optimized emotional responses while identifying methodological limitations and areas for further research.

While current studies have explored the visual transformation of cultural elements and design methodologies, many fall short in analyzing the internal mechanisms that trigger users' emotional resonance. These works often neglect dynamic emotional shifts across contexts and lack systematic user feedback collection and analysis. To address these limitations, the present study focuses on HFoJ traditional patterns and employs QFD in combination with user perception research. This integrated approach preliminarily quantifies user perceptions and offers a methodological framework for enhancing cultural integration and emotional engagement in HTD.

2.3. Design Decision—Making and Scheme Verification

To ensure that HTD effectively balances functionality, user emotion, and cultural meaning, systematic design evaluation and decision-making methods are essential. Wang et al. [14] introduced a product identity form design method that integrates various technologies. They employed the QFD method to map consumer requirements to engineering characteristics. In a subsequent study, Wang et al. [15] addressed the design of rattan-woven lamps by integrating GRA with Fuzzy QFD. The experimental results validated the feasibility and effectiveness of this combined method. In the context of sustainable residential design, Lee et al. [16] utilized the Kano model to identify the design preferences of a broad sample of homebuyers. Their analysis revealed generational differences in user demands and proposed 31 grouped strategies prioritized by importance, along with implementation challenges, offering valuable guidance for future sustainable designs. Similarly, Wang et al. [17] applied the three-level theory of emotional design and the Kano model in the design of urban furniture on Yangzhou Sanwan Street.

However, existing research still exhibits notable limitations. Many studies insufficiently differentiate user needs, resulting in engineering parameters that fail to fully align with market expectations. Moreover, in specialized fields, such as traditional pattern design and cultural and creative products, current approaches often lack robust mechanisms to match users' emotional needs with the deeper cultural significance intended by the designs.

To address these challenges, this study adopts a hybrid PCA–FAHP–GRA framework. PCA is used to extract key pattern features while the FAHP assesses the relative importance of user needs. Combined with GRA for scheme selection, this system not only optimizes product design to meet functional demands but also enhances emotional engagement and facilitates the transmission of cultural values. It provides a novel methodology and practical pathway for improving the cultural and emotional dimensions of product design in the home textile field.

3. Methodology

3.1. Proposed Framework

This study aims to integrate TPs into the home textile product design and optimize the design process by employing the Affinity Diagram, PCA, FAHP, and QFD. The goal is to enhance both emotional resonance and market feasibility. The proposed research framework involves a sequence of analytical, creative, and evaluative steps, including data analysis, identification of emotional needs, TP innovation, scheme screening, and validation based on consumer feedback. Specifically, as illustrated in Figure 1, the framework consists of the following stages:

- The Affinity Diagram is used to collect and organize 10 core affective vocabularies related to HTD. A perceptual cognition questionnaire is then constructed to collect consumer evaluations of home textile products featuring TPs, ensuring that the data reflect intuitive user perceptions of emotional and visual qualities;
- PCA is applied to the questionnaire data to extract key perceptual factors, which represent users' cognitive-emotional responses;
- The perceptual cognition factors are divided in the criterion layer, with the core affective vocabularies forming the sub-criterion layer. Design experts assign weights to the 10 affective vocabularies using the FAHP method, allowing for the calculation of the relative importance of each perceptual factor in HTD;
- A selection of 5 representative HFoJ TPs is analyzed to uncover their cultural meanings and design potential. Shape grammar is employed to reinterpret and innovate these patterns while preserving their cultural characteristics;
- Based on the weighed affective vocabularies and 10 reinterpreted TP variants, a QFD mapping model is constructed to link perceptual needs with design attributes. The model is then used to identify the optimal patterns for home textile product development;
- Using the top 3 ranked patterns, 3 home textile product design schemes are created. These schemes are refined by integrating different design elements and materials to ensure functionality and aesthetic appeal;

- Experts assess the 3 design schemes using the GRA method to determine the most effective design from an emotional and cultural standpoint;
- The selected optimal pattern is applied in actual HTD practice. Consumers are invited to evaluate the final design scheme to assess its market feasibility and emotional resonance.

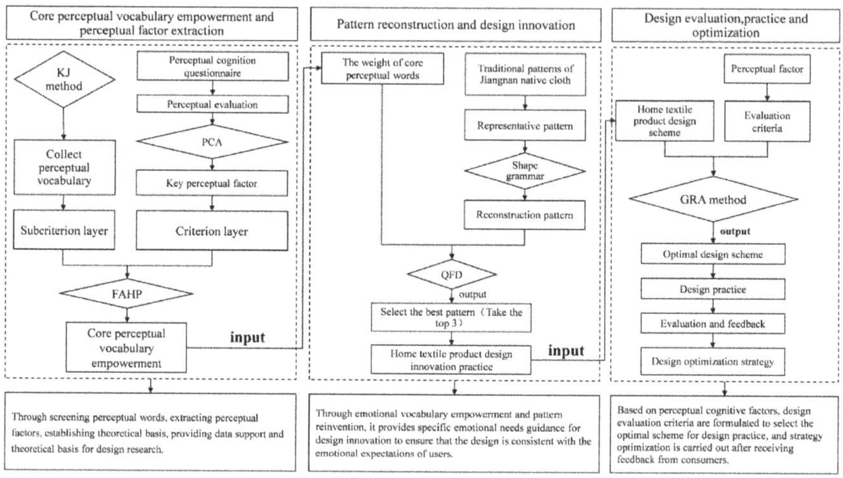

Figure 1. Proposed framework.

3.2. Affinity Diagram

The Affinity Diagram is a widely used qualitative research tool for organizing, classifying, and structuring complex or disordered information. It aims to help researchers identify the internal relationships and potential patterns among the information through a systematic process [18]. The Affinity Diagram was employed to organize users' emotional responses to HFoJ TPs collected via questionnaires. Affective vocabularies were grouped by emotional similarity and key terms were statistically analyzed to form structured data. These results informed the redesign of TPs, providing emotional grounding and guiding innovation in HTD.

3.3. Principal Component Analysis

PCA, as a commonly used dimensionality reduction technique in the design field, can effectively refine the key information of design elements, simplify the high-dimensional data structure, and help design decisions [19]. This method linearly transforms original variables into a new set, reducing data dimensionality while preserving maximum information. In this study, PCA analyzes consumers' emotional feedback on various HFoJ TPs to extract key emotional factors influencing design innovation. By simplifying data complexity, PCA provides a scientific basis for TP redesign. It enables designers to identify elements that most strongly evoke emotional resonance, ensuring design schemes meet modern consumers' emotional needs.

3.4. Shape Grammar

SG is a rule-based method used to generate and modify geometric forms, capturing a product's visual language and guiding its design logic [20]. As a structured design approach, SG enables designers to trace design evolution, organize creative ideas, and make informed decisions through clearly defined transformational rules [21]. SG generates new shapes through a series of deductive rules, which include proportional changes, mirror transformations, rotations, etc. The basic framework of SG can be expressed as:

$$SG = (S, L, R, I) \tag{1}$$

Among them, S is the set of shapes, L is the set of symbols, R is the set of deductive rules, and I is the initial shape. According to the differences in deductive rules, SG is divided into generation rules and modification rules. By combining the principal components extracted by PCA, forms that meet the design requirements can be generated through the application of deductive rules. Table 1 shows the 11 basic deductive rules of SG.

Table 1. Deductive rules of SG.

Type	Rule	Formula	Diagram
Build rules	R1 = Substitution	$TS = S_i;\ S_1 = \{x, y, z\}; TS = \{x, y, w\}$	
	R2 = Addition	$TS = S \cup S_i; S = \{a, b\}, S_i = \{c\};\ TS = \{a, b, c\}$	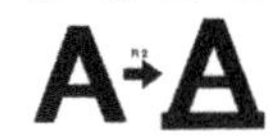
	R3 = Deletion	$TS = S - S_i;\ S = \{a, b, c\}, S_i = \{c\};\ TS = \{a, b\}$	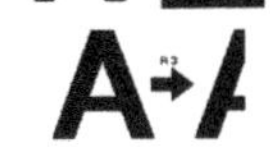
Amend rules	R4 = Scaling	$TS = pS = [xy] \cdot \begin{bmatrix} p_x & 0 \\ 0 & p_y \end{bmatrix}$	
	R5 = Duplication	$TS = (C + D)S = [xy] \cdot \begin{bmatrix} c+1 & 0 & d_x \\ 0 & c+1 & d_y \\ 0 & 0 & 1 \end{bmatrix}$	
	R6 = Mirroring	$TS = KS = [xy] \cdot \begin{bmatrix} k_x & 0 & 0 \\ 0 & k_y & 0 \\ 0 & 0 & 1 \end{bmatrix}$	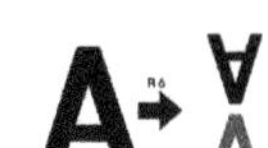
	R7 = Shearing	$TS = HS = [xy] \cdot \begin{bmatrix} h_x & 1 & 0 \\ 0 & 1 & 0 \\ 0 & 0 & 1 \end{bmatrix}$	
	R8 = Rotation	$TS = [xy] \cdot \begin{bmatrix} \cos\theta & -\sin\theta & 0 \\ \sin\theta & \cos\theta & 0 \\ 0 & 0 & 1 \end{bmatrix}$	
	R9 = Fine-Tuning	$TS = \Delta S = [xy] \cdot \begin{bmatrix} 1 & 0 & \Delta x \\ 0 & 1 & \Delta y \\ 0 & 0 & 1 \end{bmatrix}$	
Derived rules	R10 = Merging	$TS = S_1 + S_2$	
	R11 = Translation	$TS = S + (\Delta x, \Delta y)$	

SG includes 11 basic deductive rules: (1) Replacement: Replace all or part of the original shape with other shape curves. (2) Addition: Add new shape components to the original. (3) Deletion: Delete all or part of the original shape curves. (4) Scaling: Adjust the size of a shape; if $P > 1$, it enlarges; if $0 < P < 1$, it is reduced; when $P_x \neq P_y$, it performs non-uniform scaling. (5) Duplication: Duplicate a shape C times and translate it by a displacement D. (6) Mirror: Reflect the shape across a specified axis; if $k_x = 1$ and $k_y = -1$, the shape is mirrored along the Y-axis. (7) Shearing: Alter shape coordinates based on share values h_x and h_y on the x and y axes. (8) Rotation: Rotate the shape around the origin by angle θ. (9) Fine-tuning: Fine-tune the position using Δx and Δy shifts. (10) Merging:

Combine two or more shapes into one. (11) Translation: Move the shape along the x and y axes by Δx and Δy.

3.5. Fuzzy Hierarchical Analysis

The FAHP is a multi-criterion decision-making method that combines fuzzy set theory and the AHP. It is widely used in complex decision-making problems, especially when there is uncertainty and ambiguity in the decision-making process [22]. The FAHP decomposes the decision-making process into three levels: the objective layer (overall goal), the criterion layer (evaluation dimensions), and the sub-criterion layer (specific evaluation indicators):

(1) In this study, the decision problem is structured into a hierarchical model consisting of three layers. This structured model provides a clear and scientific foundation for prioritizing design elements;

(2) To evaluate the relative importance of indicators, experts perform pairwise comparisons using a 0.1–0.9 fuzzy scale (Table 2). This results in a fuzzy complementary matrix:

$$A = \begin{bmatrix} a_{11} & a_{12} & \cdots & a_{1j} \\ \vdots & \vdots & \ddots & \vdots \\ a_{i1} & a_{i2} & \cdots & a_{ij} \end{bmatrix} \quad (2)$$

where $0 < a_{ij} < 1,\ a_{ij} + a_{ji} = 1,\ a_{ij} = 0.5, (i = j)$.

Table 2. Score of the fuzzy matrix.

Score	Definition	Score	Definition
0.1	Factor i is absolutely less important than factor j	0.6	Factor i is slightly more important than factor j
0.2	Factor i is extremely less important than factor j	0.7	Factor i is relatively more important than factor j
0.3	Factor i is relatively less important than factor j	0.8	Factor i is extremely more important than factor j
0.4	Factor i is slightly less important than factor j	0.9	Factor i is absolutely more important than factor j
0.5	Factor i is equally important as factor j		

Next, the matrix A is summed by rows:

$$a_i = \sum_{k=1}^{n} a_{ik}, (i, k = 1, 2 \ldots n) \quad (3)$$

(3) Calculating Fuzzy Weights: Based on fuzzy theory, process the constructed judgment matrix to obtain the weight values of each index. Specifically, calculate the consistency index (CI) and the consistency ratio (CR) to evaluate the consistency level of the judgment matrix. When the consistency ratio of the judgment matrix meets the established criteria, the calculated weight values can be considered valid and then used for subsequent in-depth analysis and decision-making support.

Find the weight vector WI for each factor:

$$w_i = \frac{1}{n} - \frac{1}{2\alpha} + \frac{a_i}{n\alpha} \quad (4)$$

$$WI = \left[w_1, w_2 \cdots w_n\right]^T \quad (5)$$

$\alpha = \frac{n-1}{2}$ in the formula.

Constructing the weighting matrix.

$$w_{ij} = \alpha(w_i - w_j) + 0.5 \tag{6}$$

(4) Consistency check: The consistency check is an important step to ensure the consistency of expert judgments:

$$CI(A,W) = \frac{\sum_{i=1}^{n} \sum_{j=1}^{n} |w_{ij} - a_{ij}|}{n^2} \tag{7}$$

Then, calculate the consistency ratio CR and its formula is:

$$CR = \frac{CI}{RI} \tag{8}$$

Among them, RI is the random consistency index (it is an average consistency index calculated through a large number of random judgment matrices, serving as a benchmark value for measuring the consistency of judgment matrices), which depends on the number of criteria n. If the consistency ratio $CR \leq 0.1$, the judgment matrix is considered to have acceptable consistency. Otherwise, the expert's judgment needs to be re-evaluated [23].

3.6. QFD

QFD ensures the product design aligns with customer requirements (CRs) by converting emotional needs into engineering characteristics (ECs) [19]. This study integrates PCA-extracted emotional factors as CRs and evaluates ten design schemes (*P1–P10*) via the House of Quality. The relationship matrix quantifies how well each scheme satisfies CRs. Weighted calculations, based on expert-assessed CR importance and scheme relevance scores, derive design priorities [24]:

$$A_j = \frac{W_i \times R_{ij}}{\sum_{i=1}^{n} (W_i \times R_{ij})} \tag{9}$$

QFD thus offers a structured basis for optimizing HFoJ TPs, enhancing emotional appeal and cultural value.

3.7. Grey Relation Analysis

GRA is a multi-factor evaluation method suitable for incomplete or uncertain data, particularly aligning with the small sample size and limited historical data of HFoJ patterns [25]. This study applies GRA to evaluate ten application schemes of TPs in home textiles. After data preprocessing, values are normalized:

$$y_{ij} = \frac{x_{ij} - \min(x_j)}{\max(x_j) - \min(x_j)} \tag{10}$$

Then, the grey correlation coefficients ε_{ij}^{+} are calculated to assess closeness to the optimal solution:

$$\varepsilon_{ij}^{+} = \frac{\underset{i}{min}\,\underset{j}{min}\left|G_i - y_{ij}\right| + \xi \underset{i}{max}\,\underset{j}{max}\left|G_i - y_{ij}\right|}{\left|G_i - y_{ij}\right| + \xi \underset{i}{max}\,\underset{j}{max}\left|G_i - y_{ij}\right|} \tag{11}$$

Among them, ξ is the distinguishing coefficient, $\xi \in \left[0, 1\right]$, and is generally set to 0.5 and y_{ij} is the weighted normalized decision-making matrix.

Further, compute the relational degrees Z_j^+, Z_j^- and relative relational degree Z_j to rank design schemes. GRA thus provides a reliable basis for optimizing HFoJ pattern application in line with user expectations:

$$Z_j^+ = \frac{1}{m}\sum_{i=1}^{m} \varepsilon_{ij}^+ \tag{12}$$

$$z_j = \frac{Z_j^+}{Z_j^+ + Z_j^-} \tag{13}$$

4. Case Study

4.1. Collection and Classification of Affective Vocabularies

To collect the affective vocabularies of the HFoJ, this study employs the Affinity Diagram method. Participants from diverse backgrounds are invited to list the vocabulary related to the patterns of homespun cloth based on their personal, intuitive feelings and associations. Subsequently, the collected vocabulary is presented in the form of group discussions to ensure the diversity and comprehensiveness of the information. Finally, all the vocabulary is summarized and presented, providing data support for subsequent research and creative work.

To extract the key perceptual factors, this study uses PCA to conduct a further analysis of the collected emotional vocabulary. This study selects 20 representative sample pictures of the TPs of HFoJ, providing materials for the subsequent PCA. The specific samples are shown in Figure 2. To ensure the reliability and effectiveness of the analysis results, this study sets up a seven-level semantic scale for these 20 samples and forms a questionnaire. A total of 200 questionnaires were distributed in this survey (Figure 3) and 187 valid questionnaires were retrieved, with an effective recovery rate of 93.5%. Finally, statistical software is used for random calculations. After obtaining the mean value of each emotional vocabulary, the PCA is carried out.

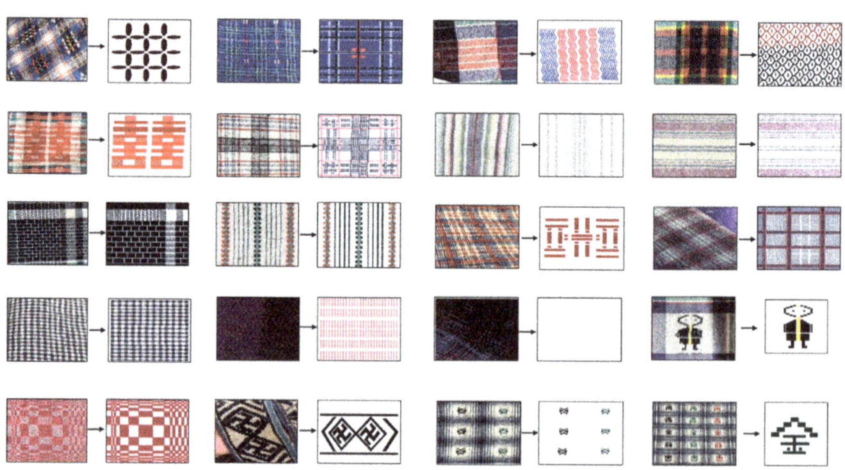

Figure 2. Pictures of TPs of HFoJ.

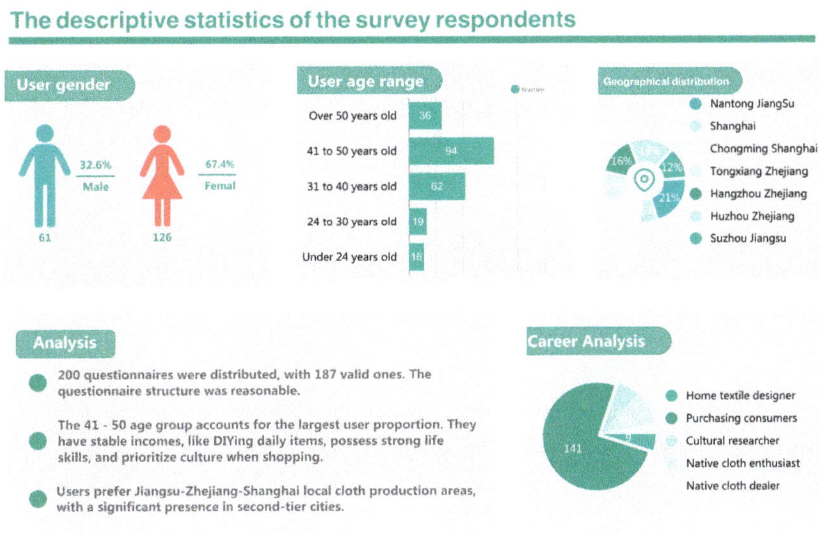

Figure 3. User infographic.

First, analyze whether the research data are suitable for PCA. As can be seen from Table 3, the KMO value is 0.605, which is greater than 0.6 and meets the prerequisite requirements for PCA, indicating that the data can be used for PCA research. In addition, the data have passed Bartlett's sphericity test ($p < 0.05$), suggesting that the research data are suitable for PCA.

Table 3. Test of KMO and Bartlett.

KMO		**0.605**
Bartlett Sphericity Check	Approximate Chi-square	211.238
	df	45
	p	0.000

According to the total variance explanation in Table 4 and the scree plot in Figure 4, the eigenvalues of the first three principal components are all greater than 1 and the cumulative variance contribution rate reaches 85.822%. Meanwhile, the slope change trend of the scree plot further supports the selection of extracting three principal components. Finally, three principal components are extracted for further analysis.

As shown in Table 5, the factor loading matrix after rotation reveals that the loading coefficients of the three principal components all exceed 0.7, including their significant explanatory effect on the data. In Principal Component 1, words like "elegant", "rhythmic", "plain", and "homely" have high loadings so it is named "Aesthetic Features". Principal Component 2, composed of "Symmetrical", "Settled", and "True quality", is named "Art Style". In Principal Component 3, words such as "Personal", "Artisanal", and "Profound" have high loadings and it is named "Life Charm". The specific classification results are summarized in Table 6.

Table 4. Explanation of total variance.

	Initial Eigenvalue			Sum of Squared Loadings Extracted			Sum of Squared Loadings After Rotation		
Element	Total	Percentage of Variance	Cumulative %	Total	Percentage of Variance	Cumulative %	Total	Percentage of Variance	Cumulative %
1	3.541	35.409	35.409	3.541	35.409	35.409	3.320	33.201	33.201
2	3.065	30.654	66.062	3.065	30.654	66.062	2.807	28.069	61.270
3	1.976	19.760	85.822	1.976	19.760	85.822	2.455	24.553	85.822
4	0.708	7.079	92.901						
5	0.375	3.750	96.651						
6	0.197	1.974	98.625						
7	0.058	0.577	99.201						
8	0.039	0.391	99.592						
9	0.033	0.329	99.922						
10	0.008	0.078	100.000						

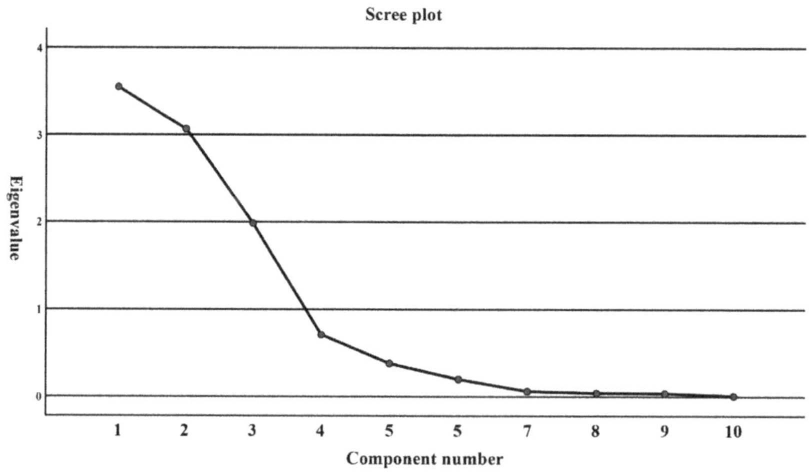

Figure 4. Scree plot.

Table 5. Component matrix after rotation.

	Component		
	Component 1	Component 2	Component 3
Elegant	0.909	−0.150	−0.158
Rhythm	0.898	−0.289	−0.255
Plain	0.833	0.393	0.127
Homely	0.811	0.392	0.031
Symmetrical	−0.065	0.921	−0.173
Settled	0.076	0.915	0.307
True quality	0.113	0.829	0.082
Personal	−0.175	0.073	0.962
Artisanal	−0.189	0.009	0.914
Profundity	0.497	0.116	0.675

Table 6. Affective vocabularies for HFoJ.

Criterion Level	Sub-Criterion Level
Aesthetic Features (E_1)	Elegant (E_{11}), Rhythm (E_{12}), Plain (E_{13}), Homely (E_{14})
Art Style (E_2)	Symmetrical (E_{21}), Settled (E_{22}), True quality (E_{23})
Life Charm (E_3)	Personal (E_{31}), Artisanal (E_{32}), Profundity (E_{33})

4.2. Pattern Sorting and Reconstruction

To select five core sample patterns from twenty HFoJ samples, the research team conducted an in-depth analysis of the patterns of the HFoJ. In addition, the team also organized experts in related fields for discussions. After discussions and analyses, five representative core sample images were finally determined. As shown in Figure 5, the codes are extracted as S, $S = \{S1, S2, S3, S4, S5\}$. Through meticulous extraction and collation of the key elements, such as the shapes and lines of these patterns, an initial pattern set is constructed.

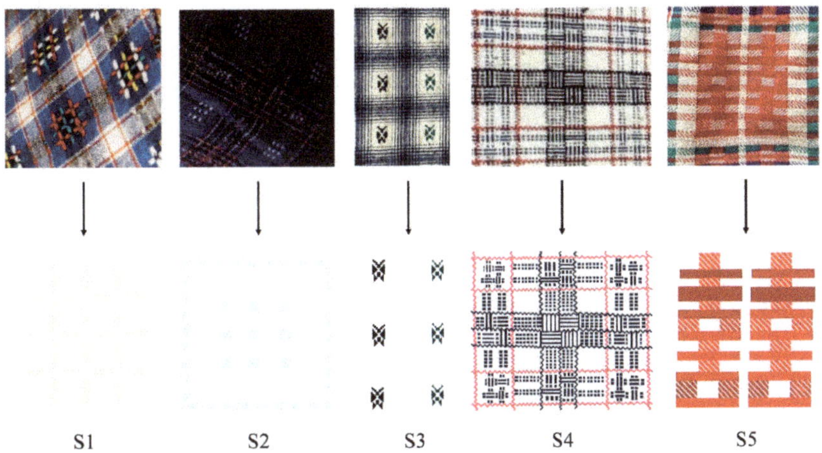

Figure 5. Extraction of core sample patterns of HFoJ.

After extracting the representative patterns of HFoJ and the characteristics of regional cultural symbols, it is necessary to formulate design restriction rules for home textile products to ensure their practicality and aesthetics. The rules mainly cover size limitations, the distribution of patterns on different fabrics, and their coordination between patterns and product shapes. Based on the above rules, SG operations are carried out through design software and, ultimately, pattern elements suitable for HTD schemes are obtained.

Scheme P1 is the variation process of the grid pattern, as shown in Figure 6. Firstly, according to Rule R3, partial deletion operations are carried out on the original grid pattern to remove redundant parts. Then, by applying Rules R5 and R8, the elements of the pattern after deletion are combined and transformed to construct a new basic element. Rule R8 is continuously applied and two rotation operations are carried out to make the outline and structure of the pattern complete and harmonious. Subsequently, Rule R5 is applied twice to copy and arrange the formed elements, enhancing the visual effect. Finally, with the help of Rule R4, the pattern is reduced in size according to the principle of equal proportion and the elements of each part are combined to finally form a new pattern.

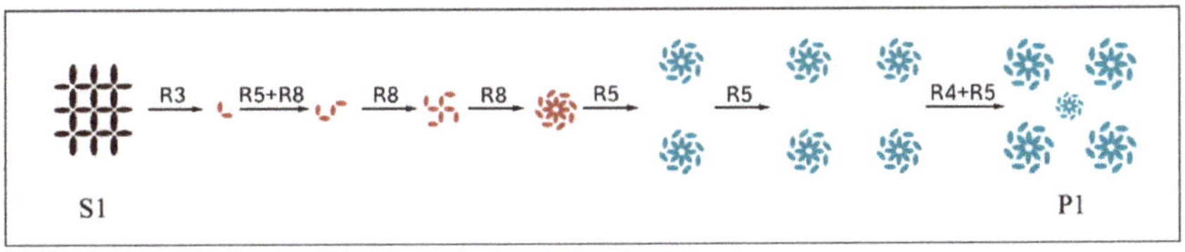

Figure 6. The deduction process of Shape Grammar for Scheme P1.

The derivation process of Scheme P2 is shown in detail in Figure 7. Firstly, according to Rule R3, a part of the original element is intercepted. Subsequently, Rule R5 and Rule R6 are applied three times to perform rotation and mirroring operations on the intercepted part, resulting in new sub-elements.

Figure 7. The deduction process of Shape Grammar for Scheme P2.

The derivation process of the "Double Happiness" cloth (S5) in Scheme P3 is shown in detail in Figure 8. Firstly, according to Rule R3, a deletion operation is carried out on the original pattern, removing one-third of it. Then, Rule R6 is applied to create an axially symmetric pattern, breaking the limitation of the original pattern. Subsequently, Rule R8 is applied twice, making the deformed pattern more visually appealing and design oriented.

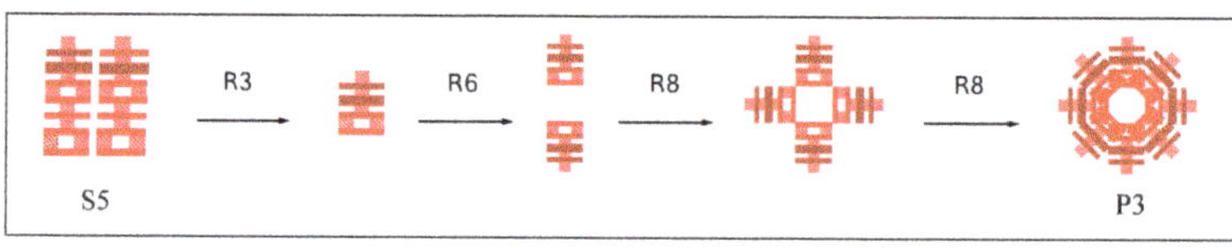

Figure 8. The deduction process of Shape Grammar for Scheme P3.

Schemes P4–P8 are designed and derived around the butterfly pattern (S3) (Figure 9). Firstly, according to Rule R3, the original butterfly pattern is deleted and only the middle part is retained. Then, Rule R6 is applied to copy the retained part, making it slightly overlap with the original pattern to add a sense of hierarchy. Finally, Rules R6 and R8 are comprehensively used to perfect the pattern, creating a new element with a fuller shape (P4).

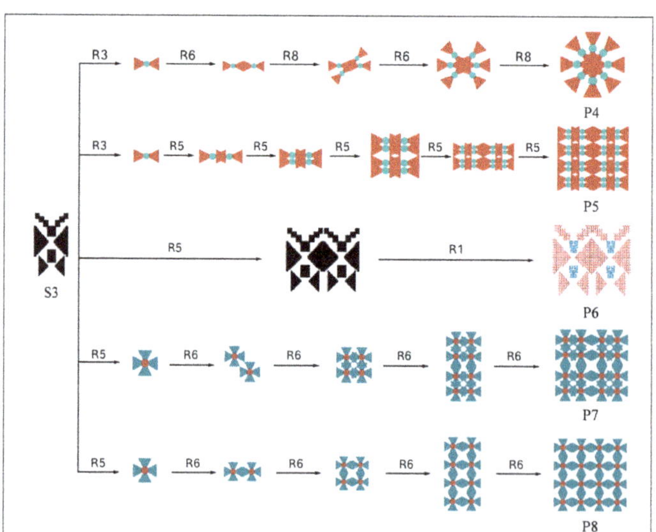

Figure 9. The deduction process of Shape Grammar for Schemes P4–P8.

Scheme P5 presents the second innovative variation of the butterfly pattern. According to Rule R3, the original butterfly pattern is screened and the middle core part is retained. Subsequently, Rule R5 is applied five times to copy and arrange the retained part, constructing a new grid-like pattern. Compared with the original pattern, the new pattern has a more compact shape and a more regular structural layout.

Scheme P6 demonstrates the third variation path of the butterfly pattern. Copy the original butterfly pattern according to Rule R5. After obtaining the copy, use Rule R1 to replace the internal structure and elements of the copy and embed new elements that conform to the design concept, enriching the content and form of the butterfly pattern.

Scheme P7 presents the fourth evolution. In the design process, according to Rule R5, the wing parts of the butterfly pattern are combined to construct the basic shape. Then, the mirror transformation operation of Rule R6 is carried out continuously three times. The combined wing patterns are mirror-copied at different angles and positions to form a new combined pattern, which improves the adaptability of the pattern and can better meet the design requirements.

The variation of Scheme P8 is similar to that of P7. At the beginning of the design, according to Rule R5, the wing parts of the original pattern are extracted and combined to construct the basic shape. Then, the transformation of Rule R6 is carried out to make all the transformed patterns closely connected without overlapping, forming a regular folding area. Through this process, the new pattern has simpler lines, a more regular layout, and a clean and neat overall visual effect.

The derivation processes of Schemes P9 and P10 are shown in detail in Figure 10. Firstly, using Rule R1, the original square outer frame is replaced with a circular one, making the pattern more concise. Subsequently, Rule R5 is applied to copy the elements. Finally, with the help of Rule R6, the elements are mirrored to create intersections between them, further adding details.

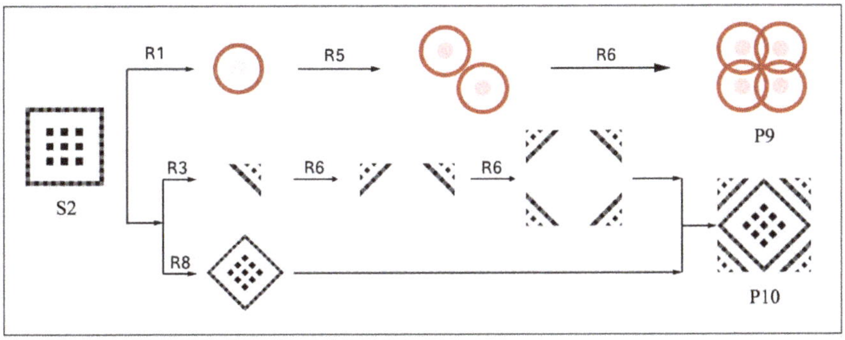

Figure 10. The deduction process of Shape Grammar for Schemes P9 and P10.

Scheme P10 presents the second innovative variation path of the cat's paw pattern (S2). According to Rule R3, a deletion operation is carried out on the original pattern to remove some redundant structures. Then, Rule R6 is applied twice to mirror-copy the elements of the pattern after deletion to enrich the visual hierarchy. Meanwhile, Rule R8 is used to rotate the original elements. A framework for the new pattern is built, shaping the base form.

4.3. Assign Weights to Affective Vocabularies

After collecting and classifying the affective vocabularies, this study uses the FAHP to assign weights to the affective vocabularies to comprehensively analyze consumers' emotional demands and preference tendencies towards the TPs of the HFoJ in HTD.

When assigning weights to affective vocabularies using the FAHP, the categories of affective vocabularies (Aesthetic Features E_1, Art Style E_2, Life Charm E_3) are defined as the criterion layer, the perceptual factors (ten affective vocabularies, such as Elegant E_{11}, Rhythm E_{12}, Plain E_{13}, etc.) are defined as the sub-criterion layer, and a model is established, as shown in Figure 11.

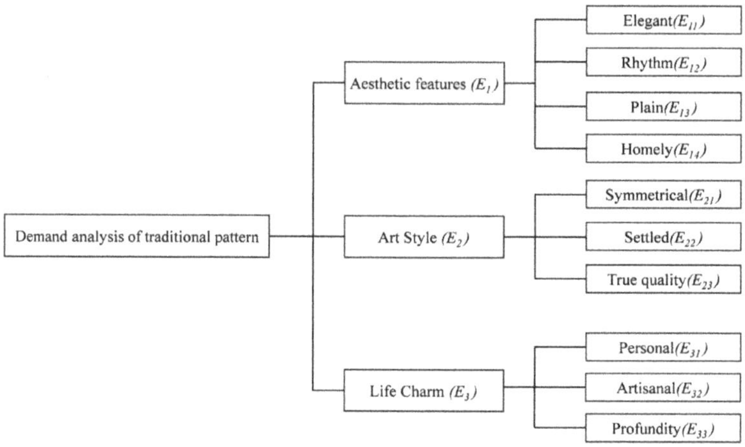

Figure 11. The evaluation system of perceptual demands for the HFoJ.

Thirteen experts (three textile history scholars, five home textile designers, and five folk culture researchers) scored aspects such as the color, pattern, and cultural connotations of the patterns. To quantify the judgment matrix, a ratio scale method ranging from 0.1 to 0.9 was adopted for assignment and numerical values were used to represent the different degrees of importance between every two elements. Through discussion and analysis, the evaluation results of the experts tended to be consistent. Calculations were carried out according to Formulas (1)–(7) and, finally, the weights of the criterion layer, the sub-criterion layer, and each evaluation index were obtained. Subsequently, a consistency test was conducted on the calculation results and the specific data are shown in Tables 7 and 8.

Table 7. Consistency test results.

	Objective Layer	Criterion Layer		
		E_1	E_2	E_3
CI	0.0067	0.005	0.022	0.0378

Table 8. Weights and rankings of affective vocabularies.

Criterion Level	Sub-Criterion Level	Same-Level Weights	Global Weights	Ranking
E_1 (0.41)	E_{11}	0.2450	0.1005	5
	E_{12}	0.2567	0.1052	4
	E_{13}	0.2283	0.0936	6
	E_{14}	0.2700	0.1107	2
E_2 (0.32)	E_{21}	0.4067	0.1301	1
	E_{22}	0.2600	0.0832	10
	E_{23}	0.3333	0.1067	3
E_3 (0.27)	E_{31}	0.3233	0.0873	9
	E_{32}	0.3467	0.0936	7
	E_{33}	0.3300	0.0891	8

4.4. Pattern Scheme Ranking and Design Practice

The previous section utilized SG to generate ten design element schemes. To accurately match user needs with pattern design, this study adopts the QFD quality house method to construct a mapping model of "users' core affective vocabularies—symbols of HFoJ patterns". To associate users' perceptual cognition of home textile products with the symbolic features of HFoJ patterns, the potential needs of users are deeply explored, providing a scientific basis for the subsequent screening of pattern designs that best meet users' expectations and optimizing the design schemes of home textile products.

In the basement part of the quality house, with the help of Formula 8, the weights of cultural symbols and the rankings of the schemes are obtained. Finally, based on the QFD method, a HOQ, as shown in Figure 12, is constructed. The research results show that the weights of cultural symbols of Schemes P3, P9, P2, and P4 are 5.3406, 4.0999, 4.099, and 4.0299, respectively, ranking among the top four in all the schemes. Therefore, Schemes P3, P9, P2, and P4 are selected as the design elements for HFoJ home textile products.

Assign values corresponding to user needs and design indicators		
◎	strongly correlated	5
○	moderately correlated	3
△	weakly correlated	1

		Comprehensive weight	P1	P2	P3	P4	P5	P6	P7	P8	P9	P10
Elegant E_{11}		0.245	◎	○	○	△	△		△		△	△
Rhythm E_{12}		0.2567			○		○					◎
Plain E_{13}		0.2283		○	○	◎					△	
Homely E_{14}		0.27				○	◎			◎	○	
Symmetrical E_{21}		0.4067						◎				
Settled E_{22}		0.26									◎	
True quality E_{23}		0.3333		◎	○							
Personal E_{31}		0.3233							◎	○		
Artisanal E_{32}		0.3467			◎	○						
Profundity E_{33}		0.33	○									○
Importance level	Absolute weight(x100%)		2.605	4.099	5.3406	4.0299	3.5539	2.0335	1.6165	3.31	4.0999	2.283
	Relative weight(%)		6.35	9.98	12.97	9.81	8.66	4.94	3.92	8.03	9.98	5.56
	Link		7	3	1	4	5	9	10	6	2	8

Figure 12. The House of Quality of the mapping model between affective vocabularies and pattern schemes.

4.5. Decision Making for Home Textile Scheme Design

Based on the four types of design elements (*P3, P9, P2, P4*) extracted by the QFD method, the design work of home textile products is carried out. The unit patterns are organically connected in series, enhancing the visual unity and harmony of the home textile products. Through a series of design practices and adjustments, three design schemes for home textile products are finally designed, and the specific scheme display is shown in Figure 13.

In the research on the innovative design of HFoJ home textile products, three design schemes (G_1–G_3) were evaluated across five dimensions: Pattern Innovation (N_1), Home Textile Applicability (N_2), Market Acceptance (N_3), Degree of Cultural Inheritance (N_4), and Personalization Potential (N_5). Home textile applicability ensures that patterns match product functions and styles, optimizing both practicality and aesthetics. Market acceptance directly reflects product viability in the market, impacting commercial value. The personalization potential caters to the trend of personalized consumption, meets diverse aesthetic needs, expands market coverage, and boosts brand competitiveness.

Figure 13. Three design schemes for home textile products.

Ten design experts were invited to score each scheme, with the final score for each scheme calculated as the average of the expert evaluations. The expert scoring scale ranged from 0.1 to 0.9, where 0.1 indicated extreme inappropriateness and 0.9 signified extreme appropriateness. The detailed scoring results are presented in Table 9. Using Formulas (9)–(12), the relevant connection numbers for each indicator and the correlation degree rankings were calculated, as shown in Table 10.

Table 9. The evaluation matrix of HFoJ home textile schemes.

Evaluation Dimensions	Reference Sequence	G_1	G_2	G_3
Pattern Innovation (N_1)	0.72	0.72	0.57	0.56
Home Textile Applicability (N_2)	0.71	0.71	0.58	0.58
Market Acceptance (N_3)	0.77	0.77	0.67	0.61
Degree of Cultural Inheritance (N_4)	0.81	0.64	0.81	0.59
Potential for Personalization (N_5)	0.76	0.76	0.57	0.59

Table 10. Correlation coefficient results.

Evaluation Dimensions	G_1	G_2	G_3
Pattern Innovation (N_1)	1.000	0.423	0.407
Home Textile Applicability (N_2)	1.000	0.458	0.458
Market Acceptance (N_3)	1.000	0.524	0.407
Degree of Cultural Inheritance (N_4)	0.393	1.000	0.333
Potential for Personalization (N_5)	1.000	0.367	0.393
Degree of correlation	0.879	0.554	0.4
Ranking	1	2	3

The relative correlation degree reflects the closeness of each scheme to the ideal state. The higher the value, the better the scheme. According to the calculation results, the ranking of the relative correlation degrees of each scheme is: $G_1 > G_2 > G_3$. Therefore, among the schemes for applying TPs of the HfoJ to modern HTD, Scheme G_1 is the best choice.

5. Discussions

5.1. Sensitivity Analysis

To assess the sensitivity of various indicators in the decision-making process and explore the impact of these changes on the final decision, this paper carried out a series of sensitivity analysis experiments. The research shows that sensitivity analysis is extremely effective in determining the weights of indicators and screening the design schemes of traditional HFoJ patterns [26]. In the experiments, adjust the weight values to test their impact on the final decision. In the case of uncertainty, sensitivity analysis is extremely effective for determining the weights of indicators and screening the optimal scheme for the traditional HTD of the HFoJ.

A total of 10 experiments were conducted and the detailed records are shown in Appendix A. In the first five experiments, we set the weights of all indicators to the same values, specifically 1, 3, 5, 7, and 9. The subsequent experiments (Experiments 6 to 10) involved setting the weight of one indicator to the highest value (9) while gradually setting the weights of the other indicators to the lowest value (1), revealing the potential impact of slight changes in each indicator. The results of the sensitivity analysis are shown in Figure 14. In the 10 experiments, Scheme G_1 consistently received the highest score, clearly indicating that Scheme G_1 is the best choice among all the design alternatives.

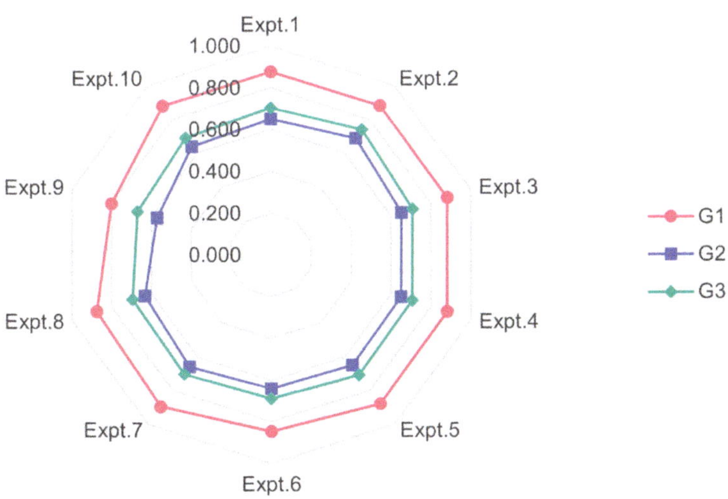

Figure 14. Three design schemes for home textile products design.

5.2. Comparison with Previous Studies

Compared with previous studies, this research demonstrates significant innovation in both methodological integration and research depth (see Table 11). Zou et al. [3] focused on outlining strategies for cross-cultural fashion design, primarily employing field investigations and the AHP, but lacked a systematic quantitative design process. Miao [4] concentrated on the application of traditional patterns in apparel, emphasizing element integration and market orientation, yet did not establish a comprehensive evaluation framework. Although Shen [5] combined the AHP and GRA to construct an evaluation system, the scope was limited to campus cultural and creative products, with insufficient depth in design innovation. In contrast, this study integrates the Affinity Diagram, FAHP, SG, QFD, and GRA to develop a user emotion–oriented systematic design process, balancing both design innovation and cultural heritage. The research not only promotes the modern transformation of traditional patterns but also expands their application in the field of HTD, demonstrating a stronger theoretical contribution and practical guidance value.

Table 11. Comparative analysis of this study and previous related works.

Study	Methodologies Employed	Key Contributions
This study	Affinity Diagram; FAHP; SG; QFD; GRA	- User-centered emotional demand analysis - Integration of qualitative and quantitative methods - Construction of a comprehensive evaluation model - Emphasis on cultural inheritance and innovation in home textile design
Zou, Y [3]	Field Investigation; Participatory Research; AHP	- Identified gaps in cross-cultural fashion design - Addressed cultural understanding and strategy formation - Lacked a systematic evaluation framework
Miao, H [4]	Case Analysis; Market Research	- Explored innovative uses of traditional patterns - Emphasized integration of clothing elements - Focused on practical design coordination rather than emotional evaluation
Shen, Y [5]	AHP; GRA; TOPSIS	- Tackled issues of product homogeneity and low innovation in campus cultural products - Developed a GC-TOPSIS-based evaluation model - Focused mainly on selection, not on creation

5.3. Home Textile Design Strategies

In the context of cultural preservation and quality-of-life enhancement, the integration of HFoJ patterns into modern home textiles presents both challenges and opportunities. Based on research on cultural symbols, KE, and form perception, the following strategies are proposed:

(1) Emotional Symbolism: HFoJ patterns serve not only functional but also cultural roles. By linking affective vocabularies with traditional symbols (e.g., wedding cloth, reed fence flowers), designers can enhance emotional resonance. Studies show that integrating elements like bamboo weaving lines and colors into modern design effectively triggers consumer identification, especially among younger users;

(2) User Experience via KE: KE helps translate consumers' emotional and sensory needs into design parameters. Emphasis should be placed on combining functionality with aesthetics while preserving the cultural essence of HFoJ patterns;

(3) Symbolic Innovation: Traditional motifs should be restructured using tools like SG to enhance modern relevance. This approach enables the cultural evolution of HFoJ patterns without losing their symbolic value;

(4) Balance of Tradition and Modernity: Symmetry and pattern rhythm play vital roles in visual stability and psychological comfort. Drawing from examples like the Republic of China cheongsam, incorporating symmetrical innovations allows HFoJ patterns to blend into minimalist modern interiors while retaining cultural depth.

6. Conclusions

This study explores the integration of TPs from the HFoJ into contemporary HTD, focusing on the interplay between pattern symmetry, user perception, and design innovation. By incorporating the Affinity Diagram, PCA, FAHP, SG, QFD, and GRA, this study constructs a comprehensive methodology to translate subjective emotional needs into quantifiable design parameters. The findings demonstrate that SG can effectively generate pattern variations with cultural depth while QFD and GRA provide robust frameworks for linking user emotions with design elements and optimizing alternatives. The optimal scheme (G1) confirms that symmetrical pattern layouts enhance visual order, promote emotional resonance, and improve user experience in home settings.

However, this study is subject to certain limitations. Due to practical constraints, the sample size for emotional and perceptual evaluation was relatively limited, potentially affecting the representativeness of the results. Furthermore, the emotional responses collected may vary across individuals due to cultural or personal cognitive differences, which introduces subjectivity into the analysis. Additionally, while emotional and sensory parameters were addressed through established methodologies, the quantification process for some emotional vocabularies remains generalized, possibly limiting the precision of design guidance.

Future research should aim to expand the sample base to include consumers with diverse cultural, demographic, and aesthetic backgrounds, thereby improving the generalizability and cultural adaptability of design outcomes. It is also essential to refine quantitative tools for emotional and sensory data analysis, particularly in the context of affective vocabulary extraction and parameter modeling. By enhancing the precision and inclusivity of emotional mapping, future studies can further advance the integration of traditional patterns into emotionally resonant, market-relevant home textile products.

Author Contributions: Conceptualization, M.Q.; Formal analysis, M.Q. and X.D.; Methodology, M.Q.; Software, M.Q.; Supervision, X.D.; Visualization, X.D.; Writing—original draft, M.Q.; Writing—review and editing, X.D., J.W. and H.Z. All authors have read and agreed to the published version of the manuscript.

Funding: This research received no external funding.

Data Availability Statement: The original contributions presented in this study are included in the article. Further inquiries can be directed to the corresponding author.

Conflicts of Interest: The authors declare no conflicts of interest.

Abbreviations

The following abbreviations are used in this manuscript:

HFoJ	Homespun Fabric of Jiangnan
TP	Traditional Patterns
CRs	Customer requirements
HTD	Home Textile Design
KE	Kansei Engineering
CI	Consistency Index
CR	Consistency Ratio
ECs	Engineering Characteristics
QFD	Quality Function Deployment
PCA	Principal Component Analysis
FAHP	Fuzzy Analytic Hierarchy Process

Appendix A

Table A1. Sensitivity analysis experiments.

NO	Definition	Sample Serial Number			Ranking
		G_1	G_2	G_3	
Expt. 1	$\omega_{N1\text{–}5} = 1$	0.879	0.554	0.400	$G_1 > G_3 > G_2$
Expt. 2	$\omega_{N1\text{–}5} = 3$	0.879	0.554	0.400	$G_1 > G_3 > G_2$
Expt. 3	$\omega_{N1\text{–}5} = 5$	0.879	0.554	0.400	$G_1 > G_3 > G_2$
Expt. 4	$\omega_{N1\text{–}5} = 7$	0.879	0.554	0.400	$G_1 > G_3 > G_2$
Expt. 5	$\omega_{N1\text{–}5} = 9$	0.879	0.554	0.400	$G_1 > G_3 > G_2$
Expt. 6	$\omega_{N1} = 1,\ \omega_{N2\text{–}5} = 9$	0.879	0.643	0.491	$G_1 > G_3 > G_2$
Expt. 7	$\omega_{N2} = 1,\ \omega_{N1,N3\text{–}5} = 9$	0.879	0.639	0.485	$G_1 > G_3 > G_2$
Expt. 8	$\omega_{N3} = 1,\ \omega_{N1\text{–}2,N4\text{–}5} = 9$	0.879	0.631	0.491	$G_1 > G_3 > G_2$
Expt. 9	$\omega_{N4} = 1,\ \omega_{N1\text{–}3,N5} = 9$	0.959	0.526	0.472	$G_1 > G_3 > G_2$
Expt. 10	$\omega_{N5} = 1,\ \omega_{N1\text{–}4} = 9$	0.879	0.649	0.492	$G_1 > G_3 > G_2$

References

1. Lee, S.K.; Koo, S. Development of three-dimensional printed cultural fashion products using symbols of longevity. *Text. Res. J.* **2022**, *92*, 4484–4500. [CrossRef]
2. Jowers, I.; Earl, C.; Stiny, G. Shapes, structures and shape grammar implementation. *Comput. Aided Design* **2019**, *111*, 80–92. [CrossRef]
3. Zou, Y.; Zhao, C.; Childs, P.; Luh, D. Cross-cultural design in costume: Case study on totemic symbols of China and Thailand. *Hum. Soc. Sci. Commun.* **2024**, *11*, 1263. [CrossRef]
4. Miao, H.; Wen, R. Wedding Bed Textiles Design Based on Chinese Traditional Auspicious Patterns. In Proceedings of the 7th International Conference on Arts, Design and Contemporary Education (ICADCE 2021), Moscow, Russia, 25–26 May 2021. [CrossRef]
5. Shen, Y. Evaluation and Selection of Cultural and Creative Design Solutions Based on Grey Correlation Multicriteria Decision Analysis. *Math. Probl. Eng.* **2022**, *2022*, 1–9. [CrossRef]
6. Chen, D.; Cheng, P.; Simatrang, S.; Joneurairatana, E. Kansei engineering as a tool for the design of traditional pattern. *Autex Res. J.* **2021**, *21*, 125–134. [CrossRef]
7. Chen, D.; Cheng, P. Research on the image design of clothing patterns. *Fibres Text. East. Eur.* **2024**, *32*, 17–24. [CrossRef]
8. An, S.; Guo, Z.; Fang, H. Study on the Kansei Image of Linear Elements of Wooden Screens on the Basis of Modern Aesthetics. *Forest Prod. J.* **2022**, *72*, 258–264. [CrossRef]
9. Song, Y.; Zhang, N.; Wu, T. Image evaluation and analysis of fabric with a geometric motif in dress style design. *Ind. Textila* **2024**, *75*, 591–598. [CrossRef]
10. Quan, H.; Li, S.; Hu, J. Product Innovation Design Based on Deep Learning and Kansei Engineering. *Appl. Sci.* **2018**, *8*, 2397. [CrossRef]
11. Gao, M.; Cao, X.; Qian, L. Cultural Echoes in Modern Design: Assessing Young Consumers' Perceptions of Traditional Bamboo Weaving Patterns. *Complexity* **2024**, *2024*, 5524490. [CrossRef]
12. Cui, J.; Tang, M. Integrating shape grammars into a generative system for Zhuang ethnic embroidery design exploration. *Comput. Aided Design* **2013**, *45*, 591–604. [CrossRef]
13. Guo, F.; Liu, W.; Liu, F.; Wang, H.; Wang, T. Emotional design method of product presented in multi-dimensional variables based on Kansei Engineering. *J. Eng. Design* **2014**, *25*, 194–212. [CrossRef]
14. Wang, C.; Zhang, J.; Liu, D.; Cai, Y.; Gu, Q. An AI-Powered Product Identity Form Design Method Based on Shape Grammar and Kansei Engineering: Integrating Midjourney and Grey-AHP-QFD. *Appl. Sci.* **2024**, *14*, 7444. [CrossRef]
15. Wang, T.; Yang, L. Combining GRA with a Fuzzy QFD Model for the New Product Design and Development of Wickerwork Lamps. *Sustainability* **2023**, *15*, 4208. [CrossRef]
16. Lee, P.; Han, Q. User-centric sustainable design in mass-customized housing using Kano model and quality function deployment. *Archit. Eng. Des. Manag.* **2025**, 1–17. [CrossRef]
17. Wang, Z.; Han, C.; Yu, B.; Wei, K.; Li, Y.; Jin, S.; Bai, P. The Emotional Design of Street Furniture Based on Kano Modeling. *Buildings* **2024**, *14*, 3896. [CrossRef]
18. Xu, H.; Song, H. Key Factors Influencing Chinese Consumers' Demand for Naturally Dyed Garments: Data Analysis through KJ Method and KANO Model. *Sustainability* **2024**, *16*, 1189. [CrossRef]

19. Apichonbancha, P.; Lin, R.; Chuang, C. Integration of Principal Component Analysis with AHP-QFD for Improved Product Design Decision-Making. *Appl. Sci.* **2024**, *14*, 5976. [CrossRef]
20. Oster, A.; McCormack, J. A Methodology for Creating Shape Rules During Product Design. *J. Mech. Design* **2011**, *133*, 61007. [CrossRef]
21. McKay, A.; Stiny, G.; de Pennington, A. Principles for the definition of design structures. *Int. J. Comput. Integ M.* **2016**, *29*, 237–250. [CrossRef]
22. Tošović-Stevanović, A.; Ristanović, V.; Ćalović, D.; Lalić, G.; Žuža, M.; Cvijanović, G. Small Farm Business Analysis Using the AHP Model for Efficient Assessment of Distribution Channels. *Sustainability* **2020**, *12*, 10479. [CrossRef]
23. Yu, S.; Liu, M.; Chen, L.; Chen, Y.; Yao, L. Emotional Design and Evaluation of Children's Furniture Based on AHP-TOPSIS. *Bioresources* **2024**, *19*, 7418–7433. [CrossRef]
24. Zheng, H.; Liu, L.; Zhang, Q.; Wang, Y.; Wei, Y. Children's Hospital Environment Design Based on AHP/QFD and Other Theoretical Models. *Buildings* **2024**, *14*, 1499. [CrossRef]
25. Wang, T.; Zhang, Q.; Chong, H.; Wang, X. Integrated Supplier Selection Framework in a Resilient Construction Supply Chain: An Approach via Analytic Hierarchy Process (AHP) and Grey Relational Analysis (GRA). *Sustainability* **2017**, *9*, 289. [CrossRef]
26. Dai, Z.; Scott, M. Product platform design through sensitivity analysis and cluster analysis. *J. Intell. Manuf.* **2007**, *18*, 97–113. [CrossRef]

symmetry

MDPI

Article

A Cognitive Load Assessment Method for Airtight Cabin Operators Based on a One-Dimensional Convolutional Neural Network

Lei Wang, Jingluan Wang *, Dengkai Chen and Jie Song

Key Laboratory of Ministry of Industrial Design and Ergonomics, Ministry of Industry and Information Technology, Northwestern Polytechnical University, Xi'an 710072, China; wang.lei@mail.nwpu.edu.cn (L.W.); chendengkai@nwpu.edu.cn (D.C.)

* Correspondence: wangjingluan1@163.com

Abstract: Airtight cabins with highly complex human–machine systems impose an excessive cognitive load on operators. However, the traditional cognitive load assessment methods often cannot fully extract physiological features such as electroencephalogram and electrocardiogram signals, relying heavily on artificial feature extraction. Therefore, this study proposes an evaluation method based on a one-dimensional convolutional neural network to evaluate the cognitive load of airtight cabin workers. This evaluation method preprocesses and intercepts raw physiological signals such as electroencephalogram and electrocardiogram signals and then inputs them into the model for evaluation. The experimental results demonstrate that the training accuracy rate of the one-dimensional convolutional neural network is 97.6%, and the test classification accuracy rate is 86.5%. Despite sample size limitations, the proposed method demonstrates valid effectiveness in this study. Finally, taking a manned submersible as an example, cognitive load in different difficult tasks is identified, evaluated, and classified.

Keywords: cognitive load assessment; one-dimensional convolutional neural network; airtight cabins; physiological signal; electroencephalography

1. Introduction

An airtight cabin represents a quintessential example of a specialized workspace and living environment. This workspace is typically confined and enclosed, with a unique working environment that limits the range of postures available to operators, thereby making it challenging to secure adequate rest. These conditions can negatively impact human physical and psychological factors. Moreover, this environment encompasses not only the traditional physical surroundings but also an information-rich environment replete with high-tech applications. In such a setting, the cognitive load on operators is likely to increase significantly, potentially compromising the safety of human–machine systems. Conducting research on the cognitive load of personnel operating within airtight cabins, as well as detecting and analyzing their cognitive states, is of paramount importance for protecting the health of these individuals, reducing human errors, and enhancing their work efficiency.

Cognitive load indicates pressure on working memory and task performance and has garnered increasing research attention in recent years. Previous studies have demonstrated that different levels of task difficulty are associated with various psychophysiological signals, such as respiration [1]; skin conductance response [2]; pupillary responses [3,4];

heart rate (HR); heart rate variability [5]; blink interval [6]; hormone levels; and measures of brain activity, particularly electroencephalography (EEG) [7,8].

There is a wealth of research cases in the study of cognitive load within airtight cabins, such as spacecraft, cockpits, and manned submersibles. Sun et al. constructed an evaluation index system and methodology for human–machine interface ergonomics, enhancing the work efficiency of astronauts and the performance of aerospace systems by addressing ergonomics evaluation issues related to spacecraft human–machine interfaces [9]. Zhang et al. analyzed the cognitive behavior of marine divers during deep-sea missions and calculated the probability of cognitive failure in these tasks [10]. Alfredson et al. studied cognitive ergonomics and applied their findings to the development of design principles for fighter aircraft cockpits [11]. Ye Cong et al. researched the design process of manned submersible cabin layouts, grounded in the principles of human–machine ergonomics and equipment layout design [12]. However, the outcomes of these evaluations are relatively subjective and susceptible to the influence of the participants' subjective perceptions.

With advances in artificial intelligence technology, evaluating cognitive load using algorithms such as support vector machines (SVMs), multilayer perceptrons, K-nearest neighbors, and convolutional neural networks (CNNs) has become a popular research direction. Hemakom et al. proposed a multimodal machine learning framework that integrated EEG and electrocardiogram (ECG) biomarkers and incorporated six classifiers (multilayer perceptron, AdaBoost, K-nearest neighbors, logistic regression, naive Bayes, and SVM) to achieve 76.55% classification accuracy across cognitive load gradations [13]. Tjolleng et al. constructed an artificial neural network using feedforward networks and scaled conjugate gradients as backpropagation learning rules to classify drivers' cognitive loads based on ECG data [14]. Tabar et al. used time–frequency transformations of EEG data based on convolutional neural networks to evaluate mental workload [15]. Jiao et al. proposed an improved convolutional neural network to classify cognitive load, not only reducing the number of parameters required for model training but also enhancing classification performance. These studies demonstrate the superiority of convolutional neural networks and classifier algorithms in assessing cognitive load.

Many studies have utilized features like root mean square and mean absolute value for physiological signals to assess cognitive load, a process that necessitates extensive experimental validation for its justification. The special nature of the airtight cabin environment makes it difficult to conduct extensive research in this area. Therefore, discovering and determining appropriate physiological features and classification methodologies from raw one-dimensional physiological signal data are crucial for evaluating operators' cognitive load levels, which can significantly improve the human design factors of airtight cabins. Symmetry and asymmetry constitute fundamental dualities in ergonomic design paradigms. Managerial asymmetries in cognitive load assessment during operator evaluations have been shown to directly compromise workforce health outcomes and productivity metrics. This is also of great importance for the physical and mental health of maintenance personnel and enhancing work efficiency.

This study proposes a method of assessing operators' cognitive load based on a one-dimensional convolutional neural network (1D-CNN). The physiological data—including EEG and ECG collected from operators within airtight cabins via wireless sensors—are directly used as inputs for the 1D-CNN to identify their cognitive loads during operations of varying difficulty levels. This approach addresses the issue of manual feature extraction encountered in traditional classification methods and simultaneously avoids interference caused by collecting wired data from operators. Compared with two-dimensional CNNs, this involves fewer training parameters, circumventing the problem of slow processing speeds due to a large number of parameters and preventing signal distortion issues that can arise from transforming one-dimensional raw signals into two dimensions.

The remainder of this study is organized as follows: Section 2 provides an overview of relevant research and background. Section 3 describes the materials and methods, including experimental design, data collection and processing, and model development. Section 4 analyzes the experimental results. Section 5 validates the method with a case study on a manned submersible. Section 6 discusses the findings. Section 7 outlines the main conclusions. Section 8 addresses the limitations of the study and discusses future work.

2. Literature Review

This subsection reviews the current state of research from three perspectives: human–machine ergonomics research in airtight cabins, worker cognitive load studies, and neural-network-based cognitive load assessment.

2.1. Human–Machine Ergonomics Research in Airtight Cabins

Human–machine ergonomics focuses on studying human–machine–environment systems, analyzing the interrelationship between the three, and exploring its mechanisms with the help of cross-field disciplines such as biomedicine and statistics. Typically, physiological indicators such as EEG and ECG are collected from operators at work, and human cognitive characteristics are used for cabin design. Using human–computer ergonomics as the basic theory, researchers have studied the layout design and human–machine interaction of airtight cabins to improve the performance and cognitive ability of operators.

Military fields such as aviation, aerospace, manned deep diving, and armored vehicles are hot areas of ergonomic research. Wang et al. studied musculoskeletal disorders and cognitive load caused by complex console layouts [16]. Shi et al. designed a shared human–machine ergonomics assessment system to solve the human–machine ergonomics assessment problem in cockpit system design, achieving real-time dynamic assessments of operators [17]. Andrews et al. developed a predictive workload model using an integrated tool with improved performance to maintain pilot cognitive load at a manageable level [18]. Lagomarsino et al. proposed a new method for evaluating cognitive load in manufacturing that can reduce the physical fatigue and discomfort of operators [19]. Wang et al. studied the comfort characteristics of the cabins of manned submersibles and proposed a JACK-based multi-source composite assessment model for comfort assessment of these spaces [20].

When operators in airtight cabins are under high cognitive loads, they are prone to fatigue, which can adversely affect their operational safety and work performance, potentially leading to safety incidents. The above studies show that ergonomics can not only guide cabin design and optimize the HMI process but also assess the operator's cognitive load level and, more importantly, improve operational capability and personnel effectiveness.

2.2. Worker Cognitive Load Studies

Cognitive load mainly refers to the level of "mental energy" taken up by a person to receive, remember, and process a large amount of information in a short period. It mainly includes work requirements, time pressure, task complexity, and operator performance. This is reflected in the fact that operators receive a lot of information and experience-corresponding sensations through their visual and auditory senses.

Xiong et al. explored automatic cognitive load pattern recognition using physiological measurements to quantify autonomic and central nervous activity by extracting 33 commonly used physiological features from EEG and ECG signals. The algorithm was optimized using particle swarm optimization to construct a cognitive load pattern recognition model, achieving 97.2% accuracy in classifying cognitive load mismatches and matches [21]. Na et al. studied three factors of cognitive load: psychological demand, time demand, and frustrated effort. The results indicated that the dual-task approach and the National Aeronautics and Space Administration Task Load Index (NASA-TLX) scale assessment could be good indicators of cognitive load [22]. Haapalainen et al. used cognitive perception and cognitive speed as assessment factors in the Ubicomp application for cognitive abilities, collecting ECG data from multiple sensors. They found that ECG median absolute deviation and median heat flux measurements were the most accurate in differentiating cognitive load levels [23].

Blink frequency and duration are also commonly used to measure states of alertness, attention, and mental load in studies related to pilots and drivers. Many studies have shown that when alertness, task demands, and fatigue increase, blink frequency and duration appear to decrease [24]. Chen et al. conducted systematic investigations on physiological signal variations in fighter pilots during flight training and combat operations, identifying EEG and ECG as sensitive biomarkers for mental workload fluctuations [25]. Through controlled psychophysiological experiments, Weelden et al. established the clinical significance of EEG theta/beta power spectral density in aviation mental workload assessment, with multimodal data in evaluation precision [26]. Dussault et al. studied changes in the EEG and ECG signal indicators of pilots during real flights and found that the β- and γ-wave power of the EEG indicators increased while the α-wave decreased when the pilots flew on standard takeoff and landing routes [27].

These studies indicate that physiological indicators such as the EEG and ECG of operators in airtight cabin environments correlate with cognitive load levels. Therefore, determining how to utilize these physiological indicators to quantitatively assess operators' cognitive load is a crucial issue, particularly for one-dimensional time series data like EEG and ECG indicators. Additionally, owing to noise in EEG and ECG signal data, preprocessing techniques such as filtering and transformation are necessary to extract more cognitive load information.

2.3. Neural-Network-Based Cognitive Load Assessment

Cognitive load assessment is an important research component in the field of ergonomics. When neural networks were not widely used, most researchers used a more traditional machine learning approach to assess cognitive load. Liang et al. developed a real-time workload classification method for car drivers based on SVMs to classify and identify the collected features, resulting in a correct classification rate of 81.1% [28]. Amin et al. proposed a discrete-wavelet-transform-based EEG signal feature extraction method that can be used for load feature classification using classifiers such as multilayer perceptrons and K-nearest neighbors [29].

In recent years, deep learning has made progress in classification tasks [30,31] and pattern recognition tasks [32]. There are many applications in the field of physiological signal processing. Han et al. architected a deep learning framework leveraging multimodal neurophysiological monitoring (EEG-ECG co-registration) for aviation human factor engineering applications [33]. Baldwin et al. used an artificial neural network for task difficulty and kind identification for three cognitive tasks using an EEG dataset as a sample, finding high accuracy in classifying task difficulty and low accuracy in classifying task kind [34]. Tjolleng et al. developed a driver cognitive load detection system based on ECG signals using multilayer artificial neural networks [35].

In addition, one of the most typical and widely used network structures in deep learning, a CNN, is also used for cognitive load classification [36,37]. Jiao et al. proposed an improved CNN for classifying cognitive load that reduced the model training parameters while also improving the classification results [38].

Existing research shows that machine learning algorithms and deep learning networks are effective in quantifying and assessing cognitive load. These studies typically involve manual feature extraction from EEG and ECG data, followed by using classification algorithms for cognitive load evaluation. This approach introduces a degree of subjectivity into the assessment of operators' cognitive load, as manual feature extraction relies on the researchers' experience and can be cumbersome. Utilizing CNNs can effectively address these issues by directly evaluating operators' cognitive load levels from one-dimensional time series data like EEG and ECG through operations such as convolution and pooling.

3. Materials and Methods

This section presents an experimental study collecting physiological signals from operators in airtight cabins. It outlines the experimental design and data-processing methods employed in this research and introduces a cognitive load assessment approach based on a 1D-CNN. The overall framework of this study is shown in Figure 1, including the cognitive load assessment experiment for airtight cabin operators, experimental data processing and analysis, the construction and training of the cognitive load assessment model, and the model application.

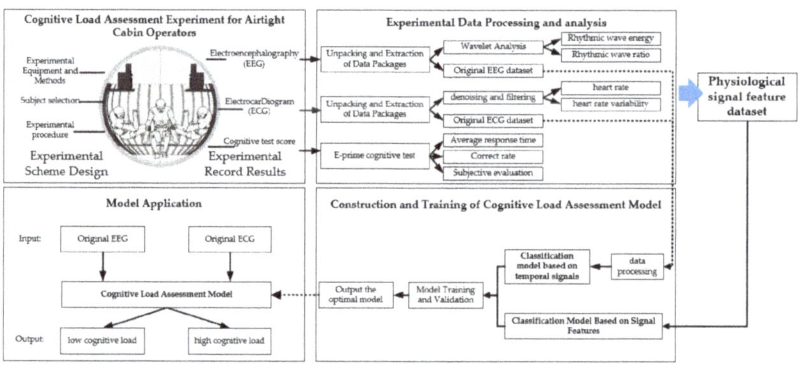

Figure 1. Research framework.

3.1. Experimental Scheme Design

This subsection details the experimental setup, equipment, participant selection, and task design for cognitive load assessment.

3.1.1. Experimental Equipment and Methods

Experiments were conducted in the airtight cabin laboratory of the Department of Industrial Design, Northwestern Polytechnic University, to study changes in the cognitive loads of operators in a confined chamber environment with different task levels. The laboratory environment fully simulates the cabin of the "Jiaolong" manned submersible. The pre-experimental preparation included a closed experimental platform, equipment for measuring physiological data such as EEG and ECG, the NASA-TLX subjective scale, and a computer.

The EEG signals were measured using the TGAM single-conductor EEG device (Shen Nian Technologies, Inc., San Jose, CA, USA). Firstly, we wiped off any grease on the subject's skin and electrodes with alcohol paper, applied an Ag/AgCl disk electrode to the left forehead, and fixed the reference electrode and ground electrode at the left and right earlobes, respectively. A matching Bluetooth adapter was plugged into the computer. After all the above operations were completed, the power switch was turned on, and the Bluetooth adapter's blinking light was on, indicating a good connection between the EEG device and the computer. Finally, the TGAM module's MindViewer (Shen

Nian Technologies, Inc., San Jose, CA, USA, https://blog.jackeylea.com/qt/mindviewer-tgam-module-graphic-application/#%E8%BD%AF%E4%BB%B6 (accessed on 5 June 2025)) software was opened, and the corresponding serial port and baud rate were selected to observe the EEG waveform.

The ECG signal was collected using a low-power ECG sensor device (ADS8881 SAR ADC, Texas Instruments, Inc., Dallas, TX, USA). The electrode pads were attached to the subject's left chest and connected to the computer's Bluetooth serial port. When the indicator light flashed and the data were output from the computational display, the real-time ECG waveform could be observed by opening the supporting software. After the subject put on the experimental equipment and prepared, the experiment was carried out according to the requirements of the main subject.

Owing to the characteristics of airtight cabins and to ensure the feasibility and convenience of subsequent on-site experiments while minimizing interference to the operator, this study selected a TGAM single-conductor EEG device and a low-power ECG sensor device. To further elucidate the interaction mechanism between EEG and ECG physiological signals and operator cognitive load, devices such as ring electrodes or integrated electrode caps should be used to collect multi-channel data.

The NASA-TLX subjective scale was used after subjects completed the experiment to rate their subjective feelings after completing each main experiment. The six dimensions of the scale include mental demand, physical demand, time demand, effort level, performance level, and frustration level. Table 1 presents detailed descriptions of each dimension of the scale.

Table 1. NASA-TLX subjective scale dimensions explained.

Dimension	Dimension Description
Mental demands	How much mental activity (thinking, memorizing, decision-making, calculating, etc.) is required to complete the task, and whether it is easy or difficult in terms of mental effort.
Physical demands	How much physical effort is required to complete the task (movement control, performing activities, etc.), and whether it is easy or difficult in terms of physical effort.
Time demands	The rate or pace at which work is performed, whether slow and relaxing or fast and flustered.
Effort level	The amount of effort required to complete the task.
Performance level	How well or poorly the task was accomplished and the level of satisfaction with the achievement.
Frustration level	The degree of frustration and annoyance felt during the completion of the task.

3.1.2. Subject Selection

Five subjects (aged between 22 and 26 years old) were selected for this experiment, all of whom were graduate students at the Department of Industrial Design at Northwestern Polytechnical University. They needed to be in good health, without any history of brain, heart, or chronic drug use. Furthermore, they needed to have normal vision (or corrected vision of 1.0 or higher) and normal hearing. All of the subjects were right-handed and positive-minded, without any depressive manifestations. The day before the experiment, they were asked to refrain from stimulating behaviors such as drinking, smoking, and coffee while ensuring adequate sleep and rest. Most importantly, from a professional standpoint, the five subjects had considerable research experience and operational expertise in human factor engineering within the fields of manned submersibles and sealed compartments. Furthermore, they had participated in designing the "Jiaolong" manned submersible, making them well acquainted with the environments of sealed compartments and the related operational processes. Due to the particularity of this research field, the selection of subjects is quite unique [16,39].

3.1.3. Experimental Procedure

To ensure the validity and accuracy of the experimental data, the temperature and humidity of the experimental environment were suitable, and the experimental time was controlled at about 10:00 am or 4:00 pm.

(1) Pre-experimental preparation

The experimental equipment was checked before the experiment to ensure proper communication between the EEG and ECG data testing equipment and the computer. The subjects were given some time to adjust to the cabin's environment so that their heart rates and EEGs were maintained in normal conditions. Subjects were asked to ensure they had adequate sleep and rest before the trial, maintain a regular schedule, and refrain from taking any stimulants. To reduce experimental errors related to the participants' adaptation to the experimental equipment, data from the first two minutes of the experiment were discarded during data processing.

(2) First experiment

The experimental flow is depicted in Figure 2. In the first experiment, subjects were initially asked to complete a primary task. After completing the primary task, their cognitive abilities, such as memory, reaction time, and attention, were assessed using E-prime 3.0 software. Lastly, they filled out the NASA-TLX subjective rating scale to subjectively evaluate the primary task.

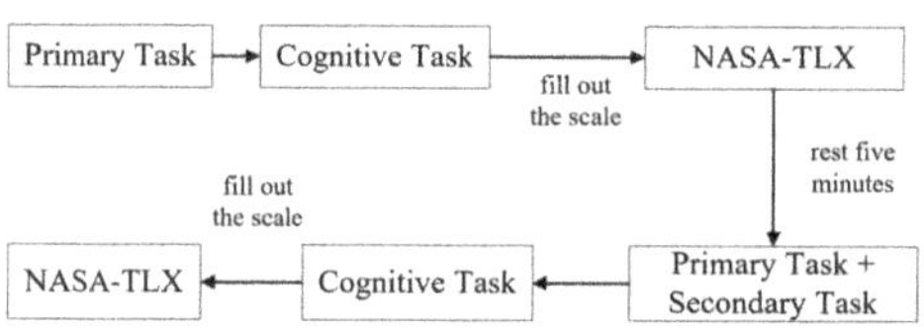

Figure 2. Experimental flow.

The primary duty of operators in an airtight cabin is to observe the external environment and the status of various instruments, providing feedback accordingly. Therefore, the primary task in this study was an observation-based work task. Participants were first assigned a specific keyword. They were then required to read information for five minutes on a computer, during which time they had to identify the number of occurrences of the assigned keyword. This was to be completed immediately after the primary task. The information read during the primary task and the assigned keyword were randomized for each trial.

(3) Second experiment

After the first experiment, we only gave the subjects five minutes of rest time for preparation before the second experiment, because tasks are continuous during operations in an airtight cabin.

In the second experiment, participants were asked to complete one main task and one secondary task. Then, as in the first experiment, E-prime was used to test their cognitive abilities after completing the task, and the NASA-TLX subjective scale was filled out.

The main task of the second experiment was consistent with the first experiment. However, the information and keywords read were random and were not exactly the same as the first experiment.

The secondary task of the airtight cabin operators was to record and calculate relevant data based on their observation results and operate relevant buttons based on calculation results. All observations, recordings, and operational procedures, as well as the principles behind these actions, were clearly explained to the participants so that they could be fully understood. Therefore, the task setting for this study was primarily focused on mental arithmetic. When the subjects completed the main task, they were asked to answer the result of an equation, that is, whether the sum of two digits can be divided by three.

Both the EEG and ECG acquisition devices were in contact with human skin through silver–silver chloride electrodes. The EEG signal was in single-channel lead mode with a sampling frequency of 512 Hz; the ECG signal was acquired through a low-power ECG device module; and data such as RR interval, heart rate, heart rate variability (HRV), and body temperature were automatically analyzed through the software.

At the end of the experiment, the subjects filled out the NASA-TLX subjective scale and scored six indicators, each with a score of 0 to 100, with higher scores representing a corresponding higher cognitive workload. In addition, the subjects were asked to rank the weighting of the six indicators, assigning different weighting values (1, 2, 3, 4, 5, and 6). Finally, a weighted average based on the scores and weights of the six indicators was used to obtain the comprehensive subjective evaluation value.

3.2. Experimental Data Collection and Processing

This subsection covers preprocessing steps for EEG, ECG, and cognitive test data, including wavelet decomposition and normalization.

3.2.1. EEG Data Processing Flow

The collected EEG packets were unpacked to obtain the raw EEG signal. The TGAM EEG module sent approximately 513 packets per second during operation, including 1 large packet and 512 small packets of data. Each large packet contained information such as signal strength, eSense focus, and relaxation; each small packet contained a set of raw signals. The raw EEG signals in all sachets needed to be acquired and extracted as follows:

The data format of each packet is AA AA 04 80 02 *xxHigh xxLow xxCheckSum*, where the first five bytes (AA AA 04 08 02) are always the same, indicating the type of the packet. The last three bytes (*xxHigh xxLow xxCheckSum*) are variable. *xxHigh xxLow* represents the raw EEG data in hexadecimal, and the raw EEG signal can be calculated with Equations (1) and (2).

$$rawdata = (xxHigh << 8)|\ xxLow \tag{1}$$

$$if(rawdata > 32768)\{\ rawdata - = 65536\} \tag{2}$$

xCheckSum indicates the checksum, which is used to check whether the packet is correct. The checksum needs to be judged before the original data are extracted. The value of the checksum is determined by adding the four bytes after byte 04, inverting it, and then taking the lower eight bits.

$$sum = ((0x80 + 0x02 + xxHigh + xxLow)\hat{}\,0xFFFFFFFF)\&0xFF \tag{3}$$

Then, the sum is compared with the value of *xxCheckSum*; if the two are equal, this is the correct packet, and the raw data value can continue to be calculated. Otherwise, this packet is skipped, and the next packet is calculated. A packet loss rate below 10% will not affect the final result.

The raw EEG signals were extracted in the above way, and the raw EEG waveforms were plotted using MATLAB R2016a, as shown in Figure 3.

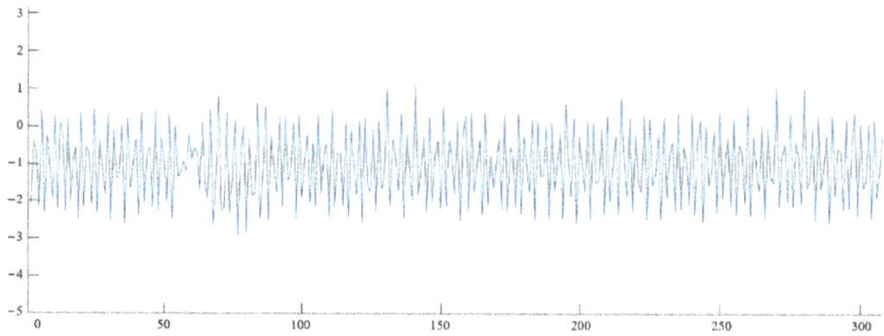

Figure 3. Original EEG waveform.

After the original EEG signal was obtained, the four rhythmic waves (α-wave, β-wave, θ-wave, and δ-wave) in the EEG signal were extracted using the wavelet packet decomposition method through a program prepared by MATLAB. Their features are shown in Table 2.

Table 2. Characteristics of the four EEG waveforms.

Rhythm Name	Frequency Range (Hz)	Amplitude (μV)	Notable Areas	Physiological Significance
α	8–13	10–40	Top occipital area	Awake, quiet, or resting with eyes closed
β	14–30	5–20	Frontal, temporal, and central regions	Concentration and wakefulness
θ	4–8	20–100	Temporal and parietal lobes	Fatigue, depressed mood
δ	0.5–4	20–200	Frontal lobe	Sleeping

The sampling frequency of the EEG signal in this study is 512 Hz, and the MATLAB program algorithm reduces the sampling frequency to 200 Hz to make the spectral features of the four decomposed rhythmic waves more obvious. We designed a wavelet packet 7-layer decomposition tree, as shown in Figure 4, and used daubechies4 wavelet basis functions for decomposition reconstruction. The frequency resolution of each layer can be expressed as Equation (4), and the frequency resolution of the 7th layer is calculated as 0.78 Hz after downsampling.

$$\Delta f = \frac{1}{2^i} \times \frac{f_s}{2} \tag{4}$$

where i denotes the i-th layer. f_s is the sampling frequency of the EEG signal.

Based on the wavelet packet decomposition frequency band characteristics, the minimum number of wavelet packet decomposition nodes contained in each spectral signal can be calculated. The nodes of the bottom layer are used as much as possible to contain the detailed data of each rhythmic wave. After wavelet packet decomposition, the 0~4 Hz frequency band in layers 6 and 7 corresponds to the δ-wave frequency range in the EEG signal. The 4~8 Hz band in layers 6 and 7 corresponds to the θ-wave frequency range in the EEG signal. The 8~12 Hz band in layers 5 and 6 combined with the 12~13 Hz band in layer 7 corresponds to the α-wave frequency range. The 18~25 Hz frequency bands in layer

4, the 15~18 Hz and 25~28 Hz bands in layer 5, the 14~15.6 Hz and 28~29.68 Hz bands in layer 6, and the 29.68~30.46 Hz band in layer 7 are combined to correspond to the β-wave frequency range. Let the j-th node of the i-th layer be the wavelet packet decomposition of the EEG signal; the decomposition nodes contained in the four rhythmic wave signals are as follows: δ: (6, 1), (7, 1), and (7, 4). θ: (6, 3), (6, 4), and (7, 5). α: (5, 3), (6, 5), and (7, 16). β: (4, 3), (5, 8), (5, 5), (6, 9), (6, 18), (7, 18), and (7, 38).

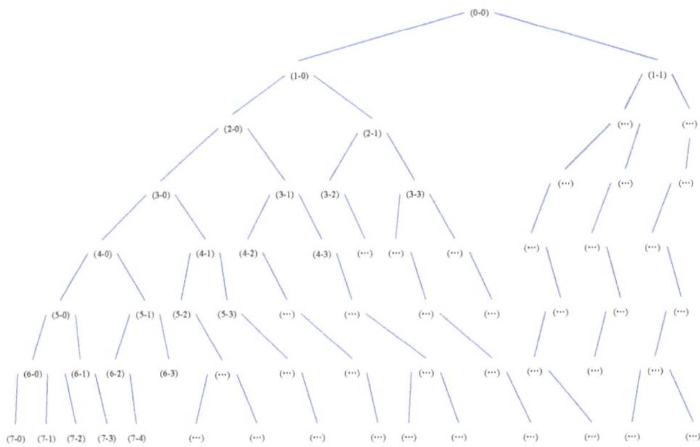

Figure 4. Wavelet packet 7-layer decomposition tree.

A MATLAB program was developed to implement the wavelet packet 7-layer decomposition of the EEG data. The wavelet packet coefficients of the four EEG rhythm waves were reconstructed and superimposed according to the frequency ranges where the four rhythm waves were located. The waveforms of the four rhythmic wave signals were calculated and are shown in Figure 5. The distribution of and variation in wavelet packet coefficients for the four rhythmic waves can be observed in the waveform diagram.

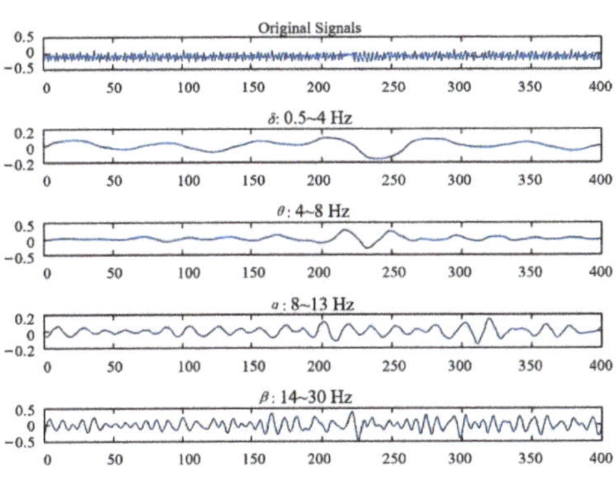

Figure 5. Four EEG rhythm waveforms.

3.2.2. ECG Data Processing Flow

Low-power ECG sensors can transmit ECG signals. Two sets of 8-bit ECG data with flag bits were received continuously through the serial port of the Bluetooth connection. The first two 01 bits were the high four bits of the AFE data, and the first two 11 bits were the low six bits of the AFE data. We removed the two sets of data flag bits and sign bits and then spliced the data into 10-bit unsigned numbers to form the ECG signal. The ECG data, heart rate data, etc., were displayed in real time after the ECG signal was received, and the table files (excel, txt, CSV, etc.) were generated. The ECG signal table files were further analyzed using MATLAB to determine the health status or workload of the subjects.

Data such as ECG and heart rate were analyzed as described above, and physiological data features were obtained after denoising and filtering. The ECG data included heart rate, heart rate variability, RR heart rate interval, and other indicators, and the data were then processed and analyzed using MATLAB.

3.2.3. Cognitive Test Score Processing and Analysis

After the subjects completed the cognitive experiment on E-prime, the software automatically recorded data indicators such as reaction time and task correctness.

Perceptual speed test: The correct rate and average time taken by the subjects to complete this test were measured, where the longer the average time, the slower the perceptual speed.

N-back test: The average time taken and number of errors when all subjects completed the N-back task twice were selected to indicate the subjects' memory abilities.

Graphical numerical coding: The performance indicators are mean reaction time and correctness, and the parameter values indicate the subject's level of comprehension and memory.

Visual search: The average reaction time and task correctness of the subjects under the selected two tasks were compared and analyzed before and after. If the second reaction time was longer than the first, it indicated that the subjects had poor attention and were at a high cognitive load level.

3.2.4. Extraction and Normalization of Physiological Signal Data

Based on the frequency relationship between EEG signals and ECG signals, EEG signal data with a fixed length of 400 and EEG signal data with a fixed length of 3 were extracted. EEG and ECG signals were concatenated along the channel dimension, forming a single 1D input vector with a length of 403 (200 Hz). This combined input preserves temporal synchronization between signals. Data expansion was achieved by using a sliding window sample interception method. This method can expand the training data by dividing it into a series of short subsequences, allowing machine learning algorithms to learn and predict separately on each subsequence, thereby improving the performance of the model [6,7]. The sliding window slides over the input physiological signal in certain steps and extracts the physiological signal into multiple samples of equal length to the window. The schematic diagram is shown in Figure 6. Assuming that the length of the original physiological signal is L, the length of the sliding window is H, and the step size is S, the number of samples, M, obtained after this segment of the signal is divided and can be expressed by the following equation:

$$M = \left\lfloor \frac{L - H}{S} \right\rfloor + 1 \tag{5}$$

where $\lfloor\ \rfloor$ is the downward rounding function.

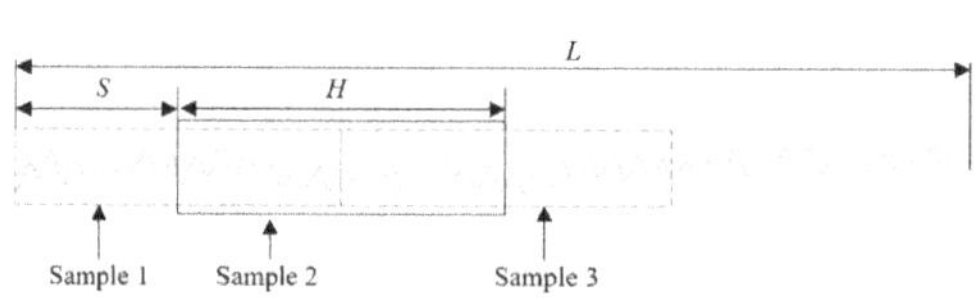

Figure 6. Sliding window for intercepting data.

If $S < H$, there is signal overlap between the samples intercepted by the two adjacent sliding windows; otherwise, if $S > H$, there is no overlap. For example, if a physiological data signal length of 1000 is collected, the training sample requires a sliding window length of 200 data with a step size of 100. This segment of the signal was calculated using Equation (5) to obtain 9 samples. In this way, the samples can be enriched to obtain the large number of data needed for subsequent algorithm model training. It is also possible to concatenate the beginning and end of the intercept data to expand the amount of information contained in a single input datum.

To reduce data complexity and speed up neural network training, a normalization operation is applied to all data with the following mathematical formula:

$$x_{norm} = \frac{x - x_{min}}{x_{max} - x_{min}} \quad (6)$$

where x_{norm} is the normalized data, x is the original data, x_{max} is the maximum value of the original data, and x_{min} is the minimum value of the original data.

3.3. *Cognitive Load Assessment Method Based on a One-Dimensional Convolutional Neural Network*

This subsection describes the architecture, parameter settings, and training protocol of the proposed 1D-CNN model.

3.3.1. Model Structure

The 1D-CNN model primarily processes one-dimensional time series data, with both the input data and convolutional kernels in a one-dimensional format. This design can reduce the number of training parameters, lower the computational complexity of the neural network, and thereby improve training efficiency. Figure 7 illustrates the structural principles of the 1D-CNN model, which consists of the input layer, convolutional layer, pooling layer, fully connected layer, and softmax layer, allowing for the direct output of cognitive load experienced by operators in a closed environment from one-dimensional EEG and ECG data.

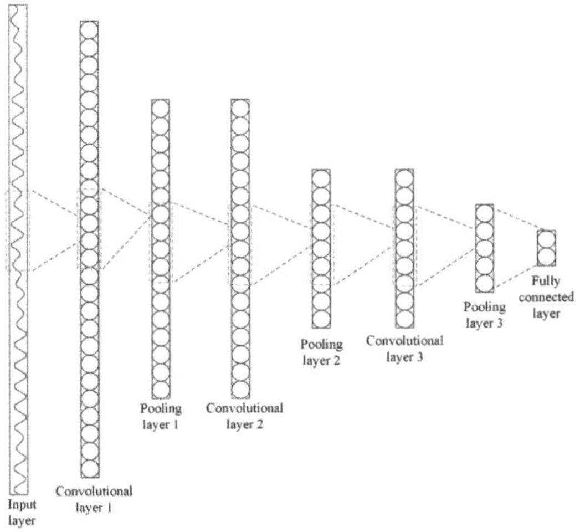

Figure 7. The structural principles of the 1D-CNN model.

The convolutional layer of the 1D-CNN model is mainly used for feature extraction from the input physiological signal data. It employs convolutional kernels that slide along one direction to perform local convolution operations. The features of physiological signals are typically distributed across different spectra. The convolutional layer of the 1D-CNN model utilizes multiple feature extraction channels to extract the corresponding physiological features, classifying the cognitive load based on this extraction. The mathematical model of the convolution process is represented in Equation (7)

$$X^n = f\left(\sum_{m=0}^{m-1} \omega^m \otimes i^k + b\right) \tag{7}$$

In the formula, X^n represents the nth value in the output physiological signal feature vector, ω^m denotes the m-th weight in the 1D-CNN convolutional kernel, $\otimes$ corresponds to the one-dimensional convolution operation, i^k refers to the k-th value in the input physiological signal sequence, b represents the bias parameter, and $f(\ )$ stands for the activation function, which uses the ReLU function.

The pooling layer primarily performs subsampling on the feature vectors obtained from the convolutional layers, reducing the feature dimensionality, expanding the receptive field, and extracting more prominent physiological signal features. The fully connected layer further classifies these features based on the physiological signal characteristics extracted from multiple convolutional and pooling layers. In this study, the fully connected layer employs the dropout technique, temporarily dropping out neural network units from the network with a certain probability to reduce model complexity and prevent overfitting. The softmax layer calculates the probability distribution of the samples being classified into different categories, with the softmax function chosen for the softmax layer in this research. Batch normalization and residual connections were incorporated to address vanishing gradients, as suggested by Abuqaddom et al. [40].

3.3.2. Model Parameter Setting

After preprocessing, the data were input into a one-dimensional convolutional neural network, and the features were extracted after three convolution and pooling operations. Max-pooling (kernel size = 2) was chosen to retain salient features and reduce dimensionality while mitigating information loss. To reduce overfitting in the neural network, the dropout layer loss rate was set to 0.3, allowing the neural network to complete training quickly and accurately. The cross-entropy function was used for the loss function. Finally, the fully connected layer was introduced, and a softmax classifier was used to output the classification results of the physiological signals, i.e., low cognitive load or high cognitive load. The network structure parameters are shown in Table 3.

Table 3. Parameter settings of 1D-CNN.

Network Layer	Size × Step Length	Quantity	Output Dimension
Input layer	/	/	403 × 1
Convolutional layer 1	8 × 1	16	396 × 16
Convolutional layer 2	8 × 1	16	389 × 16
Pooling layer 1	2 × 1	16	194 × 16
Convolutional layer 3	4 × 1	64	191 × 64
Convolutional layer 4	4 × 1	64	188 × 64
Pooling layer 2	2 × 1	64	94 × 64
Convolutional layer 5	4 × 1	256	91 × 256
Convolutional layer 6	4 × 1	256	88 × 256
Pooling layer 3	2 × 1	256	44 × 256
Global pooling layer 1	/	256	256
Fully connected layer 1	/	16	2
Softmax	/	/	2

4. Analysis of Results

To explore the mapping relationship between cognitive load and physiological signals such as EEG and ECG, this study utilized a 1D-CNN approach. This method enables automatic learning and feature extraction from the input one-dimensional EEG and ECG signal data, predicting the level of cognitive load. The 1D-CNN algorithm is particularly well suited for processing time series one-dimensional physiological signals, as it facilitates the retrieval of more subtle and useful information. Additionally, it mitigates the risk of signal distortion that may occur during the conversion of physiological signals across multiple dimensions.

4.1. Results of Experimental Data Analysis

The EEG and ECG data, the response time of the E-prime program, etc., were analyzed as follows:

(1) EEG indicators

Following wavelet decomposition processing via the protocol detailed in Section 3.2.1, EEG signals underwent rhythm-specific energy distribution analysis across four canonical frequency bands, with the normalized power spectral density allocations visualized in Figure 8. Figure 8 shows the results of the energy-sharing analysis for the four EEG rhythm waves from the first and second experiments. The proportion of delta-wave energy is relatively high, indicating that the body is in a sleep state. The proportions of theta- and alpha-wave energies are relatively low, but beta-wave energy occupies a certain proportion, suggesting slight emotional excitement. Based on this, the first experiment can also be judged to be a state of low cognitive load. During the second experiment, the participants exhibited a decrease in the percentage of delta-wave energy and an increase in the percentages of theta- and beta-wave energies. Thus, during the second experiment, the participants were in a state of high cognitive load.

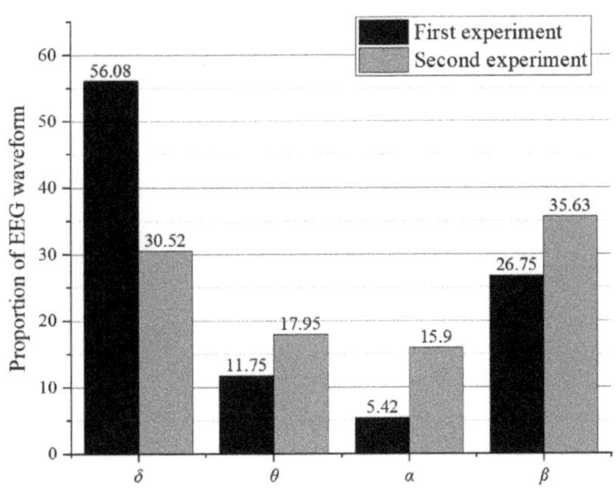

Figure 8. Results of the energy share analysis for each rhythm of the EEG signal.

(2) Electrocardiographic indicators

The variations in heart rate (HR) and heart rate variability (HRV) demonstrated by the participants in both experiments are illustrated in Figure 9. Our results suggest that the HR and HRV indices are associated with variations in task difficulty, with HR showing an upward trend as task difficulty increases and HRV exhibiting a converse pattern. However, this relationship was not distinctly observed in participants 3 and 4.

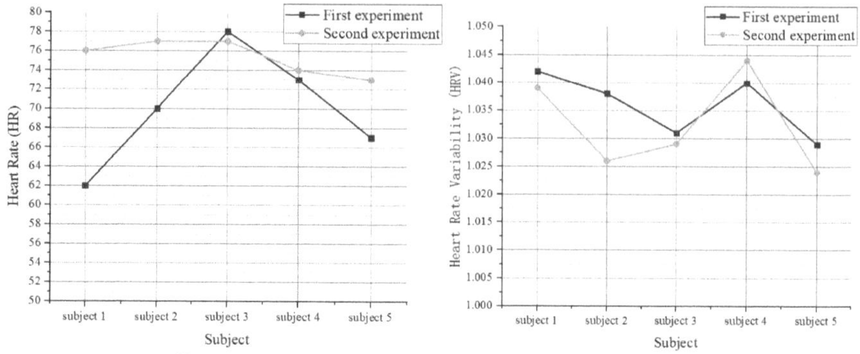

(a) Changes in HR (b) Changes in HRV

Figure 9. Subjects' HR and HRV data from the two experiments.

(3) Average response time and correct rate of cognitive experiments

After the subjects completed two cognitive experiments with E-prime, the software recorded their keystroke response times and correct rate for each question. The average response time and average correct rate obtained from the statistical analysis are shown in Figure 10.

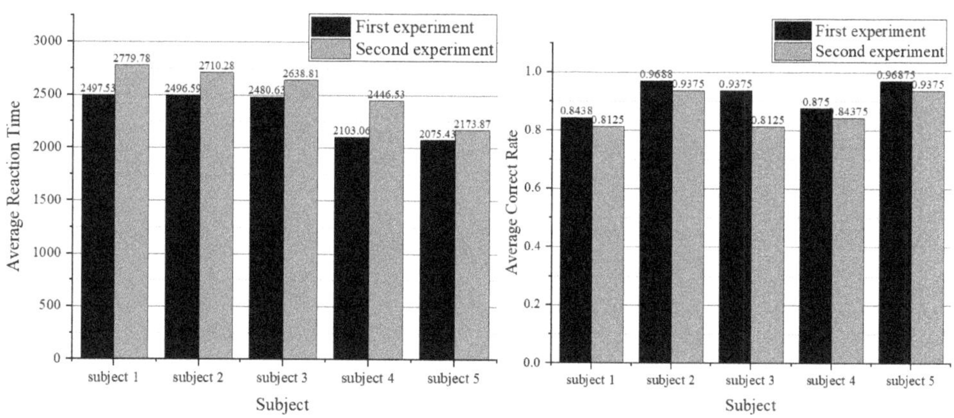

(a) Average reaction time (b) Average correct rate

Figure 10. Average reaction time and correct rate for cognitive experiments.

Figure 10 shows that the participants' average reaction time in the second cognitive experiment was generally higher than that in the first cognitive experiment. This suggests that participants engaging in the second experiment experienced greater cognitive load, leading to slower reaction times and reduced attention while completing the cognitive tasks. This may also contribute to the decreased accuracy observed in the cognitive experiments. Overall, compared with the first experiment, the two tasks arranged in the second experiment (primary task + secondary task) likely imposed a higher load on the participants, resulting in diminished reactivity.

(4) Subjective evaluation

The calculated subjective ratings and weights of the participants are presented in Figure 11. This figure illustrates the changes in subjective ratings across the two experiments. Compared with the outcomes under the low-cognitive-load state in the first experiment, the subjective ratings of participants significantly increased in the second. This indicates that the second experiment imposed a higher cognitive load on the participants than the first. Although different subjects showed differences in scoring values, the comparison between the two experiments was robust and statistically significant ($p < 0.05$). NASA-TLX scores correlated strongly with physiological classifications.

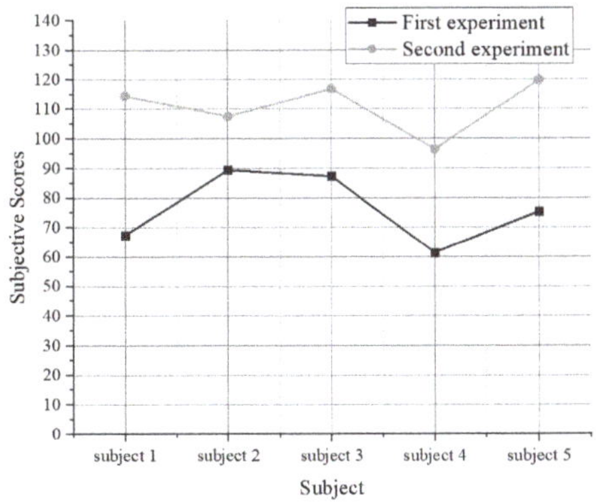

Figure 11. Subjective evaluation results of the subjects.

4.2. Model Evaluation Analysis Results

Experiments were conducted on a 64-bit Win10 system computer equipped with a 3.0 GHz CPU and 8 GB RAM to implement the 1D-CNN model via Python 3.7 on the TensorFlow platform.

After processing the EEG and ECG data, the length of each sample was chosen to be 403. The EEG and ECG data information was included in the sample, and the dimensionality of the physiological dataset was 1160 × 403. The dividing ratio of the training and test sets is 3:1.

The model was run in the TensorFlow environment on the Visual Studio platform. The experiments were run three times and averaged to reduce the randomness and chance associated with experimental results. The constructed 1D-CNN model was trained using the above dataset to test the model performance. The training process is shown in Figure 12. The model gradually converged in accuracy and loss function at the 100th iteration. The accuracy of the training set was 97.6% at this time, and the loss function was 0.1276, proving that the model has a good ability to extract physiological features.

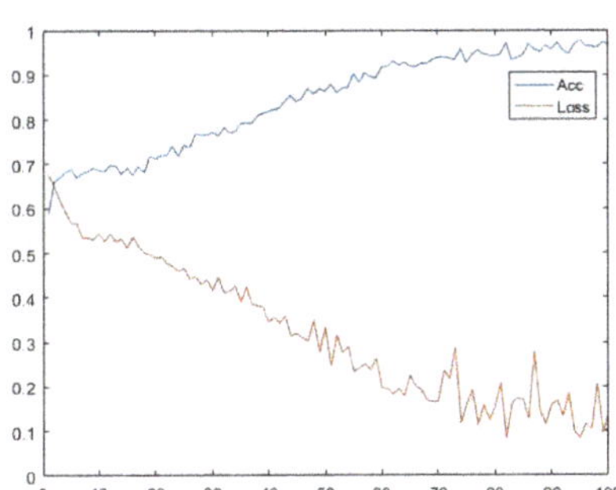

Figure 12. The training process of 1D-CNN model.

The confusion matrix obtained while testing the 1D-CNN model is shown in Figure 13. The model had a *TP* value of 0.91—that is, it had a 0.91 probability of predicting an actual low cognitive load as a low cognitive load. An *FP* value of 0.09 indicated a 0.09 probability of predicting an actual low cognitive load as a high cognitive load. An *FN* value of 0.17 indicated a 0.17 probability of predicting an actual high cognitive load as a low cognitive load. A *TN* value of 0.83 indicated a 0.83 probability of predicting an actual low cognitive load as a low cognitive load.

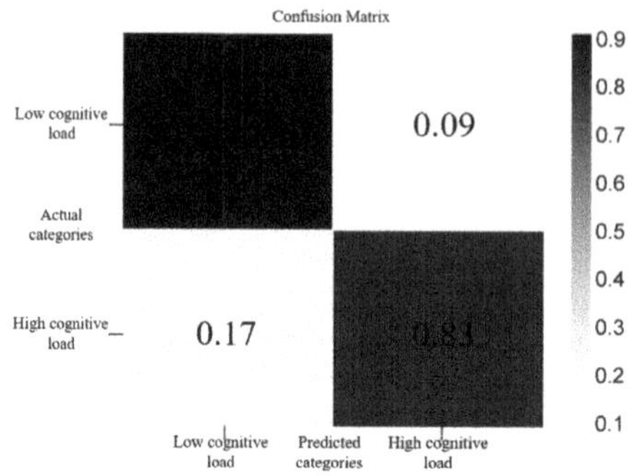

Figure 13. The 1D-CNN confusion matrix.

The values of the model's four evaluation indicators were calculated from Equation (A1), as shown in Table 4. The 1D-CNN model prediction specificity and sensitivity were 90% and 84%, respectively, with high predictive power. The overall accuracy reached 86.5%, with good classification performance. Our 1D-CNN model addresses the classification problem of cognitive load assessment based on physiological signals, and it has been experimentally demonstrated to achieve good classification results. A 1D-CNN evaluation method based on EEG and ECG signals was designed for one-dimensional signals with time series such as EEG and ECG signals. Physiological signal characteristics can be automatically and efficiently extracted from the input signal data. Compared with two-dimensional convolutional neural networks, fewer training parameters are involved, the problem of slow processing due to a large number of parameters is avoided, and classification is faster. We have also demonstrated that EEG and ECG signals can effectively characterize cognitive load.

Table 4. Prediction results of 1D-CNN.

Specificity (*Spe*)	Sensitivity (*Sen*)	Positive Prediction Rate (*PPV*)	Accuracy (*Acc*)
90%	84%	91%	86.5%

SVM and BP neural network algorithms, Long Short-Term Memory (LSTM), and Gated Recurrent Unit (GRU) were compared with the 1D-CNN to obtain classification results. All computational models underwent a rigorous 10-fold cross-validation protocol, as shown in Table 5. The total accuracy and classification accuracy in the low and high cognitive load conditions of the three network models were obtained, as shown in Figure 14. The average classification accuracy of the BP neural network was 74.5%, while the average classification accuracy of the SVM algorithm was 66.3%. By contrast, the average classification accuracy of the 1D-CNN was 86.5%. Overall, the 1D-CNN demonstrated better classification performance than the BP neural network and SVM models, particularly excelling in low-load recognition tasks. In a comparison of the 1D-CNN with LSTM and GRU (test accuracy: 79.2% and 81.5%, respectively), the 1D-CNN's localized feature extraction outperforms recurrent architectures for short-term physiological patterns.

Table 5. The accuracy of the 10-fold cross-validation method for five types of models.

Classification	Models	1	2	3	4	5	6	7	8	9	10	Average
Average classification	SVM	0.75	0.65	0.75	0.67	0.58	0.65	0.76	0.67	0.62	0.53	0.663
	BP	0.84	0.61	0.82	0.80	0.71	0.75	0.64	0.7	0.64	0.86	0.745
	LSTM	0.80	0.78	0.81	0.79	0.77	0.82	0.78	0.80	0.76	0.80	0.792
	GRU	0.82	0.81	0.83	0.80	0.81	0.84	0.82	0.83	0.80	0.81	0.815
	1D-CNN	0.85	0.88	0.87	0.86	0.84	0.89	0.86	0.87	0.85	0.88	0.865
Low cognitive load	SVM	0.68	0.64	0.69	0.66	0.53	0.68	0.74	0.63	0.55	0.53	0.633
	BP	0.92	0.61	0.93	0.86	0.73	0.79	0.70	0.96	0.68	0.90	0.808
	LSTM	0.85	0.83	0.86	0.87	0.84	0.88	0.85	0.86	0.82	0.87	0.860
	GRU	0.88	0.89	0.90	0.87	0.86	0.91	0.88	0.89	0.85	0.90	0.887
	1D-CNN	0.89	0.91	0.88	0.90	0.85	0.92	0.88	0.90	0.87	0.91	0.890
High cognitive load	SVM	0.83	0.65	0.83	0.70	0.64	0.63	0.81	0.72	0.73	0.52	0.706
	BP	0.77	0.61	0.72	0.74	0.70	0.70	0.58	0.60	0.61	0.82	0.685
	LSTM	0.75	0.73	0.76	0.71	0.70	0.76	0.71	0.74	0.70	0.73	0.724
	GRU	0.76	0.73	0.76	0.73	0.76	0.77	0.76	0.77	0.75	0.74	0.743
	1D-CNN	0.82	0.85	0.86	0.82	0.83	0.86	0.84	0.84	0.83	0.85	0.880

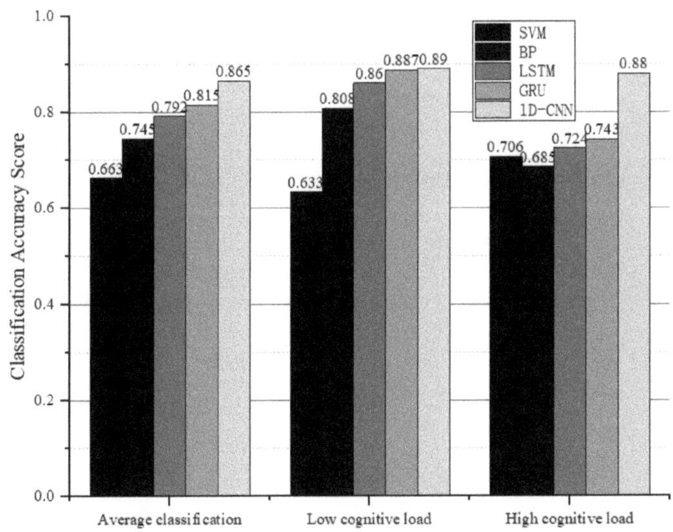

Figure 14. Comparison of prediction results of the three network models.

5. Manned Submersible Case Validation

The internal structure of the manned submersible cannot be publicly displayed, so during the validation phase, experiments were conducted only in the laboratory.

PVC panels and aluminum frames were used to build the manned submersible platform. The console buttons were positioned with different colored circular stickers to demonstrate the controls, simulating the main display device, control buttons, and display layout of the manned submersible. A schematic diagram of the platform is shown in Figure 15. The subjects were positioned in the middle of the console to complete two different tasks under different conditions. The first operation required the subject to operate the manned submersible normally according to the requirements of the main test and to press the corresponding button to complete the main task. The second involved a dual-task experiment. The subjects recorded data such as the orientation, dive depth, heading angle, and distance of the downloaded human submersible from the mother ship while performing the main task of maneuvering.

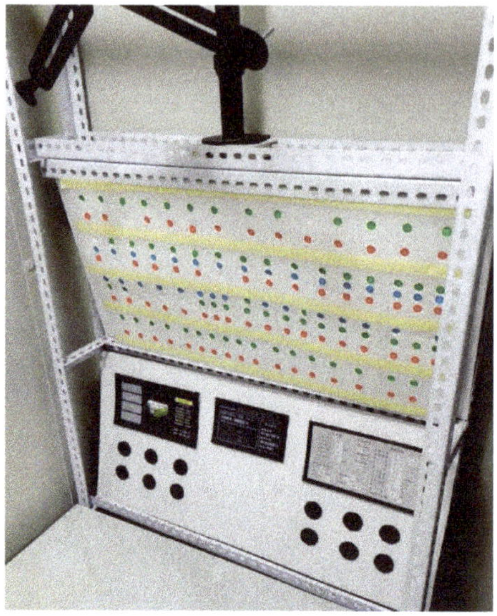

Figure 15. Manned submersible experimental platform.

5.1. Data Acquisition

Data on physiological signals such as EEG and ECG were collected from the subjects through a single-lead EEG device and a low-power ECG sensor device. The subjects were allowed to wear the device for a significant period to reduce discomfort before the experiment began. The subjects were kept awake and completely physically relaxed to avoid affecting the level of cognitive load in subsequent experiments. The physiological data were recorded continuously during the experiment as the subjects performed the manipulation task. They completed the NASA-TLX subjective scale at the end of each task and then took a 5 min break before proceeding to the next.

5.2. Data Processing

The experimentally obtained EEG physiological data were processed and analyzed as described in Section 3.

5.3. Analysis of Validation Results

The EEG and ECG data were combined to form a physiological signal dataset. The 1D-CNN model assessed the cognitive load, and an overall classification accuracy of 85.37% was obtained. The accuracy of the low cognitive load classification was 90.91%, and the high cognitive load classification accuracy was 78.95%. The values of the evaluation metrics obtained through the 1D-CNN model's validation are shown in Table 6. The results show that the model can assess the operator's cognitive load and achieve a good classification effect. It can also be used to improve cabin layout designs and optimize the ergonomics.

Table 6. Validation results of 1D-CNN model.

Specificity (*Spe*)	Sensitivity (*Sen*)	Positive Prediction Rate (*PPV*)	Accuracy (*Acc*)
90.7%	82.1%	91.9%	85.4%

6. Results and Discussion

This study proposes a 1D-CNN model that directly identifies an operator's cognitive load from EEG and ECG physiological signal data. The model effectively and comprehensively extracts features from the operator's physiological signals while avoiding signal distortion issues that may arise during data processing and transformation.

Through experiments, the 1D-CNN model's performance was validated, achieving an accuracy of 86.5% in cognitive load assessment. Compared with the BP neural network algorithm (74.5%) and the SVM algorithm (66.3%) proposed in previous studies, the 1D-CNN model converges more quickly and demonstrates better performance in cognitive load classification.

Compared with the BP neural network and SVM algorithms, the recognition rates of the 1D-CNN model improved by at least 8.2% and 19.5% for the low cognitive load and high cognitive load labels, respectively. One possible reason for this improvement is that the BP neural network and SVM algorithms are focused on global feature extraction, whereas the 1D-CNN model emphasizes local feature extraction. This allows it to effectively avoid interference noise distributed across specific frequency bands and automatically extract valid data features without manual intervention. Additionally, the modeling approach of the BP neural network is relatively simple, consisting only of hidden layers between the input and output layers with straightforward nonlinear relationships. The SVM algorithm, on the other hand, classifies data solely through hyperplanes. Compared with the 1D-CNN, these algorithms have too few parameters to extract effective features.

This study designed a six-layer convolutional pooling structure to capture features in layers. Layers 1–2 can better capture local temporal features in physiological signals, such as EEG spike detection. Layers 3–4 can effectively capture the mid-term dependence of physiological signals, such as HRV fluctuations. Layers 5–6 can capture global characteristic trends, such as sustained beta-wave elevation.

In order to rigorously demonstrate the rationality of the proposed 1D-CNN architecture, we conducted systematic ablation experiments and hyperparameter sensitivity analysis, and the results are shown in Table 7. Removing pooling degraded accuracy by 8.3%, as Model 1 failed to downsample noise-dominated features. Omitting dropout caused mild overfitting (training accuracy: 99.1%, test accuracy: 81.9%). The shallower Model 3 captured insufficient temporal features, especially for high-frequency EEG components. The optimal kernel size was 8 (accuracy: 86.5%), balancing local/global feature extraction. Smaller kernels (4) overfitted high-frequency noise, while larger kernels (16) blurred critical transient patterns. Doubling filters marginally improved accuracy (87.1%) but doubled training time. Halving filters reduced accuracy to 80.3%. Stride = 2 outperformed stride = 4 (accuracy: 86.5%, 82.6%), as aggressive pooling lost task-relevant HRV dynamics.

Table 7. The 1D-CNN ablation experiment results.

Model	Test Accuracy	Training Time (s/epoch)
Baseline	86.5%	12.3
Model 1 (No Pooling)	78.2%	18.7
Model 2 (No Dropout)	81.9%	11.5
Model 3 (3 Layers)	72.4%	8.2

In this study, experiments were conducted using the airtight cabin laboratory of the Department of Industrial Design, Northwestern Polytechnic University. The subjects performed information reading and keyword searches, and physiological data such as EEG and ECG were collected and analyzed in both low and high cognitive load states. The subjective perceptions of the subjects were measured in combination with the NASA-TLX subjective scale. Through screening, the data were compiled and analyzed to obtain the correlation characteristics of the EEG and ECG data with cognitive load.

The article's primary contributions are evident in the following areas: (1) It introduces a 1D-CNN algorithm designed for the automatic extraction of features from raw EEG/ECG signals. (2) The feasibility of wireless signal acquisition in a sealed cabin environment has been confirmed, offering a novel testing approach for physiological signal collection in subsequent research involving individuals in such environments, thereby reducing participant interference. (3) Through data analysis, the study investigates the correlation between cognitive load and EEG and ECG signals, establishing a dataset of physiological characteristics for individuals in confined spaces. This dataset is intended to be scalable, laying the foundation for future research into cognitive load assessment methodologies. (4) The algorithm demonstrates superior accuracy (86.5%) compared to SVM and BP neural networks.

7. Conclusions

This study aimed to solve the problems of low classification accuracy and tedious manual feature extraction with machine learning algorithms. The main conclusions are as follows:

(1) This study proposes a cognitive load assessment method based on a 1D-CNN model. It combines the one-dimensional nature of physiological data such as EEG and ECG with the advantages of convolutional neural networks for automatic feature extraction.

(2) In the experiments, the 1D-CNN model achieved 86.5% accuracy in cognitive load recognition, effectively and automatically extracting more features from physiological parameters. Additionally, in a simulated environment for manned submersibles, the cognitive load recognition accuracy achieved by the 1D-CNN model reached 85.4%.

(3) This study validated the feasibility of wireless collection methods for EEG and ECG signal data in assessing the cognitive load of operators in confined spaces, providing a new approach for subsequent research on collecting physiological signals from operators in enclosed environments.

(4) Through data analysis, this study examined the correlation features between cognitive load and EEG and ECG signals, establishing a physiological characteristic dataset for individuals in confined spaces.

8. Limitations and Future Developments

Airtight cabins contain highly complex human–machine relationships involving multiple factors, such as humidity, noise, temperature, and radiation. In addition, humans are extremely complex and difficult to study. Both physiological and psychological factors can impact cognitive load. In this study, we explored the cognitive load assessment methods for confined chamber operators from the perspectives of EEG and ECG. However, many issues require deeper research.

Owing to the characteristics of airtight cabins and considering the feasibility of subsequent field experiments, this study employed portable single-channel sensors to capture physiological data to minimize interference with the operators. However, this represents a significant limitation of our work, as reliance on single-channel EEG and ECG sensors may hinder a comprehensive assessment of an operator's cognitive load. More complex multi-channel data, such as those obtained from ring electrodes or integrated electrode caps, could provide deeper insights. Additionally, owing to the unique conditions faced by operators in airtight cabins, there were a limited number of suitable subjects for this experiment, resulting in a restricted dataset. But the subjects selected for this study were all relatively professional, and the 1D-CNN dataset was enhanced through the sliding window method, improving the performance of the model.

Therefore, in future research, efforts should first focus on collecting more comprehensive EEG data from multiple channels. This will better reveal how EEG signals from various regions of the brain reflect the cognitive load of operators and facilitate analyses of synchronization differences in multi-channel EEG signal data. Second, when considering a range of real-world confined space environments and more complex operational tasks, it is important to expand the sample size to enhance the performance of the proposed 1D-CNN cognitive load assessment model. This will also facilitate evaluations of the proposed methodology's effectiveness in practical applications. Third, it would be beneficial to design adaptive strategies to optimize the model parameters for the algorithms used in this study. Lastly, physiological data such as skin conductance and respiratory rate, which are one-dimensional time series data, could be trained using the proposed 1D-CNN network. Integrating more comprehensive physiological data might enhance the model strategy, making cognitive load recognition methods more broadly applicable.

This study is mainly based on the special environment of a closed cabin, and the universality of the research results is limited by the number of subjects. It is a preliminary research result, and future work will include different participants and environments.

Supplementary Materials: The following supporting information can be downloaded at: https://www.mdpi.com/article/10.3390/sym17060915/s1.

Author Contributions: Conceptualization, L.W. and J.W.; methodology, L.W. and D.C.; software, J.W.; validation, L.W. and J.S.; writing—original draft preparation, L.W.; writing—review and editing, J.W. and D.C.; visualization, J.S.; supervision, D.C. and J.W.; project administration, D.C.; funding acquisition, D.C. and J.W. All authors have read and agreed to the published version of the manuscript.

Funding: This research was funded by the National Key R&D Program of China, grant number 2021YFC2800600; the Province Key R&D Program of Shaanxi, grant number 2022GY-311; and the Innovation Foundation for Doctor Dissertation of Northwestern Polytechnical University, grant number, CX2023049.

Data Availability Statement: The original contributions presented in this study are included in the article/Supplementary Material. Further inquiries can be directed to the corresponding author.

Conflicts of Interest: The authors declare no conflicts of interest.

Abbreviations

The following abbreviations are used in this manuscript:

List of Symbols

Symbols	Explanation of Symbols
α	Alpha wave, one of the four types of brain waves; the physiological significance is awake, quiet, or resting with eyes closed.
θ	Theta wave, one of the four types of brain waves; the physiological significance is fatigue, depressed mood.
β	Beta wave, one of the four types of brain waves; the physiological significance is concentration and wakefulness.
δ	Delta wave, one of the four types of brain waves; the physiological significance is sleeping.
f_s	The sampling frequency of the EEG signal.
x_{norm}	Normalized data.
x	Original data.
x_{max}	The maximum value of the original data.
x_{min}	The minimum value of the original data.

X^n	Represents the n-th value in the output physiological signal feature vector.
ω^m	ω^m denotes the m-th weight in the 1D-CNN convolutional kernel.
$\otimes$	Corresponds to the one-dimensional convolution operation.
i^k	i^k refers to the k-th value in the input physiological signal sequence.
TP	The real category is the positive samples, and the model predicts the number of positives.
FP	The real category is the negative samples, and the model predicts the number of positives.
FN	The real category is the positive samples, and the model predicts the number of negatives.
TN	The real category is the negative samples, and the model predicts the number of negatives.
Specificity (*Spe*)	The ability of the model to predict negative samples, that is, the number of negative samples predicted to be negative among all negative samples.
Sensitivity (*Sen*)	The ability of the model to predict positive samples, that is, similar to specificity, the number of positive samples predicted as positive among all positive samples.
Positive Predictive Value (*PPV*)	The correct rate of the model predicting positive samples, that is, the number of positive samples that are predicted correctly.
Accuracy (*Acc*)	The total correct rate of model predictions, that is, the number of completely correct classifications in all samples.

List of Abbreviations

Abbreviations	The Full Name of the Abbreviation
1D-CNN	One-Dimensional Convolutional Neural Network
EEG	Electroencephalography
ECG	Electrocardiogram
HR	Heart Rate
HRV	Heart Rate Variability
CNN	Convolutional Neural Network
SVM	Support Vector Machine
LSTM	Long Short-Term Memory
GRU	Gated Recurrent Unit
NASA-TLX	National Aeronautics and Space Administration Task Load Index

Appendix A

The content of the cognitive test compiled by the E-prime software is as follows:

Perceptual speed test: Perceptual speed mainly refers to the time it takes for people to respond to objective things acting on the brain. If the reaction time is short, the perception speed is fast; otherwise, the perception speed is slow. In this experiment, digital positioning was used to examine the immediate response and discrimination ability of the subjects. A table with eight numeric intervals appears on the screen, and subjects quickly answer the correct interval based on the assigned numbers given.

N-back task: N-back, as the name suggests, means to go back n times, a cognitive task that requires memory. In this experiment, many numbers are displayed on the computer screen, and these numbers appear one after the other. The subject needs to compare the number they see now with the previous number, n, to see if they are the same. If different, they press the "F" key; otherwise, they press the "J" key. In the experiment, subjects were required to complete a two-back task, that is, to compare the number displayed on the screen with the second number back to see if they were the same.

Graphic digital coding: Graphical digital coding is a task that requires responsiveness and understanding. Three figures appear on the screen, namely, a triangle, square, and circle, corresponding to different numbers: 1, 2, and 3, respectively. The subjects need to write down the numbers corresponding to all the figures and then display a certain figure in the middle of the computer screen. They need to press the corresponding figure immediately and make sure that the time does not exceed 5 s; the experiment needs to be completed in 6. When performing the experiment for the second time, the rules of the question change; that is, the number corresponding to each figure changes, and the subject needs to write it down in a short time in order to quickly touch the figure corresponding to the next one displayed.

Visual search: Visual search is a target-specific search-aware task that requires attention. In this experiment, a picture appears in the middle of the screen. The subject searches among many triangles with tails (distractors) in the picture to find out whether there is a different triangle (target). The subjects searched for the target in the presence of interference items; if there was a target, they pressed the "J" key; otherwise, they pressed the "F" key.

Appendix B

In addition, several model evaluation indicators were derived from the above four statistics, including specificity (*Spe*), sensitivity (*Sen*), positive predictive value (*PPV*), and accuracy (*Acc*). The accuracy rate evaluates the overall performance of the model's method. The calculation formula is

$$\begin{cases} Spe = \frac{TN}{TN+FP} \\ Sen = \frac{TP}{TP+FN} \\ PVV = \frac{TP}{TP+FP} \\ Acc = \frac{TN+TP}{TN+FP+FN+TP} \end{cases} \tag{A1}$$

References

1. Hidalgo-Muñoz, A.R.; Béquet, A.J.; Astier-Juvenon, M.; Pépin, G.; Fort, A.; Jallais, C.; Tattegrain, H.; Gabaude, C. Respiration and Heart Rate Modulation Due to Competing Cognitive Tasks While Driving. *Front. Human. Neurosci.* **2019**, *12*, 525. [CrossRef] [PubMed]
2. Cisnal, A.; Antolínez, D.; Turiel, J.P.; Fraile, J.C.; De La Fuente, E. A Versatile Embedded Platform for Implementation of Biocooperative Control in Upper-Limb Neuromotor Rehabilitation Scenarios. *IEEE Access* **2023**, *11*, 35726–35736. [CrossRef]
3. Zagermann, J.; Pfeil, U.; Reiterer, H. Measuring Cognitive Load using Eye Tracking Technology in Visual Computing. In Proceedings of the Beyond Time and Errors on Novel Evaluation Methods for Visualization, BELIV '16, Baltimore, MD, USA, 24 October 2016; ACM Press: Baltimore, MD, USA, 2016; pp. 78–85.
4. Iskander, J.; Hanoun, S.; Hettiarachchi, I.; Hossny, M.; Saleh, K.; Zhou, H.; Nahavandi, S.; Bhatti, A. Eye Behaviour as a Hazard Perception Measure. In Proceedings of the 12th Annual IEEE International Systems Conference, Vancouver, BC, Canada, 23–26 April 2018; pp. 1–6.
5. Solhjoo, S.; Haigney, M.C.; McBee, E.; van Merrienboer, J.J.G.; Schuwirth, L.; Artino, A.R.; Battista, A.; Ratcliffe, T.A.; Lee, H.D.; Durning, S.J. Heart Rate and Heart Rate Variability Correlate with Clinical Reasoning Performance and Self-Reported Measures of Cognitive Load. *Sci. Rep.* **2019**, *9*, 14668. [CrossRef]
6. Lv, Z.; Zhang, J.; Oma, E. A Novel Method of Emotion Recognition from Multi-Band EEG Topology Maps Based on ERENet. *Appl. Sci.* **2022**, *12*, 10273. [CrossRef]
7. Zhou, Y.; Liu, X.; Wen, D.; Xu, S.; Wan, X.; Lu, H. Spatial Cognitive Electroencephalogram Network Topological Features Extraction Based on Cross Fuzzy Entropy Network Graph. *Symmetry* **2025**, *17*, 243. [CrossRef]
8. Cheng, E.J.; Young, K.Y.; Lin, C.T. Temporal EEG Imaging for Drowsy Driving Prediction. *Appl. Sci.* **2019**, *9*, 5078. [CrossRef]
9. Sun, J.; Jiang, T.; Wang, C.; Liu, W.; Jiang, C.; Sun, H.; Song, L.; Cui, Y.; Yang, Y.; Zhang, X. Research on Ergonomic Evaluation Indicator and Methodology for Interactive Interface of Spacecraft Software. *Manned Spacefl.* **2020**, *26*, 208–213.
10. Zhang, S.; He, W.; Chen, D.; Chu, J.; Fan, H. A dynamic human reliability assessment approach for manned submersibles using PMV-CREAM. *Int. J. Nav. Archit. Ocean. Eng.* **2019**, *11*, 782–795. [CrossRef]

11. Alfredson, J.; Holmberg, J.; Andersson, R.; Wikforss, M. Applied Cognitive Ergonomics Design Principles for Fighter Aircraft. *Lect. Notes Comput. Sci.* **2011**, *6781*, 473–483.
12. Ye, C.; Xu, W.; Liu, S. Application of ergonomics to layout design of manned submersible. *J. Northwestern Polytech. Univ.* **2021**, *39*, 233–240. [CrossRef]
13. Hemakom, A.; Atiwiwat, D.; Israsena, P. ECG and EEG based machine learning models for the classification of mental workload and stress levels for women in different menstrual phases, men, and mixed sexes. *Biomed. Signal Process. Control* **2024**, *95*, 106379. [CrossRef]
14. Tjolleng, A.; Jung, K.; Hong, W.; Lee, W.; Lee, B.; You, H.; Son, J.; Park, S. Classification of a Driver's Cognitive Workload Levels Using Artificial Neural Network on ECG Signals. *Appl. Ergon.* **2017**, *59*, 326–332. [CrossRef] [PubMed]
15. Tabar, Y.R.; Halici, U. A Novel Deep Learning Approach for Classification of EEG Motor Imagery Signals. *J. Neural Eng.* **2017**, *14*, 16003. [CrossRef] [PubMed]
16. Wang, J.; Chen, D.; Zhang, X.; Zhu, M. Real-time anthropometric data-driven evaluation method for complex console layout design. *Comput. Ind. Eng.* **2023**, *183*, 109463. [CrossRef]
17. Shi, G.; Song, Y.; Li, L.; Hu, L.; Jia, H.; Gui, C.; Zang, L.; Duan, Y.; Yu, F.; Wang, C.; et al. Design of Cockpit Ergonomic Evaluation Simulation System Based on Augmented Reality. In Proceedings of the 11th International Conference on Intelligent Human-Machine Systems and Cybernetics (IHMSC), Hangzhou, China, 24–25 August 2019; pp. 33–36.
18. Andrews, J.M.; Rusnock, C.F.; Miller, M.E.; Meador, D.P. Simulation-Based Evaluation of the Effects of Varying Degrees of Control Abstraction for Manned-Unmanned Teaming on Mental Workload of Pilots. In Proceedings of the IEEE International Conference on Systems, Man and Cybernetics, Toronto, ON, Canada, 11–14 October 2020; pp. 2680–2686.
19. Lagomarsino, M.; Lorenzini, M.; De Momi, E.; Ajoudani, A. An Online Framework for Cognitive Load Assessment in Industrial Tasks. *Robot. Comput. -Integr. Manuf.* **2022**, *78*, 102380. [CrossRef]
20. Wang, J.; Chen, D.; Zhu, M.; Wang, H.; Sun, Y. Recognition method of submarine operation posture based on convolutional pose machines. *J. Zhejiang Univ. (Eng. Sci.)* **2022**, *56*, 26–35.
21. Xiong, R.; Kong, F.; Yang, X.; Liu, G.; Wen, W. Pattern Recognition of Cognitive Load Using EEG and ECG Signals. *Sensors* **2020**, *20*, 5122. [CrossRef]
22. Na, K. The Effects of Cognitive Load on Query Reformulation: Mental Demand, Temporal Demand and Frustration. *Aslib J. Inf. Manag.* **2021**, *73*, 436–453. [CrossRef]
23. Haapalainen, E.; Kim, S.; Forlizzi, J.F.; Dey, A.K. Psycho-Physiological Measures for Assessing Cognitive Load. In Proceedings of the 2010 ACM Conference on Ubiquitous Computing, New York, NY, USA, 26–29 September 2010; pp. 301–310.
24. Baranov, V.V.; Shelupanov, A.A. Cognitive Model for Assessing the Security of Information Systems for Various Purposes. *Symmetry* **2022**, *14*, 2631. [CrossRef]
25. Chen, B.; Yu, Y.; Ding, L. Correlation analysis of physiological parameters of pilot mental workload based on flight simulation. *Biomed. Signal Process. Control* **2025**, *109*, 108024. [CrossRef]
26. van Weelden, E.; Alimardani, M.; Wiltshire, T.J.; Louwerse, M.M. Aviation and neurophysiology: A systematic review. *Appl. Ergon.* **2022**, *105*, 103838. [CrossRef] [PubMed]
27. Dussault, C.; Jouanin, J.-C.; Guezennec, C.-Y. EEG and ECG changes during selected flight sequences. *Aviat. Space Environ. Med.* **2004**, *75*, 889–897. [PubMed]
28. Liang, Y.; Reyes, M.L.; Lee, J.D. Real-Time Detection of Driver Cognitive Distraction Using Support Vector Machines. *IEEE Trans. Intell. Transp. Syst.* **2007**, *8*, 340–350. [CrossRef]
29. Amin, H.U.; Malik, A.S.; Ahmad, R.F.; Badruddin, N.; Kamel, N.; Hussain, M.; Chooi, W.-T. Feature Extraction and Classification for EEG Signals Using Wavelet Transform and Machine Learning Techniques. *Australas. Phys. Eng. Sci. Med.* **2015**, *38*, 139–149. [CrossRef]
30. Zhang, Y.; Gao, J.; Zhou, H. Breeds Classification with Deep Convolutional Neural Network. In Proceedings of the ACM International Conference Proceeding Series, Shenzhen, China, 15–17 February 2020; pp. 145–151.
31. Wang, J.; Chen, D.; Zhu, M.; Sun, Y. Risk assessment for musculoskeletal disorders based on the characteristics of work posture. *Autom. Constr.* **2021**, *131*, 103921. [CrossRef]
32. Montenegro, L.; Abreu, M.; Fred, A.; Machado, J.M. Human-Assisted vs. Deep Learning Feature Extraction: An Evaluation of ECG Features Extraction Methods for Arrhythmia Classification Using Machine Learning. *Appl. Sci.* **2022**, *12*, 7404. [CrossRef]
33. Han, S.-Y.; Kwak, N.-S.; Oh, T.; Lee, S.-W. Classification of pilots' mental states using a multimodal deep learning network. *Biocybern. Biomed. Eng.* **2020**, *40*, 324–336. [CrossRef]
34. Baldwin, C.L.; Penaranda, B. Adaptive Training Using an Artificial Neural Network and EEG Metrics for Within- and Cross-Task Workload Classification. *NeuroImage* **2012**, *59*, 48–56. [CrossRef]
35. Tjolleng, A.; Jung, K. Development of a Real-Time System for Detecting Driver's Cognitive Load Using Multi-Layer Artificial Neural Network on ECG Signals. *J. Ergon. Soc. Korea* **2020**, *39*, 625–636. [CrossRef]

36. Kim, D.; Ruy, W. CNN-based fire detection method on autonomous ships using composite channels composed of RGB and IR data. *Int. J. Nav. Archit. Ocean Eng.* **2022**, *14*, 100489. [CrossRef]
37. Wan, X.; Sun, Y.; Wu, Z.; Wen, D. Characterization of Spatial Cognitive EEG Signals Using Normalized Adjusted Permutation Conditional Mutual Information. *Symmetry* **2025**, *17*, 130. [CrossRef]
38. Jiao, Z.; Gao, X.; Wang, Y.; Li, J.; Xu, H. Deep Convolutional Neural Networks for Mental Load Classification Based on EEG Data. *Pattern Recognit.* **2018**, *76*, 582–595. [CrossRef]
39. Zhu, M.; Chen, D.; Wang, J.; Sun, Y. Analysis of oceanaut operating performance using an integrated Bayesian network aided by the fuzzy logic theory. *Int. J. Ind. Ergon.* **2021**, *83*, 103129. [CrossRef]
40. Abuqaddom, I.; Mahafzah, B.A.; Faris, H. Oriented Stochastic Loss Descent Algorithm to Train Very Deep Multi-Layer Neural Networks Without Vanishing Gradients. *Knowl. -Based Syst.* **2021**, *230*, 107391. [CrossRef]

symmetry

MDPI

Article

A Data-Driven Methodology for Industrial Design Optimization and Consumer Preference Modeling: An Application of Computer-Aided Design in Sustainable Refrigerator Design Research

Yu Chen [1,2], Haotian Liu [3], Jianwei Zhang [4] and Jiang Wu [1,*]

[1] College of Architecture and Design, Nanchang University, Nanchang 330031, China; chenyu036@email.ncu.edu.cn
[2] Haier Innovation Design Center, Qingdao 266101, China
[3] School of Electrical and Electronic Engineering, University of Sheffield, Sheffield S10 2TN, UK; hliu146@sheffield.ac.uk
[4] School of Intelligent Engineering and Automation, Beijing University of Posts and Telecommunications, Beijing 100876, China; 2024111330@bupt.cn
* Correspondence: wujiang@ncu.edu.cn

Abstract: Addressing the insufficient identification of key consumer requirements in refrigerator design and the current limitations in understanding the impacts and underlying mechanisms of product design on sustainability, this study develops an interdisciplinary methodological framework that synergizes industrial design principles with advanced computer-aided design techniques and deep neural network approaches. Initially, consumer decision preferences concerning essential product attributes and sustainability indicators are systematically elucidated through semi-structured interviews and multi-source data fusion, with a particular emphasis on user sensitivity to energy efficiency ratings, based on a high-quality sample of 303 respondents. Subsequently, a latent diffusion model alongside a ControlNet architecture is employed to intelligently generate design solutions, followed by comprehensive multi-attribute optimization screening using an integrated decision-making model. The empirical evidence reveals that the synergistic interplay between functional rationality and design coordination plays a critical role in determining the overall competitiveness of the design solutions. Furthermore, by incorporating established industrial design practices, prototypes of mini desktop and vehicle-mounted multifunctional refrigerators—derived from neural network-generated design features—are developed and assessed. Finally, a nonlinear predictive mapping model is constructed to delineate the relationship between industrial design characteristics and consumer appeal. The experimental results show that the proposed support vector regression model achieves a root mean square error of 0.0719 and a coefficient of determination of 0.8480, significantly outperforming the Bayesian regularization backpropagation neural network baseline. These findings validate the model's predictive accuracy and its applicability in small-sample, high-dimensional, and nonlinear industrial design scenarios. This research provides a data-driven, intelligent analytical approach that bridges industrial design with computer-aided design, thereby optimizing product market competitiveness and sustainable consumer value while promoting both theoretical innovation and practical advancements in sustainable design practices.

Keywords: product design; refrigerator; computer-aided design; deep neural networks; data-driven

https://doi.org/10.3390/sym17040621

1. Introduction

With the intensification of the global ecological crisis and the gradual enhancement of consumer awareness regarding sustainable consumption [1], the field of industrial design is undergoing a transformation from a traditional focus on functionality and aesthetics toward the integration of ecological considerations and user needs [2]. Among consumer products, household refrigerators represent typical durable goods, the design and usage of which not only directly affect consumers' daily life experiences but are also closely linked to energy consumption, resource utilization, and environmental sustainability [3]. Against the backdrop of global consumption upgrades and green energy efficiency trends [4], the design of household appliances now necessitates breakthroughs beyond basic functionality, extending into product aesthetics [5], energy efficiency, and user experience [6]. Despite increasing consumer demand for personalized products and sustainable lifestyles [7], a notable gap remains in the research bridging consumer demand identification and sustainable design mechanisms. On the one hand, traditional user research methods struggle to capture the dynamic interactions of multidimensional consumer demands, and the nonlinear mapping mechanisms between design features and consumer attractiveness remain inadequately explored. On the other hand, neural network technologies and generative design approaches typically emphasize form innovation, overlooking the synergistic effects among functionality, aesthetics, and sustainability. Such theoretical and practical disjunctions frequently result in sustainable designs falling into the predicament of "technically feasible yet market failure".

Addressing these gaps, this study proposes and validates an interdisciplinary methodological framework that integrates qualitative analysis, intelligent generative technologies, and nonlinear predictive modeling. The framework aims to deeply elucidate the interplay between consumer decision preferences and product characteristics within refrigerator design, exploring the underlying mechanisms through which product design features influence consumer attraction toward sustainable consumption. The main contributions of this research are as follows:

- For the first time, an LDM is integrated with empirically derived user constraints in home appliance design, innovatively employing entropy-weighted COPRAS to address multi-attribute trade-offs in generative deep neural network outputs, achieving balanced benefits among functionality, aesthetics, and sustainability.
- A closed-loop research paradigm of "demand insight—intelligent generation—decision optimization—market prediction" is established, overcoming the limitations of one-way user data transfer inherent in traditional design processes.
- The theoretical advantage of the structural risk minimization framework is validated within small-sample industrial design data scenarios, providing novel tools for decision-making analysis under limited data conditions.

First, this study employs semi-structured interviews combined with multi-source data fusion techniques to deeply explore consumers' decision-making preferences and sensitivity factors when purchasing refrigerators. Qualitative research methods effectively capture implicit consumer needs and complex decision-making psychology, uncovering variations and distribution characteristics in users' preferences regarding key attributes such as overall capacity, aesthetic design, and energy efficiency ratings. Second, to address the limitations of traditional design generation methods, which typically struggle to precisely control design details and global coherence, this research introduces an LDM combined with a ControlNet deep learning architecture to achieve high-fidelity and semantic-controllable intelligent generation of refrigerator design schemes. Furthermore, the entropy-weighted COPRAS multi-attribute decision-making method is utilized to comprehensively evaluate and optimize these generated designs, ensuring multi-dimensional coordination and optimization among functional rationality, design coherence, and complexity. Additionally, to quantitatively assess the mechanisms by which design characteristics impact consumer attractiveness, a nonlinear predictive mapping model linking industrial design features with consumer purchase intentions is established. Support vector regression (SVR) and Bayesian regularization backpropagation (BP) neural networks are comparatively analyzed, systematically evaluating their predictive accuracy and generalization capabilities to highlight the theoretical advantages of the structural risk minimization framework in small-sample, high-dimensional design data analysis scenarios. The empirical results demonstrate that the SVR model significantly outperforms the BP neural network in both predictive accuracy and generalization, validating SVR's practicality and robustness for data-driven predictive tasks involving complex design data, thereby providing clear theoretical support for quantifying the relationship between design elements and consumer attraction. This research further develops prototypes of mini desktop refrigerators and vehicle-mounted multifunctional refrigerators. By extracting intelligently generated design features and integrating detailed engineering optimizations, significant improvements are realized in market competitiveness and sustainable consumer potential, particularly in space utilization efficiency, portability, and human–machine interaction convenience. These outcomes confirm the potential and innovative value of data-driven methods within industrial design practice.

This study constructs and validates a data-driven intelligent design analysis framework, extending the theoretical boundaries within the field of industrial design. It provides a standardized and scientifically robust methodological toolkit for effectively identifying and satisfying user needs, optimizing products' market competitiveness, and enhancing sustainable consumption value (Figure 1). The research not only enriches sustainable design theory but also offers a replicable technological pathway and practical paradigm for future low-carbon transition and sustainable development in the manufacturing industry.

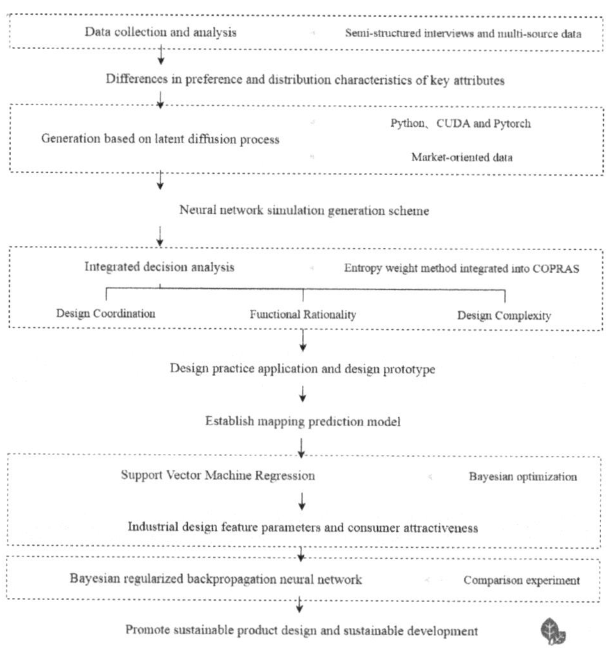

Figure 1. Research framework.

2. Related Work

The existing literature primarily comprises two research paradigms: qualitative and quantitative. On the qualitative side, studies focus on exploring user behaviors [8], providing contextual and experiential insights into product design through the analysis of demographic characteristics, purchase motivations [9], and usage scenarios [10]. For instance, Shen et al. [11] explored the relationship between consumer behavior studies and virtual business application design, while Qin et al. [12] found a positive correlation between innovative cultural product design and enhanced purchasing behavior among younger generations. Regarding sustainability analyses, Velaoras et al. [13] adopted qualitative methods to synthesize existing knowledge and evaluated the impact of hotel certifications on environmental and economic sustainability. Additionally, in sustainable product studies, Szaban et al. [14] applied conjoint analysis—a statistical method—to investigate how product attributes and individual variables influence pricing perceptions in the sustainable cosmetics industry. Although these studies provide detailed insights into sustainable product design and consumer demands, they predominantly rely on summarizing and statistically analyzing historical data to propose novel sustainability insights. However, they lack predictive analyses based on nonlinear mapping of existing data for future development, thus constraining their scalability and generalizability. On the quantitative side, research emphasizes data-driven and intelligent-driven objective design methodologies, such as generative adversarial networks (GANs) [15] and topology optimization [16]. For example, Wang and Liu [17] proposed a multi-stage artificial neural network approach integrating particle swarm optimization and the Adam algorithm for product design evaluation. Furthermore, Zhu et al. [18] investigated the impact of emotional and sustainable product design on user experience and satisfaction, developing a BP neural network optimization model for product optimization. In topology optimization, Qian and Ye [19] constructed a dual-model artificial neural network to accelerate gradient-based optimization processes. Additionally, Burnap et al. [20] combined probabilistic variational autoencoders (VAEs) with GANs for product aesthetic design. In the engineering design context, Yoo et al. [21] presented a neural network-based CAD/CAE framework for the conceptual design stage, demonstrating its efficacy through a wheel design case study. Although these quantitative approaches exhibit strong computational advantages, they frequently simplify human preferences and engineering parameters into abstract feature vectors. Moreover, they insufficiently consider constraints and trade-offs among functionality, aesthetics, and sustainability during neural network-based generation and evaluation optimization. For instance, studies employing convolutional neural networks (CNNs) in household product research [22] often overlook contextual factors such as family composition or spatial constraints, resulting in mismatches between the proposed solutions and actual usage scenarios.

In addition, Badawy et al. [23] explored predictive analytics in healthcare using machine learning and deep learning technologies. Falatouri et al. [24] analyzed and compared demand forecasting techniques within supply chain management to enhance sustainability. Aljohani [25] effectively integrated predictive analytics and machine learning into risk mitigation processes, contributing to theoretical innovations in supply chain risk management. Regarding industrial analytics, Chen et al. [26] proposed a gradient boosted partitioned regression tree model for predicting travel time based on large-scale data collected from Industrial Internet of Things infrastructures. Dawood et al. [27] employed an artificial neural network and risk analysis model to predict water quality, assessing water contamination and pipeline sustainability with an average effectiveness of 92%. Furthermore, Zhang et al. [28] applied a neural network-based forecasting method to sustainable electronic agriculture. Despite the aforementioned studies providing promising explorations of predictive analytics across diversified sustainability scenarios, limitations remain in terms of model generalization, adaptability to complex real-world contexts, and depth of empirical application. Additionally, research is still scarce regarding predictive mappings between industrial design feature parameters and consumer preferences, leading to reduced robustness in the market viability of industrial product designs. Consequently, an objective and quantitative analytical bridge between the stages of manufacturing and market entry remains insufficiently developed.

The emergence of diffusion models, particularly latent diffusion models (LDMs) [29], has enabled high-fidelity image synthesis with significantly reduced computational overhead by operating within compressed latent spaces, making them ideal for iterative design exploration. However, their application has predominantly been confined to artistic fields [30], with limited integration of user-oriented constraints or multi-criteria evaluation systems. Simultaneously, semi-structured interview techniques generate rich behavioral data [31], yet mechanisms that systematically translate these data into design guidelines remain insufficient. In response to the identified research gaps, this study develops and empirically substantiates a comprehensive cross-disciplinary research framework that synthesizes qualitative inquiry, generative design algorithms, and nonlinear forecasting models. The framework is designed to systematically investigate how consumer preferences dynamically interact with design parameters in refrigerator products and to uncover the latent pathways through which design attributes shape sustainable consumption attractiveness.

3. Methodology

3.1. Data Collection

This study adopted semi-structured interviews as the core qualitative research method to ensure the acquisition of rigorous and reliable information. This approach balanced the central research objectives with the respondents' autonomous expressions. It facilitated the exploration of underlying mechanisms and dynamic processes related to the research phenomenon. Compared with structured interviews, semi-structured interviews offer greater flexibility. They allow respondents to elaborate on and supplement specific topics. Meanwhile, the interview guidelines remain aligned with the predefined research questions. This facilitates capturing data with greater depth and richness both theoretically and practically [32]. During the research design phase, the preliminary interview outline was formulated and iteratively validated and revised by comprehensively considering theoretical saturation principles and the unique contextual factors of the study, thereby maximizing the effectiveness and credibility of the collected data [33].

To ensure the rigor and trustworthiness of the semi-structured interview protocol, a two-step validation process was implemented. First, the interview outline was reviewed by five experts—including academic scholars in design and engineering as well as senior industrial practitioners—to evaluate the semantic clarity, contextual relevance, and alignment with research objectives. Their suggestions led to refinements in item phrasing and sequencing to enhance content validity.

Second, a pilot test was conducted with six participants to verify the operational clarity and logical flow of the interview guide. Based on participant feedback and researcher observations, minor revisions were made to improve the interpretability of specific prompts and reduce redundancy.

Given the qualitative nature of the data, procedural reliability was assessed through inter-coder agreement. Two trained researchers independently coded a random subset (20%) of transcripts using the finalized codebook. The Cohen's Kappa value reached 0.81, indicating substantial inter-rater reliability. This confirmed that the data analysis process was both systematic and replicable, thereby ensuring methodological consistency.

First, this study identified several key topics based on the core research questions to establish an initial interview outline, primarily including user characteristics and habits, as well as demand-related information for refrigerator products. To ensure the reliability and heterogeneity of the qualitative data, a stratified purposive sampling strategy was adopted, complemented by elements of convenience sampling. Participants were deliberately selected to capture a diverse range of demographic and behavioral profiles relevant to refrigerator usage. Stratification was performed across key dimensions such as age group, income level, household type (e.g., urban apartment, dormitory), and refrigerator application scenario (e.g., domestic use, office use, or in-vehicle usage).

Within each stratum, participants were recruited through online user communities, product review platforms, and manufacturer-affiliated retail networks. This hybrid approach enabled the study to access a wide spectrum of consumer experiences while maintaining operational feasibility and theoretical saturation. By combining stratified design with convenience-based execution, the sampling process supported both the richness and contextual relevance of the semi-structured interview data. To ensure the relevance and depth of qualitative insights, representative respondents were selected based on predefined seniority and decision-making criteria. For industry professionals, inclusion required a minimum of five years of experience in home appliance design or manufacturing and current occupation of a mid- or senior-level role (e.g., senior product designer, product strategy lead, or sustainability officer). Academic participants were required to hold a doctoral degree and have an active track record in design-related research or sustainability studies.

Additionally, experienced consumers were included as lead-user representatives. These individuals demonstrated a history of refrigerator comparison and purchase decision making, and many had contributed to public product reviews or participated in consumer feedback forums.

This multi-dimensional sampling ensured that the perspectives captured reflected both professional expertise and advanced user insight, aligning with the study's goal of triangulating sustainable design expectations across production and consumption domains.

During the formal interview phase, representative respondents were selected as the sample source [34], considering their seniority in the research field, organizational or industrial positions, and relevant experience, thus ensuring multi-perspective discussions and informational saturation regarding the research questions.

The interviews were conducted by professionally trained researchers to ensure methodological rigor and reliability. Each interview was precisely guided and digitally recorded, followed by accurate transcription using manual proofreading methods. The transcripts were subsequently processed using qualitative analysis software (NVivo 14.0) for systematic coding and thematic synthesis. To enhance the trustworthiness of the research, the coding framework was continually refined and improved through cross-validation among researchers and multi-party discussions on the preliminary findings. Such iterative refinements contributed to the robustness of the analytical framework. To guarantee ethical rigor and precision, the interviews were meticulously transcribed with professional verification. The qualitative analysis software (NVivo 14.0) facilitated systematic coding and thematic synthesis. To enhance credibility, cross-validation among researchers and multi-party discussions of the preliminary outcomes were conducted, ensuring continuous refinement and improvement of the coding framework [35]. Consequently, this approach resulted in a comprehensive and refined coding structure. In summary, the semi-structured interviews effectively balanced maintaining research focus and flexible exploration, enhancing data richness and credibility, and they provided the study with profound insights and multidimensional evidence (Figure 2).

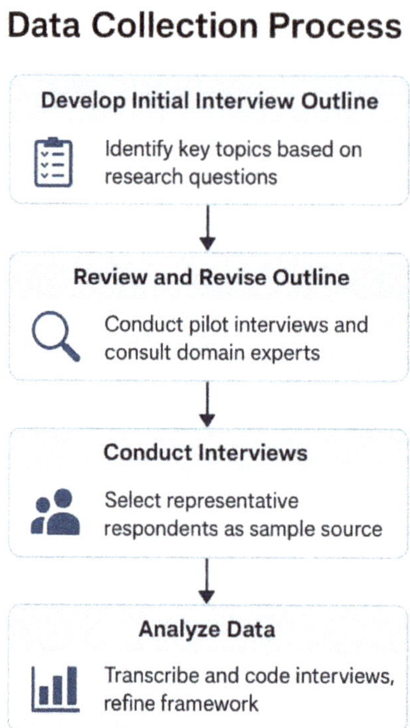

Figure 2. Flowchart of the data collection and preprocessing procedure.

3.2. Sustainable Design Research and Analysis

In this study, deep neural networks were employed to further investigate the shape design of refrigerators. Specifically, a latent diffusion model (LDM) with a deep composite neural network was used to simulate and explore the design generation process. The latent diffusion model is a generative deep learning network based on a diffusion probability process [36], designed to achieve high-fidelity and efficient image synthesis by performing stepwise denoising in latent space rather than the original pixel space. Compared to traditional pixel-level diffusion models, LDMs first utilize an encoder–decoder architecture to perform dimensionality reduction and reconstruction of the input image, thus learning the forward diffusion and reverse denoising processes in a lower-dimensional latent representation. Specifically, given an image $\mathbf{x}_0 \in \mathcal{X}$, the latent representation $\mathbf{z}_0 = E(\mathbf{x}_0)$ is first obtained through the encoder E. Then, in the latent space $\mathcal{Z}$, a forward diffusion process $q(\mathbf{z}_t \mid \mathbf{z}_{t-1})$ and a reverse process $p_\theta(\mathbf{z}_{t-1} \mid \mathbf{z}_t)$ are defined. In the forward diffusion phase, Gaussian noise is progressively injected into the latent representation at each time step, causing the distribution to gradually approach a standard normal distribution. Let the diffusion rate be β_t, the process can be represented as follows:

$$q(\mathbf{z}_t \mid \mathbf{z}_{t-1}) = \mathcal{N}\left(\mathbf{z}_t; \sqrt{1-\beta_t}\mathbf{z}_{t-1}, \beta_t\mathbf{I}\right), q(\mathbf{z}_t \mid \mathbf{z}_0) = \mathcal{N}\left(\mathbf{z}_t; \sqrt{\overline{\alpha}_t}\mathbf{z}_0, (1-\overline{\alpha}_t)\mathbf{I}\right) \quad (1)$$

where $\alpha_t = 1 - \beta_t$ and $\overline{\alpha}_t = \prod_{s=1}^{t} \alpha_s$. $\mathbf{I}$ denotes an identity covariance matrix, the dimensionality of which matches that of the latent variable $\mathbf{z}_t$. In the reverse denoising phase, a parameterized denoising network $p_\theta(\mathbf{z}_{t-1} \mid \mathbf{z}_t)$ is learned, typically modeled as a Gaussian distribution $\mathcal{N}(\mu_\theta(\mathbf{z}_t, t), \Sigma_\theta(\mathbf{z}_t, t))$, so that at each time step, the latent representation of the previous step can be accurately restored, effectively reversing the forward diffusion process layer by layer. During training, the network parameters θ are estimated by minimizing the variational lower bound from $\mathbf{z}_t$ to $\mathbf{z}_0$, which can be written as follows:

$$\mathcal{L}_{\text{VLB}}(\theta) = \mathbb{E}_{q(\mathbf{z}_0,\ldots,\mathbf{z}_T)}\left[\sum_{t=1}^{T} D_{\text{KL}}(q(\mathbf{z}_{t-1} \mid \mathbf{z}_t, \mathbf{z}_0) \parallel p_\theta(\mathbf{z}_{t-1} \mid \mathbf{z}_t)) - \log p_\theta(\mathbf{z}_0 \mid \mathbf{z}_1)\right] \quad (2)$$

where D_{KL} denotes the Kullback–Leibler divergence. The term $\mathbb{E}_{q(z_0,\ldots,z_T)}[\cdot]$ refers to the expectation taken over the joint distribution $q(z_0, \ldots, z_T)$ of the entire latent variable trajectory generated by the forward diffusion process during training. Since the encoder–decoder compresses high-dimensional images into relatively compact latent representations, the LDM performs diffusion and reverse diffusion processes in the latent space, significantly reducing memory and computational overhead while capturing global semantic and structural features of the image more effectively in this lower-dimensional representation. During the inference (sampling) phase, latent noise $\mathbf{z}_T \sim \mathcal{N}(0, \mathbf{I})$ is first sampled from a standard normal distribution, and then, through iterative steps using the reverse denoising network, it is gradually restored to $\mathbf{z}_0$. Finally, the image is decoded back to the pixel space through the decoder $D(\mathbf{z}_0)$, generating a new image (Figure 3). To further enhance the controllability of the generated designs, this study introduced the ControlNet neural network in the latent diffusion process to strengthen both the balance and control over local details and global consistency of the synthesized image design solutions [37].

To ensure rigorous and consistent evaluation of the generated design schemes, a semi-structured scoring rubric was developed for each of the three key evaluation criteria:

Design Harmony (*DH*): Assessed based on the visual coherence between product form elements, color schemes, proportional balance, and overall stylistic integrity. Experts assigned scores on a 1–10 scale using the following components:

$$DH = \frac{1}{4}\left(S_{\text{form}} + S_{\text{proportion}} + S_{\text{color}} + S_{\text{aesthetic unity}}\right) \quad (3)$$

where each subscore S_i ranges from 1 (poor) to 10 (excellent).

Functional Rationality (*FR*): Measured by evaluating the logical arrangement of functional components, user ergonomics, and contextual adaptability of the layout. Experts used a three-point structure:

$$FR = \frac{1}{3}\left(S_{\text{layout logic}} + S_{\text{usability}} + S_{\text{scenario fit}}\right) \quad (4)$$

Design Complexity (*DC*): A reverse-scored indicator reflecting the degree of design intricacy, number of components, and expected difficulty in manufacturing or user learning. A lower score indicates higher complexity. The formula was as follows:

$$DC = 10 - \left(\frac{1}{3}\left(S_{\text{parts count}} + S_{\text{interaction steps}} + S_{\text{manufacturing difficulty}}\right)\right) \quad (5)$$

All experts scored independently and were instructed to use the scoring rubric for calibration prior to formal assessment. The final scores for each scheme were computed as the arithmetic mean across all evaluators.

Next, the synthesized design solutions were optimized and filtered to ensure the quality and comprehensive value of the generated results. The proposed methodology began with integrating the multi-source expert evaluations to construct a standardized decision matrix. Multiple domain experts independently evaluated a set of candidate alternatives based on predefined criteria, which were divided into attributes that were either benefit-oriented (maximized) or cost-oriented (minimized). For each alternative i and criterion j, the aggregated score x_{ij} was calculated as the arithmetic average of all expert ratings:

$$x_{ij} = \frac{1}{K}\sum_{k=1}^{K} x_{ij}^{(k)} \tag{6}$$

where K represents the number of experts, and $x_{ij}^{(k)}$ denotes the rating from the k-th expert. Prior to aggregation, outlier detection was conducted using interquartile range (IQR) analysis. Extreme values beyond the 1.5×IQR threshold were adjusted via Winsorization at the 5th and 95th percentiles. The adjusted ratings were then averaged across experts, reducing individual variance while mitigating the influence of outliers.

To objectively quantify the relative importance of the criteria, the entropy weight method [38] was applied, using information entropy to measure the discriminating power of each criterion. Heterogeneous data were standardized, with the benefit-oriented criteria normalized as follows:

$$z_{ij}^{+} = \frac{x_{ij} - \min(x_j)}{\max(x_j) - \min(x_j)} \tag{7}$$

For the cost-oriented criteria, the conversion formula was:

$$z_{ij}^{-} = \frac{\max(x_j) - x_{ij}}{\max(x_j) - \min(x_j)} \tag{8}$$

Although min–max normalization is widely used, it is sensitive to outliers. In cases where the standard deviation or coefficient of variation of expert scores exceeded a predefined threshold, z-score-based normalization was applied as a robustness-enhancing alternative, ensuring the stability of the entropy-weighted calculation.

For the j-th criterion, its entropy E_j was calculated using a logarithm to the base N, where N is the number of alternatives:

$$p_{ij} = \frac{z_{ij}}{\sum_{i=1}^{N} z_{ij}}, E_j = -\sum_{i=1}^{N} p_{ij}\log_N p_{ij} \tag{9}$$

where N is the number of alternatives, and this formulation ensured that $E_j \in [0,1]$, thereby facilitating consistent normalization across criteria. A lower entropy value indicated less dispersion in the data, implying greater significance of the criterion.

The internal information utility of each criterion was reflected by the coefficient of variation $d_j = 1 - E_j$. The final weight w_j was obtained through normalization:

$$w_j = \frac{d_j}{\sum_{j=1}^{M} d_j} \tag{10}$$

where M is the total number of criteria. This data-driven method ensured that the weights were not influenced by subjective bias and were consistent with the characteristics of the dataset.

The COPRAS method ranked the alternatives by synthesizing the weighted criterion values [39], explicitly addressing the trade-offs between benefit and cost attributes. The calculation process was as follows:

First, the standardized matrix $Z = [z_{ij}]_{N\times M}$ was converted into a weighted matrix $V = [v_{ij}]$, using the conversion formula:

$$v_{ij} = w_j \cdot z_{ij} \tag{11}$$

Next, for each alternative i, the aggregated benefit index S_{+i} and cost index S_{-i} were calculated as follows:

$$S_{+i} = \sum_{j \in \Omega^+} v_{ij}, S_{-i} = \sum_{j \in \Omega^-} v_{ij} \tag{12}$$

where Ω^+ and Ω^- denote the sets of benefit- and cost-oriented criteria, respectively.

Then, the relative utility U_i of each alternative was calculated using the proportional principle:

$$U_i = S_{+i} + \frac{\sum_{i=1}^{N} S_{-i}}{S_{-i} \cdot \sum_{i=1}^{N} \frac{1}{S_{-i}}} \tag{13}$$

The second term introduced a penalty–reward mechanism to adjust the relative influence of the cost criteria, ensuring a balanced evaluation across competing objectives.

Finally, the alternatives were ranked in descending order of U_i, with higher values indicating better overall performance. In this study, the above steps were used for the multi-criteria evaluation of design solutions, considering key factors such as functionality, aesthetics, and cost effectiveness. This approach allowed for a comprehensive comparison and optimization ranking of different design solutions, providing a scientific basis for the final decision.

Furthermore, a support vector regression (SVR) model was employed to quantitatively predict the relationship between industrial design feature parameters and consumer attractiveness indices [40]. The SVR method facilitated the quantitative analysis of industrial design parameters and consumer attractiveness. Given a training dataset $\{(x_i, y_i)\}_{i=1}^n \subseteq \mathbb{R}^d \times \mathbb{R}$, SVR constructs the regression function $f(x) = w^T\phi(x) + b$ by solving the following convex optimization problem:

$$\begin{array}{ll} \min\limits_{w,b,\xi,\xi^*} & \frac{1}{2} \parallel w \parallel^2 + C \sum\limits_{i=1}^{n} (\xi_i + \xi_i^*) \\ \text{s.t.} & y_i - w^T\phi(x_i) - b \leq \epsilon + \xi_i \\ & w^T\phi(x_i) + b - y_i \leq \epsilon + \xi_i^* \\ & \xi_i, \xi_i^* \geq 0, \forall i = 1, \ldots, n \end{array} \tag{14}$$

where $\phi : \mathbb{R}^d \to \mathcal{H}$ is a nonlinear mapping function that projects the input space into a high-dimensional reproducing kernel Hilbert space (RKHS); $\parallel w \parallel^2$ is a regularization term used to control the model complexity; $C > 0$ is a penalty coefficient that balances the training error and the model's generalization ability; $\epsilon \geq 0$ defines the ε-insensitive zone, allowing prediction errors within $\pm\varepsilon$ to be excluded from the loss calculation; and ξ_i and ξ_i^* are slack variables used to handle outlier samples that exceed the ε-insensitive zone.

Through Lagrangian dual transformation, the original optimization problem can be converted into a dual form that depends solely on the kernel function $K(x_i, x_j) = \phi(x_i)^T\phi(x_j)$:

$$f(x) = \sum_{i=1}^{n} \left(\alpha_i - \alpha_i^*\right) K(x_i, x) + b \tag{15}$$

where α_i and α_i^* are the dual variables, with nonzero values corresponding to the support vectors. The Gaussian radial basis function (RBF) kernel is expressed as $K(x_i, x_j) = \exp\left(-\gamma \| x_i - x_j \|^2\right)$.

The hyperparameters (C, ϵ, γ) are typically determined through grid search combined with k-fold cross-validation optimization. The statistical advantage of SVR lies in the implicit realization of high-dimensional linear regression via kernel techniques, which effectively capture complex interactions among variables. The theoretical upper bound of the generalization error of this method is controlled by the Vapnik–Chervonenkis dimension, and its performance is consistently guaranteed under kernel functions that satisfy Mercer's condition, making it well suited for regression tasks characterized by small sample sizes and high-dimensional nonlinearity.

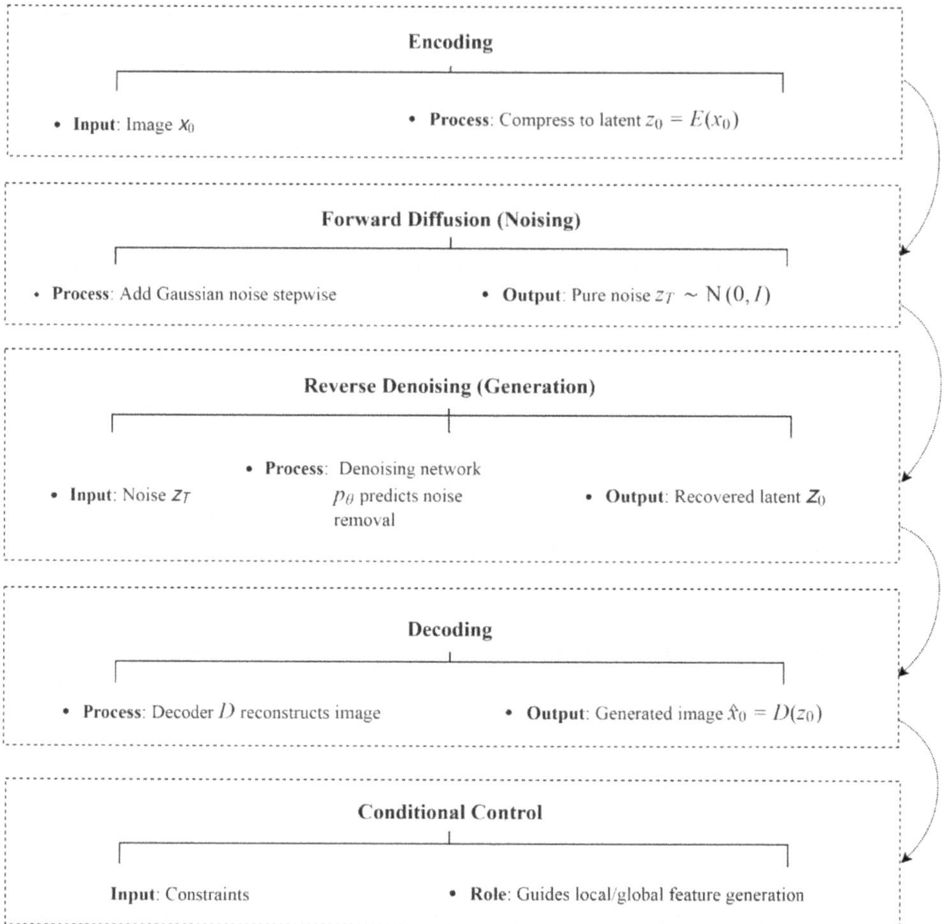

Figure 3. Operational architecture based on a deep neural network.

4. Results and Discussion

4.1. Consumer Feedback on Refrigerator Product Features and Energy Consumption

This study, through rigorous and detailed statistical analysis, obtained a sample structure, as shown in Figure 4, where the figures are expressed as percentages, N denotes the sample size, and all price units are in ¥. In addition, other multi-door refrigerators include double-door refrigerators, T-door refrigerators, French-door refrigerators, and multi-door refrigerators.

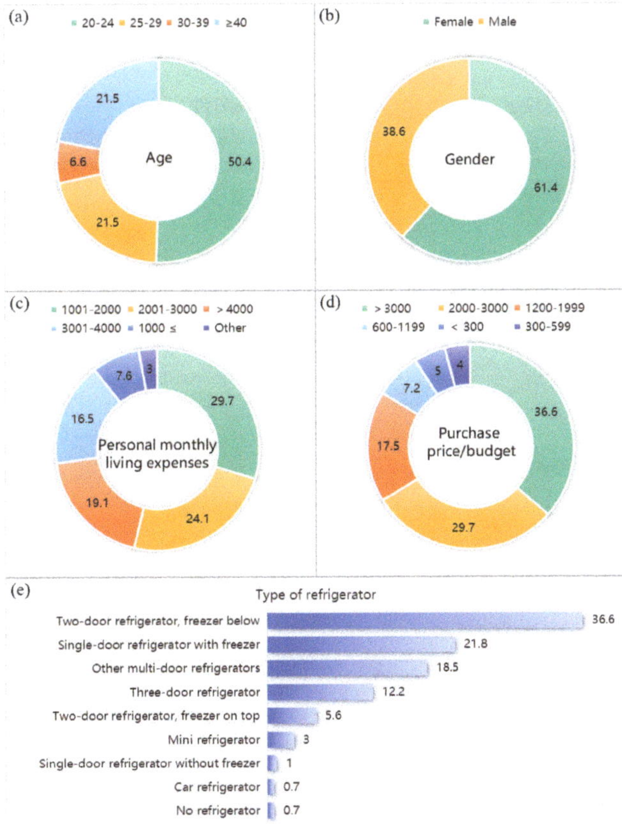

Figure 4. Sample structure: (**a**) Age, (**b**) Gender, (**c**) Personal monthly living expenses, (**d**) Purchase price/budget, (**e**) Type of refrigerator.

Figure 5a illustrates the association between the various factors that refrigerator users consider during their purchase and the factors deemed most critical. This analysis, which examined the decision criteria across different refrigerator types, revealed notable differences in consumer priorities. In this overall sample, the intrinsic qualities of the product emerged as the top consideration, with 63% of respondents prioritizing it. Price and after-sales service also ranked highly, at 71% and 60.7%, respectively, while brand recognition was slightly less emphasized. Advertising and distribution channels, on the other hand, played a minimal role, with only 4% and 10.2% consideration, respectively. For single-door refrigerator buyers, the product itself remained the primary focus. Within this group, price was the second most important factor—66.7% of users indicated its significance—while after-sales service and brand received moderate attention (52.2% and 50.7%, respectively); distribution channels and advertising were scarcely considered. In the dual-door refrigerator segment, a similar trend was observed, with users predominantly valuing the product itself. However, the importance of price was even more pronounced in this group, reaching 76.6%. After-sales service and brand maintained their relevance with contributions of 64.8% and 74.2%, respectively, yet the influences of advertising and distribution channels remained limited. For those considering triple-door refrigerators, the emphasis on the product itself continued to dominate. Here, both price and brand gained considerable attention, accounting for 56.8% and 48.6%, respectively, while after-sales service influenced 48.6% of decisions. Again, advertising and distribution channels were barely factored into the decision-making process. Among users of other multi-door refrigerators, the product's inherent characteristics were valued most highly. In this category, both price and brand were equally important, each garnering a 75% consideration rate. Notably, after-sales service was also significant at 73.2%, indicating that consumers in this segment were particularly sensitive to support services—more so than users of other refrigerator types. As with the other groups, advertising and distribution channels remained of minor importance.

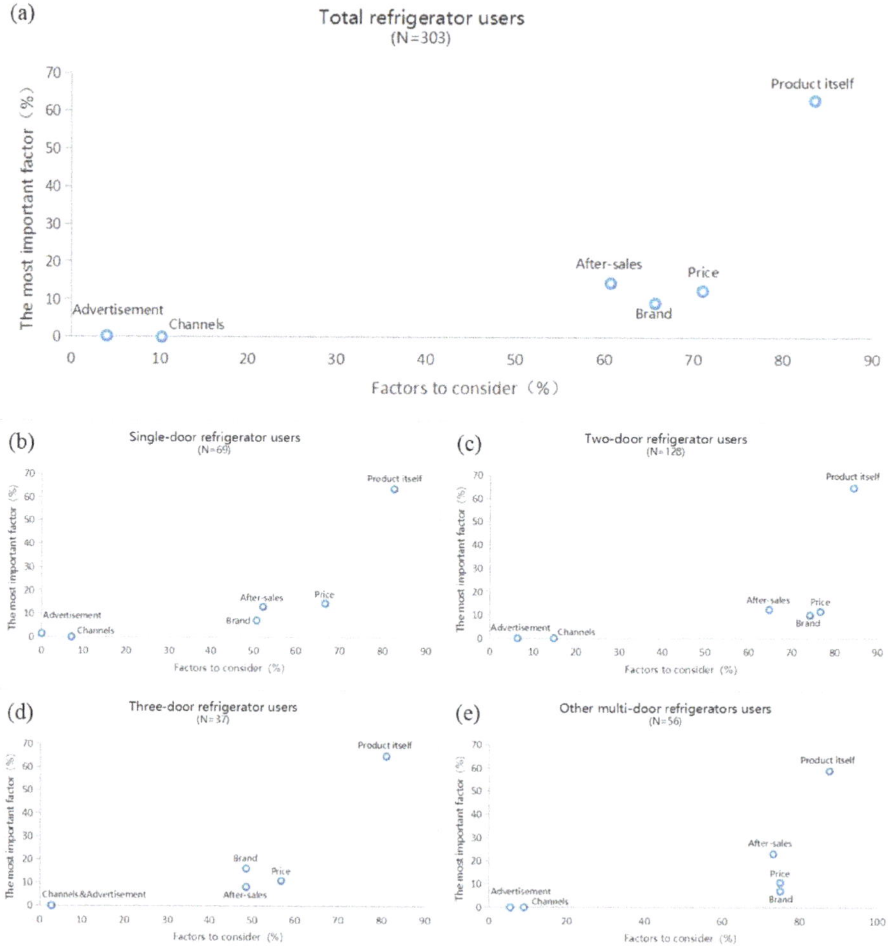

Figure 5. Factors considered when purchasing a refrigerator vs. the most important factors: (**a**) Total refrigerator users, (**b**) Single-door refrigerator users, (**c**) Two-door refrigerator users, (**d**) Three-door refrigerator users, (**e**) Other multi-door refrigerators users.

Overall, the data indicated that regardless of refrigerator type, consumers universally prioritized the product itself when making a purchase decision. Price was the immediate secondary factor, while the influences of after-sales service and brand were somewhat lower, and advertising along with distribution channels had the least impact. These findings [41] suggested that consumers place a high premium on product quality, functionality, and durability. In today's increasingly competitive market, the core value of the product is the decisive factor in consumer choice. Moreover, economic considerations exert a significant influence on purchasing behavior [42], with some consumers particularly attuned to price—an effect that is especially pronounced among dual-door refrigerator users, likely due to the specific market positioning of these products.

In Figure 6a, numerical labels denote factors related to the refrigerator itself:

1. Overall Refrigerator Capacity
2. Exterior Design
3. Energy Efficiency Rating
4. Size
5. Freezer Capacity
6. Operating Noise
7. Internal Space Layout/Compartment Design
8. Intelligent/Technological Functions
9. Refrigerator Compartment Capacity
10. Convenience of Storing Items
11. Cooling Method
12. Special Function Compartments

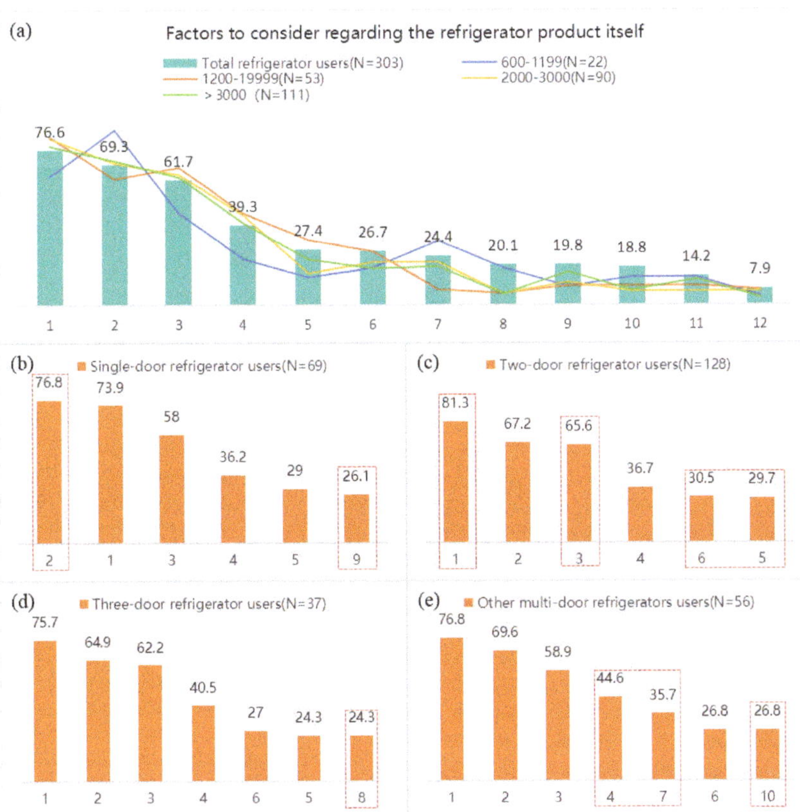

Figure 6. Considerations regarding the product itself: (**a**) Total refrigerator users, (**b**) Single-door refrigerator users, (**c**) Two-door refrigerator users, (**d**) Three-door refrigerator users, (**e**) Other multi-door refrigerators users. The red boxes indicate situations where the proportion of users of each refrigerator type who focus on factors related to the refrigerator product itself exceeds that of the overall user group.

Based on the data presented in Figure 6a, among these 12 key factors, the study found that "Overall Refrigerator Capacity" (76.6%), "Exterior Design" (69.3%), and "Energy Efficiency Rating" (61.7%) emerged as the top three priorities for users. This suggests that consumers place a high value on the fundamental functionality and fashionable appearance of refrigerators, while the focus on energy efficiency reflects concerns for environmental protection [43] as well as cost effectiveness. Following these, "Size" (39.4%), "Freezer Capacity" (27.4%), and "Operating Noise" (26.7%) indicated that consumers also have specific requirements regarding the appliance's practical compatibility and freezing performance. The dimensions influence placement and optimal space utilization within the home, and freezer capacity is directly tied to the ability for long-term food storage—a feature that becomes particularly significant during the pandemic or on special occasions.

Conversely, factors such as "Internal Space Layout/Compartment Design" (24.4%), "Refrigerator Compartment Capacity" (19.8%), "Convenience of Storing Items" (18.8%), and "Cooling Method" (14.2%) received relatively lower attention. This trend suggests that these attributes may be considered secondary by some consumers or that current market offerings have already met basic expectations, rendering them less influential in the decision-making process. The least prioritized factor was "Special Function Compartments" (only 7.9%), possibly because most users do not view such features as essential or because they are infrequently available in existing products.

Moreover, segmentation by purchase price revealed additional nuances. Consumers with a budget of ¥600–1199 exhibited a markedly higher emphasis on "Exterior Design" compared to other factors, and their concern for "Internal Space Layout/Compartment Design" was also significantly elevated relative to the overall sample. This suggests that users within this price range may prioritize a balance between economic affordability and aesthetics. In the ¥1200–1999 segment, high attention was maintained on "Exterior Design" alongside considerable concern for "Energy Efficiency Rating," possibly indicating a growing awareness of energy-saving benefits and cost efficiency. For users in the ¥2000–3000 range, "Overall Refrigerator Capacity" stood out as the most critical attribute, highlighting that at mid-range price levels, practicality and storage capacity are paramount. Meanwhile, for budgets exceeding ¥3000, although "Overall Refrigerator Capacity" and "Energy Efficiency Rating" remained highly valued, the emphasis on "Exterior Design" was slightly diminished—likely because products in this higher price bracket typically already meet established standards in both design and energy performance.

Shifting focus to different refrigerator types, Figure 6b reveals that single-door refrigerator users predominantly valued "Exterior Design" (76.8%), a proportion that exceeded the overall average. This preference may be closely associated with the typical usage scenarios for single-door models, which are often employed in small households, dormitories, or offices where the appliance's appearance must harmonize with specific interior decor. Additionally, the heightened focus on "Refrigerator Compartment Capacity" in this group may stem from the fact that single-door designs are primarily used in applications where refrigeration is the main function, thereby necessitating effective storage.

In the case of dual-door refrigerators, as illustrated in Figure 6c, "Overall Refrigerator Capacity" was the leading factor (81.3%), surpassing the overall rate. Given that dual-door models are generally used in households with substantial storage requirements, it is unsurprising that buyers in this category place special emphasis on capacity. Furthermore, the elevated attention to "Energy Efficiency Rating" (65.6%), "Operating Noise" (30.5%), and "Freezer Capacity" (29.7%) reflected concerns about long-term operating costs, a quiet home environment, and the need for diverse food storage options.

Figure 6d shows that among triple-door refrigerator users, "Overall Refrigerator Capacity" remained the most important factor (75.7%), albeit slightly lower than the overall average. Notably, "Intelligent/Technological Functions" (24.3%) received higher attention than the overall rate, suggesting that the independent compartment design of triple-door refrigerators—balancing traditional functionality with modern technological innovation—caters to users seeking enhanced space organization and convenient handling of specialized food items.

Finally, Figure 6e indicates that for users of other multi-door refrigerators, "Overall Refrigerator Capacity" was the most valued attribute (76.8%), closely aligning with the overall average, which reflected a consistent demand for storage capacity. Additionally, factors such as "Size" (44.6%), "Internal Space Layout/Compartment Design" (35.7%), and "Convenience of Storing Items" (26.8%) registered higher than average, indicating that these users have heightened expectations for optimal home compatibility, flexible internal configuration, and storage convenience. This pattern underscored the adaptability advantages of multi-door refrigerators in larger households or environments with complex culinary needs, where efficient space utilization and user-friendly design are highly prized.

In Figure 7a, the overall sample revealed that 67.6% of refrigerator users were attentive to energy efficiency ratings, 15.9% were not, and 16.5% remained neutral. In general, Chinese consumers placed significant emphasis on energy efficiency when choosing a refrigerator. Figure 7b demonstrates that users with a purchase price or budget exceeding ¥3000 exhibited the highest level of concern for energy efficiency ratings (72%), with only 2.7% indicating they were "completely indifferent". By contrast, users with a purchase price below ¥300 showed the lowest overall concern (53.3%). Notably, within this lower price range, 40% reported being "very concerned," and the proportion of users who were indifferent reached 33.4% (with 26.7% being "completely indifferent"). This bipolar distribution in this price segment suggested a polarization in attitudes toward energy efficiency. Moreover, the overall trend indicated that the higher the price or budget, the greater the concern for energy efficiency—likely because higher-priced refrigerators, being larger and equipped with more features and specialized compartments, are generally perceived to consume more energy.

Figure 7c further highlights that among different refrigerator types, users of multi-door refrigerators exhibited the highest concern for energy efficiency at 75%, followed by dual-door users at 71.1%, while single-door refrigerator users showed the lowest concern at 58%. Within the multi-door segment, the proportion of users who were "very concerned" reached 33.9%, compared to 21.6% for triple-door models. For single-door refrigerators, the attention to energy efficiency appeared to be polarized. On one hand, their smaller overall size and internal capacity lead many users to assume a lower energy consumption, prompting some to report being "completely indifferent". On the other hand, a segment of single-door refrigerator buyers cited cost-effectiveness as their primary purchasing motive, leading them to express "very concerned" views regarding energy efficiency. This duality reflected a divergence in consumer attitudes based on the perceived energy performance of single-door models. By contrast, the heightened concern among multi-door refrigerator users was attributable to the larger size, more complex compartmental designs, and richer technological features inherent in these models, which collectively lead users to assume higher energy consumption and, therefore, to prioritize energy efficiency ratings in their decision-making.

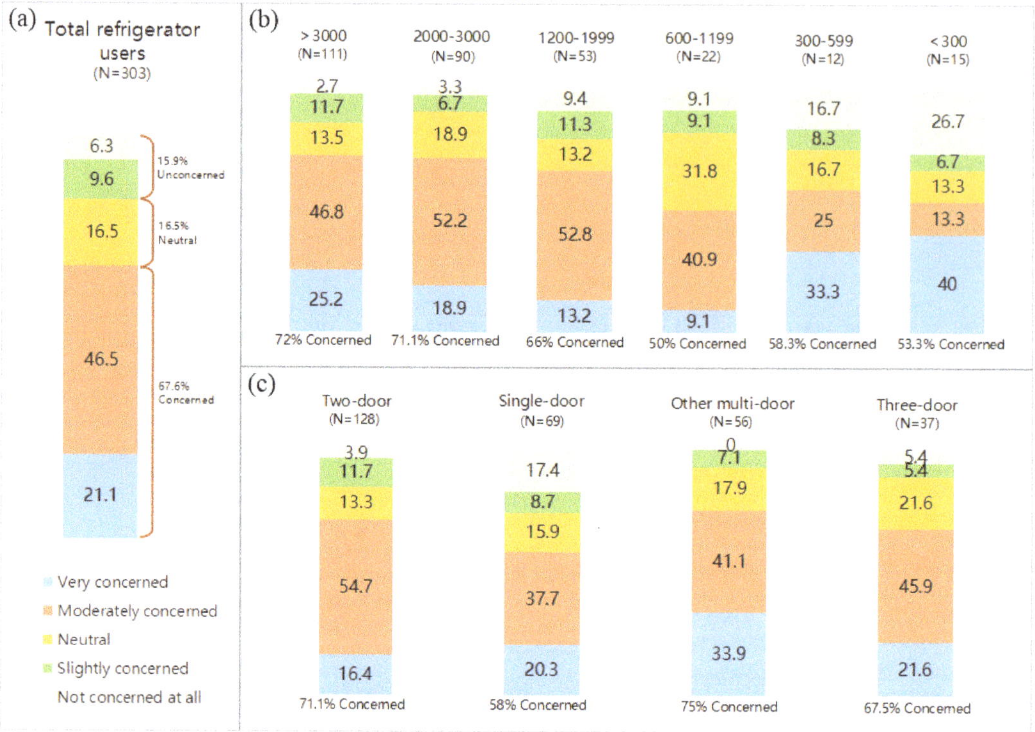

Figure 7. Concern level for refrigerator energy consumption/energy efficiency rating: (**a**) Total refrigerator users, (**b**) Users under different purchase prices and budget conditions, (**c**) Users under different refrigerator usage types.

Based on Figure 8, several aspects of Chinese consumers' attention to refrigerator energy efficiency ratings can be observed. In Figure 8a, a high proportion of overall refrigerator users (71.6%) were concerned with "energy efficiency ratings," whereas only 28.4% paid attention to "annual electricity consumption". Figure 8b,c further indicates that, regardless of refrigerator type or purchase price/budget, users tended to focus more on "energy efficiency ratings" rather than "annual electricity consumption". This trend suggested a widespread phenomenon, reflecting consumers' preference for easily accessible energy efficiency information. As a straightforward and intuitive indicator, the energy efficiency rating enables consumers to quickly assess a product energy performance, while complex information such as annual electricity consumption may not be fully understood or effectively incorporated into purchasing decisions. Even though annual electricity consumption can provide more detailed and accurate information, its complexity and the time required for its calculation may impede its practical application among consumers. For ordinary consumers without advanced technical knowledge, the energy efficiency rating, as a symbolic label, is more readily adopted and trusted than specific numerical data like annual electricity consumption.

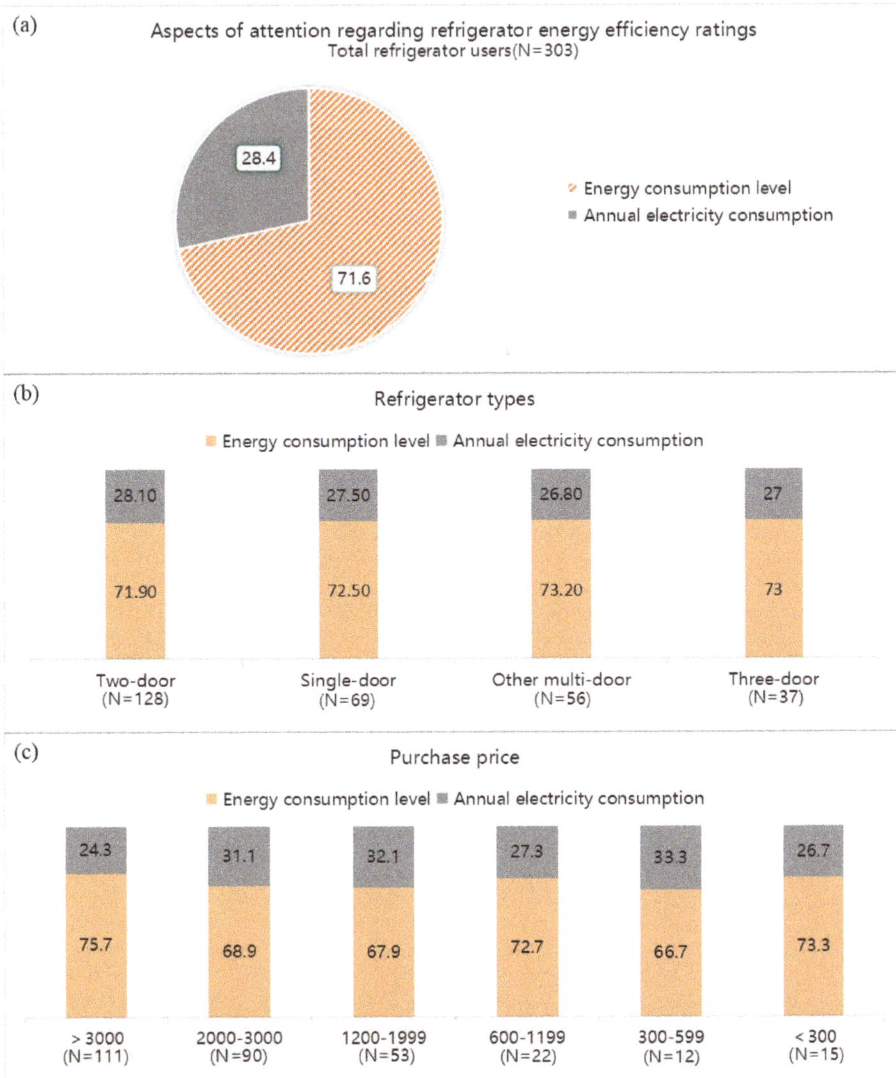

Figure 8. Concerns regarding refrigerator energy consumption/energy efficiency rating: (**a**) Total refrigerator users, (**b**) Users under different refrigerator usage types, (**c**) Users under different purchase prices and budget conditions.

The analysis of refrigerator users' attention to energy efficiency ratings in product selection revealed several significant trends and influencing factors. These findings provided key insights into consumer behavior, demonstrating that energy efficiency ratings have become an important decision-making factor in the Chinese refrigerator market. However, the notable proportion of users who were neutral or indifferent suggests that further efforts in information dissemination and consumer education are needed to ensure that a broad consumer base fully understands and utilizes energy efficiency information in their purchasing decisions. Moreover, enhancing energy efficiency knowledge, improving product transparency, and ensuring clear information delivery will help to promote more sustainable product choices and long-term ecological benefits.

To enhance the robustness of the statistical findings, we computed 95% confidence intervals (CI) for all major proportion estimates using the Wilson score method for binomial proportions. For example, the proportion of users who prioritized "Overall Refrigerator Capacity" was 76.6% (CI: 72.1–80.5%), while "Exterior Design" was rated highly by 69.3% (CI: 64.6–73.6%). These intervals confirmed the statistical reliability of the observed preferences.

Moreover, the Pearson's chi-square test was applied to examine the association between refrigerator type and key attribute preferences. The results revealed statistically significant differences in consumer emphasis on energy efficiency across product types ($\chi^2 = 18.42$, df $= 4$, $p < 0.01$) and budget levels ($\chi^2 = 23.57$, df $= 3$, $p < 0.001$). These findings indicated that consumer preferences are not uniformly distributed but vary systematically based on product configuration and purchase intention.

The addition of confidence intervals and inferential statistics provided a more rigorous empirical basis for understanding user preferences and validated the generalizability of the collected survey data.

4.2. Generation and Analysis of Sustainable Design Schemes via Computational Methods

4.2.1. Simulation-Based Generation and Discussion of Schemes

During the qualitative analysis of the interview transcripts, an emergent cross-dimensional theme was identified linking aesthetic preferences with consumer perceptions of sustainability. Specifically, multiple respondents associated visually minimalistic and organically styled refrigerator designs with environmentally responsible manufacturing and energy-saving performance. Terms such as "compact", "clean", "natural", and "uncluttered" were repeatedly mentioned as positive indicators of both aesthetic satisfaction and sustainable design consciousness.

Conversely, some participants perceived overly decorative or structurally complex designs as indicative of excessive material usage and potential energy inefficiency, implying a negative impact on environmental sustainability. This observation reveals a latent cognitive interaction wherein aesthetic qualities act as symbolic cues influencing users' sustainability judgments.

Based on the aforementioned analysis, users attach significant importance to the integration of cost effectiveness, aesthetics, and sustainability in refrigerator design; moreover, in the case of small refrigerators, the appearance is also a key factor. Given the varied usage environments for small refrigerators—including homes, dormitories, and offices—the design schemes must cater to multiple application scenarios and thus adhere to the principles of compactness and simplicity. To further investigate small refrigerator design, the experimental section employed images of best-selling small refrigerator models as the training dataset to guide the deep neural network in effectively learning and capturing market-driven design trends. Specifically, this study constructed a LoRA control model based on images of popular small refrigerators. Following expert discussions and the integration of DeepBooru tagging, emotional imagery labels were assigned to 500 small refrigerator images. Concurrently, the keyword "compact" was used as a guiding term during the training of the LoRA control model. Initially, the images underwent a multi-stage preprocessing procedure. All images were standardized to a resolution of 512×512 pixels and converted to RGB format. DeepBooru tagging was then applied to extract semantic labels representing both emotional and stylistic attributes. The label was manually reviewed, filtered, and concatenated into structured text prompts for conditioning the generative model. Minor augmentation (including horizontal flipping, brightness adjustment, and rotation) was also applied to enhance the robustness and diversity of the dataset. Subsequently, the generated tag texts were consolidated with the database to serve as input for model training. During the sampling phase, the DPM++ 2M algorithm (with the CFG scale set to 7) was utilized in combination with ControlNet to control image morphology and enable continuous iterative optimization. In addition, Canny and Scribble edge detection algorithms were introduced during preprocessing [44], which allowed the latent diffusion model to iteratively generate entirely new design schemes (Figure 9). To enhance the controllability and design coherence of the generated refrigerator concepts, the ControlNet architecture was integrated into the latent diffusion framework with two levels of conditioning input. First, semantic prompts were derived from expert-guided fusion of DeepBooru tags and interview-based user preference descriptors. These prompts encoded high-level design expectations, such as form simplicity, functional clarity, and sustainability alignment. Second, Canny edge maps were used as structural inputs to constrain spatial features such as compartment boundaries, handle positioning, or display panel alignment. The ControlNet model was trained to inject these spatial priors into the denoising steps of the latent space, enforcing consistency between the generated output and user-defined geometric structures. This dual conditioning mechanism enabled hierarchical balance between global semantic form and local structural detail.

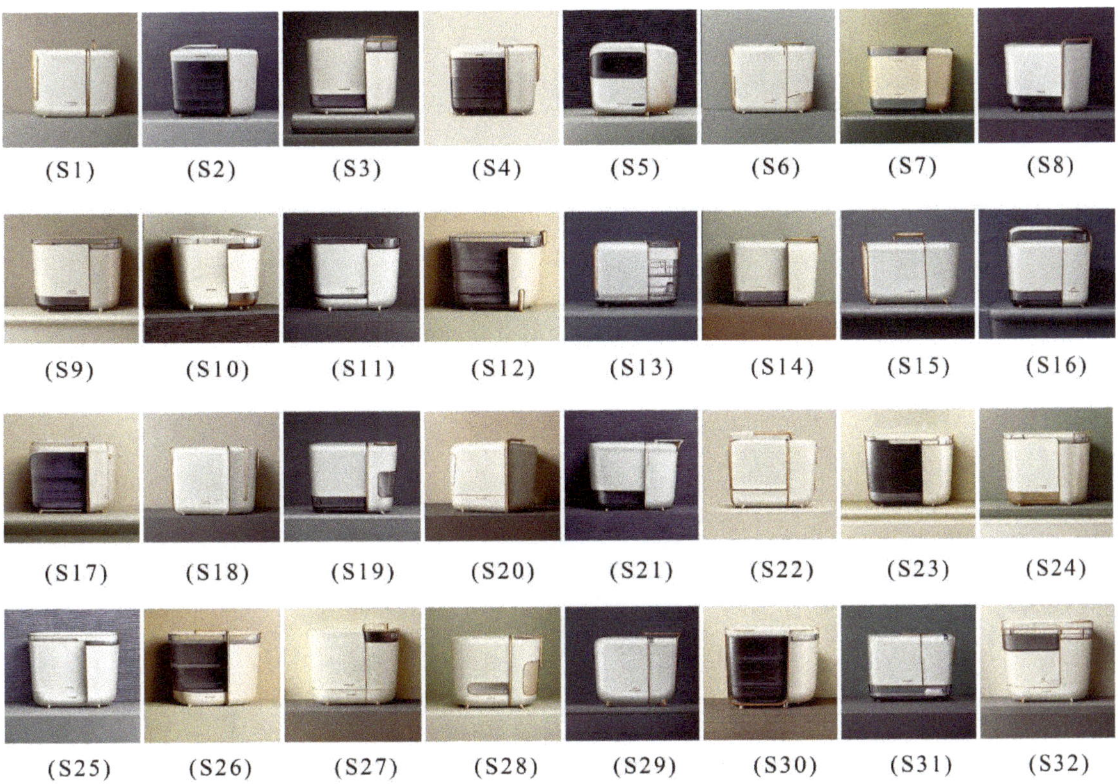

Figure 9. Computationally derived design scheme diagram:(S1)–(S32) are the detailed identifiers of design proposals generated using deep learning algorithms.

An in-depth analysis of these design schemes followed. A focus group comprising four experts with extensive backgrounds in industrial design was convened for evaluation, including two academic instructors specializing in industrial design research and two enterprise managers with profound experience in refrigerator design. All experts possessed deep insights and practical experience in sustainable development. Through focus group discussions and analysis, the following evaluation indicators were established: design harmony, functional rationality, and design complexity. A higher design harmony score indicated better overall coherence in visual appearance, structure, and user experience; a higher functional rationality score implied that the design functional layout and usage logic were clearer and more reasonable, thus better meeting target requirements; whereas design complexity was a negative indicator, with higher values suggesting more intricate components or interaction processes, potentially leading to increased manufacturing or user learning costs. Through deep decision analysis and by integrating the decision matrices from the four experts, a composite matrix was generated and subsequently normalized (Table 1, where CV stands for composite value, and SV stands for standardized value). The entropy weight method yielded indicator weights w_1, w_2, and w_3 of 0.352, 0.413, and 0.235, respectively. The normalized matrix was then combined with these weights to form a weighted normalized matrix, with the resulting values illustrated in Figure 10. Benefit values, cost values, and finally utility values were calculated, yielding analytical results for all schemes (Table 2). Employing the entropy-weighted COPRAS integrated model, Scheme 16 was identified as the optimal design, with its utility value significantly higher than those of the other schemes (Table 2). Further analysis revealed that Scheme 16 ranked within the top 10th percentile in both design harmony (8.25) and functional rationality (6.00), while its design complexity (3.75) fell within a low-risk range. This result underscored its balanced performance across key quality attributes. Compared with suboptimal schemes (Schemes 22, 8, and 29), Scheme 16 did not achieve an extreme value in any single indicator; however, its multi-criteria collaborative optimization resulted in superior overall utility. For example, although Scheme 22 excelled in functional rationality (8.50), it had a relatively high design complexity (4.25), while Scheme 8 exhibited extremely low design complexity (2.50) but its functional rationality (7.75) was somewhat lacking. This suggests that in multi-attribute decision scenarios, a balanced approach may be more competitive than excelling in any single criterion.

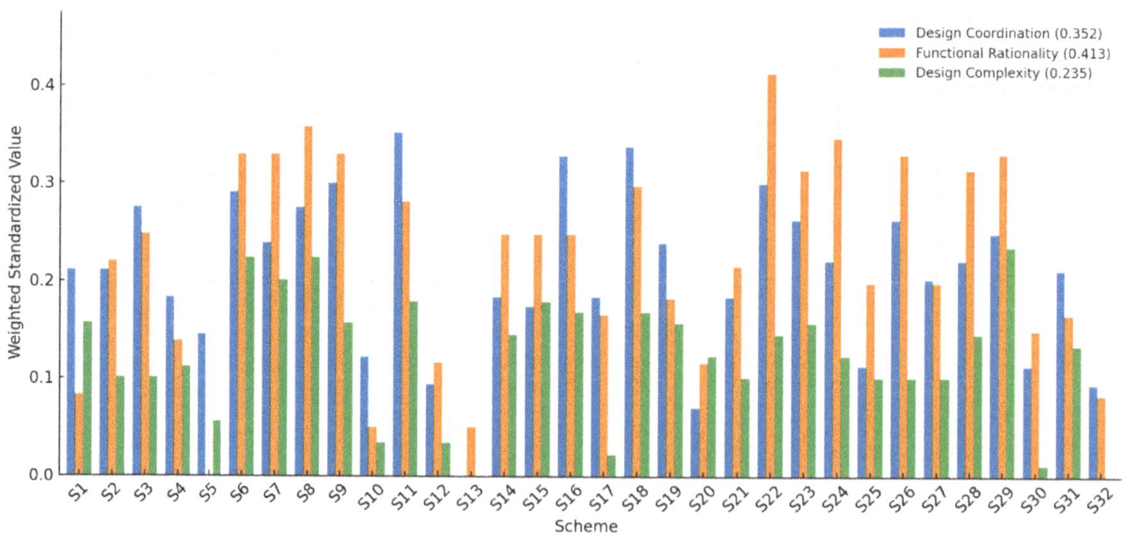

Figure 10. Weighted standardized scores for 32 schemes.

Table 1. Composite matrix and standardized matrix.

Scheme	Indicator 1		Indicator 2		Indicator 3	
	CV	SV	CV	SV	CV	SV
S1	6	0.6	3.5	0.2	4	0.667
S2	6	0.6	5.5	0.533	5.25	0.429
S3	7.25	0.78	6	0.6	5.25	0.429
S4	5.5	0.52	4.25	0.333	5	0.476
S5	4.75	0.413	2.25	0	6.25	0.238
S6	7.5	0.827	7.25	0.8	2.5	0.952
S7	6.5	0.68	7.25	0.8	3.25	0.857
S8	7.25	0.78	7.75	0.867	2.5	0.952
S9	7.75	0.853	7.25	0.8	4.25	0.667
S10	4.25	0.347	3	0.12	6.75	0.143
S11	8.75	1	6.5	0.68	3.5	0.762
S12	3.75	0.267	4	0.28	6.75	0.143
S13	2	0	3	0.12	7.5	0
S14	5.5	0.52	6	0.6	4.25	0.619
S15	5.25	0.493	6	0.6	3.5	0.762
S16	8.25	0.933	6	0.6	3.75	0.714
S17	5.5	0.52	4.75	0.4	7	0.095
S18	8.5	0.96	6.75	0.72	3.75	0.714
S19	6.5	0.68	5	0.44	4	0.667
S20	3.25	0.2	4	0.28	4.75	0.524
S21	5.5	0.52	5.5	0.52	5.25	0.429
S22	7.75	0.853	8.5	1	4.25	0.619
S23	7	0.747	7	0.76	4	0.667
S24	6.25	0.627	7.5	0.84	4.75	0.524
S25	4	0.32	5.25	0.48	5.25	0.429
S26	7	0.747	7.25	0.8	5.25	0.429
S27	5.75	0.573	5.25	0.48	5.25	0.429
S28	6.25	0.627	7	0.76	4.25	0.619
S29	6.75	0.707	7.25	0.8	2.25	1
S30	4	0.32	4.5	0.36	7.25	0.048
S31	6	0.6	4.75	0.4	4.5	0.571
S32	3.75	0.267	3.5	0.2	7.5	0

The criterion weights determined via the entropy method (functional rationality 41.3% > design harmony 35.2% > design complexity 23.5%) significantly influenced the final ranking. The high weight of functional rationality (41.3%) explained its major contribution to the utility value calculation. Among the top five schemes, the functional rationality scores were all $\geq$ 6.00 (with a global mean of 5.42), indicating that this indicator played a decisive role in scheme competitiveness. The secondary weight of design harmony (35.2%) elevated aesthetically superior schemes (e.g., Schemes 11 and 22) into the top rankings, although its impact was moderated by functional rationality. For instance, Scheme 11 achieved the highest design harmony score (8.75) but ranked fifth due to its lower functional rationality (6.50). Notably, despite having the lowest weight, design complexity still played a critical role in Scheme 16's success; its design complexity (3.75) was markedly better than that of competitors within the same utility range (e.g., Scheme 22's 4.25), demonstrating that even criteria with lower weights can influence decisions through marginal benefits. These findings suggested that, for manufacturing enterprises optimizing design under limited resources, priority should be given to enhancing functional rationality—perhaps through participatory design to better align with user needs—while adopting modular design approaches to reduce complexity, thereby balancing innovation with manufacturability. This study not only provides direct guidance for refrigerator design optimization but also presents a methodological framework that can be transferred to other industrial design scenarios, promoting a data-driven intelligent decision-making paradigm and advancing sustainable design development.

Table 2. The utility values of all schemes.

Rank	Scheme	Benefit Value	Cost Value	Utility Value
1	S16	0.596	0.168	1.145
2	S22	0.858	0.145	1.132
3	S8	0.633	0.224	1.128
4	S29	0.579	0.235	1.123
5	S11	0.633	0.179	1.117
6	S6	0.621	0.224	1.109
7	S18	0.635	0.168	1.103
8	S7	0.569	0.201	1.096
9	S23	0.577	0.157	1.088
10	S28	0.535	0.145	1.081
11	S14	0.431	0.145	1.074
12	S3	0.523	0.101	1.067
13	S24	0.568	0.123	1.059
14	S19	0.421	0.157	1.052
15	S2	0.431	0.101	1.045
16	S9	0.63	0.157	1.037
17	S31	0.376	0.134	1.03
18	S21	0.398	0.101	1.023
19	S4	0.321	0.112	1.016
20	S15	0.422	0.179	1.009
21	S25	0.311	0.101	1.002
22	S26	0.593	0.101	0.995
23	S27	0.4	0.101	0.988
24	S5	0.145	0.056	0.981
25	S17	0.348	0.022	0.974
26	S1	0.294	0.157	0.967
27	S10	0.172	0.034	0.96
28	S20	0.186	0.123	0.953
29	S30	0.262	0.011	0.946
30	S12	0.21	0.034	0.939
31	S32	0.177	0	0.932
32	S13	0.05	0	0.925

4.2.2. Design Implementation and Engineering Analysis

Based on the preliminary appearance schemes and architectures generated by the neural network—and drawing upon the design elements formed in these images—further design refinements were undertaken that incorporated a broader range of practical considerations. In conjunction with user feedback and functional requirements obtained during the data survey phase, and after thoroughly evaluating various methods for implementing each function, sketches of a mini desktop refrigerator were produced (Figure 11). During the sketching process, the overall form underwent multiple iterations. Adhering to the design philosophy of "form serving function and sustainable design," simplicity and naturalness were established as the hallmark elements of this product series. Ultimately, a minimalistic overall shape featuring a "flat top and rounded bottom" was finalized, with all detailed elements on the refrigerator maintaining a high degree of consistency. The design concept prioritized home use while also considering portability. Both the proportional design and the functional layout were carefully crafted to ensure ease of use in compact environments. With its flat top and rounded bottom, the refrigerator not only provided a visually comfortable impression but also offered a space on the top surface for small items such as succulents, decorative objects, and trinkets. The mini refrigerator's door employed a strong magnetic latch, while side grooves allowed for comfortable opening of the door. The heat dissipation vents were designed with a texture consistent with the refrigerator's overall elements, and they fully accounted for the cooling requirements of the electronic components. Internally, shelves facilitated the storage of items or food of varying sizes. The rear of the refrigerator was equipped with both a 12V DC power supply and a 220V AC power supply, fulfilling the dual functionality for home and vehicular use. Additionally, an LED display on the front enabled users to easily monitor the refrigerator's real-time status and operating mode. A leather handle with limit screws further enhanced the convenience of moving the appliance.

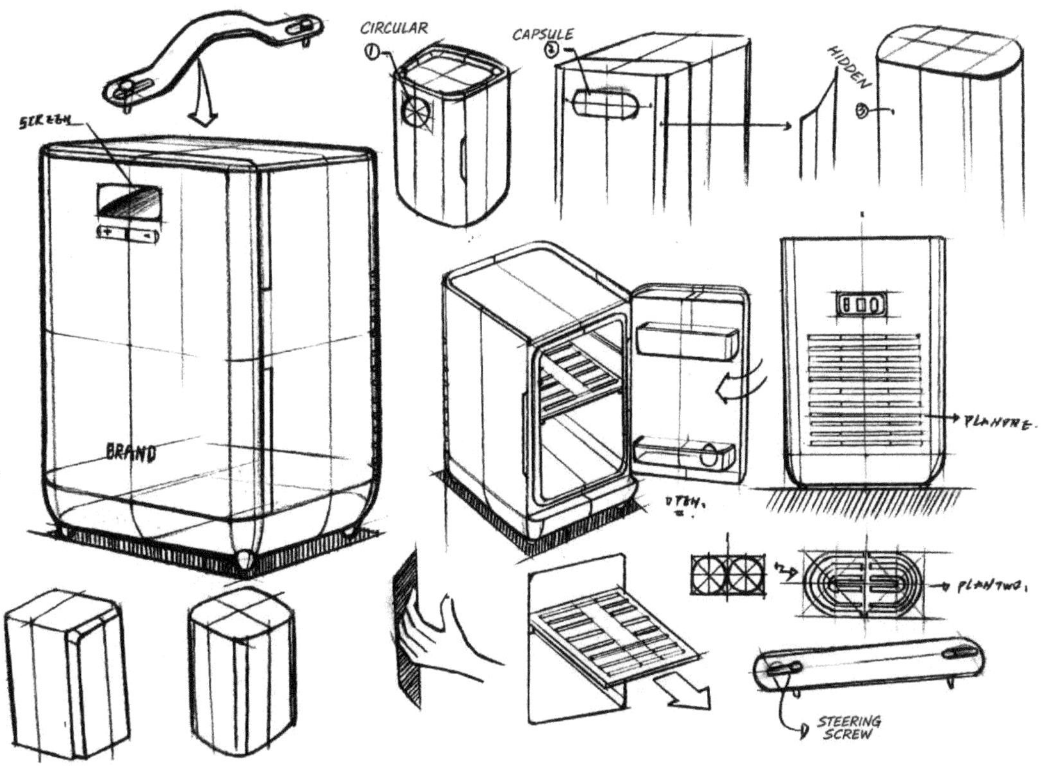

Figure 11. Mini desktop refrigerator sketch.

The design of the four "legs" was also inspired by the generated images. After appropriate optimization, they provided a "floating" visual impression by lowering the product's visual center of gravity, thereby rendering the overall appearance of the refrigerator more elongated (Figure 12). The sketches preliminarily presented the refrigerator's iconic elements and volumetric composition, offering a reference for subsequent model development and detailed refinement. The decision to increase the length and height was based on user interviews, during which the most frequently reported pain point for mini refrigerator users was insufficient internal capacity. The refrigerator employed semiconductor cooling, with dual cooling chips capable of delivering 77W of cooling and 66W of heating. The heat dissipation vents on the side and back ensured efficient overall operation (Figure 13). In

ECO mode, the system reduced both the refrigerator's power consumption and the fan speed for heat dissipation, thereby providing a quieter operating experience.

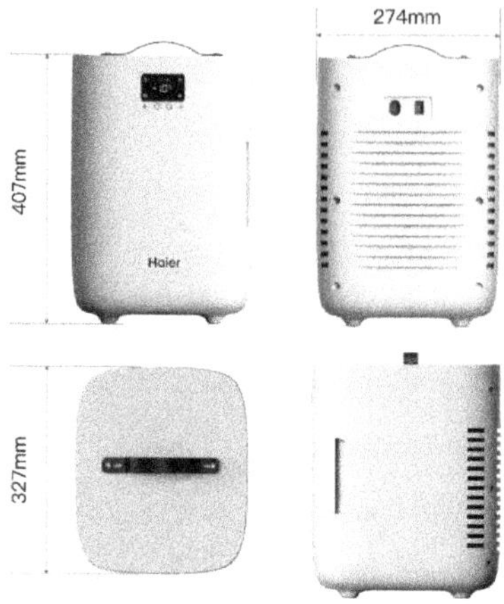

Figure 12. Mini desktop refrigerator multi-angle display.

Figure 13. Refrigerator internal details.

Based on sustainable design principles and the preliminary appearance schemes and architectures generated by the neural network, the design process primarily considered outdoor usage scenarios and functionalities. In addition to the basic refrigerator architecture, wheels, handles, a vehicular power supply interface, and interactive interfaces adapted to relevant scenarios were incorporated. After thorough consideration and analysis, sketches of a multifunctional vehicle refrigerator were produced (Figure 14). As a product in the same series, the vehicle refrigerator shared the design philosophy and detailed design elements with the mini refrigerator. However, due to differences in cooling methods and the additional challenges encountered in outdoor environments, the design of the vehicle refrigerator placed a greater emphasis on functionality. At the same time, while ensuring that functional requirements were met, attention was also paid to the overall proportions, sustainable simplicity, and aesthetic features of the appliance. This design concept prioritized "portability" and "outdoor usage" as its main considerations, leading to the development of relevant functional features. The overall size and proportions were carefully determined to ensure ease of use in the confined space of a vehicle when on the move. The refrigerator's form was particularly suited for placement in a car trunk, and the interactive interface was relocated to the side of the unit for user convenience. The appliance was equipped with a set of 160 mm diameter wheels to enhance mobility, and an extended handle—integrated into a composite handle on the opposite side—allowed users to pull the refrigerator in a manner similar to dragging a suitcase. Both side handles were designed to be foldable and were complemented by shorter handles to facilitate vertical maneuvering during loading and unloading.

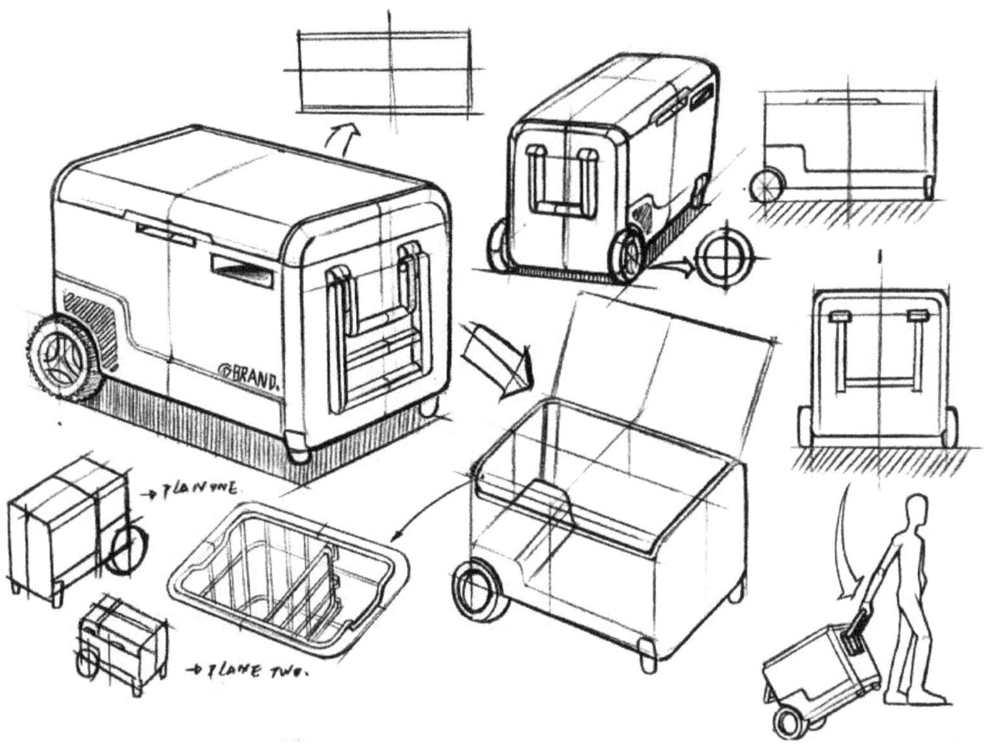

Figure 14. Multifunctional vehicle refrigerator sketch.

Internally, the refrigerator featured a stepped layout with partitioning that facilitated the storage of food and other items of various sizes and types while minimizing movement. The heat dissipation vents on the side and rear ensured the compressor's stable, long-term operation. The door employed a strong magnetic latch, maintaining the minimalistic aesthetic of the design while ensuring that the seal was not compromised by vibrations or jostling (Figure 15). After accounting for the necessary space required for the compressor, electrical control system, external accessories, and insulation layer, the final internal capacity reached 36 L, which satisfied users' storage needs. Market research indicated that an internal capacity between 30 and 35 L is the most preferred by users of vehicle refrigerators, as capacities that are either too large or too small can diminish practicality. This size was compatible with the trunk storage conditions of the vast majority of vehicles and also met the household needs of 1–2 persons, thereby achieving a dual function for both vehicle and home use. Moreover, the simplified components and exterior design contributed to reduced raw material consumption and lower human–machine interaction costs during operation.

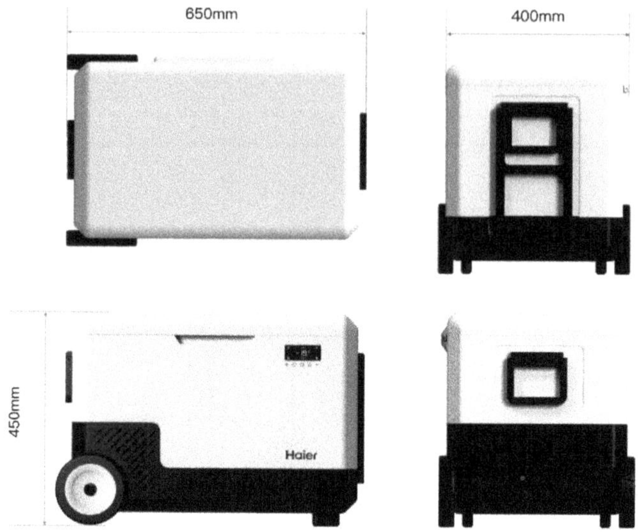

Figure 15. Multifunctional vehicle refrigerator multi-angle and dimensional display.

Figure 16 illustrates the internal details of the vehicle refrigerator. Due to the space occupied by the compressor and other electronic components, the storage compartment exhibited a stepped configuration on both the left and right sides. To address this, the interior partitioning was optimized by designing a removable grid that effectively separates different zones. This grid not only ensured the stability of stored items but also enabled efficient categorization of foods or items of varying sizes, while also being detachable for easy cleaning. An integrated lighting system was installed to assist users in retrieving items under low-light conditions. The refrigerator door featured a strong magnetic latch, and its hinge incorporated a damping mechanism—similar to that found in laptop hinges—that allowed the door to remain suspended at any angle. The contrasting black-and-white color scheme was inspired by CMF references generated by the neural network, and the overall color palette and detailing were consistent with those of the mini desktop refrigerator, forming a unified design language across the miniature refrigerator family. Given the unique environmental demands of vehicle use, all connection points likely to endure external forces—including the wheels, wheel axles, handles, door hinges, and bottom support feet—were reinforced to ensure product robustness and compliance with quality standards.

4.3. Establishment of a Sustainable Consumption Mapping Model

To further predict the consumer market and potential of sustainably designed products, a quantitative prediction model was developed using support vector regression (SVR) to map the industrial design feature parameters to the consumer appeal index. First, 300 subjects with a need for purchasing refrigerators were recruited based on stratified sampling principles. Using a 7-point Likert scale, purchase intentions for 32 sets of industrial design schemes were evaluated. The evaluation data were processed—by computing the mean and applying normalization—to transform them into data for the consumer appeal prediction variable (Figure 17). To ensure data validity, all design schemes were standardized through 3D rendering techniques. By constructing an SVR model with hyperparameter optimization, the nonlinear relationship between the product design elements and consumer appeal was systematically explored. In the experiments, design harmony, functional rationality, and design complexity were standardized using the z-score function and used as input variables, while consumer appeal (normalized to the [0,1] interval) served as the target variable. A stratified 70–30 data split was implemented using the cvpartition function (with the random seed rng(42) ensuring experimental reproducibility).

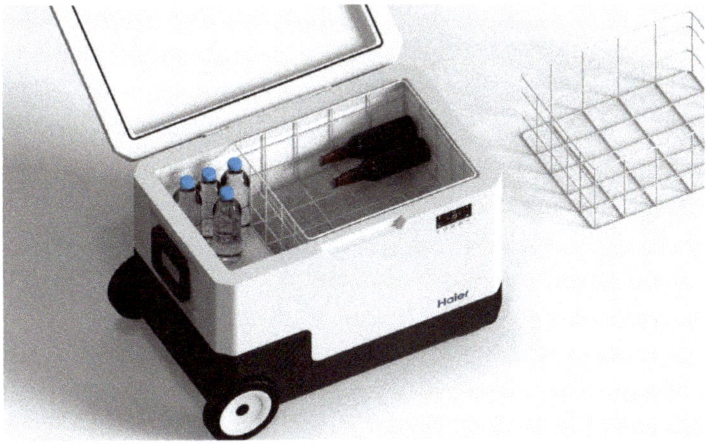

Figure 16. Multifunctional vehicle refrigerator internal details diagram.

During the model construction phase, an SVR with a radial basis function (RBF) kernel was instantiated via the fitrsvm function. A Bayesian optimization algorithm (with the optimizer parameter set to bayesopt) was employed to optimize three key hyperparameters—BoxConstraint (search space $[1 \times 10^{-3}, 1 \times 10^{3}]$), KernelScale ($[1 \times 10^{-3}, 1 \times 10^{3}]$), and Epsilon (dynamic range $[0.01 \times \mathrm{IQR}(Y), 0.2 \times \mathrm{IQR}(Y)]$)—over 50 iterations (MaxObjectiveEvaluations = 50). Throughout this process, 5-fold cross-validation was used to calculate the mean squared error (MSE) as the optimization objective function. Convergence was reached at the 35th iteration when the change in the objective function ΔMSE was less than 1e-4 for 10 consecutive iterations (Figure 18). Ultimately, the optimal hyperparameter combination was obtained: BoxConstraint = 48.72 (controlling the regularization strength), KernelScale = 2.31 (determining the RBF kernel width), and Epsilon = 0.034 (setting the boundary of the insensitive region). Under this configuration, the model's Hessian matrix condition number was $\kappa = 7.2 \times 10^3$, indicating a numerically stable parameter space. In the model validation phase, the independent test set yielded an RMSE of 0.0719 and a coefficient of determination R^2 of 0.8480. A scatter plot of predicted versus actual values further confirmed the model's accuracy (Figure 19), with data points densely distributed along the diagonal ($y = x$), demonstrating excellent predictive capability. Residual analysis revealed the error distribution characteristics of the SVR model in predicting consumer appeal (Figure 20). The observed data showed that the residuals were symmetrically distributed in the range $[-0.1, 0.2]$, with over 90% of the absolute residuals being less than 0.08, consistent with the model's RMSE of 0.0719. To further decompose the feature contributions, a permutation feature importance analysis was conducted. By randomly shuffling each feature column in the test set (with n_perm = 100 Monte Carlo simulations) and calculating the resulting RMSE increment, the results indicated that perturbing design harmony led to a greater ΔRMSE than perturbing functional rationality, and the ΔRMSE for functional rationality was greater than that for design complexity (Figure 21). This ranking aligned with theoretical expectations in design psychology, where form integration is prioritized over functional visibility. The limitations analysis revealed that the current model did not account for the temporal drift in consumer preferences. Future work will extend to include time series cross-validation (TimeSeriesSplit) and multi-objective optimization based on the gamultiobj function to enhance the model's temporal adaptability. This case study provides a standardized technical paradigm for data-driven product design optimization, with potential for generalization to other design attribute prediction tasks. Moreover, it achieves a degree of quantitative analysis and prediction related to the sustainable consumption market, offering practical value for the development of sustainable products under engineering constraints.

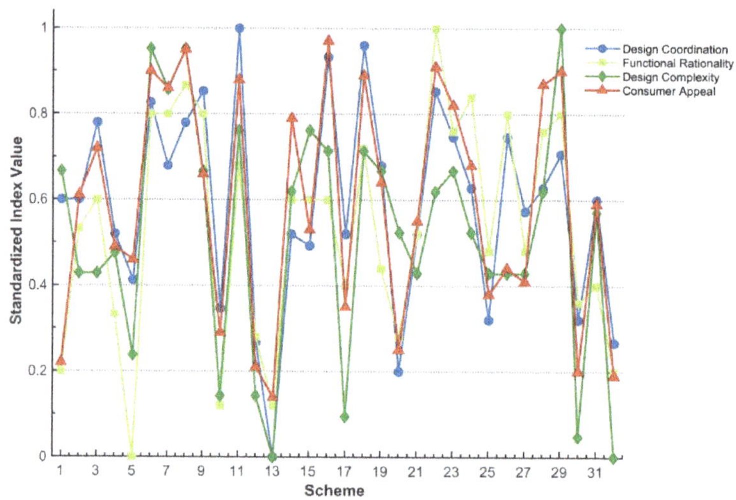

Figure 17. Visualization of the scores of the 32 design proposals.

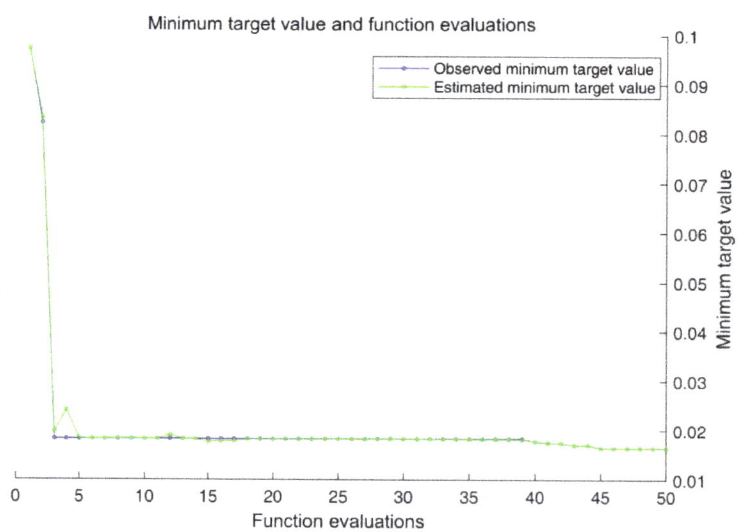

Figure 18. Process of finding the optimal solution of the objective function.

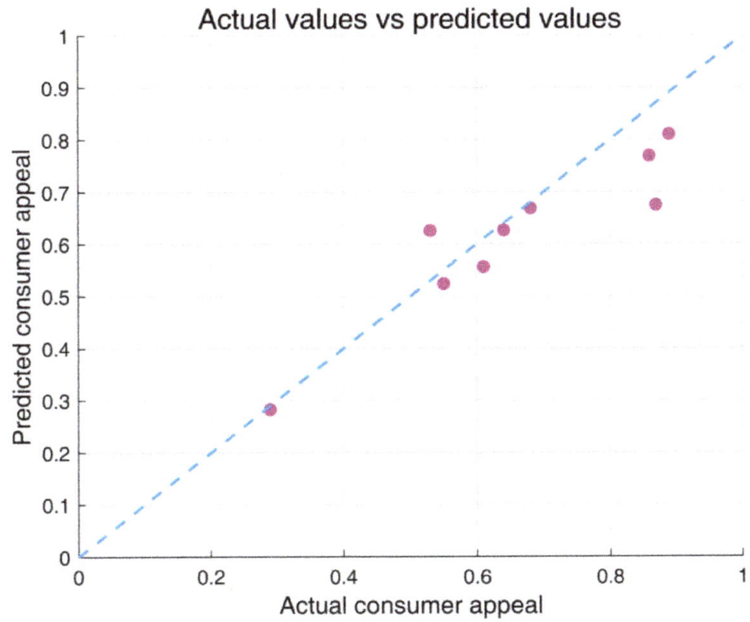

Figure 19. Predicted situation analysis scatter plot; the dashed blue line represents the ideal agreement line (y = x).

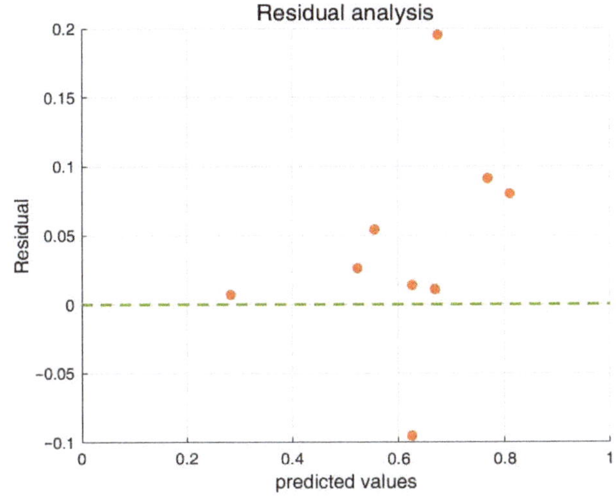

Figure 20. Residual analysis chart; the dashed green line denotes the zero-residual baseline (y = 0).

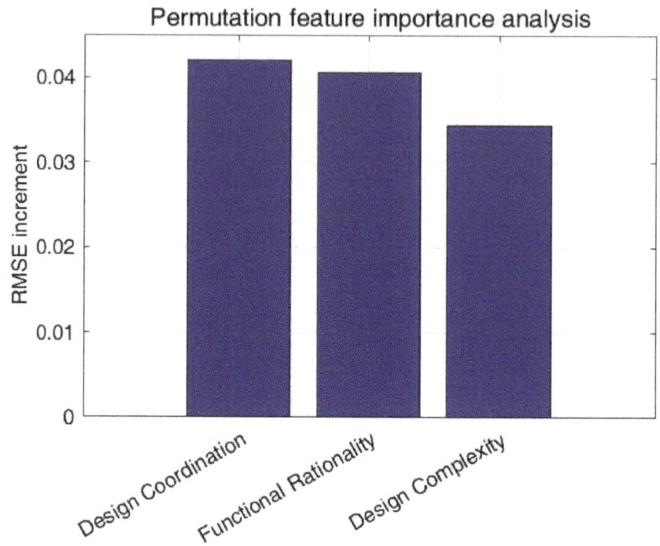

Figure 21. Deconstructing feature contributions.

4.4. Comparative Experiments and Discussions

In addition, to further analyze and validate the predictive performance, this study constructed a comparative predictive model based on a Bayesian regularization backpropagation (BP) neural network. The aim was to explore the nonlinear mapping between multidimensional design factors and consumer appeal. Using the same original dataset as the support vector regression model, data augmentation was performed via Gaussian noise injection (with standard deviation $\sigma = 0.03$) to enhance the model's generalization capability, generating 50% synthetic samples (thereby expanding the total sample size to 48 groups). Both the input and output variables were normalized to the [0,1] interval using the mapminmax function, and the transformation parameters (xPS and yPS) were saved to ensure consistency for subsequent inference. A five-fold cross-validation (CV) framework (with random seed rng = 2023) was adopted, with each fold partitioning the data into 70% training, 15% validation, and 15% testing sets. During the neural network configuration, a feedforward neural network with 8 hidden nodes was constructed using feedforwardnet (8, 'trainbr'), where 'trainbr' denotes the use of the Bayesian regularization training algorithm. This algorithm adjusted the regularization parameters to control overfitting and automatically adapts the network's complexity during training (Figure 22). In the training process, the maximum number of iterations was set to 1000 and the performance goal (net.trainParam.goal) to 1×10^{-5} to ensure a gradual reduction in error. Furthermore, an early stopping mechanism was implemented using a custom stopIfOverfitting function that monitored the validation error. Early stopping was triggered if the validation error increased for 5 consecutive iterations or if the regularization parameter (net.trainParam.mu) exceeded a preset threshold, thereby preventing overfitting.

The final model was selected as the one with the lowest MSE during CV (denoted as bestNet), achieving a coefficient of determination $R^2 = 0.786$ (RMSE = 0.112) on the original test set (unenhanced data), which indicated that the model explained 78.6% of the variance in consumer appeal. The residual analysis showed that the prediction errors followed an approximately normal distribution (with over 90% of the samples falling within ± 0.2) and did not exhibit any heteroscedasticity trends (Figure 23). Figure 24 reveals that the training error rapidly decreased during the initial stages and then plateaued.

Notably, the best training performance occurred at the 45th epoch with an MSE of 0.01157, reflecting the optimal state achieved during training. However, further training did not yield significant improvements, suggesting that the model's learning capacity might have reached a bottleneck or that additional tuning and regularization might be required to further mitigate overfitting. Figure 25 demonstrates that the error distributions for the training and test sets were relatively similar, although errors in the test set occurred less frequently and were more uniformly distributed. The training set's errors were more concentrated, particularly near-zero error (as indicated by the orange dashed line), which suggested a good fit on the training data. Despite many instances of near-zero error in the training data, the test data exhibited comparatively fewer zero-error cases, indicating that while the model fit the training data well, some errors persisted on the test set. Figure 26 shows that throughout the training process, the network's gradient gradually converged, indicating that training became progressively stable and the parameter updates stabilized. The marked fluctuations in the regularization parameter (mu) suggested that Bayesian regularization played a crucial role in controlling overfitting, especially during the later stages of training. Other factors, such as the number of model parameters, chi-square values, the sum of squared parameters, and input normalization parameters, remained stable, demonstrating that no abnormal fluctuations occurred in the model structure or training process and that overall training stability was satisfactory. The number of validation checks further indicated that neither overfitting nor excessive bias in the validation set occurred, underscoring the reliability of the training process. Figure 27 illustrates that the BP neural network's fitting performance varied across different datasets. The training set achieved excellent performance with an R^2 of 0.93075, indicating that the model could explain approximately 93% of the variance in the training data, and the fitted curve had a slope of 0.86 and an intercept of 0.074, indicating a strong linear relationship between the output and target values. By contrast, the test set's performance was relatively poor, with R^2 decreasing to 0.86802, a noticeable reduction in the slope to 0.5, and an increased intercept of 0.39, signifying a decline in fitting accuracy. The overall dataset exhibited intermediate performance (R^2 = 0.9116), with a fitted slope of 0.82 and an intercept of 0.11, reflecting a compromise between the strong training performance and the shortcomings on the test set.

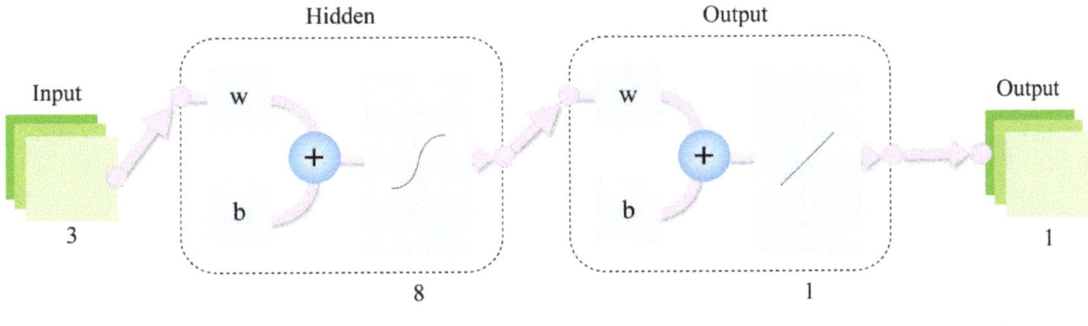

Figure 22. Neural network architecture.

In summary, although the model performed exceptionally on the training data, its generalization ability on the test data remained insufficient. To improve generalization, future work could explore additional regularization methods, increase the diversity of training data, or optimize the model's structure and parameters to enhance prediction accuracy and stability on new data.

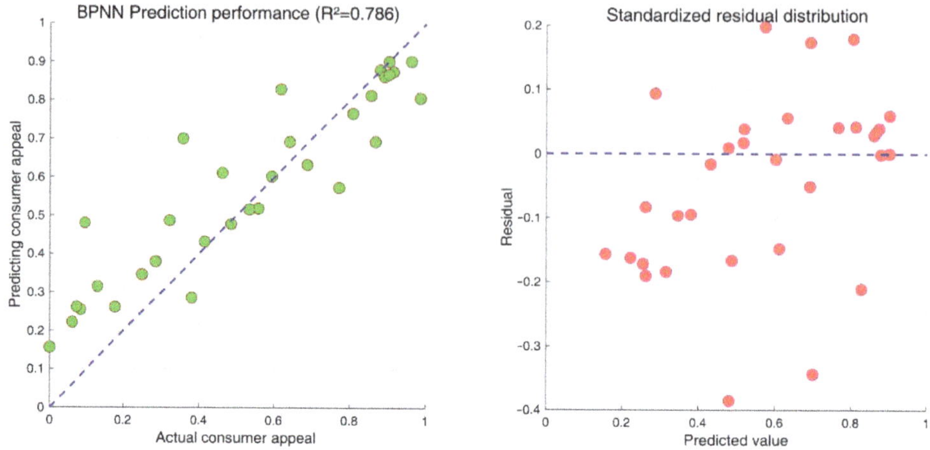

Figure 23. Prediction result analysis chart. BPNN prediction performance: the dashed blue line denotes the ideal agreement (y = x). Standardized residual distribution: the dashed blue line marks the zero-residual baseline (y = 0). Points represent individual design cases.

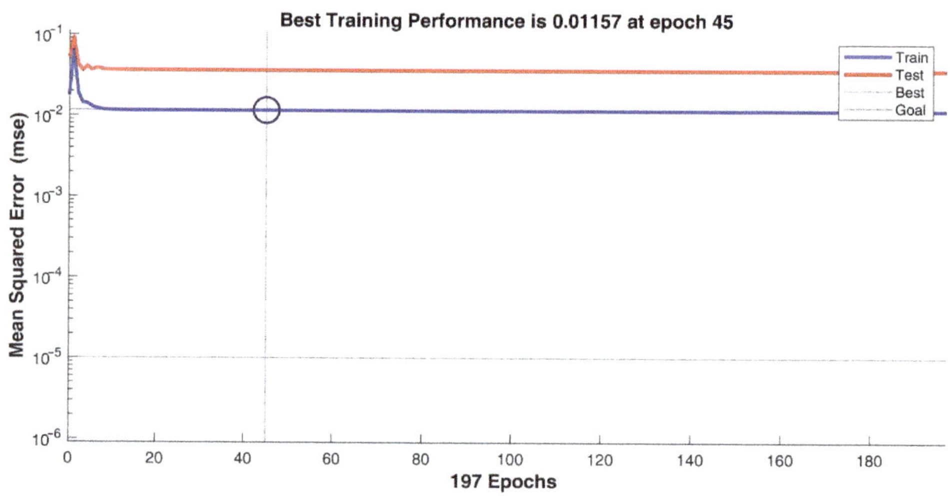

Figure 24. MSE curve during the training process.

This study compared the performance differences between support vector regression (SVR) and Bayesian regularization backpropagation (BP) neural networks in predicting consumer appeal based on industrial design features, revealing the interplay between the models' intrinsic mechanisms and the characteristics of the data. The superiority of SVR (test set RMSE = 0.0719, R^2 = 0.848) stemmed from its structural risk minimization (SRM) framework. By combining the ε-insensitive loss function with a radial basis function kernel, SVR balanced model complexity and empirical error in nonlinear mapping. Its hyperparameter optimization via Bayesian methods suppressed overfitting by maximizing the margin and retaining only a small subset of training samples as support vectors, demonstrating the adaptability of sparse solutions to high-dimensional, small-sample (n = 32) scenarios. By contrast, the BP neural network (test set RMSE = 0.112, R^2 = 0.786), despite employing Bayesian regularization (trainbr) and an early stopping strategy, sufferred from parameter redundancy in its 8-node hidden layer, which resulted in an empirical risk minimization

(ERM) tendency. This issue was further exacerbated after data augmentation (with synthetic samples comprising 50%), introducing a potential covariate shift that intensified overfitting on the training set (training $R^2 = 0.931$) and diminished generalization on the test set. This phenomenon was consistent with VC-dimension theory: shallow models (like SVR) are preferable under limited data due to controllable complexity, whereas deep networks (like BP) require larger datasets to avoid the "double descent" effect.

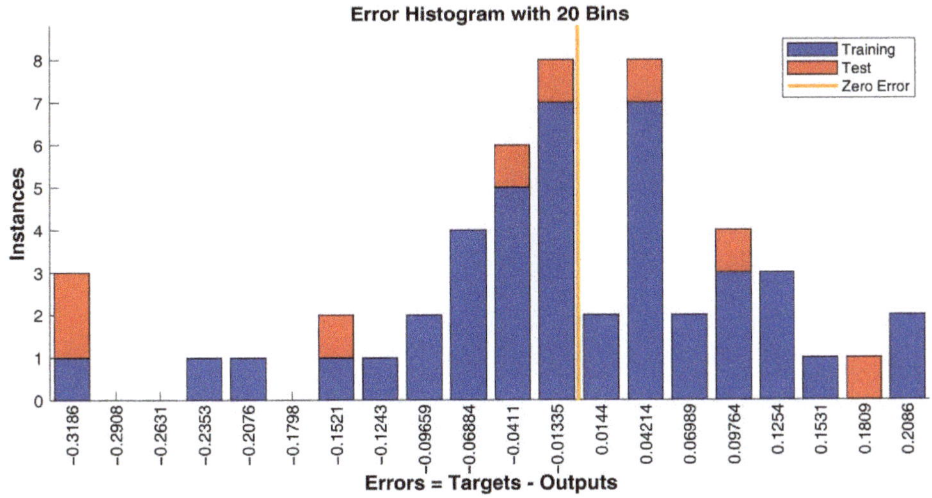

Figure 25. Error distribution chart.

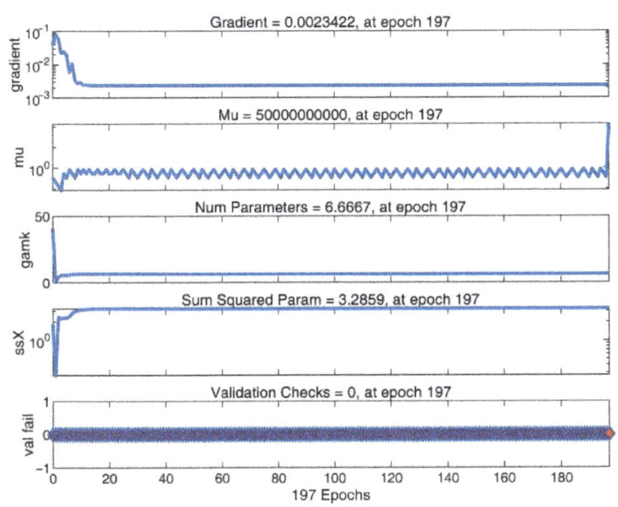

Figure 26. Training process parameter variation trends.

Furthermore, SVR's regularization directly controlled the slack of the margin through the BoxConstraint parameter, and when combined with a dynamically adjusted ε-insensitive region (based on the target variable's IQR), it formed a dual regularization constraint. The condition number of its Hessian matrix ($\kappa = 7.2 \times 10^3$) indicated strong stability in the parameter space. By contrast, although the BP neural network's Bayesian regularization adjusted the hyperparameter μ to balance weight decay and data fitting, its non-convex loss function caused the optimization path to become trapped in local minima—as evidenced by early stopping at the 45th epoch (MSE = 0.01157) and significant fluctuations in the validation error. Moreover, the permutation feature importance analysis of SVR showed that the ΔRMSE for design harmony exceeded that for functional rationality, which in turn exceeded that for complexity (i.e., design harmony ΔRMSE > functional rationality ΔRMSE > complexity ΔRMSE). This result was consistent with design psychology theory and underscored the interpretability of the SVR model. By contrast, the nonlinear transformations in the BP network's hidden layers obscured the contribution of individual features, limiting causal inference regarding design elements.

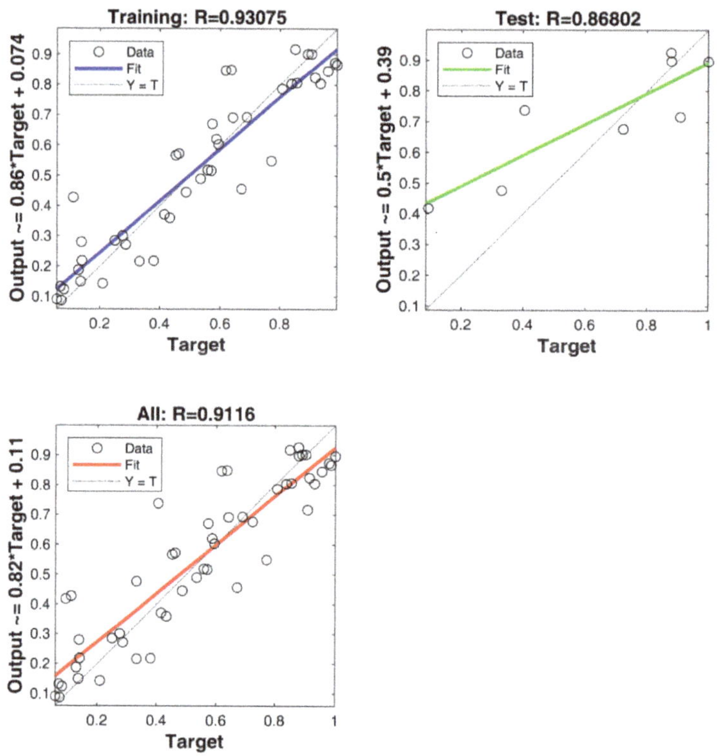

Figure 27. Neural network fitting performance diagram.

Although the BP neural network used Gaussian noise injection (σ = 0.03) to expand the sample size to 48 groups, the distribution shift of the synthetic data may have weakened the learning of true feature–response relationships. By contrast, SVR, relying on critical boundary samples (support vectors), was more robust to noise, as its residual distribution (with 90% of samples within ±0.08) was much more concentrated than BP's (±0.2), thereby verifying the suppressive effect of the ε-insensitive constraint on outliers. Additionally, SVR's R^2 of 0.848 indicated that it can explain 84.8% of the target variance—significantly higher than BP's 78.6%—reflecting the superior nonlinear expressive power of the kernel function in high-dimensional spaces.

SVR demonstrated superior prediction accuracy and stability in analyzing small-sample, high-dimensional design data; its SRM framework and sparse solution properties were key advantages. Conversely, the BP neural network was limited by parameter redundancy and non-convex optimization challenges, necessitating further data augmentation or network compression to enhance generalization. The fundamental performance differences between the two models arose from the compatibility of their inductive biases with the data characteristics. Future research should select the appropriate paradigm based on task requirements or explore collaborative strategies—for example, integrating SVR's kernel techniques with neural networks' hierarchical feature extraction to construct Kernelized Neural Networks—which may achieve both interpretability and nonlinear modeling capability in small-sample scenarios.

5. Limitations and Future Research Directions

Although the sampling strategy aimed to achieve demographic and behavioral diversity through stratified purposive selection, partial reliance on convenience sampling introduced certain limitations in sample representativeness. Notably, the sample was skewed toward individuals with medium to high levels of product awareness, technological familiarity, and education, which may result in the underrepresentation of marginalized or less-engaged consumer groups.

Nonetheless, the dataset encompassed a broad spectrum of the target market, including variations in income level, age, region, and usage scenarios. This ensured the inclusion of key consumer archetypes typically observed in the Chinese refrigerator market. While the possibility of selection bias cannot be fully eliminated, the internal validation metrics of the predictive models, along with the consistency of thematic patterns across subgroups, support the robustness and indicative generalizability of the findings.

Future work will incorporate a probabilistic sampling framework to further improve representativeness and external validity, particularly for applications requiring population-level inference.

While the SVR model demonstrated robust performance in predicting consumer appeal for refrigerator designs, its application to products with different characteristics requires several domain-specific adaptations. First, the input feature set must be redefined to reflect the relevant design attributes of the target product category. Second, the consumer appeal index must be reinterpreted and normalized based on market-specific expectations. Lastly, retraining with representative and sufficiently diverse data is essential due to the limited extrapolation ability of SVR's kernel function across dissimilar domains.

In terms of scalability, standard SVR implementations exhibit computational complexity of $O(n^2)$, rendering them less suitable for large-scale datasets. Additionally, the generalization capability of SVR diminishes when the input distribution shifts significantly from the original training data, particularly in cases involving complex consumer behavior or structurally divergent product categories.

To overcome these challenges, future directions may include the use of hybrid frameworks (e.g., SVR + deep feature extractors), kernel transfer learning, or sparsified SVR variants. These approaches can enhance scalability and adaptability while retaining the interpretability and structural risk minimization advantages of SVR.

To further enhance the model's applicability in dynamic market environments, future work will focus on integrating temporal and behavioral dimensions into the prediction framework. Specifically, time series variables such as quarterly market trend shifts, seasonal feature preferences, and longitudinal sentiment evolution will be incorporated as structured predictors. These may be encoded through lagged variables, moving averages, or exogenous regressors within a time-aware SVR or sequence-learning model. In parallel, the model will be adapted to account for diverse consumer engagement levels. Recognizing that first-time buyers, repeat purchasers, and segment-specific users (e.g., students vs. professionals) exhibit differentiated design expectations, future modeling iterations will include consumer segmentation metadata. Mixed-effects regression, stratified SVR models, and hierarchical neural architectures will be explored to reflect group-dependent decision mechanisms and contextualize preference modeling.

6. Conclusions

This study addresses the issues of insufficient user need identification and inadequate exploration of the intrinsic mechanisms of sustainable design in current refrigerator product design. It proposes and validates an interdisciplinary intelligent design framework that integrates qualitative research with deep neural network technology. Through semi-structured interviews and multi-source data fusion analysis, the study found that consumers place high importance on overall capacity, exterior design, and energy efficiency ratings when selecting refrigerators and that different types of refrigerator users exhibit significant differences in specific considerations such as price sensitivity and functional requirements. Based on an intelligent generative system employing a latent diffusion model and a control network architecture, the framework achieves semantic-controllable synthesis of high-fidelity design schemes, and the synergistic optimization effects of functional rationality and design harmony are validated using an entropy-weight COPRAS multi-criteria decision-making model.

In constructing the predictive model, support vector regression (SVR) significantly outperformed the Bayesian regularization neural network (test set $R^2 = 0.848$ vs. 0.786) due to its structural risk minimization framework and kernel space mapping mechanism. Its permutation feature importance analysis revealed that design harmony (ΔRMSE = 0.15) holds cognitive priority in influencing consumer appeal. Modular prototype development further verified the transformation pathway of intelligent feature engineering practice. The mini desktop and vehicle refrigerator designs achieved improvements in energy efficiency and material intensification through innovative functions such as dual-mode cooling and magnetic sealing. The established closed-loop system comprising "demand insight—intelligent generation—decision optimization—market forecasting" provides full-cycle methodological support for sustainable product development. The interdisciplinary integration paradigm and quantitative decision-making tools proposed in this study not only extend the theoretical boundaries of industrial design optimization but also offer a reproducible technical pathway for the manufacturing industry's low-carbon transition and sustainable development. Future research could further enhance the system's spatiotemporal adaptability and ecological benefits by integrating time series analysis of preference drift and full lifecycle environmental impact assessment.

Author Contributions: Conceptualization, Y.C. and H.L.; methodology, Y.C.; software, J.Z.; validation, H.L. and J.Z.; formal analysis, Y.C. and H.L.; investigation, J.Z.; resources, J.W.; data curation, Y.C.; writing—original draft preparation, Y.C. and H.L.; writing—review and editing, Y.C. and J.W.; visualization, Y.C.; supervision, J.W.; project administration, J.W. All authors have read and agreed to the published version of the manuscript.

Funding: This research received no external funding.

Data Availability Statement: The data presented in this study are available upon request from the corresponding author. The data are not publicly available due to confidentiality and ethical restrictions.

Conflicts of Interest: Author Yu Chen was employed by Haier Group Corporation. The remaining authors declare that the research was conducted in the absence of any commercial or financial relationships that could be construed as a potential conflict of interest.

References

1. Anwar, R.S.; Ahmed, R.R.; Streimikiene, D.; Strielkowski, W.; Streimikis, J. Customer Engagement, Innovation, and Sustainable Consumption: Analyzing Personalized, Innovative, Sustainable Phygital Products. *J. Innov. Knowl.* **2025**, *10*, 100642. [CrossRef]
2. Ceschin, F.; Gaziulusoy, I. Evolution of Design for Sustainability: From Product Design to Design for System Innovations and Transitions. *Des. Stud.* **2016**, *47*, 118–163. [CrossRef]
3. Xiao, R.; Zhang, Y.; Liu, X.; Yuan, Z. A Life-Cycle Assessment of Household Refrigerators in China. *J. Clean. Prod.* **2015**, *95*, 301–310. [CrossRef]
4. Kwilinski, A. Mapping Global Research on Green Energy and Green Investment: A Comprehensive Bibliometric Study. *Energies* **2024**, *17*, 1119. [CrossRef]
5. Wang, S.; Sun, W.; Liu, J.; Nah, K.; Yan, W.; Tan, S. The Influence of AR on Purchase Intentions of Cultural Heritage Products: The TAM and Flow-Based Study. *Appl. Sci.* **2024**, *14*, 7169. [CrossRef]
6. Đurić, I.; Medić, S.; Ecet, D.; Grgić, S.; Atanacković Jeličić, J. Enhancing Public Space Experiences: Evaluating Perception of Digital and Digitized Sculptures in Augmented Reality. *Appl. Sci.* **2025**, *15*, 870. [CrossRef]
7. Basu, S. Personalized Product Recommendations and Firm Performance. *Electron. Commer. Res. Appl.* **2021**, *48*, 101074. [CrossRef]
8. Sreen, N.; Mehrotra, A.; Alghafes, R.; Agarwal, V. Interplay between Minimalism, Moral Identity, and Ethically Minded Consumer Behavior in Retail Context: Cross-Cultural Investigation of Indian and American Consumers. *J. Retail. Consum. Serv.* **2025**, *84*, 104191. [CrossRef]
9. Zheng, S.; Chen, J.; Liao, J.; Hu, H.-L. What Motivates Users' Viewing and Purchasing Behavior Motivations in Live Streaming: A Stream-Streamer-Viewer Perspective. *J. Retail. Consum. Serv.* **2023**, *72*, 103240. [CrossRef]
10. Wang, Z.; Chen, C.-H.; Li, X.; Zheng, P.; Khoo, L.P. A Context-Aware Concept Evaluation Approach Based on User Experiences for Smart Product-Service Systems Design Iteration. *Adv. Eng. Inform.* **2021**, *50*, 101394. [CrossRef]
11. Shen, B.; Tan, W.; Guo, J.; Zhao, L.; Qin, P. How to Promote User Purchase in Metaverse? A Systematic Literature Review on Consumer Behavior Research and Virtual Commerce Application Design. *Appl. Sci.* **2021**, *11*, 11087. [CrossRef]
12. Qin, Z.; Song, Y.; Tian, Y. The Impact of Product Design with Traditional Cultural Properties (TCPs) on Consumer Behavior Through Cultural Perceptions: Evidence from the Young Chinese Generation. *Sustainability* **2019**, *11*, 426. [CrossRef]
13. Velaoras, K.; Menegaki, A.N.; Polyzos, S.; Gotzamani, K. The Role of Environmental Certification in the Hospitality Industry: Assessing Sustainability, Consumer Preferences, and the Economic Impact. *Sustainability* **2025**, *17*, 650. [CrossRef]
14. Szaban, M.; Szymkowiak, A.; Zdziennicka, A. Unpacking Consumer Price Perceptions: The Role of Sustainability and Ethical Labels in the Cosmetics Market. *J. Clean. Prod.* **2025**, *490*, 144730. [CrossRef]
15. Navidan, H.; Moshiri, P.F.; Nabati, M.; Shahbazian, R.; Ghorashi, S.A.; Shah-Mansouri, V.; Windridge, D. Generative Adversarial Networks (GANs) in Networking: A Comprehensive Survey & Evaluation. *Comput. Netw.* **2021**, *194*, 108149. [CrossRef]
16. Zhang, Z.; Li, Y.; Zhou, W.; Chen, X.; Yao, W.; Zhao, Y. TONR: An Exploration for a Novel Way Combining Neural Network with Topology Optimization. *Comput. Methods Appl. Mech. Eng.* **2021**, *386*, 114083. [CrossRef]
17. Wang, L.; Liu, Z. Data-Driven Product Design Evaluation Method Based on Multi-Stage Artificial Neural Network. *Appl. Soft Comput.* **2021**, *103*, 107117. [CrossRef]
18. Zhu, Q.; Li, J.; Lin, X.; Lu, F.; Jang, J. A BP Neural Network Product Design Optimization Model Based on Emotional Design and Sustainable Product Design. *Appl. Sci.* **2024**, *14*, 6225. [CrossRef]
19. Qian, C.; Ye, W. Accelerating Gradient-Based Topology Optimization Design with Dual-Model Artificial Neural Networks. *Struct. Multidiscip. Optim.* **2021**, *63*, 1687–1707. [CrossRef]
20. Burnap, A.; Hauser, J.R.; Timoshenko, A. Product Aesthetic Design: A Machine Learning Augmentation. *Mark. Sci.* **2023**, *42*, 1029–1056. [CrossRef]
21. Yoo, S.; Lee, S.; Kim, S.; Hwang, K.H.; Park, J.H.; Kang, N. Integrating Deep Learning into CAD/CAE System: Generative Design and Evaluation of 3D Conceptual Wheel. *Struct. Multidiscip. Optim.* **2021**, *64*, 2725–2747. [CrossRef]
22. Ding, M.; Cheng, Y.; Zhang, J.; Du, G. Product Color Emotional Design Based on a Convolutional Neural Network and Search Neural Network. *Color. Res. Appl.* **2021**, *46*, 1332–1346. [CrossRef]
23. Badawy, M.; Ramadan, N.; Hefny, H.A. Healthcare Predictive Analytics Using Machine Learning and Deep Learning Techniques: A Survey. *J. Electr. Syst. Inf. Technol.* **2023**, *10*, 40. [CrossRef]
24. Falatouri, T.; Darbanian, F.; Brandtner, P.; Udokwu, C. Predictive Analytics for Demand Forecasting–A Comparison of SARIMA and LSTM in Retail SCM. *Procedia Comput. Sci.* **2022**, *200*, 993–1003. [CrossRef]
25. Aljohani, A. Predictive Analytics and Machine Learning for Real-Time Supply Chain Risk Mitigation and Agility. *Sustainability* **2023**, *15*, 15088. [CrossRef]
26. Chen, Y.-T.; Sun, E.W.; Chang, M.-F.; Lin, Y.-B. Pragmatic Real-Time Logistics Management with Traffic IoT Infrastructure: Big Data Predictive Analytics of Freight Travel Time for Logistics 4.0. *Int. J. Prod. Econ.* **2021**, *238*, 108157. [CrossRef]
27. Dawood, T.; Elwakil, E.; Novoa, H.M.; Gárate Delgado, J.F. Toward Urban Sustainability and Clean Potable Water: Prediction of Water Quality via Artificial Neural Networks. *J. Clean. Prod.* **2021**, *291*, 125266. [CrossRef]

28. Zhang, L.; Huang, Z.; Liu, W.; Guo, Z.; Zhang, Z. Weather Radar Echo Prediction Method Based on Convolution Neural Network and Long Short-Term Memory Networks for Sustainable e-Agriculture. *J. Clean. Prod.* **2021**, *298*, 126776. [CrossRef]
29. Rombach, R.; Blattmann, A.; Lorenz, D.; Esser, P.; Ommer, B. High-Resolution Image Synthesis with Latent Diffusion Models. In Proceedings of the IEEE/CVF Conference on Computer Vision and Pattern Recognition (CVPR) CoRR, Nashville, TN, USA, 20–25 June 2021.
30. Yang, W.; Zhao, Y. Artistic Intelligence: A Diffusion-Based Framework for High-Fidelity Landscape Painting Synthesis. *IEEE Access* **2024**, *13*, 26037–26049. [CrossRef]
31. Adeoye-Olatunde, O.A.; Olenik, N.L. Research and Scholarly Methods: Semi-Structured Interviews. *JACCP J. Am. Coll. Clin. Pharm.* **2021**, *4*, 1358–1367. [CrossRef]
32. Mukurunge, E.; Nyoni, C.N.; Hugo, L. Context of Assessment in Competency-Based Nursing Education: Semi-Structured Interviews in Nursing Education Institutions in a Low-Income Country. *Nurse Educ. Today* **2025**, *146*, 106529. [CrossRef] [PubMed]
33. Yang, Y.N.; Kumaraswamy Mohan, M.; Pam, H.J.; Mahesh, G. Integrated Qualitative and Quantitative Methodology to Assess Validity and Credibility of Models for Bridge Maintenance Management System Development. *J. Manag. Eng.* **2011**, *27*, 149–158. [CrossRef]
34. Galvin, R. How Many Interviews Are Enough? Do Qualitative Interviews in Building Energy Consumption Research Produce Reliable Knowledge? *J. Build. Eng.* **2015**, *1*, 2–12. [CrossRef]
35. Stanca, L.; Dabija, D.-C.; Câmpian, V. Qualitative Analysis of Customer Behavior in the Retail Industry during the COVID-19 Pandemic: A Word-Cloud and Sentiment Analysis Approach. *J. Retail. Consum. Serv.* **2023**, *75*, 103543. [CrossRef]
36. Taye, M.M. Understanding of Machine Learning with Deep Learning: Architectures, Workflow, Applications and Future Directions. *Computers* **2023**, *12*, 91. [CrossRef]
37. Zhang, L.; Rao, A.; Agrawala, M. Adding Conditional Control to Text-to-Image Diffusion Models. *arXiv* **2023**, arXiv:2302.05543. [CrossRef]
38. Chen, P. Effects of the Entropy Weight on TOPSIS. *Expert. Syst. Appl.* **2021**, *168*, 114186. [CrossRef]
39. Balali, A.; Valipour, A.; Edwards, R.; Moehler, R. Ranking Effective Risks on Human Resources Threats in Natural Gas Supply Projects Using ANP-COPRAS Method: Case Study of Shiraz. *Reliab. Eng. Syst. Saf.* **2021**, *208*, 107442. [CrossRef]
40. Surucu, O.; Gadsden, S.A.; Yawney, J. Condition Monitoring Using Machine Learning: A Review of Theory, Applications, and Recent Advances. *Expert. Syst. Appl.* **2023**, *221*, 119738. [CrossRef]
41. Cox, J.; Griffith, S.; Giorgi, S.; King, G. Consumer Understanding of Product Lifetimes. *Resour. Conserv. Recycl.* **2013**, *79*, 21–29. [CrossRef]
42. Victor, V.; Joy Thoppan, J.; Jeyakumar Nathan, R.; Farkas Maria, F. Factors Influencing Consumer Behavior and Prospective Purchase Decisions in a Dynamic Pricing Environment—An Exploratory Factor Analysis Approach. *Soc. Sci.* **2018**, *7*, 153. [CrossRef]
43. Bogusz, M.; Matysik-Pejas, R.; Krasnodębski, A.; Dziekański, P. The Concept of Zero Waste in the Context of Supporting Environmental Protection by Consumers. *Energies* **2021**, *14*, 5964. [CrossRef]
44. Huang, Y.-C.; Tung, Y.-S.; Chen, J.-C.; Wang, S.-W.; Wu, J.-L. An Adaptive Edge Detection Based Colorization Algorithm and Its Applications. In Proceedings of the 13th Annual ACM International Conference on Multimedia, Singapore, 6–11 November 2005; Association for Computing Machinery: New York, NY, USA, 2005; pp. 351–354.

symmetry

MDPI

Article

Research on Symmetry Optimization of Designer Requirements and Prototyping Platform Functionality in the Context of Agile Development

Zheng Wen [1,2], Jianming Yang [1], Bowen Sun [1,3,*] and Yuanwei Liu [4]

1 School of Design and Arts, Beijing Institute of Technology, Beijing 100086, China; 3120225968@bit.edu.cn (Z.W.); yangjianming66@sina.com (J.Y.)
2 Goldsmiths, University of London, London SE14 6NW, UK
3 School of Fine Arts and Design, Lanzhou University of Arts and Science, Lanzhou 730010, China
4 The College of Architecture and Art, North China University of Technology, Beijing 100144, China; xyw@ncut.edu.cn
* Correspondence: sunbowen@bit.edu.cn

Abstract: Aligning designer requirements with prototyping platform functionalities remains a challenge in agile development (AD) environments, as existing tools often fail to accommodate evolving needs. This study proposes a systematic approach to optimizing prototyping platforms by bridging the gap between user needs and functional design. First, a designer requirement architecture was constructed using grounded theory, identifying three core elements: interaction needs, collaboration needs, and visualization and testing needs. The F-KANO model was used to categorize requirements, while DEMATEL was used to prioritize them based on interdependencies. Finally, quality function deployment (QFD) was used to map designer needs to functional specifications, deriving an optimization strategy. Empirical evaluation through user testing indicated notable improvements in workflow efficiency, usability, and collaboration effectiveness. This research offers a systematic framework for refining prototyping platforms in AD, improving design efficiency and UX.

Keywords: interface prototyping; user requirements; agile development; user experience; design optimization

1. Introduction

In the era of digital transformation, agile development (AD) has been widely adopted in design and development processes. The core principles of AD encompass iterative development, user-driven design, and cross-functional collaboration [1], focusing on the frequent release of functional software in short development cycles to swiftly adapt to evolving market demands [2]. Compared with traditional waterfall development, AD prioritizes cross-functional collaboration and swift user feedback integration, requiring rapid requirement validation and iterative functionality updates within tight timeframes [3]. However, while AD enhances software iteration efficiency, it also introduces multifaceted challenges for designers. In an AD environment, designers must swiftly and effectively access essential tools for interface design, prototyping, and user testing. They are required not only to adapt to frequent design changes but to complete interface design, optimize user experience (UX), and facilitate cross-team communication within constrained time limits to ensure that the final product aligns with user expectations [4]. Consequently, enhancing design efficiency has become a critical factor influencing the overall effectiveness and quality of product development within an AD framework.

With the increasing challenges posed by AD, an increasing number of scholars have conducted research from the perspectives of design tools, design strategies, and team structures to address these issues. Design tools (e.g., Figma, Sketch, Adobe XD) integrate key functionalities such as visual prototyping, assisting designers in improving design efficiency. Although these tools play a crucial role in design and prototyping, they still fail to fully meet designers' core needs in AD environments, such as efficient version iteration management, enhanced collaboration and requirement synchronization, and improved consistency in visual standard [5]. For instance, while some prototyping platforms offer real-time collaboration features, studies have shown that these tools often lack efficient mechanisms for managing design requirements dynamically, which can lead to workflow inefficiencies and inconsistencies in team-based design environments [6].

Some studies suggest that leveraging componentization and reusable assets can effectively enhance design efficiency. Some studies contend that creating a unified design language or component library not only minimizes redundant effort but enhances development teams' comprehension of design principles [7]. However, these studies mainly focus on visual consistency and technical implementation, without delving into how requirement management can be efficiently integrated at the design tool level. Other research has explored design process optimization, such as Magistretti's study, which recommended incorporating UX sprints or design sprints into team structures to rapidly focus on UX goals at the beginning of each iteration [8]. However, these studies predominantly emphasize internal workflow optimization within teams, without proposing actionable design strategies for prototyping platforms. Despite the growing number of studies on prototyping tools and agile workflows, existing research still lacks a structured methodology for translating designer needs into concrete platform functionalities. Research has highlighted shortcomings in design platforms' handling of version control, interaction complexity, and multiuser collaboration [9], but there is no unified framework that systematically prioritizes and implements optimizations to bridge these gaps.

While existing research has explored various aspects of prototyping tools in AD, it lacks a structured methodology to systematically align designer needs with platform functionalities. Current studies focus mainly on isolated tool optimizations [10] or workflow refinements [11] without prioritizing user needs in a data-driven manner. Moreover, existing approaches lack an integrated prioritization mechanism, often relying on ad hoc feature additions rather than a strategic alignment with designer workflows. This leads to inefficiencies in iteration, usability, and collaboration. By taking designers as the primary demand subjects within AD environments, this research refines their requirement hierarchies and priorities, ultimately exploring how structured optimization methods can improve platform usability, enhance collaboration, and support high-frequency iteration cycles. The proposed framework offers a systematic approach to bridging the gap between user needs and design functionalities, ensuring that prototyping platforms in AD environments effectively facilitate iterative design and cross-team collaboration.

The core objective of this study is to optimize prototyping platforms in AD environments, ensuring a more precise and efficient alignment between designer needs and platform functionalities, thereby improving design efficiency and UX. This research aims to explore the core demands of designers in AD environments, identify the major challenges they face when using design platforms, and apply scientific methods to classify, prioritize, and map designer needs, ultimately enhancing workflow efficiency, information management, and UX.

First, interviews were conducted with 12 designers, including UI designers, UX designers, and product managers, all of whom had at least three years of experience in agile development environments. Grounded theory was employed to construct a conceptual framework for designers' needs in AD environments. Subsequently, the fuzzy Kano (F-KANO) model was employed to categorize and filter user requirements, followed by the decision-making trial and evaluation laboratory (DEMATEL) method to prioritize the filtered user needs and determine key design requirements. Quality function deployment (QFD) analysis was then used to map designer needs to design specifications. Finally, based on the above requirement analysis, an optimized prototyping platform tailored for AD environments was developed, and designers were invited to test the optimized platform, with user feedback collected for evaluation.

Section 2 provides a comprehensive literature review, examining the latest research developments in AD, user interface (UI) design, and prototyping platforms, establishing the theoretical foundation for this study. Section 3 presents the methodology, detailing the research framework based on grounded theory, the F-KANO model, the DEMATEL method, and QFD analysis. Section 4 shows the systematic extraction of core designer needs in AD environments through interviews and survey data analysis. By classifying requirements, assigning weights and priority rankings, this chapter establishes a mechanism for aligning user needs with technical requirements. Section 5 exhibits an empirical analysis to validate the effectiveness of the optimized requirement framework, proposing a demand management optimization strategy for product design platforms in AD environments. Finally, Section 6 summarizes the findings and contributions of this study, discussing its practical implications for improving design efficiency in AD workflows and outlining future research directions.

2. Literature Review

2.1. Interface Design in the Context of AD

Currently, UI research in the context of AD focuses primarily on adaptability and usability, often centering on diverse user scenarios across different user groups to optimize UX and enhance interaction efficiency. Choi conducted usability testing on interface interaction patterns for mobile e-commerce applications and proposed a design strategy that simplifies information hierarchy to reduce the user's cognitive load [12]. Lei, in a study on online education platforms, integrated survey data and eye-tracking technology to examine the effects of text–image combinations and information architecture logic on learning efficiency [13]. Similarly, Cappiello's research focused on multidevice consistency, emphasizing that cross-platform interfaces should maintain visual and interaction coherence to ensure a seamless transition between devices [14]. These studies, employing experimental methods and field studies, assessed specific user groups (e.g., students, consumers, and mobile users) by measuring task completion time, error rates, or subjective satisfaction, thereby providing insights into interface design strategies for external users across various task scenarios. However, existing research concentrates primarily on product usability for external users, with limited attention given to the unique requirements of UI design for professional tools. As a result, while these findings offer valuable design perspectives for AD-driven design tasks, there remains a research gap in the interface design of professional tools used internally, particularly in prototyping platforms.

Several studies have highlighted that professional design tools (e.g., Axure, Sketch, and Figma) serve as critical hubs for prototype creation, interactive demonstration, and requirement communication within agile teams. However, existing research is largely confined to tool functionalities and team collaboration efficiency, with limited exploration of workflow usability and interaction design in these tools. Hussain, Slany, and Holzinger observed that while prototype tools are frequently utilized during agile sprints, research focuses predominantly on the comprehensiveness of tool functionalities and the accuracy of deliverables, rather than the usability and workflow of the tool interfaces [15]. Tohidi, from the perspective of rapid prototype validation, emphasized that implementing low- or mid-fidelity prototypes in early development stages enhances creative quality [16]. However, this study did not further investigate the specific interface requirements of design tools in this process. These findings indicate that current research on tool interfaces is primarily descriptive or fragmented, lacking a systematic investigation into the information architecture, interaction modalities, and visual layout of prototyping platforms in professional design workflows.

While agile design teams continuously iterate and refine external product interfaces, the prototyping platforms used internally often fail to undergo similar adaptations and optimizations to align with agile workflows [17]. A review of existing literature suggests that there may be a significant misalignment between designers' needs and platform interface functionalities. Currently, there is a lack of systematic research on how prototyping platforms address key professional requirements, such as high-frequency collaboration, rapid task switching, visual annotations, and multiversion management at the interface level. Hinderks and Winter emphasized the crucial integration of UX principles within agile methodologies for product development. However, their research focused primarily on optimizing the UX of end-user products [18], with limited exploration of the operational bottlenecks and information design deficiencies encountered by designers when using prototyping platforms. Building in this gap, the present study aims to systematically examine the structure and characteristics of designers' needs within AD contexts and propose a structured approach to analyzing and optimizing prototyping platform interfaces and functionalities. The objective is to mitigate the misalignment between prototyping platform design and the specialized requirements of designers, thereby enhancing efficiency and usability in agile workflows.

2.2. Interface Design from User Requirements

User-centered design methodologies have been widely adopted in interaction design and UX research. Whaiduzzaman systematically reviewed usability studies and HCI methodologies, highlighting that techniques such as interviews and usability testing effectively capture user needs and provide objective foundations for product interface iteration [19]. Through a literature analysis of multiple design studies, Palopak and Huang observed that many teams, when developing product prototypes, tend to collect requirements directly from target consumers or business stakeholders, while rarely considering professional tool users as part of the user base [20]. Additionally, Pichler, in his exploration of agile product management, emphasized the relationship between requirement prioritization and user stories, revealing that requirement management focuses primarily on market and customer value [21], with limited frameworks addressing the specific needs of internal professional users such as designers and engineers when using software tools.

Some studies have explored the unique requirements of technology and creative professionals. In a study on design team collaboration, He conducted preliminary interviews with designers and found that version control and team discussion features are essential in prototyping tools [22]. However, their study did not conduct an in-depth analysis of specific interface components or information presentation methods. Another study developed a rapid prototyping platform for outdoor game design, enabling designers to iterate and test game prototypes more efficiently [23]. Similarly, Kahlon and Fujii, from a design cognition perspective, investigated how designers employ metaphorical descriptions to facilitate understanding and task execution when interacting with design representations [24]. However, their findings remained at the conceptual level, without offering practical interface optimization strategies. Current research on designers as a user group focuses primarily on creative processes and cognitive models, while efficiency-related issues in operational interfaces remain largely overlooked. The perspectives on designer requirements are fragmented, lacking a systematic classification of different need types, such as interaction needs, collaboration needs, and prototyping needs. As a result, existing studies fall short in proposing targeted solutions from an architectural perspective that bridges designer needs with technical implementations.

Existing UI design research focuses predominantly on general users, with objectives centered on enhancing UX and service satisfaction for the broader audience. However, there is a lack of in-depth investigation into the multifaceted needs of professional users, particularly designers using design tools. While some studies have acknowledged the differences between designer needs and those of general users, they have focused primarily on team collaboration workflows or creative thinking methodologies rather than the specific operational challenges designers encounter in prototyping tools. In an AD environment, teams must rapidly construct and validate many prototypes within extremely short iteration cycles, yet research on whether prototyping platform interfaces can effectively support high-density creative output and rapid adjustments remains limited. A misalignment often exists between designer needs and platform functionalities, where tools offer a plethora of plugins and complex interactive components but lack intuitive, efficiently navigable interface mechanisms. Therefore, this study focuses on optimizing the design of prototyping platforms in AD environments to better accommodate designer requirements. By efficiently collecting, filtering, analyzing, prioritizing, and aligning designer needs, this research establishes a mapping mechanism between designer requirements and technical functionalities. The goal is to enhance platform interfaces to support high-frequency tasks in AD workflows while proposing scientifically grounded design optimization strategies.

3. Methodology

3.1. Research Framework

This study aims to address the misalignment between product design platforms and designers' needs in AD environments. To achieve this, the F-KANO model, DEMATEL method, and QFD analysis were employed to establish a mapping mechanism between user requirements and platform technical specifications, ultimately enhancing designers' UX and work efficiency. To fulfill this objective, a systematic research framework is proposed, encompassing the entire process from collecting designer requirements to platform optimization and evaluation. The framework is illustrated in Figure 1 and consists of the following key components:

- User Research: A qualitative interview analysis approach is employed to construct designer personas in AD environments, ensuring representative sampling. Additionally, the interview protocol is refined to enhance the specificity and accuracy of requirement collection.
- User Requirement Collection and Analysis: Grounded theory is applied to conduct in-depth interviews and analyses of designers' needs in AD contexts. Open coding, axial coding, and selective coding are utilized to extract key designer requirements, leading to the construction of a conceptual framework for these needs.
- Requirement Classification and Filtering: The F-KANO model is used to classify and filter requirements, retaining M (must-be), O (one-dimensional), and A (attractive) categories, while eliminating I (indifferent) requirements, ensuring that optimization efforts focus on the most valuable designer needs.

- Requirement Prioritization: The DEMATEL method is applied to prioritize the retained designer requirements, establishing a hierarchy of needs to ensure that technical implementations effectively support designers' core requirements.
- Identification and Prioritization of Design Requirements: Based on the ranked user needs, corresponding design requirements are identified. QFD analysis is then employed to map designer needs to specific design requirements, ensuring alignment between technological development and user expectations.
- Design Implementation and Feedback Analysis: Interface optimizations for the product design platform are executed according to prioritized technical requirements. User testing is conducted to evaluate and refine the optimized design. Ultimately, an optimized interface design solution is formulated, leading to the development of strategic guidelines for prototyping platform optimization in AD environments.

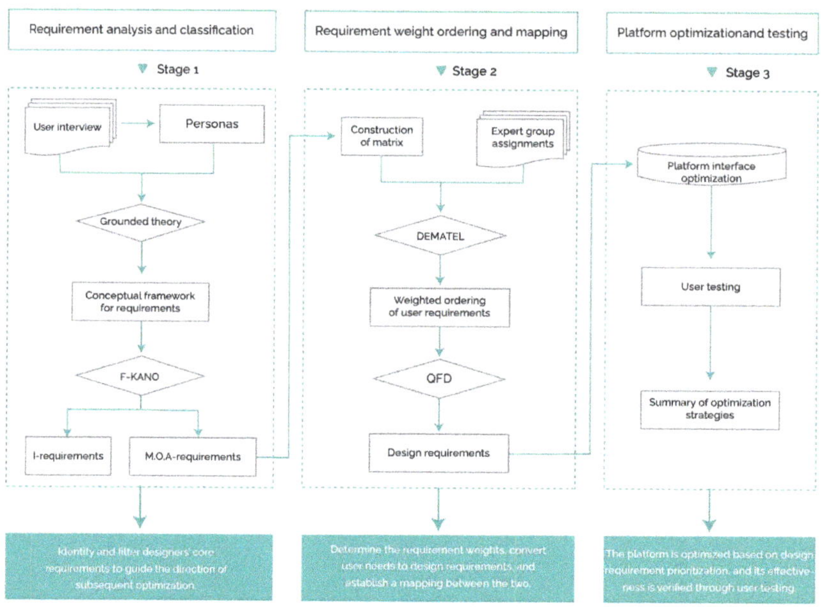

Figure 1. Proposed Framework.

To ensure the rigor of this study, semistructured interviews were conducted to collect qualitative data, and structured surveys were used to support quantitative analysis. Participants were selected based on their professional experience in agile development environments to ensure representativeness. All participants provided informed consent, and personal data were anonymized in accordance with research ethics guidelines. The study was reviewed and approved by the institutional ethics committee. This integrated methodological approach ensures a systematic and data-driven optimization process rather than an arbitrary selection of techniques. By linking user-driven insights (grounded theory), requirement prioritization (F-KANO and DEMATEL), and functional alignment (QFD), this study constructs a coherent and rigorous pathway for improving prototyping platform efficiency in AD environments.

3.2. Grounded Theory

Grounded theory is an inductive qualitative research methodology designed to derive concepts and theories from data, enabling the interpretation of phenomena within specific contexts [25]. In this study, grounded theory was employed to collect and analyze the core needs of designers in AD environments. A semistructured interview approach is utilized to gather insights into designers' actual requirements and pain points when using prototyping platforms. The collected data were systematically processed through open coding, axial coding, and selective coding, ultimately leading to the construction of a conceptual framework that encapsulated designer needs within AD contexts. To ensure the authenticity and reliability of the research data, follow-up validation with interviewees was conducted when necessary. This ensured that the extracted designer requirements were firmly grounded in real-world AD scenarios, thereby providing a robust data foundation for subsequent requirement classification and design optimization.

3.3. F-KANO Model

The F-KANO model is an advancement of the traditional Kano model, integrating fuzzy mathematics to enhance the accuracy of user requirement classification and mitigate the issue of discrete categorization [26]. Under the framework of this study, the F-KANO model was utilized to classify and refine designers' requirements, ensuring that optimization efforts were concentrated on the most impactful needs. Based on the classification principles of the Kano model (Figure 2), requirements were divided into the must-be (M), one-dimensional (O), attractive (A), and indifferent (I) categories. To quantify user preferences, an F-KANO questionnaire was administered, where participants assigned fuzzy values ranging from 0 to 1 to indicate satisfaction and dissatisfaction levels, ensuring that the total sum equaled 1. This methodology allowed for a more precise interpretation of how different design elements influence user experience, effectively capturing the nonlinear relationship between satisfaction levels and product attributes. By transforming subjective perceptions into quantifiable factors, the F-KANO model serves as a crucial tool for evaluating product performance, identifying priority features, and guiding user-centric design enhancements. Consequently, this approach ensured that prototyping platform optimizations were data-driven and strategically aligned with designer expectations. The satisfaction coefficient S_i and dissatisfaction coefficient D_i for a given requirement *i-th* were derived using Equations (1) and (2), respectively.

$$S_i = \frac{A_i + O_i}{A_i + O_i + M_i + I_i} \tag{1}$$

$$D_i = -1 \cdot \frac{M_i + O_i}{A_i + O_i + M_i + I_i} \tag{2}$$

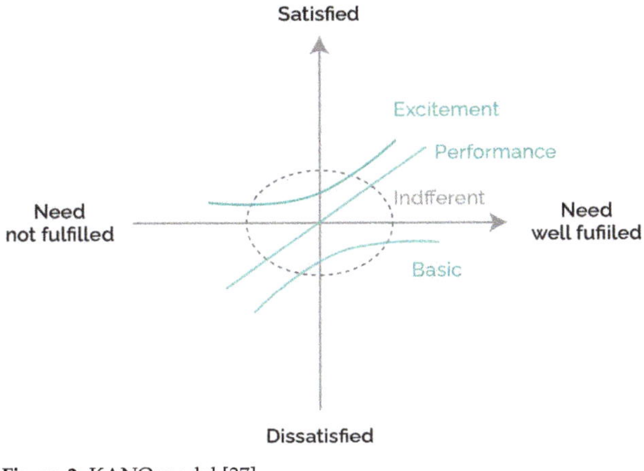

Figure 2. KANO model [27].

3.4. DEMATEL Method

The DEMATEL method is a multicriteria decision-making approach based on expert evaluation, designed to identify causal relationships among influencing factors and quantify their relative importance [28]. In this study, the DEMATEL method was employed to analyze and rank the weight of core designer requirements, ensuring that optimization strategies prioritize the most critical needs.

(1) Direct Influence Matrix: A direct influence matrix was constructed based on the M, O, and A requirements filtered through the F-KANO model. Experts and senior designers were invited to evaluate the degree of influence between each pair of requirements, generating an $n \times n$ direct influence matrix A (Equation (3)). A five-point Likert scale was used to quantify the influence level, ranging from no influence (1) to very strong influence (5).

$$A = \begin{bmatrix} 0 & a_{12} & \cdots & a_{1n} \\ a_{21} & 0 & \cdots & a_{2n} \\ \vdots & \vdots & 0 & \vdots \\ a_{n1} & a_{n2} & \cdots & 0 \end{bmatrix} = \left(A_{ij}\right)_{n\times n} \quad (3)$$

In the equations, the direct influence of factor i on factor j is denoted as A_{ij}, where i and j are integers satisfying $1 \leq I \leq n$, $1 \leq j \leq n$, and n represents the total number of influencing factors. Since self-influence is not considered, $A_{ij} = 0$ when $i = j$.

(2) Normalization Matrix: To mitigate potential biases resulting from multiple expert evaluations or dimensional inconsistencies, the direct influence matrix A was normalized (Equation (4)) to obtain the normalized matrix X, ensuring that $0 \leq x_{ij} \leq 1$.

$$X = A / \max_{1\leq i\leq n} \sum_{j=1}^{n} A_{ij} = \left(x_{ij}\right)_{n\times n} \quad (4)$$

(3) Total Influence Matrix Calculation: The comprehensive relationship between direct and indirect influences among requirements was computed using Equation (5).

$$Z = X_1 + X_2 + \cdots + X_n = X(I-X)^{-1} = \left(Z_{ij}\right)_{n\times n} \quad (5)$$

(4) Causal Relationship Measurement: The influence degree (f), affected degree (e), centrality degree ($m = f_i + e_i$), and causal degree ($n = f_i - e_i$) were determined using Equations (6) and (7).

$$f_i = \sum_{j=1}^{n} Z_{ij} (1 \leq i \leq n, 1 \leq j \leq n) \quad (6)$$

$$e_i = \sum_{j=1}^{n} Z_{ij} (1 \leq i \leq n, 1 \leq j \leq n) \quad (7)$$

(5) Influence Network Relationship Map Construction: The graph (Figure 3) was generated by categorizing factors into four quadrants based on the average values of horizontal vector centrality ($f_i + e$) and vertical vector causality ($f_i - e_i$). This visualization illustrates the hierarchical position of each requirement within the system and its overall impact. Key requirements with the highest system influence are identified, establishing their optimization priority.

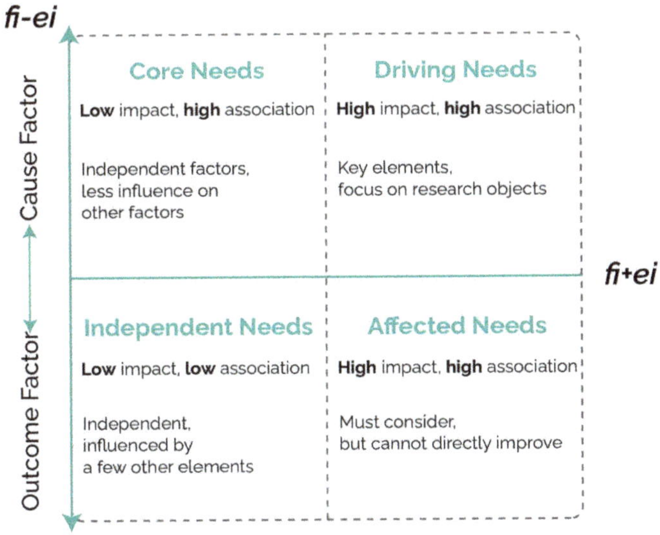

Figure 3. Influence network relationship map graph [29].

(6) User Requirement Weight Calculation: The importance weight (W_{Ui}) of each user requirement was determined based on Equation (8).

$$W_{U_i} = \frac{(f + e_i)}{\sum_{i=1}^{N'} (f_i + e_i)} \tag{8}$$

3.5. QFD Analysis

QFD is a systematic product development methodology, with its core tool being the House of Quality (Figure 4). QFD enables the quantitative transformation of user requirements into design requirements based on weighted priorities, ensuring that prototyping platform optimization aligns with target user needs. In this study, QFD analysis was employed to convert the prioritized core requirements, as determined through the DEMATEL method, into corresponding design requirements. Additionally, the prioritization of design requirements was established, providing a structured framework to guide the optimization of the prototyping platform.

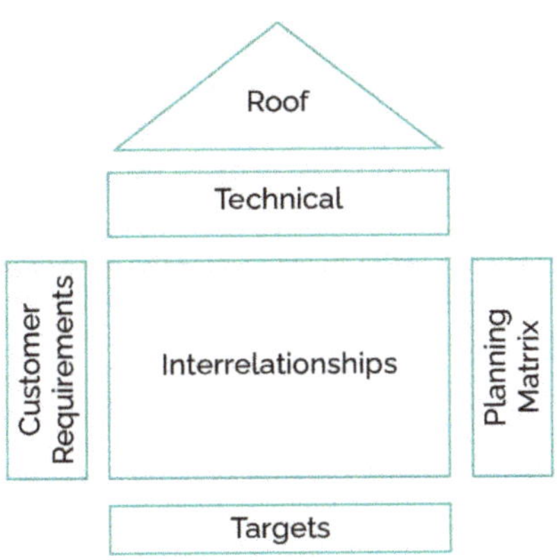

Figure 4. House of Quality [30].

(1) Construction of a Matrix of User Requirements and Design Requirements:

The collected user requirements were first analyzed and translated into specific design requirements. A panel of interaction design experts was invited to discuss and establish the mapping relationships between user requirements and design requirements. The expert group categorized user needs based on their functional attributes and interaction characteristics, ensuring that each design requirement accurately reflected core user requirements. The core designer requirement weights (W_{Ui}) obtained from the DEMATEL method served as input for constructing the correlation mapping matrix. In this matrix, rows represented user requirements, while columns corresponded to design requirements. A panel of experts composed of senior designers, product managers, and software engineers assessed the strength of the association between each user requirement and design requirement. They assigned relevance scores to establish a decision-making framework for the relationship between user requirements and design requirements. Let the set of user requirements be $U = \{U_1, U_2, \ldots, U_n\}$, and the set of design requirements be $D = \{D_1, D_2, \ldots, D_m\}$. The user requirement–design requirement mapping matrix W_{UD} is formulated as follows:

$$W_{UD} = \begin{bmatrix} w_{11} & w_{12} & \cdots & w_{1m} \\ w_{21} & w_{22} & \cdots & w_{2m} \\ \vdots & \vdots & \ddots & \vdots \\ w_{n1} & w_{n2} & \cdots & w_{nm} \end{bmatrix} \quad (9)$$

where W_{nm} represents the relevance score between user requirement U_n and design requirement D_m.

(2) Calculation of Design Requirement Weights:

$$S_T = \sum_{i=1}^{n} (W_{U_i} \times W_{UD}) \quad (10)$$

where S_{Tj} represents the weighted score of design requirement T_j, W_{Ui} denotes the user requirement weights derived from the DEMATEL method, and W_{UD} represents the correlation between user requirement U_n and design requirement D_m.

After computing the weighted scores for all design requirements, they were ranked in descending order to prioritize the most critical design elements for implementation. This study successfully applied the QFD methodology to translate user requirements into design requirements, and the user requirement–design requirement mapping matrix was utilized to quantify the importance of each design requirement.

4. Case Study

4.1. User Research

This study identified the key pain points and requirements of designers in AD environments and constructed three user personas. Additionally, a semistructured interview framework was designed to support subsequent user requirement collection and analysis, requirement classification, and prototyping platform optimization. UI designers focus primarily on the usability of design tools and the automatic updating of design specifications, aiming to reduce the cost associated with repeated searches and modifications while ensuring quick access to relevant information when requirements change. UX designers emphasize tracking requirement changes and adjusting interaction logic, requiring a high degree of linkage between requirement documentation and design files to reduce cross-team communication costs and enhance design consistency. Product managers are concerned with the standardization of design workflows and project progress management, aiming to achieve traceability of design modifications through systematic tools and to quantify design team efficiency and output. Figure 5 presents a visual representation of the user information collected in this study.

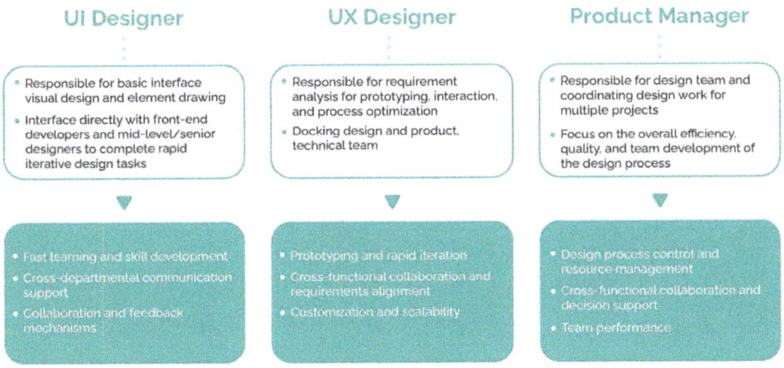

Figure 5. User personas of designers in AD environments.

4.2. User Requirement Analysis

In-depth interviews were conducted with 12 product designers experienced in AD to thoroughly explore their requirements and challenges in using product design systems (see Table 1). Following the interview protocol, all conversations were recorded and transcribed immediately after the interviews. The transcripts were then reviewed and verified to ensure accuracy and completeness. To maintain data fidelity and credibility, follow-up validation with interviewees was conducted when necessary. A systematic grounded theory approach was applied, following the three-stage process of open coding, axial coding, and selective coding [31]. Next, open coding was performed on the raw interview transcripts. The interview data were examined line by line to identify key information related to the design platform, which was then conceptualized and assigned labels. Through this process, 41 initial concepts were extracted and categorized into 19 scopes. Analysis of the open coding results revealed logical relationships among the identified scopes. These 19 scopes were further clustered and abstracted, ultimately forming three core categories. The axial coding process and category definitions are detailed in Table 2.

Table 1. Summary of interviewees' information.

Category	Details
Age Distribution	26–35 years old, average 30.1 years
Gender Ratio	Male: 7 (58.3%), Female: 5 (41.7%)
Education Level	Master's: 9 (75%), Bachelor's: 3 (25%)
Field of Study	Design, Interaction Design, Computer Science, Software Engineering, etc.
Job Roles	UI Designer (4), UX Designer (4), Product Manager (3), Product Designer (1)
Work Experience	3–12 years, average 7.5 years

Based on grounded theory, designer requirements were extracted from real-world AD environments, and a comprehensive conceptual framework of user needs was constructed. This framework provided systematic theoretical support for aligning designer requirements with the optimization of product design platforms. The results of the requirement analysis were then further refined to determine requirement priorities and drive platform optimization, as discussed in the next section.

Table 2. Designer requirement architecture.

Main Scope	Scope	Scope Connotation	Initial Concept
Layout and Basic Visuals (C_1)	Drag-and-Drop Layout (B_1)	Arrange components quickly on the canvas through drag-and-drop, reducing the need for manual coordinate adjustments	Dragging Components (A_1); Smart Snapping (A_2); Auto Snap Lines (A_3)
	Grid and Alignment (B_2)	Provide grid and alignment rules to ensure consistent interface layout	Grid Display (A_4); Alignment Guides (A_5)
	Multicanvas and Responsive Layout (B_3)	Support multiple canvas pages and allow quick switching between different screen sizes	Customizable Canvas Size (A_6); Multidevice Canvas (A_7)
	Quick Theme Configuration (B_4)	Define global settings for colors, fonts, and brand identity	Theme Color Switching (A_8); Brand Identity Set (A_9)
	Reusable Component Library (B_5)	Offer commonly used UI elements such as buttons, input fields, and navigation bars, enabling reuse and batch updates	Component Reusability (A_{10}); Customizable Properties (A_{11})
	Automated Visual Standard Compliance (B_6)	Perform basic validation for colors, contrast, and other visual parameters	Accessibility Detection (A_{12}); Color Contrast Alerts (A_{13}); Font Size Warnings (A_{14})
	Basic Graphic and Image Editing (B_7)	Enable basic image editing within the platform, including cropping, transformation, and annotation	Crop/Scale (A_{15}); Opacity Adjustment (A_{16})
Interaction and Prototype Iteration (C_2)	Basic Interaction Triggers (B_8)	Add interactive events such as click, hover, and drag actions to interface elements	Click-to-Jump (A_{17}); Drag-and-Sort (A_{18})
	Animation and Transition Effects (B_9)	Provide page transitions and animation effects, such as fade-ins and slide transitions, to enhance prototype immersion	Page Transitions (A_{19}); Timing and Delay Control (A_{20})
	Quick Prototype Preview (B_{10})	Generate interactive preview links with a single click	Interactive Preview Links (A_{21}); QR Code Mobile Viewing (A_{22})
	Version History and Rollback (B_{11})	Save snapshots of each design iteration	Snapshot Timeline (A_{23}); Change Annotations (A_{24}); One-Click Restore (A_{25})
	Integrated Usability Testing (B_{12})	Integrate or connect with basic usability testing features, such as click heatmaps and feedback collection	Click Tracking (A_{26}); Embedded Survey Pop-ups (A_{27})
Collaboration and Management (C_3)	Real-Time Multiuser Collaboration (B_{13})	Support real-time collaboration among multiple designers or team members, allowing visibility of each other's cursor positions	Autosave in Real Time (A_{28}); Online User Status Display (A_{29})
	Canvas Annotations and Comments (B_{14})	Enable teams to leave comments directly on interface elements	Pinpointed Annotations (A_{30}); Threaded Discussions (A_{31})
	Role-Based Access Control (B_{15})	Differentiate user roles such as read-only, editable, and admin access, with options to restrict external access	Read-Only Links (A_{32}); Operation Log Tracking (A_{33})
	Requirement Integration with External Tools (B_{16})	Integrate with external tools for requirement management and synchronization	Status Synchronization (A_{34}); Change Notifications (A_{35})
	Task Management Kanban (B_{17})	Provide a simple task management board to help designers track iteration progress	To-Do/In-Progress/Completed Tasks (A_{36}); Priority Tags (A_{37})
	Code and Annotation Export (B_{18})	Convert designs into frontend annotations (size, spacing, color values) or generate basic HTML/CSS code	Automated Asset Export (A_{38}); Basic Code Generation (A_{39})
	Design Documentation and Handoff Files (B_{19})	Automatically generate design documentation based on styles and components used in the canvas	Operation Manual (A_{40}); Online Sharing Link (A_{41})

4.3. Requirement Classification and Filtering

This section discusses the categorization and filtering of designer requirements in AD environments based on the user requirement conceptual framework, with the F-KANO questionnaire utilized to capture designers' judgments on different requirement types. A total of 109 valid responses were obtained from UI designers, UX designers, and product managers. Following data collection, fuzzy mathematics was applied to transform subjective user evaluations into measurable indicators, ensuring an objective classification process.

To analyze the collected data, satisfaction and dissatisfaction matrices were formulated for each requirement. Specifically, a fulfilled requirement matrix P and an unfulfilled requirement matrix N were constructed based on user responses. Subsequently, an interaction matrix S was derived using $S = P^T \times N$, which enabled the identification of requirement classification attributes. By correlating the dataset in Table 3 with matrix S, the membership vector T was computed for each requirement category, effectively determining their classification within the F-KANO framework.

Table 3. F-KANO Evaluation.

Demands Satisfied or Not		Dissatisfied				
		Like	Must-Be	Indifferent	Tolerable	Dislike
Satisfied	Like	Q	A	A	A	O
	Must-be	R	I	I	I	M
	Indifferent	R	I	I	I	M
	Tolerable	R	I	I	I	M
	Dislike	R	R	R	R	Q

Must-be requirements (M), one-dimensional requirements (O), attractive requirements (A), indifferent requirements (I), reverse requirements (R). (Q: contradictory user responses indicating inconsistent or conflicting perception of the requirement).

Taking B_1 from Table 4 as an example, the unfulfilled requirement matrix N is represented as:

$$S = \begin{bmatrix} 0 & 0 & 0 & 0.06 & 0.24 \\ 0 & 0 & 0 & 0.12 & 0.48 \\ 0 & 0 & 0 & 0.02 & 0.08 \\ 0 & 0 & 0 & 0 & 0 \\ 0 & 0 & 0 & 0 & 0 \end{bmatrix}$$

Table 4. F-KANO questionnaire (part).

Type	No.	Demand		Like	Must-Be	Indifferent	Tolerable	Dislike
Layout and Basic Visuals (C_1)	B1	Drag-and-Drop Layout	Satisfied	0.3	0.6	0.1		
			Dissatisfied				0.2	0.8
Interaction and Prototype Iteration (C_2)	B8	Basic Interaction Triggers	Satisfied	0.8	0.2			
			Dissatisfied			0.1	0.2	0.7
Collaboration and Management (C_3)	B12	Integrated Usability Testing	Satisfied	0.1	0.3	0.6		
			Dissatisfied			0.7	0.2	0.1

By mapping the data from Table 3 to the interaction matrix S, the membership vector T_1 for each requirement can be obtained.

$$T_1 = \left(\frac{0.56}{M'}, \frac{0.24}{O'}, \frac{0.06}{A'}, \frac{0.14}{I'}, \frac{0}{R'} \right)$$

Based on a confidence level of $\alpha = 0.4$, the membership vector T_1 was used to classify requirements. If the α value in the membership vector T was greater than or equal to 0.4, the requirement was assigned $t = 1$ [27]. Otherwise, it was assigned $t = 0$. If the sequence contained at least two occurrences of 1, the requirement priority order followed (*M*, *O*, *A*, *I*, *R*). For example, given $T_1 = (1, 0, 0, 0, 0)$, the corresponding requirement was classified as *M* in the F-KANO questionnaire.

By systematically applying this process to all collected questionnaires and conducting individual calculations, the occurrence frequency of each requirement category was determined. The category with the highest frequency was assigned as the final classification of the design requirement. Furthermore, the better–worse satisfaction coefficient was computed using Equations (1) and (2) to quantify the impact of each requirement on user satisfaction. A coefficient with an absolute value approaching 0 suggests minimal influence on user satisfaction, whereas values nearing 1 indicate a significant impact. The comprehensive classification outcomes are detailed in Table 5.

Table 5. Statistical results on design requirements for the prototyping platform.

No.	Attribute Number					Attribute Classification	Better	Worse
	M	O	A	I	R			
B_1	72	16	13	5	3	*M*	0.28	−0.75
B_2	78	11	9	7	4	*M*	0.31	−0.82
B_3	27	17	47	16	2	*A*	0.64	−0.47
B_4	22	15	51	17	4	*A*	0.59	−0.54
B_5	29	45	20	14	1	*O*	0.52	−0.60
B_6	20	17	58	13	3	*A*	0.66	−0.44
B_7	20	16	17	48	8	*I*	0.45	−0.38
B_8	78	14	11	6	0	*M*	0.24	−0.76
B_9	24	11	63	8	3	*A*	0.64	−0.49
B_{10}	17	13	54	20	5	*A*	0.57	−0.51
B_{11}	67	16	12	10	4	*M*	0.29	−0.71
B_{12}	19	21	51	16	2	*A*	0.61	−0.56
B_{13}	20	54	19	15	1	*O*	0.55	−0.62
B_{14}	24	44	20	15	5	*O*	0.59	−0.68
B_{15}	19	12	16	57	5	*I*	0.42	−0.39
B_{16}	19	55	18	13	4	*O*	0.54	−0.61
B_{17}	19	18	14	56	2	*I*	0.41	−0.36
B_{18}	17	12	16	60	4	*I*	0.45	−0.40
B_{19}	22	21	13	52	1	*I*	0.43	−0.44

As presented in Table 6, the analysis of prototyping platform requirements identified four must-be (M) requirements, four one-dimensional (O) requirements, six attractive (A) requirements, and five indifferent (I) requirements. According to the F-KANO model, I-type requirements have a negligible impact on user experience (UX) and are not considered essential for platform optimization. Consequently, this study focused on M, O, and A-type attributes, retaining only those that significantly influenced UX, while excluding I-type attributes. The retained attributes served as the primary evaluation criteria for optimizing the prototyping platform.

Table 6. Classification of design requirements for the prototyping platform.

Designer Requirement Classification	Requirements
M (reserved)	Drag-and-Drop Layout (B_1); Grid and Alignment (B_2); Basic Interaction Triggers (B_8); Version History and Rollback (B_{11})
O (reserved)	Reusable Component Library (B_5); Real-Time Multiuser Collaboration (B_{13}); Canvas Annotations and Comments (B_{14}); Requirement Integration with External Tools (B_{16})
A (reserved)	Multicanvas and Responsive Layout (B_3); Quick Theme Configuration (B_4); Automated Visual Standard Compliance (B_6); Animation and Transition Effects (B_9); Quick Prototype Preview (B_{10}); Integrated Usability Testing (B_{12})
I (excluded)	Basic Graphic and Image Editing (B_7); Role-Based Access Control (B_{15}); Task Management Kanban (B_{17}); Code and Annotation Export (B_{18}); Design Documentation and Handoff Files (B_{19})

4.4. Weighting Calculations

To ensure the accuracy and objectivity of the evaluation results, ten experts were invited to participate in the assessment, including seven professors specializing in UX design and three UX designers. A 0 to 4 rating scale was applied to quantify the judgment matrix, where 0 signifies no influence, 1 indicates a weak influence, 2 represents a moderate influence, 3 corresponds to a significant influence, and 4 denotes a very significant influence. After multiple rounds of discussion and analysis, the expert panel reached a consensus, as presented in Table 7.

Table 7. Direct impact matrix.

No.	B_1	B_2	B_8	B_{11}	B_5	B_{13}	B_{14}	B_{16}	B_3	B_4	B_6	B_9	B_{10}	B_{12}
B_1	0	1.2	2.7	3	3.4	2.8	2.2	2.4	3.5	2.6	2.2	3.4	3.4	3.2
B_2	1.2	0	2.4	2.8	3.2	2.7	3.1	2.2	3.2	2.7	2.2	2.8	3.2	3
B_8	0.6	1.2	0	1.5	2.1	2	1.2	1.7	2.6	2.1	1.2	1.8	2.7	2.4
B_{11}	0.4	1	1.3	0	3.2	2.2	2.7	3	3.2	2.3	2.8	2.6	3	2.7
B_5	1.3	1	0.7	1.3	0	2.5	1.2	1.3	1.2	1	3.2	2.1	1	1.2
B_{13}	2.3	1.3	1.1	0.7	2.7	0	2.3	2.2	3.2	2.7	3.2	2.7	2.4	1.3
B_{14}	2.2	2	2.2	2.6	3	2.4	0	2	2.9	2.5	2	2.5	2.8	2.7
B_{16}	2.5	2.4	2.2	3.2	1.2	2.3	1	0	3	2.6	2	2.4	2.5	2.4
B_3	1	1.8	2	2.5	1	2	0.5	1.2	0	2.2	1.2	2	2.4	2
B_4	1.2	2	2.2	2.3	1.6	2.3	1	1.2	2	0	3.3	2.3	2.3	2.2
B_6	2.5	3.2	2.5	3.2	2.3	2.8	1.8	2	2.6	2.8	0	3	3.2	3.2
B_9	2	2.2	1.8	2.4	1.7	2.2	1.3	1.7	2.3	2.4	3	0	2.8	2.6
B_{10}	2.4	2.5	2.6	2	2.2	2.5	2	2.3	1	2.2	2.6	2.8	0	3.2
B_{12}	2	1.8	2.2	1.8	1.2	2	1.5	2	1.2	2.5	2.4	2.5	1.5	0

Using the DEMATEL calculation formulas, the total influence matrix Z was derived, followed by the computation of the influence degree (f_i) and affected degree (e_i) for each factor. Subsequently, the centrality degree (m) and causality degree (n) for each requirement indicator were determined. Finally, the weight values (W_{Ui}) for each requirement in the system were calculated. The detailed results are presented in Table 8.

Table 8. DEMATEL calculated indicator values.

No.	Influence Degree (*fi*)	Influenced Degree (*ei*)	Central Degree ($mi = fi + ei$)	Cause Degree ($ni = fi - ei$)	Weights
B_1	4.531	2.863	7.394	1.668	0.072
B_2	4.393	3.132	7.525	1.260	0.073
B_8	2.947	3.364	6.311	−0.417	0.061
B_{11}	3.862	3.762	7.624	0.100	0.074
B_5	2.563	3.667	6.230	−1.104	0.060
B_{13}	3.649	3.957	7.606	−0.308	0.074
B_{14}	4.059	2.841	6.900	1.218	0.067
B_{16}	3.859	3.279	7.138	0.579	0.069
B_3	2.850	4.036	6.886	−1.187	0.067
B_4	3.390	3.953	7.342	−0.563	0.071
B_6	4.512	4.088	8.600	0.424	0.083
B_9	3.713	4.227	7.940	−0.515	0.077
B_{10}	3.948	4.237	8.185	−0.288	0.079
B_{12}	3.253	4.121	7.374	−0.868	0.072

To visually represent the causal and influence relationships among the requirement indicators, an influence network relationship map was generated for the prototyping platform requirements, with centrality plotted on the horizontal axis and causality on the vertical axis, with a defined threshold value (Figure 6). The importance ranking of design factors for the prototyping platform was as follows: $B_1 > B_2 > B_{14} > B_{16} > B_6 > B_{11} > B_{10} > B_{13} > B_8 > B_9 > B_4 > B_{12} > B_5 > B_3$.

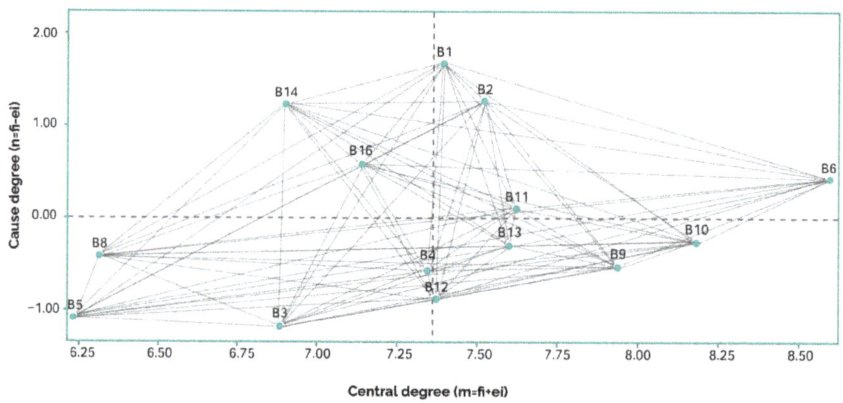

Figure 6. The influence network relation map.

4.5. Analysis of the Importance of Design Requirements

Based on the user requirement data in Table 7, the corresponding design requirements were derived (see Table 9). Subsequently, the design requirements, user requirements, and requirement weights were input into the House of Quality matrix, where their associations were analyzed. Following the evaluation criteria, the determined relationships were mapped onto the House of Quality, ensuring alignment between user needs and design specifications.

Table 9. Mapping of user requirements to design requirements.

Criterion Layer	User Requirements	Design Requirements
Interaction	Drag-and-Drop Layout (B_1)	Free Dragging and Alignment (DR_1)
	Grid and Alignment (B_2)	Mesh Adsorption (DR_2)
	Basic Interaction Triggers (B_8)	Interactive Trigger Configuration (DR_3)
Design Management	Version History and Rollback (B_{11})	Versioning (DR_4)
	Reusable Component Library (B_5)	Component Library (DR_5)
	Real-Time Multiuser Collaboration (B_{13}); Canvas Annotations and Comments (B_{14})	Multiplayer Collaboration (DR_6)
	Requirement Integration with External Tools (B_{16})	Requirement Synchronization (DR_7)
	Multicanvas and Responsive Layout (B_3)	Multicanvas (DR_8)
Visualization and Feedback	Quick Theme Configuration (B_4); Automated Visual Standard Compliance (B_6)	Visual Specification (DR_9)
	Animation and Transition Effects (B_9)	Animation (DR_{10})
	Quick Prototype Preview (B_{10}); Integrated Usability Testing (B_{12})	Preview and Testing (DR_{11})

In the matrix shown in Figure 7, the degree of association between user requirements and design requirements is represented using a (9–3–1–0) scale, where 9 indicates a strong correlation; 3, a moderate correlation; 1, a weak correlation; and 0, no correlation. The final weights of the design requirements were computed by integrating user requirement weights into the matrix. The results indicated that DR_9 (Visual Specification, 2.254) had the highest weight, underscoring the critical role of automated validation and theme management in enhancing designers' workflow efficiency. DR_3 (Interactive Trigger Configuration, 2.232) also exhibited a high weight, suggesting that designers strongly emphasize configurability in interactive behaviors and animation transitions. Additionally, DR_{11} (Preview and Testing, 1.805) and DR_{10} (Animation, 1.791) fell within the high-weight range, highlighting the importance of prototype visualization and interaction experience optimization for designers. Furthermore, DR_6 (Multiplayer Collaboration, 1.758) held a significant weight, indicating that real-time collaboration is indispensable for designers in AD environments. The platform must therefore facilitate robust real-time collaboration mechanisms, supporting multiuser editing, cursor visualization, and commenting/annotation functionalities, to enhance cross-functional team communication efficiency. Moreover, DR_4 (Versioning, 1.643) and DR_5 (Component Library, 1.537) warranted particular attention to ensure effective version management, component reuse, and synchronized updates, thereby maintaining design consistency and traceability.

Overall, the research findings reveal the complex mapping relationships between user requirements and design requirements, providing a clear representation of core designer needs in AD environments. In particular, the study highlights the critical importance of visual experience optimization, interactive animations, prototype preview, and multiuser collaboration as essential functionalities for enhancing the efficiency and effectiveness of design workflows.

User Requirements	Weight	DR1	DR2	DR3	DR4	DR5	DR6	DR7	DR8	DR9	DR10	DR11
		Design Requirements										
B1	0.072	●	○	△					○	△		
B2	0.073	○	●	△					○	△		
B8	0.061	△	△	●	△				△	○	○	△
B11	0.074			△	●	○	○	△				
B5	0.060				○	●	△	○				
B13	0.074				○	○	●	○				
B14	0.067				○	△	●	○				
B16	0.069				○	○	○	●				
B3	0.067	○	○						●			
B4	0.071			○						●	○	△
B6	0.083			○						●	○	△
B9	0.077			●						○	●	○
B10	0.079			○						○	○	●
B12	0.072			△						△	○	●
Weight		1.129	1.135	2.232	1.537	1.258	1.758	1.298	1.099	2.254	1.791	1.805
Rank		10	9	2	6	8	5	7	11	1	4	3

Design Requirements				
Relevance	strong	medium	weak	none
Symbol	●	○	△	
Mark	9	6	3	0

Figure 7. House of Quality of user requirements.

4.6. Prototyping Platform Optimization

In this study, the core objective is to optimize the prototyping platform's UX, ensuring that it meets AD requirements while precisely aligning user needs with design requirements. First, grounded theory was applied to analyze user needs, and the F-KANO model was used to classify these needs, identifying key design directions for optimizing the prototyping platform. Next, QFD analysis was used to construct a mapping model between user requirements and design requirements. By evaluating the strength of associations between user needs and design requirements and incorporating requirement weight results, the weight of each design requirement was calculated to determine optimization priorities. The results indicated that Visual Specification (DR_9) and Interactive Trigger Configuration (DR_3) were the most critical design requirements, exerting the greatest impact on UX optimization, as shown in Figure 8.

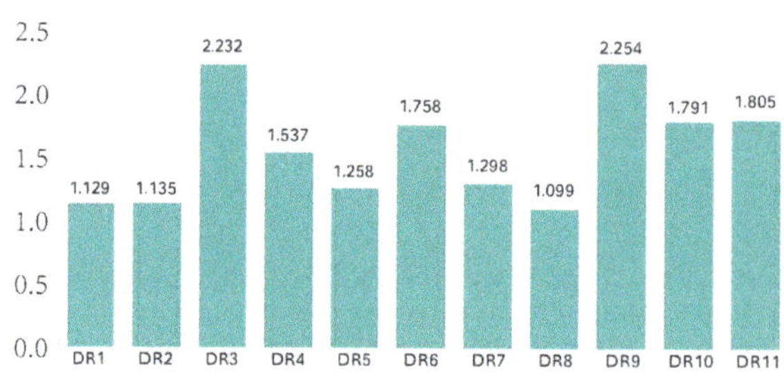

Figure 8. Prototyping platform design requirement ranks.

The optimized prototyping platform enhances user experience by systematically aligning designer needs with platform functionalities in AD environments. By refining interaction workflows, improving component and version management, and integrating data-driven testing mechanisms, the platform significantly enhances design efficiency and collaboration (Figure 9).

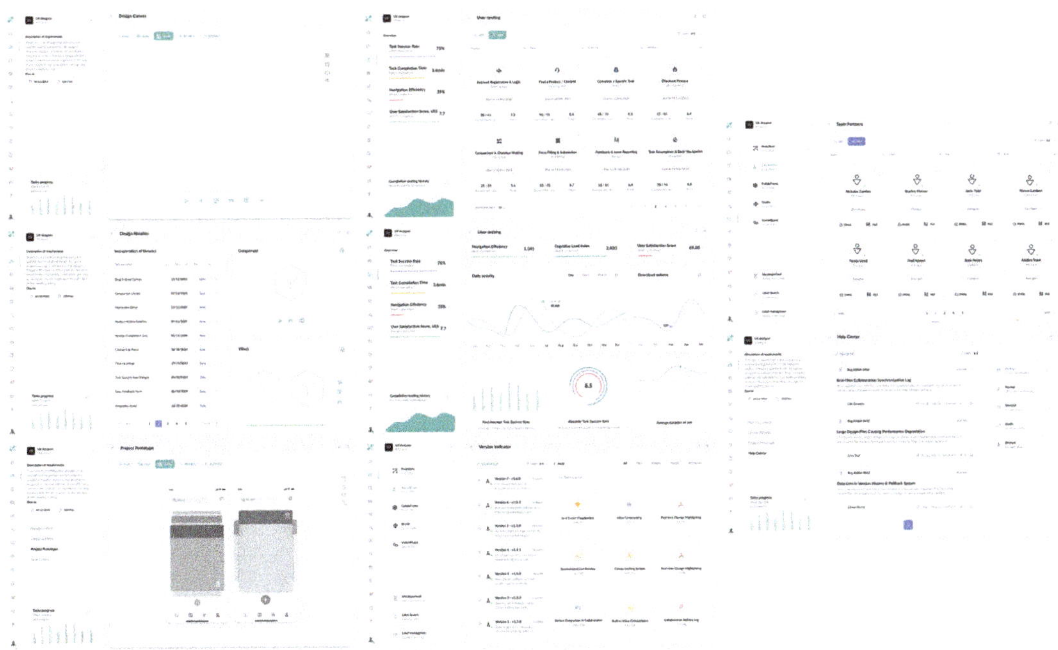

(a) (b) (c)

Figure 9. Optimized prototyping platform interface. (**a**) Canvas page: enhances free dragging, intelligent alignment, and mesh adsorption for improved precision; (**b**) system center and version page: integrates component management, version control, and requirement synchronization, enabling cross-project sharing and automated updates; (**c**) testing page: supports prototype preview, remote testing, click heatmaps, and task tracking for data-driven optimization.

(a) Canvas Page: Enhancing Interaction Efficiency

The canvas page introduced improvements in Free Dragging and Intelligent Alignment and Mesh Adsorption (DR_1 and DR_2), ensuring that elements snap accurately into place with minimal manual adjustment. The Interactive Trigger Configuration (DR_3) was optimized to provide a more intuitive method for linking components with animations and dynamic behaviors, reducing the complexity of interaction design. Additionally, Animation (DR_{10}) was integrated, allowing designers to quickly implement smooth transitions and state changes without repetitive configuration, streamlining the prototyping process.

(b) System Center and Version Page: Strengthening Collaboration and Asset Management

The system center and version management module introduced key enhancements in Versioning (DR_4), Component Library (DR_5), and Requirement Synchronization (DR_7). The version control system supported snapshot archiving, version comparison, and rollback features, allowing designers to track design iterations with greater flexibility. The component library was upgraded to support cross-project reuse and automated updates, ensuring that assets remain consistent across different design tasks. Multiplayer Collaboration (DR_6) and Multicanvas (DR_8) further enhanced real-time teamwork, enabling designers to share cursors, track changes, and leave annotations in collaborative projects.

(c) Testing Page: Data-Driven Evaluation and Optimization

The testing page focused on Preview and Testing (DR_{11}), equipping designers with tools for remote usability testing, click heatmaps, and task completion tracking. These features allow designers to analyze user interactions based on empirical data, making informed decisions about usability improvements.

In summary, based on user requirement weighting and design requirement mapping analysis, the proposed optimization strategy for the prototyping platform improved the alignment between user needs and design requirements while simultaneously enhancing efficiency in AD environments. Compared with existing commercial solutions, the proposed platform enables designers to rapidly respond to high-frequency iterations and dynamic requirement changes, addressing limitations in requirement tracking and information alignment present in current tools. Additionally, the proposed solution reinforces visual standardization management, reducing the cost of repetitive modifications caused by visual inconsistencies through standardized application processes. Furthermore, in terms of efficient version control and component reuse mechanisms, the optimized platform enhances change management, design traceability, and cross-project component synchronization, offering greater traceability and reusability compared with existing products, thereby improving design asset management efficiency. The optimized platform demonstrates significant improvements in interaction fluidity, collaboration efficiency, and visual consistency. Moreover, by integrating a data-driven testing feedback mechanism, designers can now execute prototyping tasks with greater precision and efficiency. Overall, this study introduces an optimized prototyping platform that is more efficient and better aligned with AD requirements, fostering innovation and advancement in modern design workflows.

5. Discussion

5.1. Design Feedback and Evaluation

To assess the feasibility and user satisfaction of the optimized prototyping platform in real-world applications, 20 designers were invited to evaluate its performance. The evaluation criteria covered six key task dimensions: dragging and alignment, interaction creation, preview and testing, team collaboration, version management, and component management. A five-point rating scale was used, where 1 indicated "very dissatisfied" and 5 indicated "very satisfied". By conducting statistical analysis on the designers' feedback data, the average score for each evaluation metric was calculated. The results were visualized using a radar chart to provide an intuitive representation of user satisfaction (Figure 10).

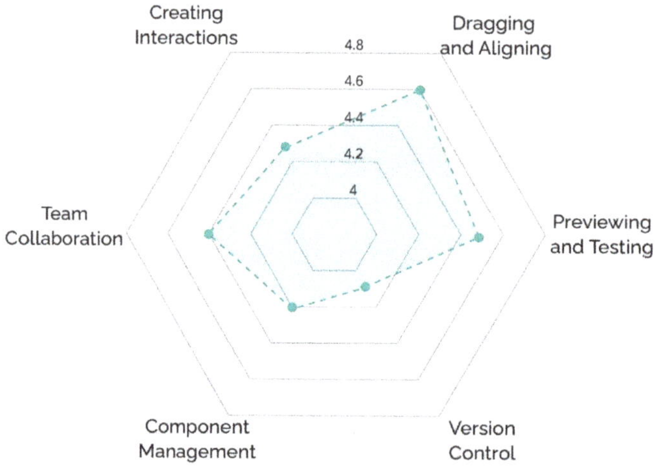

Figure 10. Radar chart showing designers' satisfaction ratings across six key task dimensions of the optimized prototyping platform.

The evaluation results indicate that designers exhibited a high level of overall satisfaction with the optimized design, as all evaluation metrics received average scores above 4.0. This suggests that the optimized design requirements effectively addressed core user needs. Among the evaluation criteria, dragging and alignment (4.6) and previewing and testing (4.5) received the highest scores, highlighting that the precise component alignment mechanism and efficient prototype preview functionality were highly valued by designers. Team collaboration (4.4) and creating interaction (4.3) also received strong ratings, emphasizing the importance of multiuser collaboration mechanisms and enhanced interaction configuration tools in improving workflow efficiency. Additionally, component management (4.2) and version control (4.1) were widely recognized by designers, reflecting that the optimized component synchronization, archiving mechanisms, and version control system significantly enhanced the stability and consistency of the design process.

The user feedback validates the overall feasibility of the optimization strategy, providing data-driven support for future design iterations and platform deployment. The positive designer responses not only confirm the effectiveness of the proposed optimization approach but offer practical insights for further refinement of prototyping tools and UX improvements.

5.2. Comparative Analysis of Interface Design Methods

To ensure the reliability of our findings and address methodological differences, we conducted an additional round of expert evaluations and employed two alternative weighting methods (entropy weight method and CRITIC) to compare with our original DEMATEL-based analysis (see Table 10 and Figure 11). The entropy weight method assesses the diversity of user demands [32], while the CRITIC method identifies the most discriminative factors based on variance and correlation [33]. After integrating these newly obtained expert scores into the QFD model, we observed that the highest-priority design requirements remained largely consistent across all three weighting approaches (see Table 11). The convergence of results across different computational methods underscores the robustness of our optimization framework. Even when weighting schemes were adjusted or new data were introduced, the key design priorities exhibited minimal variation. This stability reaffirms that the integration of grounded theory, F-KANO classification, and QFD provides a solid foundation for capturing and prioritizing user needs, regardless of the decision-making technique applied. By demonstrating that multiple methodologies converge on similar conclusions, our comparative analysis further strengthens confidence in the proposed prototype platform optimization, confirming that it is both data-driven and resilient to methodological variations.

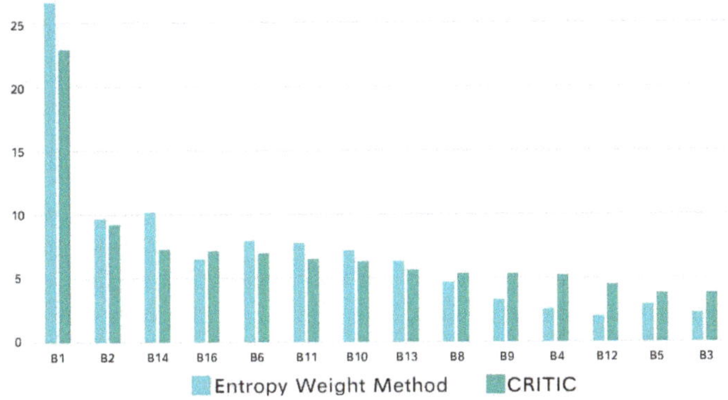

Figure 11. Comparison of entropy weight method and CRITIC weights.

Table 10. Comparison of weight methods.

Number	Method	Measuring Unit	Rank Results
1	DEMATEL	DEMATEL Centrality	$B_1 > B_2 > B_{14} > B_{16} > B_6 > B_{11} > B_{10} > B_{13} > B_8 > B_9 > B_4 > B_{12} > B_5 > B_3$
2	Entropy Weight Method	Entropy Value in EWM	$B_1 > B_{14} > B_2 > B_6 > B_{11} > B_{10} > B_{16} > B_{13} > B_8 > B_9 > B_5 > B_4 > B_3 > B_{12}$
3	CRITIC	Information Content	$B_1 > B_2 > B_3 > B_{14} > B_6 > B_{16} > B_{11} > B_{13} > B_5 > B_9 > B_{10} > B_8 > B_4 > B_4$

Table 11. Comparison of design requirement results.

Control Method	DR_1	DR_2	DR_3	DR_4	DR_5	DR_6	DR_7	DR_8	DR_9	DR_{10}	DR_{11}
Entropy Weight Method	0.087	0.074	0.223	0.049	0.025	0.024	0.022	0.063	0.211	0.176	0.122
CRITIC	0.083	0.079	0.208	0.060	0.038	0.035	0.031	0.065	0.221	0.178	0.106

5.3. Optimization Strategies for Prototyping Platforms

In AD environments, prototyping platforms play a crucial role in enhancing design efficiency and cross-team collaboration. However, existing research has focused primarily on isolated improvements, such as AI-assisted interaction design [34,35] and collaborative design [36,37], without systematically addressing the alignment between user needs and platform functionalities. While these approaches contribute to specific aspects of UX, they often lack an integrated framework for prioritizing and implementing optimizations. To address these challenges and more accurately meet designers' core needs in AD environments, this study, based on grounded theory, the F-KANO model, the DEMATEL method, and QFD analysis, proposes the following four optimization strategies:

(I) Integration of Interaction Experience and Design Efficiency

Current prototyping tools still present a high learning curve in interaction configuration and animation adjustments, making it difficult for designers to quickly implement complex interaction logic within short iteration cycles. Wang's study highlighted that the complexity of interaction configuration in existing tools may create communication barriers, limiting designers' ability to achieve intricate interactions efficiently in fast-paced environments [38]. To optimize interaction triggers and animation configuration, the platform should offer an intuitive interaction editing interface, simplifying interaction setup workflows while supporting visual logic connections and providing a preset library of interactive animations to reduce redundant operations. Additionally, enhancing real-time preview and rapid testing features would enable designers to immediately refine interaction effects, reducing cognitive load caused by frequent tool-switching or manual debugging, thereby improving workflow fluidity and overall design efficiency.

(II) Optimization of Multiuser Collaboration and Requirement Management

AD environments require real-time design progress sharing and rapid adaptation to requirement changes. However, existing prototyping platforms still face challenges such as editing conflicts and unclear requirement change tracking during multiuser collaboration. In the industrial design and manufacturing domain, Wang proposed a multiuser collaborative AR system that effectively optimizes these issues by improving collaborative editing, real-time synchronization, and annotation management [39]. To address the asymmetry between multiuser collaboration and requirement synchronization, the platform should incorporate features such as real-time cursor display and traceable change logs, ensuring that team members can view and annotate modifications in real time, thereby reducing design discrepancies caused by miscommunication. Additionally, the platform should integrate a requirement management system, enabling direct mapping of product requirement changes to prototype designs, with automatic change notifications and version comparison features, ensuring that all design adjustments are aligned with the latest requirement updates.

(III) Standardization and Automated Detection of Visual Guidelines

During cross-team collaboration and high-frequency iterations, the absence of visual standardization management often leads to inconsistent interface styles and unstable design quality [40]. To address insufficient visual standardization, the platform should provide automated visual guideline detection, allowing designers to identify deviations in color, spacing, and typography hierarchy in real time, with automated optimization recommendations. Additionally, the theme management functionality should be enhanced to support one-click application of brand colors, typography, and component styles, ensuring that all interfaces adhere to predefined visual rules. Furthermore, the platform should allow teams to establish global visual templates, enabling different projects to inherit a unified design language, thereby improving style consistency across projects.

(IV) Optimization of Version Management and Component Library

Existing prototyping tools still have significant room for improvement in version management and component library maintenance, particularly in version rollback and component synchronization. The lack of functionality in these areas makes it challenging for designers to efficiently manage design assets during iterative development cycles. To address the limitations of design asset management, the platform should optimize version history archiving and snapshot rollback functionalities, supporting version comparison, change annotations, and one-click reversion. This ensures that designers can flexibly adjust design plans without the risk of losing critical versions due to accidental modifications. Additionally, component library management should be enhanced to support global component updates, cross-project reuse, and automatic synchronization, ensuring that teams can maintain design consistency across multiple projects. This would significantly increase design asset reusability, reduce redundant design work, and improve overall maintenance efficiency.

This study addresses the misalignment between user needs and design requirements by proposing four key optimization strategies: reducing interaction design complexity, enhancing multiuser collaboration and requirement synchronization, unifying visual guideline management, and improving version control and component reuse. These optimization strategies not only enhance the functional adaptability of prototyping platforms but significantly improve the UX for designers, enabling them to complete prototyping tasks more efficiently in AD environments. In the future, as design tools become more intelligent, further exploration is needed into AI-assisted design, automated interaction generation, and other emerging technologies, providing new directions for enhancing design efficiency and innovation in prototyping platforms.

6. Conclusions

This study systematically explores the optimization of prototyping platforms in AD environments, addressing the misalignment between user needs and design requirements. By integrating user requirement weight computation and structured prioritization, this study enhances the adaptability of prototyping platforms in four key areas: interaction experience optimization, multiuser collaboration, visual standardization, and version management and component reuse. These improvements enhance both designers' operational efficiency and collaboration experience in AD workflows.

The primary contribution of this study is the user requirement weight-based optimization framework, ensuring a systematic alignment between designer needs and platform functionalities. Using grounded theory, F-KANO, DEMATEL, and QFD analysis, we developed a structured methodology to classify, prioritize, and map designer needs into platform optimizations. User evaluation results confirmed the effectiveness of this framework, demonstrating improvements in interaction fluidity, collaboration efficiency, and visual consistency.

Despite its contributions, this study has several limitations. First, the participant sample ($N = 12$) consistedprimarily of experienced designers working in agile environments, which may not fully represent the diversity of prototyping tool users across industries. Future research should incorporate a broader sample, including novice designers and interdisciplinary teams. Second, while the study optimized platform functionalities, it did not fully address the evolving nature of designer needs in highly dynamic AD environments. Future research could explore adaptive requirement management mechanisms that integrate real-time user feedback into platform iterations. Third, this study evaluated immediate usability and efficiency improvements but did not assess the long-term impact on real-world design workflows. Longitudinal studies and field deployments are needed to measure how well these optimizations sustain efficiency gains over time.

Future research could explore several directions beyond the direct extensions of this study. One promising avenue is AI-driven prototyping enhancements, where artificial intelligence could be leveraged to automate component suggestions and recognize intelligent design patterns. Such advancements would not only streamline the design process but improve the adaptability of prototyping platforms to evolving user needs. Another important direction is real-world validation through industry partnerships, where optimized platforms could be deployed in live projects to assess their practical impact. Conducting field studies in professional settings would provide valuable insights into the usability and long-term effectiveness of the proposed framework, ensuring its applicability beyond controlled experimental conditions.

Author Contributions: Conceptualization, Z.W.; formal analysis, Z.W.; methodology, Z.W.; software, Z.W.; supervision, B.S.; visualization, Z.W.; writing—original draft, Z.W.; writing—review and editing, B.S., J.Y. and Y.L. All authors have read and agreed to the published version of the manuscript.

Funding: This research received no external funding.

Data Availability Statement: The data used to support the findings of this study are available from the corresponding author upon reasonable request.

Conflicts of Interest: The authors declare no conflicts of interest.

Abbreviations

The following abbreviations are used in this manuscript:

AD	Agile Development
UX	User Experience
UI	User Interface

References

1. Klunder, J.; Trommer, F.; Prenner, N. How agile coaches create an agile mindset in development teams: Insights from an interview study. *J. Softw. Evol. Process.* **2022**, *34*, e2491. [CrossRef]
2. Rego, G.E.; Pitukhin, E.A. Method of Collaboration between Humans and Generative Artificial Intelligence in the Development of Information Systems. *Program. Ingeneria* **2025**, *16*, 13–27. [CrossRef]

3. Ijomah, T. Advancements in project management methodologies: Integrating agile and waterfall approaches for optimal outcomes. *World J. Adv. Sci. Technol.* **2024**, *5*, 2216–2231. [CrossRef]
4. Reiche, B. Between interdependence and autonomy: Toward a typology of work design modes in the new world of work. *Hum. Resour. Manag. J.* **2023**, *33*, 1001–1017. [CrossRef]
5. Gren, L.; Goldman, A.; Jacobsson, C. Agile ways of working: A team maturity perspective. *J. Softw. Evol. Process.* **2020**, *32*, e2244. [CrossRef]
6. Ye, X.; Frens, J.; Hu, J. Design Tools for Supporting the Remote Collaborative Design Process: A Systematic Review. In Proceedings of the Tenth International Symposium of Chinese CHI, New York, NY, USA, 5–6 November 2022; pp. 83–95.
7. Kathirvelkumaran, D.L.; Moorthy, D.R.S. An Architectural Pattern for Dynamic Component Integration. *Int. J. Sci. Res. Comput. Sci. Eng. Inf. Technol.* **2023**, *26*, 101–106. [CrossRef]
8. Magistretti, S.; Dell'Era, C.; Doppio, N. Design sprint for SMEs: An organizational taxonomy based on configuration theory. *Manag. Decis.* **2020**, *58*, 1803–1817. [CrossRef]
9. Zhang, Z.; Jiang, Y.; Zhang, P.; Qian, C. Remotely Muti-Collaboration for the Online Teaching of Architectural Design: A Pilot Study Based on a Distributed Version Control Solution. In Proceedings of the 2023 IEEE Frontiers in Education Conference (FIE), College Station, TX, USA, 18–21 October 2023; pp. 1–5.
10. Adeleke, A.G.; Sanyaolu, T.O.; Efunniyi, C.P.; Akwawa, L.A.; Azubuko, C.F. Leveraging UX design and prototyping in agile development: A business analyst's perspective. *Eng. Sci. Technol. J.* **2024**, *5*, 2670–2693. [CrossRef]
11. Hansen, C.A.; Arlitt, R.; Eifler, T.; Deininger, M. Design by Prototyping: Increasing Agility in Mechatronic Product Design through Prototyping Sprints. *Proc. Des. Soc.* **2022**, *2*, 201–210. [CrossRef]
12. Zayim, N.; Yıldız, H.; Yüce, Y.K. Estimating Cognitive Load in a Mobile Personal Health Record Application: A Cognitive Task Analysis Approach. *Healthc. Inform. Res.* **2023**, *29*, 367–376. [CrossRef]
13. Lei, Z.; Zhou, H.; Ye, S.; Hu, W.; Liu, G.; Wei, Z. Interactive and Visualized Online Experimentation System for Engineering Education and Research. *J. Vis. Exp. (JoVE)* **2021**, *177*, e63342. [CrossRef]
14. Zhang, J.; Xiang, Y. AHFE InternationalUser Interface Consistency Experience in Composite Cross-device Interaction. In Proceedings of the 14th International Conference on Applied Human Factors and Ergonomics (AHFE 2023), Orlando, FL, USA, 20–24 July 2023.
15. Kausar, M.; Ishtiaq, M.; Hussain, S. Distributed Agile Patterns-Using Agile Practices to Solve Offshore Development Issues. *IEEE Access* **2022**, *10*, 8840–8854. [CrossRef]
16. Lee, H.; Park, J. Designing a New Empathy-Oriented Prototyping Toolkit for the Design Thinking Process: Creativity and Design Sensibility. *Int. J. Art Des. Educ.* **2021**, *40*, 324–341. [CrossRef]
17. Lester, C. Combining agile methods and user-centered design to create a unique user experience: An empirical inquiry. In Proceedings of the Fourth International Conference on Advances in Computer-Human Interactions (ACHI 2011), Guadeloupe, France, 23–28 February 2011.
18. Hinderks, A.; Winter, D.; Mayo, F.; Escalona, M.; Thomaschewski, J. UX Poker: Estimating the Influence of User Stories on User Experience in Early Stage of Agile Development. *Int. J. Interact. Multimed. Artif. Intell.* **2022**, *7*, 97–104. [CrossRef]
19. Whaiduzzaman, M.; Sakib, A.; Khan, N.; Chaki, S.; Shahrier, L.; Ghosh, S.; Rahman, M.; Mahi, M.; Barros, A.; Fidge, C.; et al. Concept to Reality: An Integrated Approach to Testing Software User Interfaces. *Appl. Sci.* **2023**, *13*, 11997. [CrossRef]
20. Palopak, Y.; Huang, S. Perceived impact of agile principles: Insights from a survey-based study on agile software development project success. *Inf. Softw. Technol.* **2024**, *176*, 107552. [CrossRef]
21. Yang, B.; Ma, X.; Wang, C.; Guo, H.; Liu, H.; Jin, Z. User story clustering in agile development: A framework and an empirical study. *Front. Comput. Sci.* **2023**, *17*, 176213. [CrossRef]
22. Martins Pacheco, N.M.; Vazhapilli Sureshbabu, A.; Dieckmann, E.; Apud Bell, M.; Green, S.; Childs, P.; Zimmermann, M. Challenges and Opportunities in Remote Prototyping: A Case-Study during COVID-19. *Proc. Des. Soc.* **2022**, *2*, 231–240. [CrossRef]
23. Berglund, A.; Jaarsma, T.; Oradd, H.; Jedel, I.; Fallstrom, J.; Stromberg, A.; Klompstra, L.; Berglund, E. Player-centered, iterative, and interdisciplinary design and development of a mobile exergame for older cardiac patients. *Eur. J. Cardiovasc. Nurs.* **2023**, *22*, I164–I165.
24. Kahlon, Y.; Fujii, H. Visualization and inquiry into mental content in design activity: A case study of design interpretation. *AI EDAM* **2022**, *36*, e2. [CrossRef]
25. Turner, C.; Astin, F. Grounded theory: Whatmakes a grounded theory study? *Eur. J. Cardiovasc. Nurs.* **2021**, *20*, 285–289. [CrossRef] [PubMed]
26. Hu, Z. Jewelry Packaging User Demand Analysis Based on Fuzzy Kano Model. *Adv. Math. Phys.* **2022**, *2022*, 1776150. [CrossRef]
27. Qu, M.; Ren, Z.; Wu, J. Design and evaluation of smart blood pressure monitor oriented to user needs. *J. Eng. Des.* **2024**, *35*, 290–319. [CrossRef]

28. Smidovnik, T.; Groselj, P. Solution for Convergence Problem in DEMATEL Method: DEMATEL of Finite Sum of Influences. *Symmetry* **2023**, *15*, 1357. [CrossRef]
29. Si, S.; You, X.; Liu, H.; Zhang, P. DEMATEL Technique: A Systematic Review of the State-of-the-Art Literature on Methodologies and Applications. *Math. Probl. Eng.* **2018**, *2018*, 3696457. [CrossRef]
30. Wang, J.; Liu, H.; Shi, H.; Guo, W.; Zhu, J. New approach for quality function deployment based on social network analysis and interval 2-tuple Pythagorean fuzzy linguistic information. *Comput. Ind. Eng.* **2023**, *183*, 109554. [CrossRef]
31. Holt, N.; Pankow, K.; Ormond, I.; Jorgensen, H.; Deal, C.; Pynn, S. Grounded theory. *Int. Rev. Sport Exer. Psychol.* **2022**, *15*, 199–225. [CrossRef]
32. Zhang, X.; Lv, M.; Yuan, X. Research on cloud-CRITIC-PDR method for hybrid multi-criteria decision making. Research on cloud-CRITIC-PDR method for hybrid multi-criteria decision making. *J. Intell. Fuzzy Syst.* **2023**, *45*, 8789–8803. [CrossRef]
33. Roszkowska, E.; Wachowicz, T. Impact of Normalization on Entropy-Based Weights in Hellwig's Method: A Case Study on Evaluating Sustainable Development in the Education Area. *Entropy* **2024**, *26*, 365. [CrossRef]
34. Han, S.; Xie, T.; Chih-Lin, I.; Chai, L.; Liu, Z.; Yuan, Y.; Cui, C. Artificial-Intelligence-Enabled Air Interface for 6G: Solutions, Challenges, and Standardization Impacts. *IEEE Commun. Mag.* **2020**, *58*, 73–79. [CrossRef]
35. Grigera, J.; Espada, J.; Rossi, G. AI in User Interface Design and Evaluation. *IT Prof.* **2023**, *25*, 20–22. [CrossRef]
36. Lewis, C.C.V.; Miroslava, T.E.R.; Henry, I.E.W.; Elizabeth, S.J.M. Development of a Collaborative Information Management Prototype through a gamification App for Android in the prevention, response and recovery of natural, technological and human disasters. In Proceedings of the 2023 18th Iberian Conference on Information Systems and Technologies (CISTI), Aveiro, Portugal, 20–23 June 2023; pp. 1–6.
37. Hidayat, T.S.; Siregar, K.; Damayanti, R. Agile Open Innovation Platform: Managing Value Cocreation to Face Health Challenges in the Post-pandemic Era. *Open Access Maced. J. Med. Sci.* **2023**, *11*, 322–325. [CrossRef]
38. Wang, J.; Ranscombe, C.; Eisenbart, B. An integrated prototyping tool to enhance interdisciplinary communication in smart product design. *Ergonomics* **2024**, 1–19. [CrossRef]
39. Wang, J.; Qi, Y. A Multi-User Collaborative AR System for Industrial Applications. *Sensors* **2022**, *22*, 1319. [CrossRef]
40. Valtolina, S.; Neri, L. Visual design of dialogue flows for conversational interfaces. *Behav. Inf. Technol.* **2021**, *40*, 1008–1023. [CrossRef]

symmetry

MDPI

Article

A Failure Touchpoint Identification and Reconfiguration Approach for Enhancing Product–Service Symmetry

Zhuo Liu [1,2], Suihuai Yu [1], Wenjun Du [1,*] and Fangmin Cheng [3,*]

1 Key Laboratory of Industrial Design and Ergonomics, Ministry of Industry and Information Technology, Northwestern Polytechnical University, Xi'an 710072, China; liuzhuo@tjut.edu.cn (Z.L.); caid@nwpu.edu.cn (S.Y.)
2 School of Art & Design, Tianjin University of Technology, Tianjin 300384, China
3 School of Design, Xi'an Technology University, Xi'an 710021, China
* Correspondence: duwenjun@mail.nwpu.edu.cn (W.D.); chengfangmin@xatu.edu.cn (F.C.)

Abstract: Asymmetry of product–service systems, that is, the presentation of services that does not match the expectations of stakeholders, often leads to inefficient services. To address design asymmetry in service systems, this study proposes a stakeholder-centric methodology for failure touchpoint identification and service reconfiguration. Grounded in the principles of multi-stakeholder value co-creation, the framework involves a three-phase process: systematic identification of failure-prone touchpoints through tripartite analysis (enterprise, service personnel, and user perspectives), generation of reconfiguration alternatives aligned with prioritized stakeholder requirements, and multi-criteria decision-making to optimize service configuration. The methodology achieves design symmetry by integrating stakeholder evaluations across failure diagnosis, causal analysis, and solution validation phases. A case study on a visitor management system demonstrates significant improvements in service quality (overall score increased from 0.70 to 0.81), validating the approach's efficacy. This research bridges the gap in existing studies by balancing multi-stakeholder interests, offering a novel contribution to service design literature.

Keywords: service design symmetry; product–service system; failure touchpoint; service reconfiguration; multi-stakeholder collaboration

1. Introduction

The product–service system is a new type of production system with symmetry formed under the product full life-cycle service mode in product manufacturing enterprises [1]. Against the background of the rapid development of the experience economy, the concept and method of product–service have been widely recognized and applied [2]. In the product–service system, the service touchpoint refers to the critical moment when all participants involved in the service process interact with the service, mainly existing in the interactive activities between the service provider and the service receiver [3]. Good service touchpoint design is the foundation for the high quality and symmetry of the entire product–service system [4]. If the interaction quality of service touchpoints is poor, failing to bring good experience to relevant participants and resulting in the asymmetry of the product–service system, it is called a failure touchpoint. Failure touchpoints seriously affect the quality of the service system [5]. Effectively identifying failure touchpoints and carrying out reconfiguration and design are important ways to improve the quality of the product–service system.

Some achievements have been made in the research on the identification of failure touchpoints and service redesign to solve the asymmetry problem of product–service systems. In terms of failure touchpoint identification, since the failure of touchpoints depends on the subjective experience of service participants, the existing research has mainly adopted expert or user evaluation methods for failure point identification. For example, Wei et al. [6] proposed a service failure evaluation model, which combined the fuzzy failure mode and effect analysis (FMEA) method with the TOPSIS method to construct a human–computer interaction service failure evaluation model. Moosavi et al. [7] aimed at the bus service and selected four reliability indicators to evaluate the bus service system, identifying the service touchpoints with poor reliability. Hao et al. [8], in order to optimize the urban postal service network in Norway, proposed a location optimization model and reallocated the positions of postal counters according to different location characteristics and user needs, improving the accessibility of postal services. The evolution of artificial intelligence (AI) technologies has prompted innovative approaches to service asymmetry challenges. Ozuem et al. [9] analyzed emotional influences on user loyalty and technology adoption efficacy at human–AI touchpoints, Wang et al. [10] established deep learning-driven frameworks for quality prediction and event detection in classification tasks, while Li et al. [11] developed cross-failure-type mechanical fault prediction systems utilizing advanced neural architectures.

Existing studies have employed diverse methods for service system evaluation and failure touchpoint reconfiguration, yet they have predominantly focused on user perspectives, neglecting the multi-stakeholder nature of service design. Wang et al. [12] employed a research-through-design methodology to develop a systematic design modeling framework, while Chen et al. [13] complemented this by proposing the "BEDFITA" model—a smart technology-integrated service touchpoint design paradigm that formalized stakeholder interactions through algorithmic parameterization. Extending this paradigm, Wang's team further established a failure analysis and reconfiguration framework for service touchpoints, incorporating weighting metrics derived from user perceptual evaluations to quantify failure determinants [14]. However, the above research has mainly evaluated service systems from the perspective of users (service recipients), without considering other stakeholders in the service system. An important distinction between service design and traditional product design is that service design involves more diversified and complex stakeholders during the service execution process [15–17]. In service design, stakeholders refer to all people or organizations involved in the entire service cycle and even include quasi-human (service robots) or non-human (such as animals) subjects [18]. Although various stakeholders have different importance in the service system, they are all directly or indirectly affected by the operation process of the service system. A good service system should not only pursue the maximization of the interests of a certain stakeholder but also enhance the comprehensive interests of all stakeholders as much as possible, so as to achieve the symmetry of the system and obtain the higher overall interests of the service system [19,20]. Therefore, unlike the "user-centered" design concept emphasized in the field of product design, the field of service design emphasizes the "stakeholder-centered" or "system-centered" design concept [21]. If a service touchpoint results in low satisfaction of any type of stakeholder, this touchpoint should be regarded as a failure touchpoint and needs to be improved. Therefore, when identifying and reconfiguring failure touchpoints, the interests of all stakeholders should be comprehensively considered so as to improve the overall interests of the service system. Based on this, this paper proposes a failure touchpoint identification and reconfiguration method for the interests of the service system, that is, for the overall interests of stakeholders. Since users, enterprises, and service personnel are the most common and important stakeholders in common service systems [22], and for the universality of the method, only these three types of stakeholders are considered in this method. The proposed method addresses asymmetry in service systems by harmonizing stakeholder interests, thereby achieving design symmetry—a core focus of the *Symmetry* journal.

2. Method Construction

Based on the above analysis, a framework for failure touchpoint identification and reconfiguration was proposed. The framework construction follows the idea of "discover the problem-propose the solution-decide the solution", which is often used in the design field. This framework contributes to the accurate identification and reconstruction of failure contact points in two ways. First, the opinions of all stakeholders were considered in the construction of the framework, and second, evaluation indicators and quantitative evaluation methods with strong operability were proposed according to the characteristics of different stakeholders. The framework is shown in Figure 1.

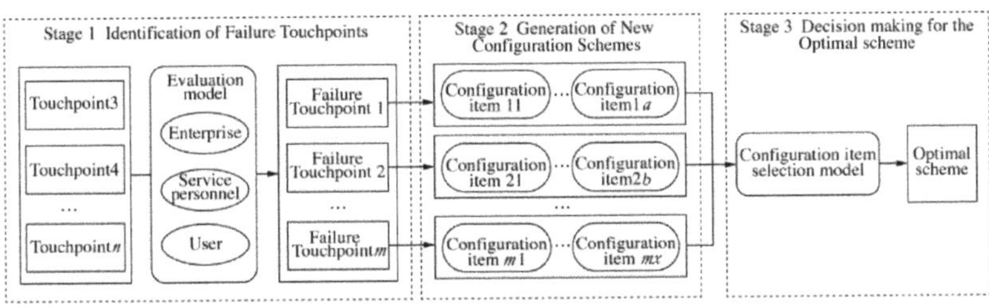

Figure 1. The framework for failure touchpoint identification and reconfiguration.

The method was divided into three stages:

- Identification of Failure touchpoints: On the basis of sorting out all touchpoints in the service cycle, build evaluation models for different stakeholders, evaluate all touchpoints, and identify the failure touchpoints with poor service quality.
- Generation of New Configuration Schemes: Analyze the causes of failure at the failure touchpoints, put forward multiple candidate service configuration items in a targeted manner, and generate multiple new service configuration schemes through different combinations of configuration items.
- Decision-making for the Optimal Scheme: Evaluate the new configuration schemes and make decisions to obtain the optimal one.

2.1. Identify Failed Touchpoints

2.1.1. Sort Out Service Touchpoints

The main methods for sorting out service touchpoints include observations, situational interviews, role-playing, questionnaires, and other methods [23]. After obtaining all the touchpoints, we analyzed the stakeholders involved. If only enterprises and users were involved, it was recorded as $P(S)$; if enterprises, service personnel and users were involved, it was recorded as $P(M)$. We sorted and coded all the touchpoints according to the typical user behavior process to obtain the touchpoint set $TP = \{P(S)_1, P(S)_2, \ldots, P(S)n, P(M)_{n+1}, P(M)_{n+2}, \ldots, P(M)_{n+m}\}$, where n and m are the number of two types of touchpoints, respectively, and the total number of touchpoints in the service system is $n + m$. We recorded them in the form of a user journey map or table.

2.1.2. Failure Touchpoint Determination Rules and Evaluation Model Construction

Failure touchpoints refer to service touchpoints with poor interaction quality. When identifying failure touchpoints, the interests of different stakeholders need to be considered simultaneously. For example, a hospital has set up a service process of "official APP appointment registration-sign in to the clinic according to the appointment time-waiting area for a call-medical treatment". In the touchpoint of "waiting area for a call", if the patient waits for the doctor on time but fails to see a doctor, this touchpoint does not meet the interests of the patient and is a failure touchpoint. If the patient waits for the doctor on time and visits the doctor, but the doctor's workload is too large, then this touchpoint does not meet the doctor's interests, and it is also a failure touchpoint.

Based on the above analysis, two judgment rules for failure touchpoints were formulated:

Rule 1: For the evaluation result of a single touchpoint. If the interests of a certain stakeholder or the comprehensive interests of all stakeholders of the touchpoint are lower than the threshold, this touchpoint will be judged as a failure point.

Rule 2: For the evaluation result of the service system. If the overall interests of the service system are lower than the threshold, in addition to improving the failure points identified by Rule 1, the touchpoints with high importance and low comprehensive interests should also be focused on improving so as to efficiently improve the overall quality of the service system. In this case, the touchpoints with importance higher than the threshold and comprehensive score lower than the threshold will be identified as failure points.

In the service system, three types of stakeholders have different interests. According to the main interests of each stakeholder, the touchpoint evaluation indexes are set, respectively. For enterprises, economic interests are the most important interests, and the operating cost of touchpoints is taken as the evaluation index of economic interests. For service personnel, the job satisfaction index represents their attitude and appeal [24], so obtaining higher job satisfaction is their main interest. According to the literature [25–28], the factors that affect job satisfaction and are universally applicable to all industries include salary, promotion system, workload and so on. In the case of touchpoints in the service system, the impact of factors such as salary and promotion system on job satisfaction can be ignored. Therefore, the workload is taken as an index to evaluate the job satisfaction of touchpoints. On the basis of the above literature research results, secondary indexes such as total working hours, single cycle working hours, total service population, single cycle service population, physical workload, and mental workload were proposed. For users, the main interest is to achieve the predetermined goals comfortably, efficiently and conveniently through receiving services to meet the needs and realize the value. This paper took user satisfaction as the evaluation index. User satisfaction refers to the comparative value between the actual feeling of users when receiving products and services and their expected degree [29,30], which is a common user evaluation index in the field of service design. Based on several studies on user satisfaction evaluation in service design [31–33], target achievement degree, service speed, clarity, comfort, convenience, and economy were set as secondary indicators. In different application scenarios of the service system, the second-level indicators can be adjusted and expanded. Accordingly, the service touchpoint evaluation index system shown in Figure 2 is constructed. In Figure 2, service touchpoint evaluation indicators are sorted out from three dimensions: enterprise, service personnel and users, and two levels of indicators are proposed. The evaluation indicator system can be modified and expanded according to the specific situation.

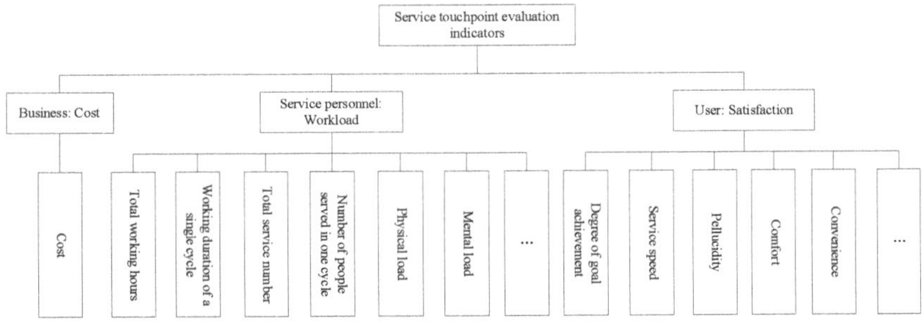

Figure 2. Evaluation indicator system for service touchpoints.

2.1.3. Evaluation of Touchpoints

A certain number of enterprise representatives, service personnel, and users were invited to evaluate the touchpoints based on their respective interests, taking the touchpoint Pi $(1 \leq i \leq n + m)$ as an example.

- Business Evaluation Method: For enterprises, the cost of evaluation indicators is a quantitative metric. Enterprises calculate the actual operational cost C_{ir} of P_i based on the real operating costs of the service system. According to market analysis results and the business conditions of the enterprise, the maximum tolerable cost for P_i was set as C_{imax}, and the optimal cost was C_{imin}. The evaluation score S_{ic} of P_i's cost was calculated using Equation (1), where 1 represents the best and 0 represents the worst.

$$S_{ic} = \begin{cases} 0, & C_{ir} > C_{i\max} \\ \frac{C_{i\max} - C_{ir}}{C_{i\max} - C_{i\min}}, & C_{i\min} < C_{ir} < C_{imax} \\ 1, & C_{ir} \leq C_{i\min} \end{cases} \quad (1)$$

- Service Personnel Evaluation Methods: For service personnel, there are many evaluation indicators. The weights of each indicator should be evaluated first, and then each indicator is evaluated to obtain the comprehensive evaluation value. Service personnel are more suitable for evaluation with semantic variables rather than precise numerical expressions. Five semantic variables {very important, important, medium, unimportant, very unimportant} were used to evaluate the importance of indicators, and five semantic variables {very good, good, medium, bad, very bad} were used to evaluate the performance of touchpoints under various indicators. This paper used triangular fuzzy numbers to express and process semantic evaluation variables. The relationship between semantic variables and triangular fuzzy numbers is shown in Table 1.

Table 1. Conversion relationship between semantic evaluation variables and triangular fuzzy numbers.

Semantic Evaluation Variables	Very Important	Important	Moderate	Unimportant	Very Unimportant
Triangular Fuzzy Numbers	(0.7, 1, 1)	(0.5, 0.7, 0.9)	(0.3, 0.5, 0.7)	(0, 0.3, 0.5)	(0, 0, 0.3)

We developed the evaluation method with reference to the method proposed in [34]. There was a total of p service personnel participating in the evaluation of P_i. There were q evaluation indicators, denoted as $IF_1, IF_2, \ldots, IF_q$. Each service personnel F_j $(1 \leq j \leq p)$ evaluates the importance and score of each indicator using the above semantic variables. Let $\widetilde{w}_k^j$ represent the evaluation of the importance of indicator IF_k $(1 \leq k \leq q)$ by service personnel F_j. The group decision value $\widetilde{w}_k$ for calculating the importance of the indicators was obtained using the arithmetic mean method:

$$\widetilde{w}_k = \frac{1}{p} \otimes \left(\widetilde{w}_k^1 \oplus \widetilde{w}_k^2 \oplus \cdots \oplus \widetilde{w}_k^q \right) \tag{2}$$

Let $\widetilde{s}_k^j$ represent the evaluation value of the touchpoint P_i under the indicator IFk by service personnel F_j. The group decision value $\widetilde{s}_k^j$ for calculating the importance of the indicators was obtained using the arithmetic mean method:

$$\widetilde{s}_{ik} = \frac{1}{p} \otimes \left(\widetilde{s}_{ik}^1 \oplus \widetilde{s}_{ik}^2 \oplus \cdots \oplus \widetilde{s}_{ik}^q \right) \tag{3}$$

The evaluation score of touchpoint P_i is given by

$$\widetilde{S}_{if} = \sum_{k=1}^{q} \widetilde{w}_k \cdot \widetilde{s}_{ik} \tag{4}$$

In Formula (4), both $\widetilde{w}_k$ and $\widetilde{s}_k$ are triangular fuzzy numbers. They need to be converted into precise values. Using Formula (5), we calculated the normalized weight of $\widetilde{w}_k = (w_{kl}, w_{km}, w_{ku})$:

$$w_k = \frac{w_{kl} + 2w_{km} + w_{ku}}{\sum\limits_{i=1}^{q} (w_{il} + 2w_{im} + w_{iu})} \tag{5}$$

Assuming $\widetilde{s}_{ik} = (s_{ikl}, s_{ikm}, s_{iku})$, we can use Equation (6) to calculate its expected value:

$$s_{ik} = \frac{s_{ikl} + 2s_{ikm} + s_{iku}}{4} \tag{6}$$

Finally, the precise evaluation score of the touchpoint P_i by the service personnel was obtained as follows:

$$S_{if} = \sum_{k=1}^{q} w_k \cdot s_{ik} \tag{7}$$

- User Evaluation Method: The user evaluation method is similar to the service personnel evaluation method. Using the same approach, the evaluation score S_{iu} for the touchpoint P_i was calculated.
- Touchpoint Importance Evaluation: Each touchpoint's importance to the service system varies. To assess the overall performance of the service system, it was necessary to evaluate the importance of each touchpoint. The touchpoint importance was evaluated by all evaluators using the Analytic Hierarchy Process (AHP), a classical evaluation method [35]. The importance of touchpoint P_i is denoted as W_i. The sum of all touchpoint importance values is equal to 1.

2.1.4. Failure Touchpoint Determination

Through the above process, we have obtained the evaluation results of various touchpoints from the three categories of stakeholders. Considering the evaluations from all three stakeholders, we calculated the comprehensive evaluation results for each touchpoint. If $P_i \in P(S)$, which means the touchpoint does not involve service personnel, its comprehensive evaluation result was calculated as follows:

$$S_i = w_{sc} S_{ic} + w_{su} S_{iu} \tag{8}$$

where w_{sc} and w_{su}, respectively, represent the weights of the enterprise and the user, with $w_{sc} + w_{su} = 1$.

If $P_i \in P(M)$, indicating that the touchpoint involves service personnel, its comprehensive evaluation results were calculated as follows:

$$S_i = w_{mc}S_{ic} + w_{mf}S_{if} + w_{mu}S_{iu} \tag{9}$$

where w_{mc}, w_{mf}, and w_{mu}, respectively, represent the weights of the enterprise, service personnel, and users, with $w_{mc} + w_{mf} + w_{mu} = 1$. The determination of the weight can be based on the discussion of the relevant stakeholders, or it can be determined by a more objective group decision-making method [36].

Based on the failure point determination rules established in the previous context, two standard criteria were formulated to determine failure touchpoints:

- If the evaluation results of P_i are below the set threshold, i.e., if the evaluation results of P_i satisfy Equation (10), then it is determined as a failure point.

$$\begin{array}{c} S_{ic} < S_{c\min} \\ \text{or } S_{if} < S_{f\min} \\ \text{or } S_{iu} < S_{u\min} \\ \text{or } S_i < S_{\min} \end{array} \tag{10}$$

where S_{cmin}, S_{fmin}, S_{umi}, and S_{min}, respectively, represent the minimum threshold values for enterprise rating, service personnel rating, user rating, and comprehensive rating.

- The overall rating of the service system is the weighted sum of the evaluation scores of each touchpoint. If the overall rating of the service system is below the threshold, i.e., it satisfies Equation (11), then touchpoints with higher importance but lower evaluation scores are considered as failure touchpoints.

$$S^{overall} = \sum_{i=1}^{n+m} W_i \cdot S_i < S_{\min}^{overall} \tag{11}$$

where $S_{\min}^{overall}$ is the minimum threshold value for the overall rating of the service system. Threshold values W_o and S_o are set. Under the condition of satisfying Equation (11), if P_i meets Equation (12), then P_i is determined as a failure touchpoint.

$$W_i > W_o \text{ and } S_i < S_o \tag{12}$$

2.2. Generating New Configuration Plans

After identifying a total of $r + s$ failure touchpoints, they were re-encoded to form the failure point set $WTP = \{P'(S)_1, P'(S)_2, \ldots, P'(S)_r, P'(M)_{r+1}, P'(M)_{r+2}, \ldots, P'(M)_{r+s}\}$. Reconfiguration of service configuration items was performed for the identified failure touchpoints. Firstly, the triggering conditions for the failure touchpoints were analyzed, followed by further analysis of the evaluation results to clarify the failure reasons. Subsequently, service designers proposed several corresponding service configuration items in response to the failure reasons. Multiple service configuration plans could be generated for several failure points, offering various decision options for different stakeholders to make optimal decisions.

2.3. Optimal Decision-Making

To select the best scheme from numerous candidate configuration schemes, it was necessary to predict the evaluation scores of each scheme and choose the scheme with the highest predicted evaluation score as the final scheme.

The scheme evaluation scores were determined by the evaluation scores of the service configuration items selected for each touchpoint, and different methods were used to predict the evaluation results for different stakeholders. For enterprises, the cost of the service configuration items can be more accurately determined by experts based on market analysis and enterprise operation analysis and then converted into points according to Equation (1). For service personnel and users, if conditions permit, a real service system can be constructed for small sample experiments, and the same evaluators can be invited for real evaluation. If there are too many candidate configuration items, or if it is impossible to construct experiments due to cost and other limitations, it is difficult for service personnel and users to have real experience with service configuration items and to give more objective evaluation. In this case, service design experts predict the evaluation results of configuration items based on item performance. Two methods were adopted according to the characteristics of indicators, and the specific methods are as follows:

- Data-based evaluation indicators, such as total working hours, total number of service personnel, etc.: Let IF_k be a data-based evaluation indicator. For the failure point P'_i, its actual value of IF_k is measured as N_{ik}, and based on Equation (3) and Equation (6), the evaluation score is obtained as S_{ik}. For P'_i, the service designers propose a total of g service configuration items, forming the set of configuration items $D = (D_{i1}, D_{i2}, \ldots, D_{ig})$. Based on their experience, the service design experts provide data prediction values for each configuration item under the indicator, denoted as $N = (N_{ik1}, N_{ik2}, \ldots, N_{ikg})$. Assuming that the service configuration item D_{ia} ($D_{ia} \in D$) performs the best under this indicator, its score S_{ika} is set to 1. According to existing research, the user experience of a product or service is often linearly related to relevant parameter variables [31,32]. Based on this, if IF_k is a cost-type indicator, meaning that lower values are preferable, the predicted evaluation score for the service configuration item D_{ix} ($D_{ix} \in D_i$) under this indicator is:

$$s_{ikx} = \frac{s_{ika} - s_{ik}}{N_{ik} - N_{ika}}(N_{ikx} - N_{ika}) + s_{ik} \tag{13}$$

If IF_k is a benefit-type indicator, meaning that higher values are preferable, the predicted evaluation score for the service configuration item D_x ($D_x \in D$) under this indicator is:

$$s_{ikx} = \frac{s_{ik} - s_{ika}}{N_{ik} - N_{ika}}(N_{ikx} - N_{ika}) + s_{ika} \tag{14}$$

- Experience-based evaluation indicators, such as workload, comfort, convenience, etc.: These types of indicators cannot be evaluated based on quantitative data. Therefore, service design experts use semantic evaluation methods for assessment. They predict the scores of candidate service configuration items under various indicators based on the scores of the current service system's failure point service configuration items and the performance of candidate service configuration items.

After obtaining the scores of candidate service configuration items under various indicators, the predicted evaluation results of service personnel and users for these items were calculated using Equation (7). Subsequently, based on Equations (8) and (9), the predicted comprehensive evaluation results of each candidate service configuration item were calculated according to the touchpoint type, using Equation (10) to filter the configuration items and eliminate those with scores below the threshold.

Let $P'_I \in P(S)$ be a failure touchpoint, and after filtering, there are a total of k_i candidate service configuration items. Similarly, let $P'_j \in P(M)$ be another failure touchpoint, and after filtering, there are a total of k_j candidate service configuration items. To maximize the predicted scores of the plans, the service configuration item optimization model was constructed as follows:

$$\begin{aligned} \max S_p &= \sum_{i=1}^{r}\sum_{v=1}^{k_i} W_i \cdot x_{iv} \cdot S_i + \sum_{j=1}^{s}\sum_{w=1}^{k_j} W_j \cdot x_{iw} \cdot S_j \\ &= \sum_{i=1}^{r}\sum_{v=1}^{k_i} W_i \cdot x_{iv} \cdot (w_{sc} \cdot S_{icv} + w_{su} \cdot S_{iuv}) + \sum_{j=1}^{s}\sum_{w=1}^{k_j} W_j \cdot x_{iw} \cdot \left(w_{mc} \cdot S_{jcw} + w_{mf} \cdot S_{jfw} + w_{mu} \cdot S_{juw}\right) \\ &\text{s.t.} \sum_{v=1}^{k_i} x_{iv} = \sum_{w=1}^{k_j} x_{jw} = 1,\ i = 1, 2, \ldots, r,\ j = 1, 2, \ldots, s \\ &\qquad x_{iv}, x_{jw} \in \{0,1\} \end{aligned} \tag{15}$$

The variables x_{iv} and x_{jw} in the formula are both binary variables with values between 0 and 1. x_{iv} = 1 indicates selecting the v-th candidate service item as the final service configuration item for the failure touchpoint P'_i, while x_{iv} = 0 indicates not selecting the v-th candidate service item as the final service configuration item for P'_i. Similarly, x_{jw} follows the same interpretation. W_i and W_j represent the importance of touchpoints i and j, respectively, which are evaluated by all evaluators based on AHP. Additionally, there might be compatibility issues among candidate service configuration items for different touchpoints, and specific constraints should be added accordingly.

By solving the service configuration item optimization model, the optimal service configuration plan that maximizes the overall benefits of the service system was determined.

3. Case Validation

To achieve service symmetry in pandemic conditions, we engineered a dual-mode visitor ecosystem, harmonizing digital pre-screening tools with adaptive physical infrastructure, which balanced stakeholder needs (enterprise efficiency, user convenience, and public health compliance). The system has been in operation for several months at a Chinese company. The company attaches more importance to trade secrets, so the management of visitors is stricter. During this period, both visitors and relevant enterprise personnel have expressed dissatisfaction with the operation of the system, believing that there are problems such as inefficiency and chaotic management in the operation process of the system. To enhance the quality of the service system, the methods proposed in this paper were adopted to assess and reconfigure the failure touchpoints.

3.1. Identification of Failure Service Touchpoints

Service design experts reviewed all the touchpoints within the service system and identified 13 touchpoints, assigning unique identifiers to each. Additionally, they documented the corresponding service content and stakeholders for each touchpoint, as shown in Table 2. In this service system, visitors acted as users, while the service personnel consisted of various positions of enterprise employees responsible for providing services at different stages.

Table 2. Summary of service touchpoints.

Service Stage	Touchpoint ID	Service Touchpoint	Service Content	Stakeholders
Preparing for Visit	$P(M)_5$	Confirming the visit requirements	Informing the visitors about the visit application process	Enterprise, Visitors, Interviewees
Apply for Visit	$P(S)_1$	Mini-program registration	Mini-program registration interface	Enterprise, Visitors
	$P(S)_2$	Fill in visitor information	Visitor Information Entry Interface	Enterprise, Visitors
	$P(M)_6$	Entry of Interviewee Information	Entry of Interviewee Information Interface	Enterprise, Visitors, Interviewees
	$P(S)_3$	Filling COVID-19 Information	COVID-19 Related Information Form	Enterprise, Visitors
Approval for Visit	$P(M)_7$	Approval	Approval personnel review the visit application	Enterprise, Visitors, Approvers
	$P(S)_4$	Notification of approval result	Notification to the visitor of the approval result	Enterprise, Visitors
Arrival at the company	$P(M)_8$	Proceed to visit	Assist visitors in planning their itinerary and route	Enterprise, Visitors, Interviewees
	$P(M)_9$	Enter the company premises	Enter the company premises through the access control system	Enterprise, Visitors, Security guards
	$P(M)_{10}$	Information registration	Recording visitor information	Enterprise, Visitors, Security guards
	$P(M)_{11}$	Waiting for the person to be visited	Guiding the visitor to the rest area to wait	Enterprise, Visitors, Security guards
visiting	$P(M)_{12}$	Receiving the visitor	Escorting the visitor to the relevant department	Enterprise, Visitors, Interviewees
ending	$P(M)_{13}$	Departure	The host escorts the visitor to leave the company	Enterprise, Visitors, Interviewees

Various stakeholders were invited to participate in the study. Among the candidates who accepted the invitation, the users who had used the service system more times were preferentially selected to participate in the case study. In the end, 20 stakeholders who had participated in the service system multiple times were invited to be part of the current service system improvement project. All evaluation participants were informed and consented to this project. This group comprised two enterprise managers; four individuals each for the roles of visitors, approvers, and gatekeepers; and six visitors. A combination of offline interviews and online questionnaires was used to collect their opinions.

The two enterprise managers calculated the costs for each touchpoint based on the service system's operational data. The costs for each touchpoint varied. For the application access stage, the costs mainly consisted of the development and maintenance expenses of the WeChat mini-program ($P(S)_1$, $P(S)_2$, $P(M)_6$, $P(S)_3$, $P(S)_4$). The touchpoints associated with approvers primarily involved the labor costs of the approval personnel ($P(M)_7$). The costs related to visitors entering and leaving the enterprise encompassed the labor costs of gatekeepers, expenses for developing and maintaining the access control system, as well as design and manufacturing costs for lobby signage in the office building ($P(M)_9$, $P(M)_{10}$, $P(M)_{11}$, $P(M)_{13}$). The costs during the visit stage mainly included dining expenses and other hospitality costs for visitors ($P(M)_{12}$). The remaining touchpoints were considered to have zero costs ($P(M)_5$, $P(M)_8$). Subsequently, based on the actual situation of the enterprise and relevant market conditions, the enterprise managers provided the maximum tolerable costs and optimal costs for each touchpoint. The evaluation scores for each touchpoint were then calculated using Equation (1).

Considering the unique characteristics of the service system, a comprehensive evaluation indicator system was developed for both service personnel and users. The weights of the evaluation indicators were determined using Equations (2) and (5). For service personnel, the evaluation indicators included working hours, total number of services, number of services during peak hours, and service difficulty, with corresponding weights of 0.28, 0.19, 0.31, and 0.22, respectively. For users, the evaluation indicators comprised target achievement level, service speed, clarity, comfort, and convenience, with corresponding weights of 0.27, 0.24, 0.16, 0.15, and 0.18, respectively. The research participants first used semantic variables to assess the importance of each indicator and then evaluated the quality of the touchpoints related to themselves using semantic variables. Based on Equations (2)–(7), evaluation scores were obtained for each touchpoint.

To assess the reliability of the evaluation data, Kendall's coefficient of concordance was separately computed for the three categories of service personnel and visitor assessment results. Kendall's coefficient of concordance is a widely used measure of inter-rater reliability [37], with values closer to 1 indicating higher inter-rater reliability and more reliable assessment results. The data were analyzed using SPSS 22.0 software, and the results are presented in Table 3.

Table 3. Inter-rater reliability test.

Scorers	Kendall's Coefficient of Concordance	*p*
Interviewees	0.796	<0.001
Approvers	0.875	<0.001
Security guards	0.824	<0.001
Visitors	0.759	<0.001

Based on the data presented in Table 3, the Kendall consistency coefficients of the four types of raters were high (all > 0.75) and had significant significance, indicating a high level of consistency and inter-rater reliability among the different evaluators, resulting in more reliable assessment outcomes.

Following this, all evaluators utilized the Analytic Hierarchy Process (AHP) to evaluate the importance of each touchpoint. The comprehensive scores for each touchpoint were subsequently computed using Equations (8) and (9). A focus group was held with the participation of multiple stakeholders and experts, according to which a common view was obtained with equal weight for each stakeholder; thus, in Equation (8), $w_{sc} = w_{su} = 1/2$, and in Equation (9), $w_{mc} = w_{mf} = w_{mu} = 1/3$. Finally, the overall assessment score for the service system was determined using Equation (11).

The evaluation results are summarized in Table 4, which includes the assessment scores assigned by stakeholders for each touchpoint, the total score for each touchpoint. The importance weight of each contact point was calculated according to Equations (2)–(5). The overall score for the service system was calculated according to Equation (11).

Following the established design objectives of the enterprise service system, evaluation thresholds were determined for both stakeholders' ratings and the total scores of touchpoints, with both thresholds set to 0.70, i.e., $S_{c\min} = S_{f\min} = S_{u\min} = S_{\min} = 0.70$. Consequently, the threshold for the overall score of the service system was set to 0.75. Using Equation (11), $S^{overall} = 0.70 < S^{overall}_{\min} = 0.75$, the threshold values for Equation (12) were set to $W_o = 0.10$, $S_o = 0.75$. Based on the application of Equation (10), the identified failure touchpoints were determined to be $P(M)_6$, $P(M)_7$, $P(M)_4$, $P(M)_9$, $P(M)_{10}$. Furthermore, employing Equation (12) led to the identification of $P(S)_2$ as an additional failure touchpoint. In total, six failure points were recognized.

Table 4. Evaluation results.

Touchpoint (Pi)	Enterprise Rating (Sic)	Service Personnel Rating (Sif)	User Rating (Siu)	Total Score of Touchpoints (Si)	Importance Weight of Touchpoints (Wi)	Total Score of Service System (Si)
$P(M)_5$	1	0.79	0.88	0.89	0.02	
$P(S)_1$	0.72	-	0.75	0.74	0.04	
$P(S)_2$	0.72	-	0.77	0.75	0.11	
$P(M)_6$	0.72	0.64	0.86	0.74	0.09	
$P(S)_3$	0.72	-	0.88	0.80	0.13	
$P(M)_7$	0.81	0.53	0.43	0.59	0.08	
$P(S)_4$	0.82	-	0.38	0.60	0.11	0.70
$P(M)_8$	1	0.76	0.80	0.85	0.03	
$P(M)_9$	0.58	0.66	0.49	0.58	0.05	
$P(M)_{10}$	0.76	0.44	0.54	0.51	0.13	
$P(M)_{11}$	0.76	0.85	0.71	0.77	0.06	
$P(M)_{12}$	0.74	0.78	0.92	0.81	0.13	
$P(M)_{13}$	1	0.90	0.81	0.90	0.02	

3.2. Generating Configuration Plans

Based on the order of failure touchpoints in the service system, they were renumbered and mapped as follows: $P(S)_2 \rightarrow P'(S)_1$, $P(S)_4 \rightarrow P'(S)_2$, $P(M)_6 \rightarrow P'(M)_3$, $P(M)_7 \rightarrow P'(M)_4$, $P(M)_9 \rightarrow P'(M)_5$, $P(M)_{10} \rightarrow P'(M)_6$. Service designers analyzed the reasons for the failure points and proposed targeted new service configurations. Taking $P'(S)_1$, the visitor information filling, as an example, its enterprise rating, user rating, and total score all exceeded the thresholds. However, due to its high importance and relatively low total score, it was identified as a failure point according to Equation (12). Therefore, new configurations should be proposed from the perspectives of both enterprise and user stakeholders. After further analysis, it was found that the cost of developing a new small program was high, so the main improvement should focus on the user's perspective. Based on further user interviews, it was revealed that the main drawbacks of this touchpoint were the redundant visitor information required and a slightly chaotic interface, leading to a poor user experience. Accordingly, four new visitor information filling pages were redesigned as candidate configurations for this failure point. Table 5 lists the candidate service configurations for each failure point. Different combinations of these configurations led to the generation of several new service configuration plans.

Table 5. Candidate service configuration options for failure points.

Evaluation Results' Failure Point	Candidate Configuration Options			
$P'(S)_1$	D_{11}: Visitor Information Entry Interface Option 1	D_{12}: Visitor Information Entry Interface Option 2	D_{13}: Visitor Information Entry Interface Option 3	D_{14}: Visitor Information Entry Interface Option 4
$P'(S)_2$	D_{21}: Enterprise WeChat Notification	D_{22}: SMS Notification	D_{23}: SMS and WeChat Notification	D_{24}: Phone Call Notification
$P'(S)_3$	D_{31}: Visited Person Information Entry Interface Scheme 1	D_{22}: Visited Person Information Entry Interface Scheme 2	D_{33}: Visited Person Information Entry Interface Scheme 3	
$P'(S)_4$	D_{41}: 2 approvers, approval cycle within 1 h.	D_{42}: 2 approvers, approval cycle within 0.5 h.	D_{43}: 3 approvers, approval cycle within 1 h.	D_{44}: 3 approvers, approval cycle within 0.5 h.
$P'(S)_5$	D_{51}: Access control system upgrade plan 1		D_{52}: Access control system upgrade plan 2	
$P'(S)_6$	D_{61}: 2 security guards, information registration form Scheme 1.	D_{62}: 2 security guards, information registration form Scheme 2.	D_{63}: 3 security guards, information registration form Scheme 1.	D_{64}: 3 security guards, information registration form Scheme 2.

3.3. Decision-Making for Optimal Service Configuration Plans

Stakeholders evaluated the candidate configuration options, and the cost of each option was provided by enterprise experts, along with the calculation of their evaluation scores. For the candidate configurations of $P'(S)_1$ and $P'(M)_3$, which involved small program interface designs, an experimental approach was adopted to assess the interface design proposals by visitors and interviewees. However, for the candidate configurations of other touchpoints, due to cost or experimental difficulty constraints, it was challenging to conduct experiments. Therefore, service designers evaluated these configurations following the methods proposed in Section 1. The evaluation scores for all candidate configurations exceeded the threshold. Specific evaluation scores are presented in Table 6.

Table 6. Evaluation results of candidate service configuration options.

Failure Point (P′i)	Configuration Item (Di)	Enterprise Score (Sic)	Service Personnel Score (Sif)	User Score (Siu)	Total Score (Si)
$P'(S)_1$	D_{11}	0.72	-	0.75	0.74
	D_{12}	0.72	-	0.81	0.77
	D_{13}	0.72	-	0.86	0.79
	D_{14}	0.72	-	0.79	0.76
$P'(S)_2$	D_{21}	1	-	0.75	0.88
	D_{22}	0.86	-	0.87	0.87
	D_{23}	0.77	-	0.92	0.85
	D_{24}	0.73	-	0.86	0.80
$P'(M)_3$	D_{31}	0.72	0.74	0.76	0.74
	D_{32}	0.72	0.82	0.80	0.78
	D_{33}	0.72	0.79	0.87	0.79
$P'(M)_4$	D_{41}	0.76	0.78	0.89	0.81
	D_{42}	0.76	0.74	0.94	0.81
	D_{43}	0.71	0.92	0.89	0.84
	D_{44}	0.71	0.87	0.94	0.84
$P'(M)_5$	D_{51}	0.75	0.91	0.88	0.85
	D_{52}	0.70	0.84	0.85	0.80
$P'(M)_6$	D_{61}	0.76	0.72	0.75	0.74
	D_{62}	0.76	0.79	0.87	0.81
	D_{63}	0.71	0.78	0.82	0.77
	D_{64}	0.71	0.86	0.91	0.83

Upon analysis, there were no mutually exclusive relationships among the candidate configurations of each failure point and between the candidate configurations and the effective touchpoints. Based on the service configuration optimization model, the Lingo 13.0 software was employed to obtain the optimal service configuration plan. The optimization model was a single-objective optimization model, and the objective function was strictly concave, so the optimization model had a unique solution. The selected configurations were D_{13}, D_{21}, D_{33}, D_{43}, D_{51}, and D_{64}, with an objective function value of 0.4724. Considering the effective touchpoints together, the predicted total score for the new service system was 0.82.

Following the configuration plan, the enterprise upgraded the service system. After running the new service system for several weeks, the same evaluation participants were invited to assess the new configured touchpoints, and the evaluation results are shown in Table 7.

Table 7. Actual ratings of new configured touchpoints.

Touchpoint (Pi)	Enterprise Rating (Sic)	Service Personnel Rating (Sif)	User Rating (Siu)	Total Score (Si)
$P(S)_2$	0.72	-	0.83	0.78
$P(S)_4$	1	-	0.74	0.87
$P(M)_6$	0.72	0.85	0.89	0.82
$P(M)_7$	0.71	0.84	0.82	0.79
$P(M)_9$	0.72	0.76	0.81	0.76
$P(M)_{10}$	0.71	0.86	0.83	0.80

Based on Table 7, it can be observed that the evaluation scores of each stakeholder for the newly configured touchpoints were higher than the threshold, indicating a comprehensive improvement over the previous failure points. A comparison between Tables 6 and 7 reveals that the predicted scores were relatively close to the actual scores. The calculated overall evaluation score for the new service system was 0.81, indicating a significant improvement compared to the previous version. The experimental results demonstrate the feasibility and effectiveness of the proposed approach as presented in this paper.

4. Discussion

In this case, the importance of the three types of stakeholders was set as equal. However, in current service design research, users are mostly regarded as the most important stakeholders. In order to explore the influence of stakeholder importance on failure point identification and configuration item optimization, two groups of sensitivity analysis were carried out, respectively.

- The influence of stakeholder opinion weight on failure point identification

Three sensitivity analysis experiments were carried out to increase the weight of user opinions and correspondingly reduce the weight of opinions from enterprises and service personnel. In the three groups of experiments, the user weights in Equations (8) and (9) were set to 0.5, 0.6, and 0.7, respectively, and the failure points were re-identified using the method in this paper. The results are shown in Table 8. According to the results in Table 8, the change in stakeholder weights had a minor influence on the total score of the service system and the failure point identification results. The main reason for this result was that, in this case, most of the failure points were identified based on Rule 1, which was independent of the weights of stakeholders.

Table 8. User importance sensitivity analysis experiment 1.

Weight Value	Service System Total Score	Failure Point
Original weight	0.70	$P(S)_2$, $P(S)_4$, $P(M)_6$, $P(M)_7$, $P(M)_9$, $P(M)_{10}$
$w_{su} = w_{mu} = 0.5$, $w_{sc} = 0.5$, $w_{mc} = w_{mf} = 0.25$	0.71	$P(S)_2$, $P(S)_4$, $P(M)_6$, $P(M)_7$, $P(M)_9$, $P(M)_{10}$
$w_{su} = w_{mu} = 0.6$, $w_{sc} = 0.4$, $w_{mc} = w_{mf} = 0.2$	0.71	$P(S)_4$, $P(M)_6$, $P(M)_7$, $P(M)_9$, $P(M)_{10}$
$w_{su} = w_{mu} = 0.7$, $w_{sc} = 0.3$, $w_{mc} = w_{mf} = 0.15$	0.71	$P(S)_4$, $P(M)_6$, $P(M)_7$, $P(M)_9$, $P(M)_{10}$

- The influence of stakeholder opinion weight on configuration scheme decision-making

Similarly, three sensitivity analysis experiments were carried out. In the three groups of experiments, the user weights in Equations (8) and (9) were set to 0.5, 0.6, and 0.7, respectively, and the preferred decision-making was conducted for the configuration items generated in Section 2.2 using the method in this paper. The results are shown in Table 9. According to Table 9, the change in stakeholder weights affected the selection of configuration items for failure points $P'(S)_2$ and $P'(M)_4$. Combining Table 6, it can be seen that when there was a large score difference among candidate configuration items from a certain type of stakeholders, this influence was relatively significant. In order to obtain the best configuration scheme, it was necessary to determine appropriate stakeholder weights according to the actual situation of the service system. For example, in service systems involving more service personnel, non-profit service systems provided by enterprises (such as the case in this paper), etc., attention should be paid to balancing the interests of different stakeholders. For profit-making service systems of enterprises, the importance of users should be higher so as to enhance user stickiness and attract more users, thus achieving good economic benefits and realizing a win–win situation for all stakeholders.

Table 9. User importance sensitivity analysis experiment 2.

Weight Value	Configuration Item Selection Results	Objective Function Value
Original weight	D_{13}, D_{21}, D_{33}, D_{43}, D_{51}, D_{64}	0.4724
$w_{su} = w_{mu} = 0.5, w_{sc} = 0.5, w_{mc} = w_{mf} = 0.25$	D_{13}, D_{21}, D_{33}, D_{44}, D_{51}, D_{64}	0.4797
$w_{su} = w_{mu} = 0.6, w_{sc} = 0.4, w_{mc} = w_{mf} = 0.2$	D_{13}, D_{22}, D_{33}, D_{44}, D_{51}, D_{64}	0.4827
$w_{su} = w_{mu} = 0.7, w_{sc} = 0.3, w_{mc} = w_{mf} = 0.15$	D_{13}, D_{23}, D_{33}, D_{44}, D_{51}, D_{64}	0.4912

To verify the superiority of this method, the method proposed in [38] was used to conduct comparative experiments on the same case. The SERVUQAL-AHP-TOPSIS comprehensive evaluation method was established in [38] to evaluate the quality of the service system. SERVUQAL is a widely recognized service quality evaluation scale, which evaluates service design quality in five dimensions: Tangibility, Reliability, Responsiveness, Assurance, and Empathy. In this case, the evaluation object is still the service touchpoint listed in 2. In the approach proposed in [38], the assessment was performed by a single stakeholder. In this case, the service system was evaluated by 10 visitors according to the evaluation model. The evaluation results are shown in Table 10, where the full score of 1. 0.70 was still used as the threshold value.

Table 10. Evaluation results based on two methods.

Touchpoint	Evaluation Score Base on [38]
$P(M)_5$	0.86
$P(S)_1$	0.80
$P(S)_2$	0.72
$P(M)_6$	0.86
$P(S)_3$	0.80
$P(M)_7$	0.63
$P(S)_4$	0.48
$P(M)_8$	0.76
$P(M)_9$	0.62
$P(M)_{10}$	0.68
$P(M)_{11}$	0.76
$P(M)_{12}$	0.88
$P(M)_{13}$	0.84

As can be seen from Table 10, there were four failure contact points obtained by the method proposed in [New 3], which were $P(M)_7$, $P(S)_4$, $P(M)_9$, and $P(M)_{10}$. There were six failure contact points identified by this method, which were $P(M)_6$, $P(M)_7$, $P(S)_4$, $P(M)_9$, and $P(M)_{10}$ and $P(S)_2$. The comparison results show that the failure contact points identified by the two methods coincided, but more failure points were identified by this method. The reason for this is that the views of other stakeholders were not taken into account. According to this result, the design of failure points was improved. Obviously, the optimization scheme obtained by this method will be more conducive to the overall quality improvement of the service system.

There are still some deficiencies in this study. Firstly, to ensure the universality, the method was simplified in some respects. For example, only three key stakeholders were considered. However, regulators, competitors, and third-party service providers can also be important in the real world. The framework provided by this approach is extensible and should take into account a wider range of stakeholders in different application areas. The method adopts the single-objective optimization model, which is also a simplification of the real problem. In the service system improvement problem, more goals, such as shorter project completion time and lower economic cost, can also be optimization goals.

In this case, the multi-objective optimization model is closer to the reality. Secondly, the evaluations of stakeholders were mostly subjective with low objectivity. Finally, this approach did not take into account the time factor, but the quality of the service system and the opinions of stakeholders were constantly changing over time. In future research, these issues will be addressed emphatically.

5. Conclusions

Based on the stakeholder-centered service design concept, this paper proposed a method for identifying and re-configuring failure points in service systems aimed at improving the overall interests of the service system, that is, enhancing the total interests of all stakeholders. Through the evaluation of the service system by three types of stakeholders, namely enterprises, service personnel, and users, failure points were identified and re-configured. The effectiveness of the method was demonstrated through a case study. Compared with most existing service design research, which has mainly focused on users, this paper comprehensively considered important participants in the service system, which is more in line with the characteristics of service design and is a useful complement to existing research ideas.

For the identification and enhancement of heavy failure contact points in service systems, rapidly evolving AI technology may have an important impact on this field. AI technology can not only improve the efficiency and accuracy of identification but also help to real-time monitoring of service processes, optimize service processes, and promote the development of personalized services. Together, these impacts drive improved service quality and increased customer satisfaction.

This framework is adaptable to diverse service contexts, from health care to smart manufacturing, where stakeholder symmetry is critical. In the future, the generality of the present approach will be tested in different areas.

Author Contributions: Conceptualization, Z.L. and S.Y.; methodology, Z.L.; validation, Z.L., W.D. and F.C.; formal analysis, W.D.; investigation, F.C.; resources, Z.L.; data curation, Z.L. and F.C.; writing—original draft preparation, Z.L. and S.Y.; writing—review and editing, Z.L. and W.D.; visualization, F.C.; supervision, S.Y.; funding acquisition, Z.L. All authors have read and agreed to the published version of the manuscript.

Funding: This work was supported by the Tianjin Art Science Planning Project (B24024).

Data Availability Statement: The original contributions presented in this study are included in the article. Further inquiries can be directed to the corresponding authors.

Conflicts of Interest: The authors declare no conflicts of interest.

References

1. Song, W.; Cao, J. A rough DEMATEL-based approach for evaluating interaction between requirements of product-service system. *Comput. Ind. Eng.* **2017**, *110*, 353–363.
2. Lin, C.J.; Cheng, L.Y. Product attributes and user experience design: How to convey product information through user-centered service. *J. Intell. Manuf.* **2015**, *28*, 1743–1754.
3. Yee, R.W.Y.; Yeung, A.C.L.; Cheng, T.C.E. The impact of employee satisfaction on quality and profitability in high-contact service industries. *J. Oper. Manag.* **2008**, *26*, 651–668. [CrossRef]
4. Ojiako, U.; Chipulu, M.; Graesser, A. Correlating service touch-point preferences with engagement parameters. *Ind. Manag. Data Syst.* **2012**, *112*, 766–785. [CrossRef]
5. Dadfar, H.; Brege, S. Differentiation by improving quality of services at the last touch point. *Int. J. Qual. Serv. Sci.* **2012**, *4*, 345–363.
6. Wei, T.; Shi, Y. A service failure assessment model for smart product consumption experience based on customer perception. *Sci. Rep.* **2024**, *14*, 23097.
7. Moosavi, S.; Ismail, A.; Yuen, C.W. Using simulation model as a tool for analyzing bus service reliability and implementing improvement strategies. *PLoS ONE* **2020**, *15*, e0232799.

8. Yu, H.; Sun, X.; Solvang, W.D.; Laporte, G. Solving a Real-World Urban Postal Service System Redesign Problem. *Sci. Program.* **2021**, *2021*, 3058472. [CrossRef]
9. Ozuem, W.; Ranfagni, S.; Willis, M.; Salvietti, G.; Howell, K. Exploring the relationship between chatbots, service failure recovery and customer loyalty: A frustration–aggression perspective. *Psychol. Mark.* **2024**, *41*, 2253–2273.
10. Wang, B.; Li, Y.; Luo, Y.; Li, X.; Freiheit, T. Early event detection in a deep-learning driven quality prediction model for ultrasonic welding. *J. Manuf. Syst.* **2021**, *60*, 325–336. [CrossRef]
11. Li, Z.; Kristoffersen, E.; Li, J. Deep transfer learning for failure prediction across failure types. *Comput. Ind. Eng.* **2022**, *172*, 108521.
12. Wang, X.; Yang, D.; Zha, L.; Liao, B. Enhancing Income as a Starting Point for Designing Sustainable Health Product-Service Systems for Chronically Ill Elderly in Rural Areas. *Sustainability* **2023**, *15*, 14404. [CrossRef]
13. Chen, J.; Li, Z.; Wang, W.; Wang, Y.; He, Z. Research on a Service Touchpoint Design Model Driven by Smart Technology Based on Kano–Failure Modes and Effects Analysis. *Sensors* **2024**, *24*, 7854. [CrossRef] [PubMed]
14. Wang, W.; Song, J.; Chen, J.; Wang, Y.; Yang, Y.; Liao, K. Failure analysis method in the service design user touchpoint reconstruction process. *Comput. Integr. Manuf. Syst.* **2022**, *28*, 1524–1536.
15. Yu, G.D.; Yang, Y.; Liu, A.J. Joint optimization of complex product variant design responding to customer requirement changes. *J. Intell. Fuzzy Syst.* **2015**, *30*, 397–408.
16. Naude, K.; Andrew, N.E.; Srikanth, V.; Parker, E.; Marsh, L.; Beare, R.; McNaney, R.; Snowdon, D.A. Using a multi-stakeholder co-design process to develop a health service organisation-wide patient reported outcome measure collection system. *Qual. Life Res.* **2024**, *33*, 619–636. [PubMed]
17. Collins, M.; Higgs, P. Improving suicide awareness in rural service providers: Some considerations arising from stakeholder consultations. *Aust. J. Rural Health* **2021**, *29*, 999–1001.
18. Krucken, L.; Meroni, A. Building stakeholder networks to develop and deliver product-service-systems: Practical experiences on elaborating pro-active materials for communication. *J. Clean. Prod.* **2006**, *14*, 1502–1508.
19. Jaakkola, E.; Alexander, M. The Role of Customer Engagement Behavior in Value Co-Creation: A Service System Perspective. *J. Serv. Res.* **2014**, *17*, 247–261. [CrossRef]
20. Touloum, K.; Idoughi, D.; Seffah, A. User Experience in Service Design: A Case Study from Algeria. *It Prof.* **2017**, *19*, 56–58.
21. Demartini, M.; Ferrari, M.; Govindan, K.; Tonelli, F. The transition to electric vehicles and a net zero economy: A model based on circular economy, stakeholder theory, and system thinking approach. *J. Clean. Prod.* **2023**, *410*, 137031. [CrossRef]
22. O'Sullivan, B.G.; Giddings, P.; Mcgrail, M.R. Perceived stakeholder benefits of continuously training general practitioners in the same rural or remote practice: Interviews exploring the Remote Vocational Training Scheme. *Med. J. Aust.* **2024**, *221*, S29–S34. [CrossRef]
23. Clatworthy, S. Service innovation through touch-points: Development of an innovation toolkit for the first stages of new service development. *J. Exerc. Sci. Physiother.* **2011**, *5*, 15–28.
24. Daoud, H.; Sellami, I.; Ben Chabene, C.; Haddar, A.; Ghrab, M.A.; Hammami, K.J.; Hajjaji, M.; Masmoudi, M.L. Assessment of job satisfaction and work ability in a confectionery factory: A Cross-Sectional Study. *Eur. Psychiatry* **2024**, *67* (Suppl. S1), S596. [CrossRef]
25. Atefi, N.; Lim Abdullah, K.; Wong, L.P.; Mazlom, R. Factors influencing job satisfaction among registered nurses: A questionnaire survey in Mashhad, Iran. *J. Nurs. Manag.* **2015**, *23*, 448–458. [CrossRef]
26. Akintola, O.; Chikoko, G. Factors influencing motivation and job satisfaction among supervisors of community health workers in marginalized communities in South Africa. *Hum. Resour. Health* **2016**, *14*, 54. [CrossRef] [PubMed]
27. Chen, P.; Sparrow, P.; Cooper, C. The relationship between person-organization fit and job satisfaction. *J. Manag. Psychol.* **2016**, *31*, 946–959. [CrossRef]
28. Tadese, T.; Mohamed, A.; Mengistie, A. Assessment of factors influencing job satisfaction among health care providers, federal police referral hospital, Addis Ababa, Ethiopia. *Ethiop. J. Health Dev.* **2015**, *29*, 119–126.
29. Ami, M.A.; Abou-Ashour, M.A.; Al-Shanwany, S. Measuring user's satisfaction for open aggregate spaces within malls in Egypt. *NeuroQuantology* **2023**, *21*, 638–656.
30. Fu, Y.; Wang, J.; Lu, L.; Tang, Q.; Zhang, S. Reputation-based joint optimization of user satisfaction and resource utilization in a computing force network. *Front. Inf. Technol. Electron. Eng.* **2024**, *25*, 685–700. [CrossRef]
31. Mao, H.F.; Chen, W.Y.; Yao, G.; Huang, S.L.; Lin, C.; Huang, W.N.W. Cross-cultural adaptation and validation of the Quebec User Evaluation of Satisfaction with Assistive Technology (QUEST 2.0): The development of the Taiwanese version. *Clin. Rehabil.* **2010**, *24*, 412–421. [CrossRef]
32. Gil-Gómez, J.-A.; Manzano-Hernández, P.; Albiol-Pérez, S.; Aula-Valero, C.; Gil-Gómez, H.; Lozano-Quilis, J.A. USEQ: A Short Questionnaire for Satisfaction Evaluation of Virtual Rehabilitation Systems. *Sensors* **2017**, *17*, 1589. [CrossRef]
33. Du, Y.; Liu, D.; Morente-Molinera, J.A.; Herrera-Viedma, E. A data-driven method for user satisfaction evaluation of smart and connected products. *Expert Syst. Appl.* **2022**, *210*, 118392.

34. Dong, J.; Wan, S. A new method for multi-attribute group decision making with triangular intuitionistic fuzzy numbers. *Kybernetes* **2016**, *45*, 158–180. [CrossRef]
35. Violante, M.G.; Vezzetti, E. Virtual interactive e-learning application: An evaluation of the student satisfaction. *Comput. Appl. Eng. Educ.* **2015**, *23*, 72–91. [CrossRef]
36. Fan, J.; Yu, S.; Chu, J.; Chen, D.; Yu, M.; Wu, T.; Chen, J.; Cheng, F.; Zhao, C. Research on multi-objective decision-making under cloud platform based on quality function deployment and uncertain linguistic variables. *Adv. Eng. Inform.* **2019**, *42*, 100932.1–100932.16. [CrossRef]
37. Franceschini, F.; Maisano, D. Aggregating multiple ordinal rankings in engineering design: The best model according to the Kendall's coefficient of concordance. *Res. Eng. Des.* **2021**, *32*, 91–103. [CrossRef]
38. Ma, P.; Yao, N.; Yang, X. Service Quality Evaluation of Terminal Express Delivery Based on an Integrated SERV-QUAL-AHP-TOPSIS Approach. *Math. Probl. Eng.* **2021**, *2021*, 8883370. [CrossRef]

MDPI AG
Grosspeteranlage 5
4052 Basel
Switzerland
Tel.: +41 61 683 77 34

Symmetry Editorial Office
E-mail: symmetry@mdpi.com
www.mdpi.com/journal/symmetry

www.ingramcontent.com/pod-product-compliance
Lightning Source LLC
Chambersburg PA
CBHW061822210926
51850CB00006B/785
9783725872503